A First Guide to Horse and Pony Care

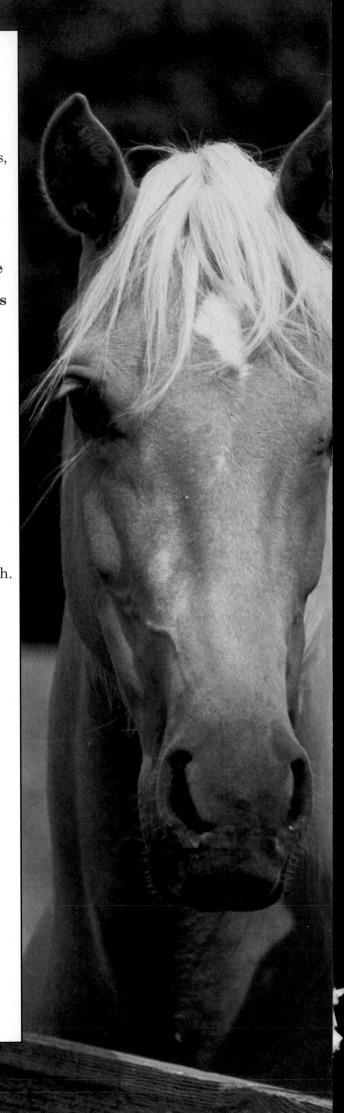

Howell Book House
Macmillan Publishing USA
1633 Broadway
New York, NY 10019

visit us online at http://www.mop.com/mgr/howell

Library of Congress Cataloging-in-Publication Data
  A first guide to horse and pony care/Jane Kidd. – 1st
American ed.
    p. cm.
Includes index.
ISBN 0-87605-833-0
1. Horses. 2. Ponies. 3. Horses–Health. 4. Ponies–Health.
I. Kidd, Jane.
SF2853.C62 1991
636. 1–dc20   91–8800   CIP

First American Edition 1991

10 9 8

Printed in China

A First Guide to Horse and Pony Care

Consulting Editor
Jane Kidd

HOWELL BOOK HOUSE
New York

Contents

1 Basic biology

Points of a horse

Each part of the horse has a different name – called a 'point'. Knowing the points of the horse is the first stage in learning about conformation (shape) and is the basis of recognizing a good or bad horse.

When learning to ride, your instructor often refers to the different parts of the horse so it's important to memorize the correct names as soon as possible. It's also useful to know the names whenever you want to describe any affected areas to a vet.

The most important points are shown below and those most often talked about are printed in capital letters.

★ **MEASURING A HORSE**

Horses are measured in 'hands' – one hand is 4in (about 10cm). When a horse is not an exact number of hands high, the inches in between are shown by a point. For example, a pony which measures 12 hands and 2 inches is said to be 12.2 hands high.

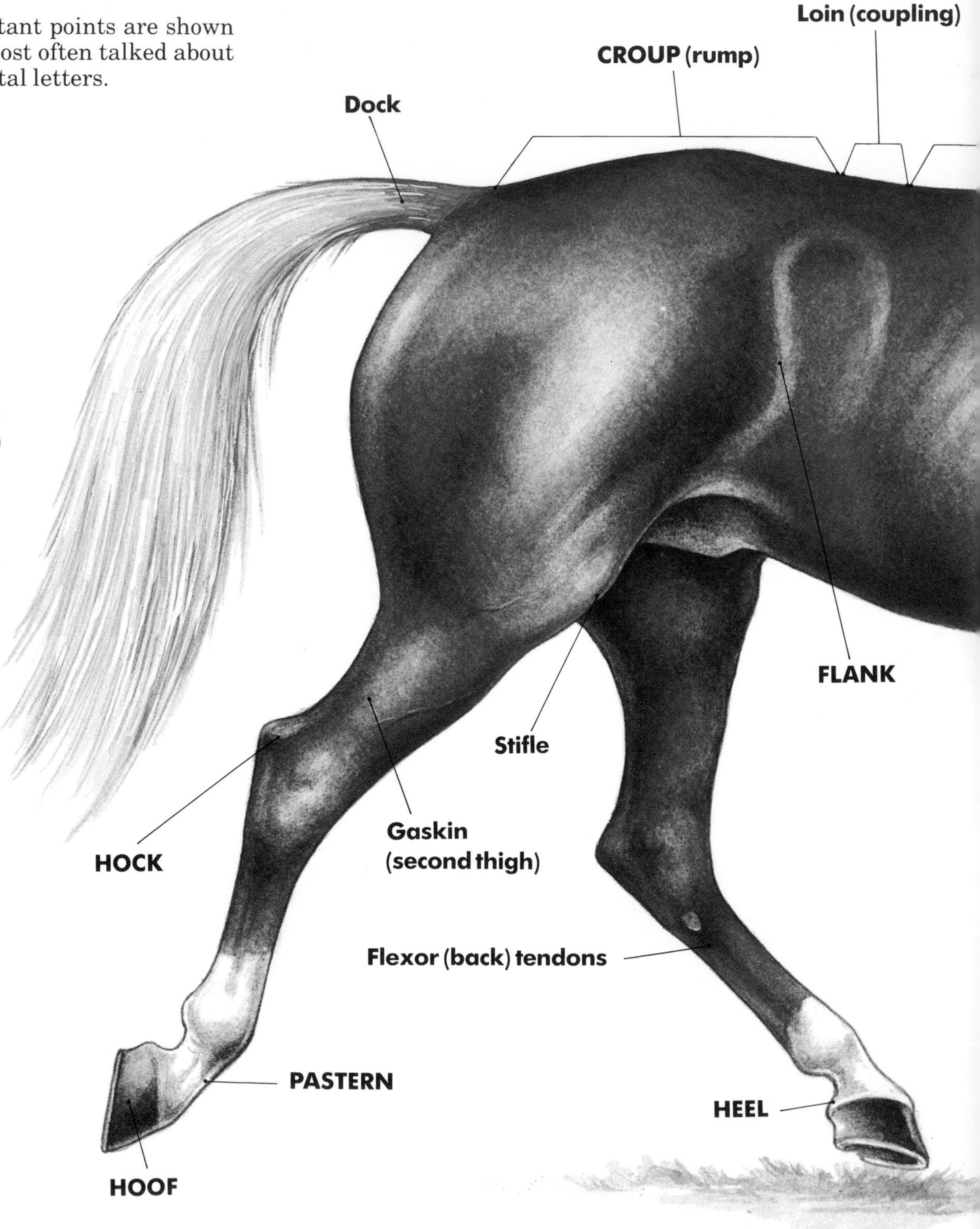

Loin (coupling)

CROUP (rump)

Dock

FLANK

Stifle

HOCK

Gaskin (second thigh)

Flexor (back) tendons

PASTERN

HEEL

HOOF

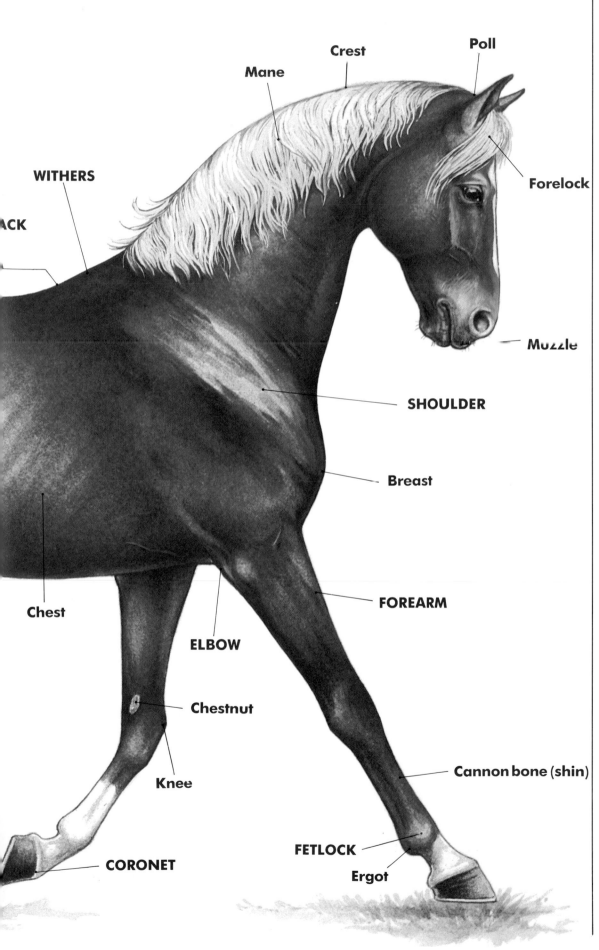

Crest

Mane

Poll

Forelock

WITHERS

ACK

Muzzle

SHOULDER

Breast

Chest

FOREARM

ELBOW

Chestnut

Knee

Cannon bone (shin)

FETLOCK

CORONET

Ergot

★ **HIGHEST POINTS**

Apart from the ears, the **poll** is the horse's highest point when it is standing upright.

But, because horses have a tendency to toss their heads about, a horse's height is measured from the **withers** to the ground.

From a side or back view, the **croup** (rump) is the highest point of the hindquarters.

DID YOU KNOW?

The horse's four **chestnuts** (the growths about halfway down the inside of the leg) are as individual to him as our fingerprints are to us. Because of this, colour photographs of a horse's chestnuts make useful clues for identifying stolen animals.

Conformation 1: front/back

Front view

When viewed from in front, an imaginary line drawn from the point of the horse's shoulder should pass through the centre of his knee, fetlock and foot. The distance between the imaginary lines down each limb should stay the same from the chest to the feet.

Conformation means a pony's make and shape – the features he has inherited from his parents, the characteristics of his type or breed and the individual appearance that makes him unique.

What can go wrong?

Very few horses possess perfectly shaped legs. Most horses are sound with minor blemishes, which would only mark them down in the showing ring and are not important athletically. But there are some defects which make a pony more prone to lameness.

Often these faults are due to uneven distribution of the horse's weight down his leg. The legs should be straight – if the limb bends inward or outward, extra pressure is placed on some parts. This can lead to injury and causes uneven wear of hooves or shoes.

Forelegs

There are a number of defects that put strain on the legs and affect movement.

Bench knees: The cannon bones are offset outward below the knee. This can cause splints.

Knock knees: The limbs bend inward at the knee. This puts strain on the ligaments.

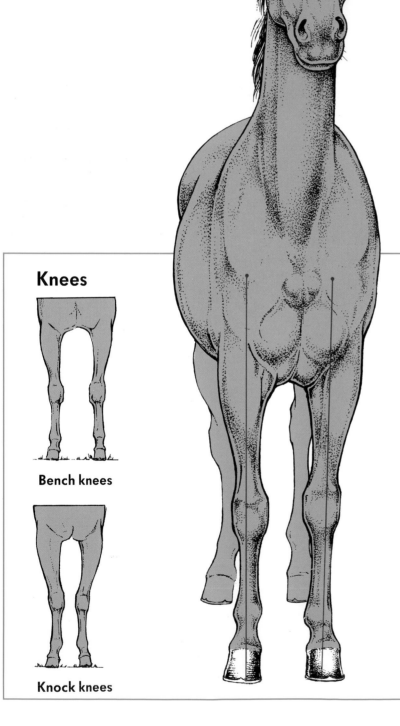

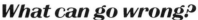

Knees

Bench knees

Knock knees

Foreleg defects

Splay footed

Pigeon toed

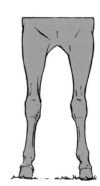

Base wide

Base narrow

Splay footed or pigeon toed, where the toes turn out or in below the fetlock, are more serious faults. Such animals have an altered action, tending to paddle or 'dish'. These defects put extra strain on the fetlock and pastern joints, which can be a cause of arthritis. They also lead to wear of the foot or shoe, on the opposite side to the way the foot is turned.

Base wide (feet set too far apart), puts more weight on the inside of the foot, which means that the inside of the limb is subjected to strain.

Base narrow (feet too close together), strains the outside of the limb.

Hindlegs

Hindleg defects cause similar problems to those of the forelegs.

Cow hocked: The hocks turn inward, which also makes the toes turn out. This can be one of the most problematic hindlimb conformations because of the strain on the hock joint, which can lead to spavin.

Bow legged (hocks too far outward), also places excessive strain on the limb.

Base wide and base narrow place strain on the inside or the outside of the limb, respectively.

Hindleg defects

Cow hocked

Bow legged

Base wide

Base narrow

Back view
When viewed from behind, an imaginary line dropped from the point of the buttock should pass through the centre of the hock, fetlock joint and foot. Like the forelimbs, the distance between the lines should stay the same all the way down the legs.

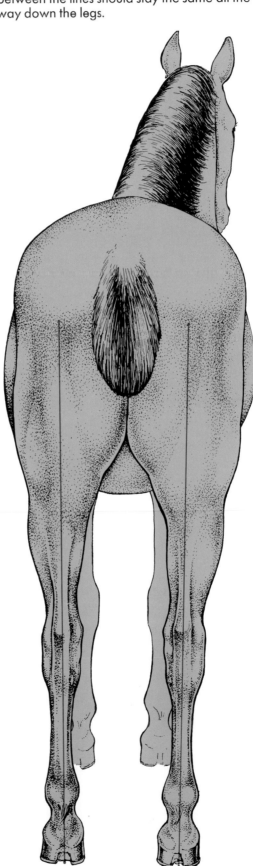

ASSESSING CONFORMATION
To assess a pony's conformation properly you need someone else to hold him. The pony should stand on a hard, level surface with his forelegs and hindlegs together (this is known as 'standing square').

Look at him carefully from directly in front and from directly behind — standing about 4.5m (15ft) away. Check that the two sides of the body are evenly balanced and well proportioned. Look at the width of the chest and hindquarters, and then examine the fore and hindlimbs.

Note whether or not the limbs are straight and how they are placed in relation to imaginary lines from the point of the shoulder and point of the buttock.

Conformation 2: side view

Faults in back conformation affect the horse's appearance and balance – especially when he is ridden. They may also make the back weak. There are a number of serious limb defects, which can cause lameness.

Back conformation

The normal outline of the back dips slightly. A very *hollow* ('sway') *back* is a sign of weakness and is liable to lead to back injuries. It can also be a sign of old age. *Roach back*, in which the back actually curves upward, reduces the athletic ability of the horse. It also causes problems in finding a correctly fitting saddle.

A horse with a *short back* has a tendency to strike his forelegs with his hindlegs while moving (called 'overreaching'), while a *long back* tends to be weak. Some horses have prominent bones along the back (*razorbacked*). This is more common in old horses.

The withers *should* be prominent, as this shows that there is a firm support for the neck muscles. If they are very narrow, the horse is likely to suffer from pressure sores (saddle galls), and it may be difficult to find a saddle that fits comfortably.

Forelimbs

When viewed from the side, there should be a straight line running from the middle of the shoulder blade, down the forearm, and through the middle of the knees and fetlock. Problems can occur if the line is not straight.

Stands under in front: The leg is angled too far back. This tends to shorten the horse's strides, making him catch his toes and stumble, and causes excessive wear of the leg joints.

Camped in front: The leg is angled too far forward. At each stride the horse is landing on the back of his feet. This places excessive weight on the heels, and can cause laminitis and navicular disease.

Back at the knee: The centre of the knee runs behind the line. This is rarer, but more serious as it can lead to strained ligaments and small ('chip') fractures of the knee bones.

Over at the knee: The centre of the knee runs in front of the line. This puts less strain on the flexor tendons.

Hindlimbs

If you look at the hindlegs from the side, a line dropped from the point of the buttock should pass through the hock, down the back of the leg to the fetlock joint. Very few horses have this ideal conformation.

Camped behind: The hock and fetlock lie behind the line, making the pasterns very straight and prone to wear.

Stands under behind: The fetlock is in front of the line. This is usually associated with sickle hocks.

Sickle hocks: The hocks are excessively angled and weak, leading to strains of the joint. This conformation is also called 'curby hocks', because it tends to cause a hock problem known as curb.

Straight hocks: The hocks are subjected to strain, commonly causing bog spavin (swelling of the hock joint).

▼ **Eclipse**, shown in this detail of a painting by George Stubbs, is one of the most famous racehorses in history.

Born in 1764, Eclipse was never beaten in his entire career. He was the great-great-grandson of Darley Arabian (one of the three founding sires of the English Thoroughbred), and was thought to have superb conformation for a racehorse.

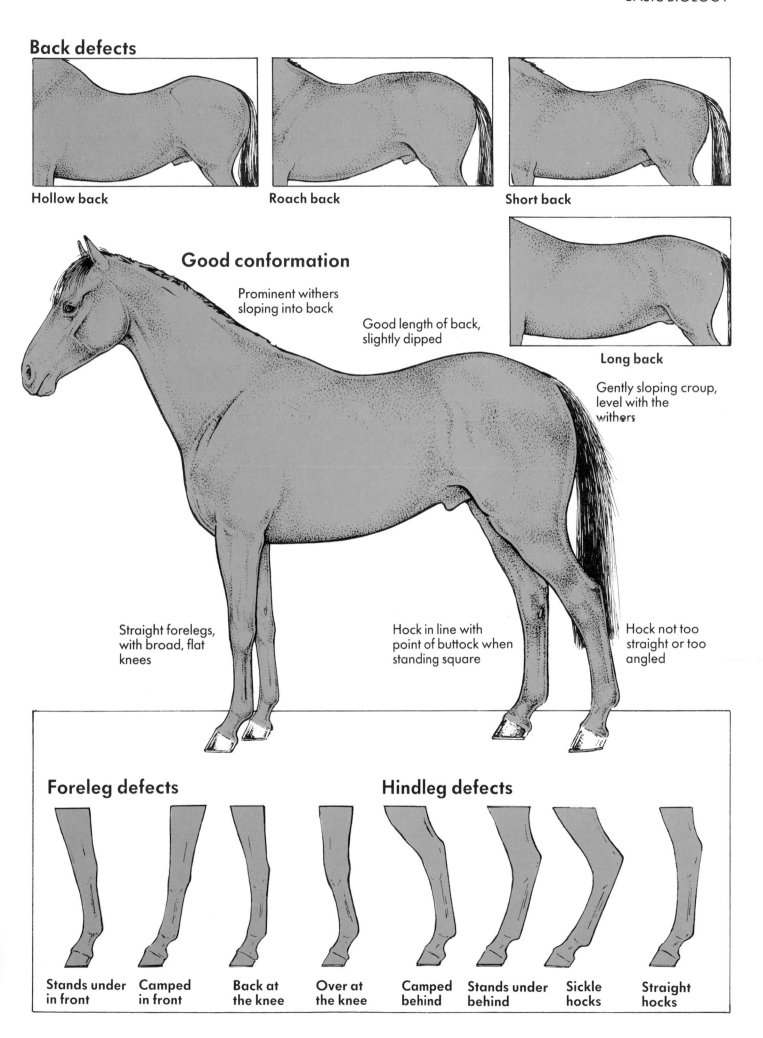

Back defects

Hollow back

Roach back

Short back

Long back

Good conformation

Prominent withers sloping into back

Good length of back, slightly dipped

Gently sloping croup, level with the withers

Straight forelegs, with broad, flat knees

Hock in line with point of buttock when standing square

Hock not too straight or too angled

Foreleg defects

Stands under in front

Camped in front

Back at the knee

Over at the knee

Hindleg defects

Camped behind

Stands under behind

Sickle hocks

Straight hocks

All about hooves

DID YOU KNOW?
Over 55 million years ago horses had four splayed-out toes so that they could move about in marshy swamps without sinking into the ground.

As the climate changed and the ground hardened, the horse began to rely more and more on its middle toes, making the rest unnecessary.

Gradually the other toes disappeared, leaving us with the single-toed horse!

The horse's foot consists of everything within the hoof. Hooves are box-like protective shells and help absorb shock to the legs created when the horse moves.

How is the hoof designed?

The hoof is made up of three parts – the **sole**, **wall** and **frog**.

The sole should be arched and is designed to take weight from above – a well-formed sole shouldn't touch the ground. A **white line** runs around its rim where the sole meets the hoof wall.

The hoof wall is formed at the coronet where horny tissue mixes with special skin-like cells to form the hard hoof wall. This wall is like our nails. But, unlike us, the horse balances and moves around on his tip toes!

The hoof wall has an inner layer of laminae ('fingers' of bone). These inter-lace with a second set of laminae which are attached to the **pedal bone** and lock the hoof firmly into place.

The frog: At the **heel**, the hoof wall turns inward toward the frog, forming the **bars** of the foot. When these make contact with the ground they give slightly, helping to absorb some of the impact.

A well-shaped frog touches the ground as the horse moves and presses upward against the large, fatty pad, known as the **plantar cushion**.

Blood enters and leaves the foot by a **digital artery** and vein on either side of the leg. Two nerves run alongside these vessels, carrying any sensation into the deeper layers of the foot.

How a horse moves

The **pedal joint** lies within the hoof. This acts like a hinge, linking the pedal

---

Outside of the foot

The hoof grows at a rate of 8-10mm (about ¼in) a month. It takes eight to ten months for a completely new hoof wall to form. The hoof wall is protected by a thin waterproof outer layer. Like our nails, the wall has no nerve supply. A farrier can, therefore, drive nails into the hoof wall without causing the horse any discomfort.

Cross-section of the foot

Because the hoof wall takes the entire weight of the horse, it has to be extremely strong – so the foot is one of the most important parts of the horse. There's even an old saying, 'No foot, no horse'!

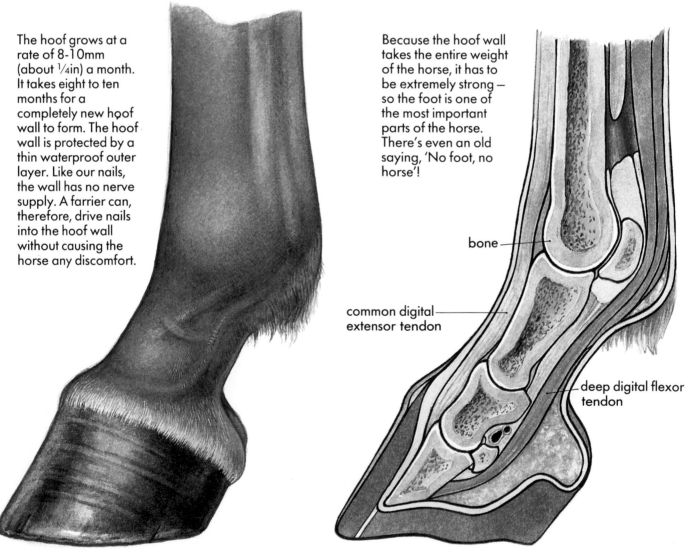

bone

common digital extensor tendon

deep digital flexor tendon

bone to the **short pastern bone**, and makes it possible for the horse to move his foot.

Two large tendons (sinews) move the pedal bone. One (the **common digital extensor**) enters the hoof at the front, while the other (the **deep digital flexor**) runs down the back of the pastern to enter the hoof at the heels.

Behind the pedal bone is a second small bone, known as the **navicular bone**, over which the deep digital flexor tendon runs. When the tendon stretches over this bone it helps to absorb further the shock of impact.

The horse's weight is taken by the hoof wall, not the sole. For brief moments during a jump or gallop, the whole weight of the horse (around 500kg/1100lb) is supported on a single foreleg showing the tremendous strength of the horse's hooves.

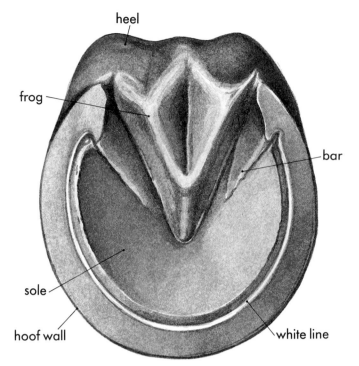

Ground surface of the hoof

Circulation in the foot

Blood is circulated around the foot by the digital artery and vein, which run alongside each other. When the frog makes contact with the ground it presses upward against the plantar cushion which in turn pumps blood back up the horse's legs.

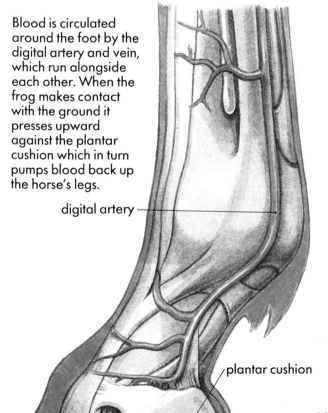

The bones of the foot

The horse's foot can be compared to our fingers. The hoof wall is like our finger nails, the tips of our fingers are the equivalent of the pedal bone, our middle bone is like the short pastern and our third bone is similar to the long pastern.

The anatomy

The body of the horse is not really designed to suit the needs of a rider. In the wild, horses gallop in short bursts and only jump to escape danger. So the two most popular tasks we ask our horses to perform are also the most demanding.

Simply sitting on a horse puts strain on him and affects his balance. The horse has to adjust to your weight whenever you ride. But by riding correctly – and sensitively – you can make life much easier for him.

The framework
The anatomy (skeleton) is the framework of bones which protects the internal organs like the heart and lungs. It also supports the muscles and helps to provide movement. It is made up of about 210 bones (excluding the tail).

The spine
The horse has a rigid spine and a heavy body, unlike other agile animals. Because of this the joints are under strain when he moves, particularly when he gallops over several miles or jumps.

To cope with this, the ends of each bone are made up of hard, dense cells. These are covered by cartilage (padding) which acts as a shock absorber and protects the horse as his hooves hit the ground.

The horse has a weak point at the end of the rib cage and before the pelvis begins – a small row of vertebrae are the only supporting bones. Never sit here or put weight on this point.

The limbs
Joints in the hindlegs are angled. They help to propel the horse forward so all movement begins from here. After a jump the horse comes down on the forelegs which, with the shoulders, absorb most of the shock.

The head and neck
The skull is long to accommodate the teeth. The neck is also long, and together they enable the horse to reach short grass or leafy branches!

A horse's weight shifts forward when he lowers his head, and shifts backward when he lifts it. You can feel this when you're riding. You are automatically tipped forward when the horse puts his head down and, if he tosses his head up, your weight goes backward.

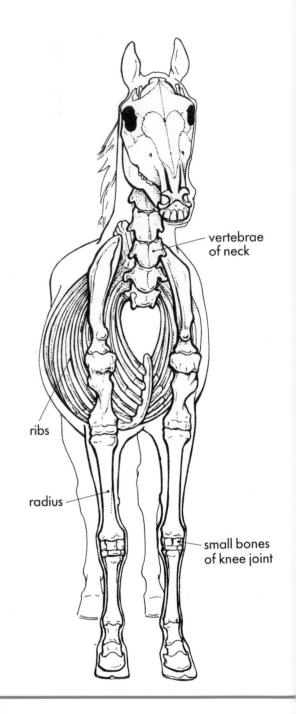

vertebrae of neck

ribs

radius

small bones of knee joint

The spine and speed
Although we think of horses as being speedy animals, they're actually quite slow relative to their size. The horse has a rigid spine which gives it a limited degree of movement. Racehorses can reach about 64kmph (40mph) over a short period, but compare this with the cheetah — an animal less than half its size.

The cheetah can run at 113kmph (70mph), making it the fastest animal on earth. This is largely due to its flexible spine which curves up and down when it runs. The leg bones swivel with the spine. So the cheetah can increase its speed and lengthen its stride, alternately extending all four legs and bunching them underneath its body. A single bound can extend a massive 7m (23ft).

What the skeleton looks like

A side view of the horse's anatomy shows clearly the strong, interlocking bones in the legs which provide the power to move fast. The bones in the forelegs (best seen from the front) take the strain after a jump.

skull (cranium)

shoulder blade (scapula)

hip joint

spinal cord

dock

elbow joint

stifle joint

long pastern

cannon bone

short pastern

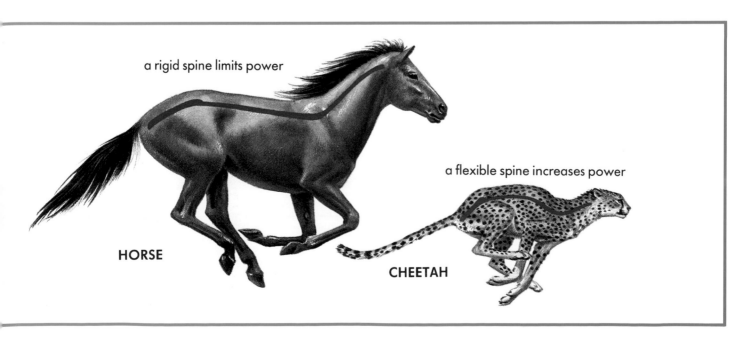

a rigid spine limits power

a flexible spine increases power

HORSE

CHEETAH

Muscles and movement

★ **SPEED OR ENDURANCE?**
Some horses perform best at speed events, others excel at endurance competitions – just like athletes who are good at either sprinting or long-distance running.

The make-up of the fibre in the muscle determines where a horse's strength lies. There are two main groups – 'slow twitch' and 'fast twitch' fibres.

Slow twitch fibres contract slowly and require plenty of oxygen. They are important in long-distance performance.

Fast twitch fibres contract quickly and do not need as much oxygen. They are important for speed events.

Muscle fibre is determined at birth and cannot be altered by training.

★ **SMOOTH MUSCLE**
A different type of muscle, smooth muscle, is found in the arteries and bowel wall. Smooth muscle enables the arteries to pump blood around the body and helps the bowel wall push food along by contracting.

Smooth muscle is also in the airways to the lungs allowing a horse to cough if he is allergic, for instance, to the dust in his bedding.

The main purpose of the muscles is to support the horse's weight – about 500kg (1100lb). The muscles also give a horse the power to move around quickly and over long distances.

What are muscles?

Muscles are made up of thousands of minute fibres which create energy by contracting.

When standing, only a few of the fibres in the muscles are needed to hold up the weight. But when a horse is involved in strenuous exercise or work, all the fibres in the muscle contract to meet the animal's needs.

The main muscles are situated on the shoulders, trunk, loins and hindquarters. The moving parts, such as the legs, have very little heavy muscle tissue. This cuts down their weight and reduces the level of wind resistance.

The horse's speed and stamina – which come from the muscles – have played a major part in the horse's survival over millions of years. The strong and finely co-ordinated system of muscles has given it the power to escape danger fast.

How the muscles work

Most of the horse's muscles are attached to its bones by fibres known as ligaments. But in the case of the legs the energy is transferred from the muscles in the forearm and thigh to the limbs by long fibrous bands called tendons.

Tendons run over pulley-like structures such as the sesamoid bone in the fetlock and the navicular bone in the hoof. These act as supports and increase the power that the muscles can exert.

The main areas of muscle

This diagram shows the outer muscles of a horse. Beneath these muscles lies a deeper, hidden layer which also helps provide movement and energy.

The main force which propels the horse forward comes from the **hindquarters**. This thick mass of complex muscle covering the buttocks does most work during galloping.

The horse's **skin** has many more muscles than ours. This gives horses and ponies the enviable ability to twitch any part of their body to dislodge flies!

The main energy comes from the pendulum-like motion of the **legs**.

Strong **back muscles** hold the back bones together tightly.

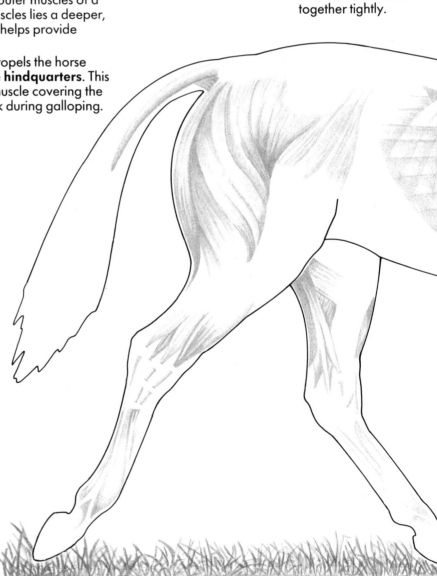

The importance of exercise

When the muscle contracts to provide energy, waste products are produced.

One of these waste products, lactic acid, can cause fatigue if it is allowed to accumulate.

To prevent this from happening the muscles must have an efficient blood supply. This helps the process of absorbing oxygen and getting rid of waste products.

Regular exercise improves the blood supply to the muscles by keeping the blood moving around the body. This maintains a healthy circulation and keeps the muscles in good shape.

Horse power?

The idea of 'horsepower' in cars dates from the earliest days of motorized transport. Horsepower was calculated on an average horse lifting about 15 tons over 30cm (1ft) in one minute. This 12 horsepower racing car — pictured in 1906 — was unbeaten at 40 miles an hour!

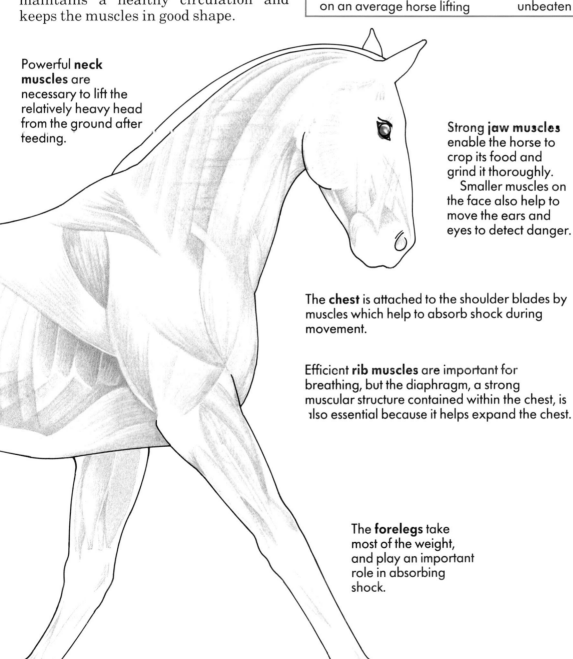

Powerful **neck muscles** are necessary to lift the relatively heavy head from the ground after feeding.

Strong **jaw muscles** enable the horse to crop its food and grind it thoroughly.
 Smaller muscles on the face also help to move the ears and eyes to detect danger.

The **chest** is attached to the shoulder blades by muscles which help to absorb shock during movement.

Efficient **rib muscles** are important for breathing, but the diaphragm, a strong muscular structure contained within the chest, is also essential because it helps expand the chest.

The **forelegs** take most of the weight, and play an important role in absorbing shock.

★ **NON-STOP HEARTBEAT**

The heart is composed of extremely strong muscle — cardiac muscle — so that it can perform the arduous task of pumping blood around the body.

To keep the blood moving, the muscle in the heart has to expand and contract non-stop. Even when a horse is at rest, the heart beats between 30–40 times a minute.

Horses have no control over the muscle in the heart. But it automatically contracts more often if a horse is involved in exercise or if he needs to escape danger. At a gallop the heart beats about 220 times a minute.

How the blood circulates

The blood has the important task of carrying oxygen and nourishment to all the cells within the horse's body. It also plays a vital role in preventing disease and helping to keep a horse healthy.

The contents of the blood

Blood is made up of liquids and solids. The liquid, called serum, carries the solids around the body and takes waste products to the **kidneys** to be discharged.

The solids are divided into two parts – red blood cells and white blood cells. The red blood cells transport oxygen round the body and carry waste gases from the tissues to the lungs. White blood cells, on the other hand, act as an army helping to combat the enemy – disease.

How blood pumps round

The horse has a highly efficient **heart** which acts as a pump. It sends blood to every part of the body.

Blood leaves the heart and flows toward the **lungs** where it absorbs oxygen. It then returns to the heart and begins its journey through a major network of **arteries**.

The thick muscular walls of the **aorta**, the main artery leading from the heart, squeeze blood along into smaller arteries. These eventually link up with minute vessels called **capillaries**. Here oxygen and nutrients are absorbed and waste products discharged.

The **liver** acts as a filter sorting out and storing nutrients. Worn-out red blood cells pass into the **spleen** where they are destroyed.

Capillaries connect the arteries to veins. Once the oxygen has been absorbed the blood starts its homeward journey to the heart through the **veins**.

Veins have thin walls with little muscle in them and so rely on movement of the surrounding tissues to squeeze blood back along them. They

The vital organs requiring oxygen

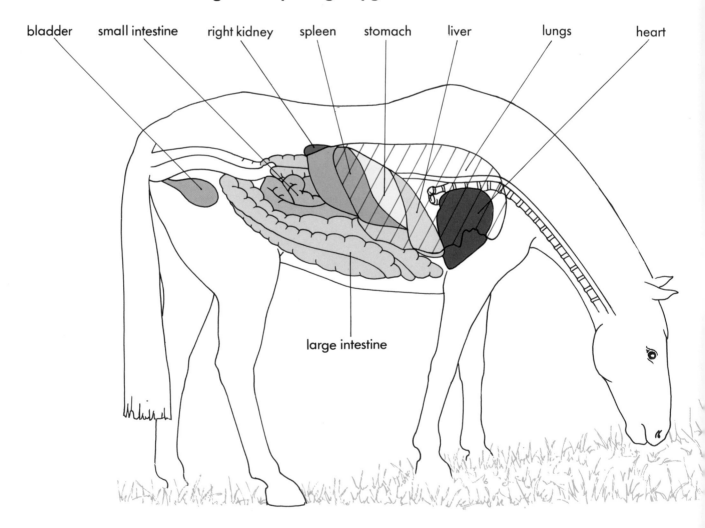

bladder   small intestine   right kidney   spleen   stomach   liver   lungs   heart

large intestine

also have valves which allow blood to flow in one direction only. So when a horse puts his head down to graze, the blood does not rush to his head. It continues on its way back to the heart.

Additional help

Blood returning to the heart from the feet has an uphill struggle. It tends to collect in the feet.

To overcome this, there is an in-built pump within the foot which helps force blood back up the legs. When a horse's hoof hits the ground, the V-shaped frog makes contact and presses against the shock-absorbing plantar cushion lying beneath it. This squeezes the veins in the foot and helps pump blood up the leg.

Painful parts

When a part of the body is deprived of its normal blood supply the cells die and it becomes extremely painful. Colic is frequently caused by the lack of blood supply to a part of the **bowel**. This in turn is often caused by a blockage in a blood vessel.

Another most painful condition in horses and ponies – laminitis – results from changes in the blood supply to the feet.

Regular exercise is one of the keys to maintaining an efficient circulation system – this is what is meant by getting a horse fit. It helps improve the movement of blood in the feet and keeps the muscles well supplied with oxygen.

★ **HEAVY HEART**
A horse's heart weighs about 4k (8½lb) and is relatively large compared to the size of its body. Compared to this, the human heart is light – between 300-350gm (10-12oz).

Its size and efficiency usually determine a horse's powers of speed and stamina – a small horse with a large heart can often out-run a larger one with a smaller heart.

The heart, therefore, can have an effect on the performance of a race horse.

For instance, the heart of the legendary unbeaten race horse, 'Eclipse' weighed over 6.5k (14lb)!

Veins and arteries

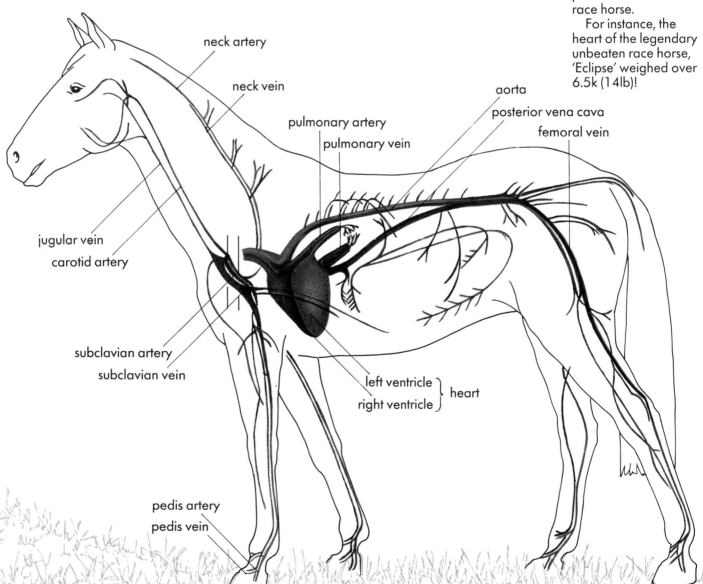

neck artery

neck vein

pulmonary artery

pulmonary vein

aorta

posterior vena cava

femoral vein

jugular vein

carotid artery

subclavian artery

subclavian vein

left ventricle
right ventricle } heart

pedis artery

pedis vein

21

How the horse digests food

Horses and ponies have an efficient digestive system designed to cope with their natural diet – grass.

How the horse eats

Grass is fairly indigestible so, for a horse to get enough goodness out of it, he needs to eat large amounts. But the stomach is so small that he has to eat little and often.

The horse's stomach works best when it is two-thirds full. An over-full stomach can cause pain (colic) and slows down the process of passing food from the stomach into the small intestine.

In a field, horses feed throughout the day. Stable-kept horses should be given frequent small feeds to imitate their natural pattern – never give a horse a large feed that he cannot cope with.

A horse has sharp front (incisor) teeth which enable him to graze tight to the ground. Horses also have mobile lips, which they use as 'fingers' to pick up small grains. The tongue moves food to the teeth at the back of the mouth where it is crushed thoroughly before being swallowed and passed down the **digestive tract**.

Breaking down the food

The grass is washed down with plenty of liquid to help reduce the food to a pulp. Horses produce vast quantities of saliva a day – about 10-12 litres (2-2½ gallons). Compare this with the amount of

Four to one

The horse has an extremely small stomach for its size. It holds between 8 and 15 litres (1½-3½ gallons). This is very different from the other main group of grass-eaters – ruminants – who chew their food twice. The cow, for example, has four stomachs which hold from 140 to 235 litres (30-50 gallons).

The cow's stomach occupies the left flank; the other organs the right. So that all the organs are visible, the stomach has been drawn further forward and to the right of its true position.

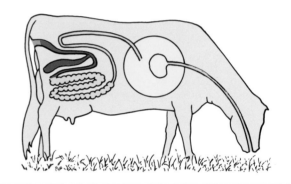

COLOUR CODING
The parts of the horse's digestive system are colour coded so that you can easily distinguish them.

- digestive tract
- stomach
- small intestine
- caecum (pronounced *sea-cum*)
- large colon
- small colon
- rectum

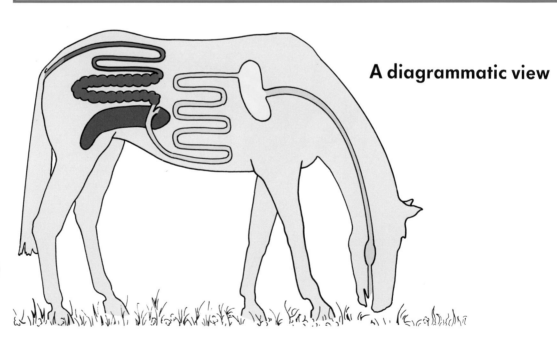

A diagrammatic view

The digestive system

The digestive system of the horse and cow shown in diagram form on this page illustrate just how much smaller the horse's stomach is compared to that of the cow.

The cow's four stomachs hold about 20 times as much food as that of the horse. This is because food breaks down in the cow's rumen, the biggest of its four stomachs. In the horse, this process takes place in the large intestine, which is correspondingly bigger than that of the cow.

saliva we produce – between 1-1½ litres (2-3 pints) a day.

When food reaches the **stomach** and **small intestine**, digestive juices are added. Some nutrients are absorbed in the small intestine – particularly sugars and proteins – from concentrated food such as nuts and oats.

Food then moves on and breaks down further in the large intestine (which consists of the **caecum**, the **large colon** and the **small colon** and passes into the **rectum**.

The horse's caecum (pronounced sea-cum) is the equivalent of the human appendix. But our appendix has become unnecessary over the years as grass is no longer a part of our diet.

The large intestine can hold 80 to 120 litres (18-26 gallons) of fermenting food. Here, bacteria break up the grass into nutrients that the horse can absorb. The bacteria even produce some vitamins themselves, so the horse has its own built-in vitamin factory! Bacteria are absorbed with the dissolved nutrients, at the end of the large intestine.

The end result

Once the fluid has been absorbed, the horse passes waste matter through the rectum. Droppings should be soft enough to break up on hitting the ground.

If stabled horses eat too much dry food, don't have enough to drink or lack exercise their bowel movements may slow down. This allows more time for fluid to be absorbed, makes the dropping hard, and can cause constipation. So it is important to give laxative foods (such as a bran mash) to stabled horses before a day off, or if they cannot be exercised due to illness.

DID YOU KNOW?
A horse is unable to vomit because of the anatomy of the back of the mouth. If a horse chokes, or its stomach becomes swollen (this happens in some cases of colic) food must be brought back through the nostrils.

All the words in **heavy print** are shown on the diagrams.

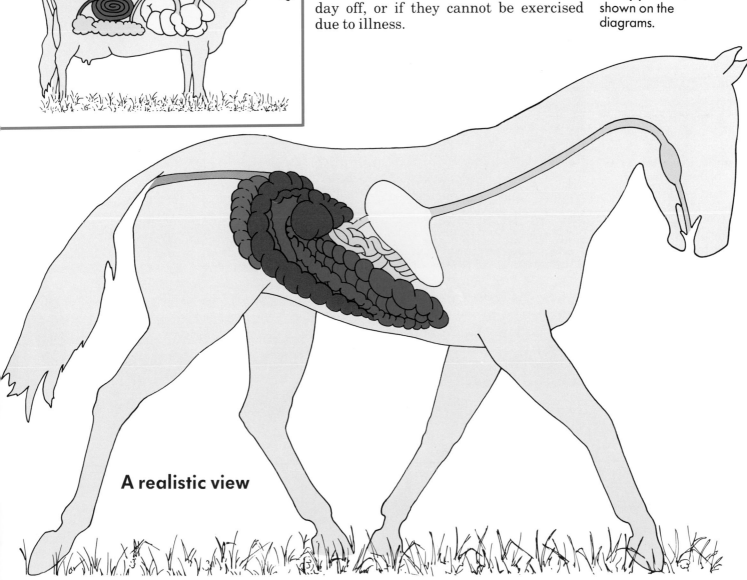

A realistic view

Sight and hearing

In the wild, a horse is naturally defensive. When threatened, his instinct is to escape. But he needs advance warning to run away in enough time to avoid the danger.

The horse's eyes and ears work together to give this warning. The eyes are geared for sideways vision, backed up by acute hearing.

Seeing sideways

Horses have prominent eyes which are set well apart on the sides of the face. This means that a horse can see almost all around his body with one or other eye and can detect danger.

However, this eye position presents a problem. Most of a horse's vision is one eyed and he cannot see directly in front or behind – he has a blind spot.

The sensitive ear

To help their sight, horses have extremely sensitive hearing. They can locate the *exact* source of sound, picking up softer noises than the human ear.

A horse has 16 muscles controlling each ear and can move his ears separately toward the sound, rather than moving the whole head. The funnel shape of the ears helps to make sounds seem louder and clearer.

▼ **The position of a horse's eyes** limits sight directly in front and behind.

When a horse looks straight ahead with his head in its normal resting position, the eyes focus on a point about 2m (7ft) from his muzzle. A horse cannot see immediately in front of him. This area is known as the blind spot.

► **Horses sometimes wear blinkers** to restrict their sideways vision.

Blinkers stop a horse being distracted from the work in hand and help to keep his concentration.

▼ **Horses cannot focus** on obstacles straight in front of them. If a horse cannot see or remember a fence, he may refuse to jump (below). Once he has investigated the obstacle (below right), he should jump clear.

sight with right eye only

unsighted

24

◄ **When startled** by a strange or unusual noise a horse often prepares for flight. He pricks up his ears, points them toward the sound (left), tries to identify it and then decides whether or not he needs to take flight (below).

unsighted

ight with
eft eye only

► **Horses can move their ears** to point in every direction around their body.

This mare points her ears backward to check what is behind her, so that she is always ready to protect her foal. The foal in turn listens to his mother to check that everything is safe.

Touch and sensation

Sensory nerves, which respond to touch, heat, cold and pain, are scattered throughout the horse's skin. But a horse's sensitivity varies over the different parts of its body, depending on the number of nerves supplied to each area.

STANDING STILL
A horse's sensitive skin can be helpful in restraining a naughty horse.

You can make a horse stand still for a few moments by pinching a small fold of skin in the middle of the neck.

How horses feel
The nose and muzzle are so sensitive that horses can use them much as we use our fingers. Nerves in the highly sensitive whiskers around the muzzle send messages to the brain whenever they come into contact with something. These messages help the horse to judge how far away an object is and whether or not it may be dangerous. Similar hairs surround and protect the eyes.

Horses also have extremely sensitive backs. They can easily detect flies landing on them and, if you run your finger or a brush gently along a horse's spine, it often dips down in reaction to the contact. Indeed, some horses have such sensitive skin that they dip their backs whenever the saddle is put on. This is known as a 'cold back'.

Continual pressure on a sensitive

▼ **Scratching** an itchy area can be difficult for ponies. This Dartmoor pony finds the solution by rubbing himself against a rock.

area tends to dull feeling. For this reason, pulling at the bit deadens the bars of the mouth and can make a horse insensitive and unresponsive.

Feeling the heat
Nerves in the skin are not only sensitive to touch. They also respond to heat and cold. When the skin is hot, its blood vessels open up to lose heat. More fluid enters the sweat glands to produce extra sweat and so help cool the horse.

In summer, horses also change their coat and the hair lies flat to prevent a warming layer of air from being trapped between the hairs.

Out in the cold
In cold weather, the horse's nerve centre responds to produce the opposite effect. The vessels close up and produce less sweat. If the temperature drops even lower, the hairs stand on end, trapping air in the coat and providing a warm, insulating blanket.

In really cold weather, ponies often indulge in a bit of do-it-yourself 'loft insulation'. They roll about in mud so that they become caked in a messy but effective coat that helps prevent heat loss from the surface of the skin!

◄ **The long sensitive whiskers** help horses determine the texture of the pasture when grazing. This Haflinger has been furrowing in the snow for fresh green grass.

⅄ **In the heat** of the midday sun, a herd of Mustangs seek shelter in the shade of trees. Horses can suffer from sunburn if they have any fleshmarks (unpigmented skin) on their coat.

DID YOU KNOW?
When horses moult in summer, their coats produce a waterproofing oil known as sebum. This protects the coat and helps keep out the rain so the horse stays cool but dry.

◄ **During the winter,** horses usually grow a thick coat to protect them from the low temperatures. In extreme cold, the long hair on these ponies stands on end to trap air and so warm up their bodies.

Smell and taste

The senses of smell and taste play a very important part in the lives of horses because they act as a warning system. Smell is useful for sorting out the familiar from the unknown and taste helps a horse to distinguish between healthy and harmful food or water.

Recognizing each other

A horse uses its acute sense of smell to investigate strange objects. When a pony enters an unfamiliar stable or paddock the first thing he does is sniff and snort at his new surroundings.

Horses recognize their friends and rivals through body smell – each individual has its own scent. Horses usually sniff each other's breath when they greet one another. This is the equine equivalent of a hand-shake.

Scent is particularly important in the bond between mare and foal. A mare works out which foal belongs to her by the smell it gives off.

Horses even get used to a person's natural odour and any unusual smell such as perfume confuses them and can upset them.

When a horse wants to study a smell more closely, he takes a deep breath, raises his head and curls the top lip upward, over the nostrils, to trap the smell in his nose. This behaviour is known as '*flehmen*'.

In the wild

Horses can detect smells over long distances. A stallion can pick up the scent of a mare that is in season when she is up to 600m (780yds) away. Horses can tell where there is water from a long way away as well.

Smells also form a part of boundary marking. Horses deposit droppings and urine around their personal territory so that others can recognize the borders and avoid 'trespassing'.

A horse's strong sense of smell discourages it from grazing near droppings because they send out an unpleasant odour. This is important in preventing the spread of worms.

The sweet tooth

Horses choose their food firstly by smell and then by taste. Their muzzles act like

▲ **Treat your horse** to sweet titbits every now and then. But try not to give him too many because he'll expect them all the time and it may make him bad mannered.

► **Smell** is one of the horse's most important senses. A horse recognizes his friends by their body smell. Here a couple of wild horses sniff each other's breath in recognition.

fingers in helping to sort out what they want to eat and what they want to leave behind.

Having passed the 'sniff' test, food can then be distinguished by its sweet, bitter, sour or salty taste. Generally horses dislike bitter tastes and have a sweet tooth.

Because of this, they usually love sugar lumps and are also often very fond of sugar-beet. They also like unusual or spicy tastes, including peppermints and ginger.

The 'taste' test is a final safety mechanism: poisonous plants, such as ragwort, yew and laburnum, taste extremely bitter and are quickly rejected. Even if a horse or pony is tempted to take a bite of something dangerous, in most cases he spits it out straight away.

▲ **Although horses do not eat buttercups** from choice, they sometimes munch them with a mouthful of grass because these flowers do not taste as bitter as other poisonous plants. Fortunately buttercups are only harmful if they are eaten in great quantities so the odd one will not upset a pony.

▼ **Horses enjoy all types of titbits** from carrots and apples to hard mints and treats. Horses have an exceptionally sweet tooth — but never give a horse soft mints as he cannot cope with chewy foods.

peppermint treats

carrots

apples

carrot treats

hard mints

All about teeth

The horse's teeth are well designed to cope with his main source of food – grass. Although constant chewing and grinding of grass wears away the tooth surface, horses' teeth continue to grow throughout their lives – unlike ours, which do not grow at all once they have fully developed. Growth normally occurs in a tooth at the same rate at which it is being worn away. This means that the teeth always *appear* to be the same, unchanging length.

How the teeth work

The horse's teeth begin the digestive process by cutting and crushing the food, so it is in a suitable state for the rest of the digestive system to work on. A horse's front teeth (incisors) act like very sharp scissors, cutting the grass and enabling the animal to graze very close to the ground.

After it has been cut, the grass is transferred to the back of the mouth by the tongue, which is very mobile. Here the grass is thoroughly ground between the cheek teeth before being swallowed.

The horse's teeth

All adult horses have at least 36 teeth – 12 front teeth (incisors) and 24 cheek teeth (molars). Male horses usually have four extra teeth, called 'tushes' (canines).
The front teeth (incisors): There are six incisor teeth in each jaw (upper and lower). They must meet exactly for the animal to eat effectively. When the upper teeth are in front of the lower ones ('parrot' mouth), or the other way round ('under-shot'), it is difficult for the animal to graze properly.
Cheek teeth (premolars and molars): There are six cheek teeth on each side of the upper jaw, and the same number in the lower jaw. Technically, there are three

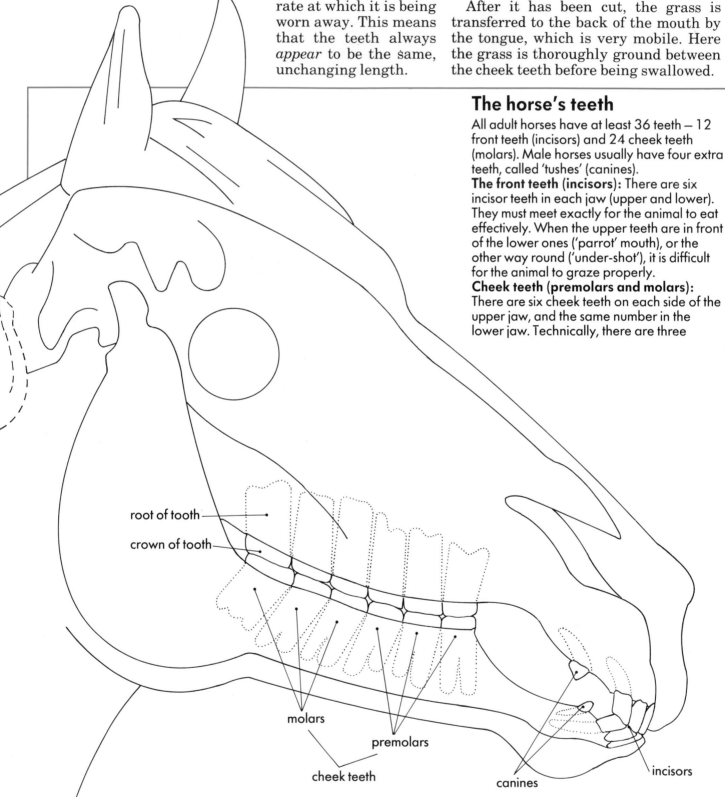

root of tooth

crown of tooth

molars

premolars

cheek teeth

canines

incisors

► **Not just for eating:** These two horses are using their teeth for mutual grooming. This is where they scratch each other's withers, back or the top of the tail. Not only does this relieve itching in difficult-to-reach places, but it is a sign of friendship and trust.

premolar teeth and three *molar* teeth, but there is no real difference between them.

These teeth are covered with a hard substance called enamel, but the grinding surface is folded into many ridges and crevices in which there is an even harder material known as cement.

Canine teeth (tushes): Stallions and geldings usually develop small canine teeth at four years old, but three out of four mares do not possess them at all. They are found in the space between the front teeth and the cheek teeth. As they do not meet with the same tooth in the opposite jaw, they cannot be used for eating, and may become quite sharp.

Teeth and diet

The horse is a *herbivore* (he eats grass and other vegetation) and the tiger is a *carnivore* (meat-eater). Because of their opposite diets, their teeth are shaped completely differently. The horse's incisors (front teeth) are well-developed chisels for cutting grass — unlike those of the tiger, which are tiny and of little importance. In contrast, the tiger has large, pointed canines for catching and holding prey. The horse's canines are either small or absent because they have no eating function.

Prehistoric teeth

The earliest prehistoric horses lived in swamps some 60-70 million years ago. Here they ate juicy fruits and succulent plants. These animals had very small, soft teeth which were well suited to their diet. Over millions of years, the climate changed. The swamps were replaced by dry plains where there was only a sparse covering of much tougher food material – grass.

During this period the teeth of the horse's ancestors gradually altered to cope with their new diet. The small soft teeth were replaced by much bigger ones with a tougher grinding surface. The horse's facial bones lengthened to make room for these large teeth. Powerful jaw muscles also developed, so the horse could crush the grass to pulp.

Wolf teeth

A few horses have extra, tiny cheek teeth, known as 'wolf' teeth. They lie in front of the upper cheek teeth and, rarely, in front of the lower cheek teeth as well.

These teeth can be very sharp. When the bit pulls the horse's cheeks against them, the cheeks may be cut and become sore. This can make the horse unwilling to respond to his rider's instructions. So these 'useless' teeth are sometimes removed by the vet, under a painless local anaesthetic.

RASPING THE TEETH
If the surface of the tooth wears down unevenly, the edges may become sharp and cut the cheeks and tongue, so the horse cannot chew his food properly.

When this happens, a vet must 'rasp' the teeth (file them down to make the surfaces level). Tooth problems are very common in old horses, and their teeth should be checked regularly.

Telling a horse's age

Horses' front teeth (incisors) show characteristic signs of wear with age. These changes can be used to tell a pony's age fairly accurately up to the age of 8. Beyond this, it is only possible to give an estimate, so horses and ponies over 8 are often described as 'aged'.

Milk teeth

A pony has a full set of six temporary *(milk)* incisor teeth in each jaw by the time he is 9 months old. The two innermost teeth in each jaw are called *centrals*, those on each side of them are called *laterals* (or *middle* incisors), and those at the corners of the mouth are known as *corners*.

Between 2½ and 4½ years, the temporary teeth are replaced by permanent ones. You should be able to distinguish the white, shell-like milk teeth from the bigger, yellowish, adult ones, when ageing young horses.

The tables

The next step is to inspect the grinding surfaces of the teeth (called *tables*). The outline of the tables changes with age – it is oval in young horses (5 years), becomes circular by 8, then more and more triangular.

In the middle of the tables of young horses is a hole known as the *infundibulum*. As the teeth wear down, this hole becomes less obvious and eventually disappears. Wear also exposes a

Birth to 4 weeks

The two innermost temporary incisors ('centrals') are either present at birth, or emerge soon afterwards. These teeth have a large hole in the centre – the *infundibulum*.

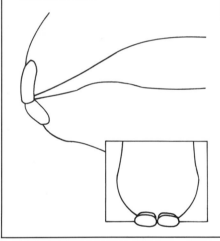

4 to 6 weeks

The second pair of temporary incisors ('laterals' or middle incisors) have now emerged through the gums on each side of the centrals.

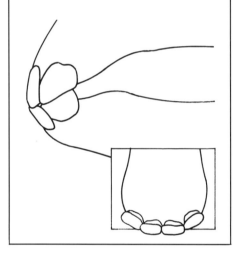

6 to 9 months

The third pair of temporary incisors ('corners') come through at about 9 months, but are not 'fully in wear' (meet with the opposite teeth) until 3 to 5 months later.

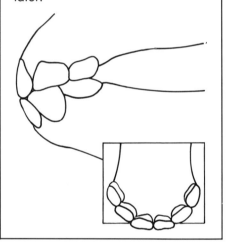

6 years

The infundibulum has become faint and has almost disappeared from the central teeth. Up to this age, the central incisors meet vertically.

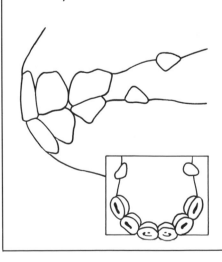

7 years

The upper corner incisors have developed the typical '7 year hook'. The centrals are becoming rounder in outline than the oval shape of younger horses.

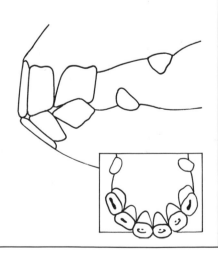

8 years

The black *dental star* is becoming apparent, just in front of the remains of the infundibulum in the centrals and laterals. The teeth now meet at an angle, not vertically.

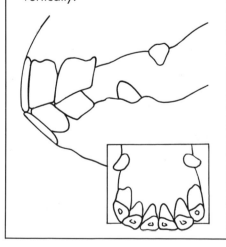

ridge of dentine which is first seen as a black, elongated line in front of the infundibulum at 8 years. This is known as the *dental star*. It becomes progressively more circular as the horse gets older.

Long in the tooth

In young horses (up to 8 years) the teeth meet vertically when viewed from the side. Beyond the age of 8, the angle between upper and lower teeth becomes increasingly more acute, until, at 20, the teeth meet at right angles. In old horses, too, the gums recede from the teeth — they become 'long in the tooth'.

In some horses and ponies (but not all) there is a stained groove on the outer surface of the upper corner incisors. This is known as *Galvayne's groove*. It first appears at the gum at 10, has grown half way down the tooth by 15, and reaches the grinding surface at 20.

Looking at teeth: a tricky business!

3 years
The temporary central incisors are replaced by larger, permanent ones at 2½ years old, but these do not come fully into wear until the horse is 3.

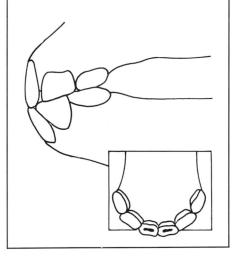

4 years
The temporary lateral (middle) incisors have been lost and replaced by permanent ones at 3½. They will not come fully into wear until the horse is 4 years old.

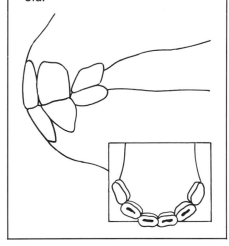

4½ years
The temporary corner incisors are being replaced by permanent ones. The pony will have a complete set of adult teeth when he is 5. The canine teeth ('tushes') have emerged after 4.

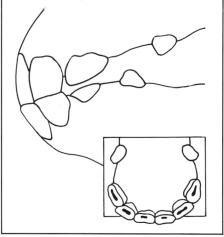

10 years
Dental stars are present in all teeth. The centrals are becoming more triangular in outline. *Galvayne's groove* is just appearing at the gum on the upper corner teeth.

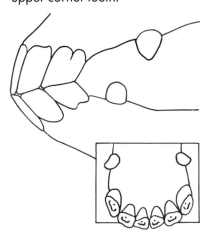

13 years
The infundibulum has just about disappeared from all six teeth. The dental stars are becoming wider and rounder. The teeth are more triangular in outline, and meet at a much greater angle.

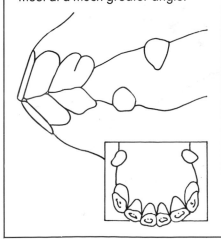

20 years
The angle between the two sets of teeth is now almost 90°. The tables are triangular in outline, and Galvayne's groove has reached the tip of the upper corner teeth.

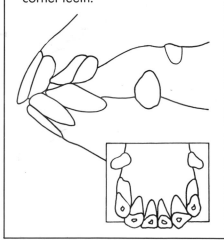

Breeding: the stallion

► **A stallion** uses his sense of smell to test whether or not a mare is ready for mating. When she is, she gives off special scents called pheromones. To study these smells closely, the stallion traps them in his nose by curling his top lip over his nostrils — this is known as 'flehmen'.

▼ **In any herd of horses** only the dominant stallion can mate with the mares. Here he herds his team of mares away from rival males.

Watching a herd of wild horses during the breeding season can be fascinating — particularly if you know how stallions and mares show their attraction for each other.

In a wild herd there is one dominant stallion who has the right to mate with any mature mare. Females can start to breed from about the age of two and they may continue well into their 20's.

The mating season

Horses naturally breed in spring. From late winter the increasing hours of daylight stimulate chemicals called hormones in the bodies of both mares and stallions. These hormones prepare the horses mentally and physically for breeding.

When mares are ready for mating, they give off special scents — called pheromones — from their flanks and

◄▲ **As a stallion woos a mare** he sniffs and nibbles her. If she isn't ready for mating, she might well kick so he takes care never to approach her from behind. If she is ready to mate, she pricks her ears and allows him to nuzzle her.

around their tails. The stallion can detect them from up to a mile away, and when he does pick up a mare's scent the courtship begins. A domesticated stallion acts in exactly the same way and the presence of a mare in season can make him difficult to control for a novice rider.

Courtship

The stallion raises his head, opens his nostrils wide, pricks his ears and sniffs the air. He then walks toward the mare with his neck arched, head tossing and tail raised. He may circle her and follow her around squealing and nickering. Then he sniffs and nibbles her sides, flanks and around her tail. He curls his top lip over his nostrils to trap her smell in his nose.

An experienced stallion always approaches a mare from the side to avoid being kicked if she is not ready to mate. If she is ready, mating often takes place several times until the mare becomes pregnant or 'goes out of season'. When she is pregnant, a mare carries her foal for 11 months.

Rival males

In the wild each male must know his place. The dominant stallion chases out of the herd any outsider trying to take over and any junior male able to mate. He herds his team of mares away from the other males, who often try to approach a mare when the dominant

stallion isn't looking. They even try to steal young mares to start herds of their own. If they are unsuccessful, young males often go around together in 'gangs'. Females, on the other hand, always like to stay in family groups.

Only the strongest, bravest and cleverest stallions win the right to mate – old, defeated stallions often lead solitary lives.

Foaling time

To give foals the best start in life, nature works out the timing of their birth carefully. With the mating season in spring and an 11-month pregnancy, foals are usually born the following spring. The weather is warmer and the grass is growing.

If a foal is born too early, he can suffer badly from harsh weather. There may also be little grass around, which means his mother won't be able to provide enough milk for him.

If a foal is born too late, he may not survive the winter.

Pregnancy in horses can last from 321 days to 361 — nearly a year!

Pregnancy: a new life

A foal starts its long journey into the world when an egg from the mare's ovary meets the sperm from the stallion after mating. From the moment of conception it then takes about 336 days – roughly 11 months – for the foal to develop and grow inside the mare.

This interval of time – known as the gestation period – may not be the same for every mare. Some breeds have a longer gestation period than others: it can be as short as 321 days or as long as 361 days. Sometimes mares of the same breed have different gestation periods – one individual may produce her foals early and another always foal late.

The first signs

About two and a half weeks after conception the mare usually stops showing the signs of coming into season (when she is ready to mate).

In some cases, when the season has finished and the mare has successfully conceived, there may be no obvious changes in her condition until the time of foaling.

Usually, however, it should be obvious that a mare is pregnant. Caring owners know when their mare is not coming into season and whether it is possible that she has conceived.

Mares can be tested for pregnancy by a vet. There are many different methods: ultrasound scanning of the uterus and developing foal (a method similar to that used by doctors for pregnant women); an internal examination when the vet feels the developing structures directly through the wall of the mare's rectum (back passage); and urine or blood testing.

All these methods are used at different stages of pregnancy and the vet is the best judge of which is most suitable for a particular mare.

Inside the mare

After conception, the fertilized egg becomes attached to the lining of the mare's **uterus** (womb), where the process of development begins.

The egg divides, first into two cells, then four, then eight, 16 and so on. At first a ball of cells forms and this develops into a hollow sphere. Gradually the shape changes as the body of the foal grows and its internal organs start to form.

A little later on the **membranes** form and **fluid** surrounds the foal for protection. Also, the **placenta** develops. This is the structure which links the foal to the mother's uterus and supplies food and oxygen to the foal via the **umbilical cord**.

The foal's blood also contains waste products from its own body. These are transferred to the mother's blood and taken away in her bloodstream to be expelled from her body.

▲ **By the last few weeks** it usually becomes obvious that the mare is pregnant.

► **Diagrammatic view** of the position of the womb and the developing foal.

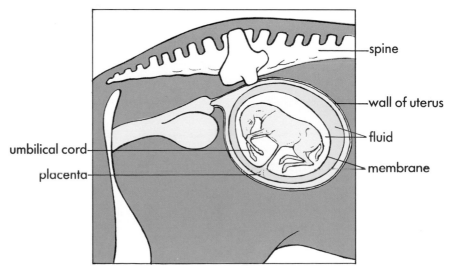

spine

wall of uterus

fluid

membrane

umbilical cord

placenta

The stages of development

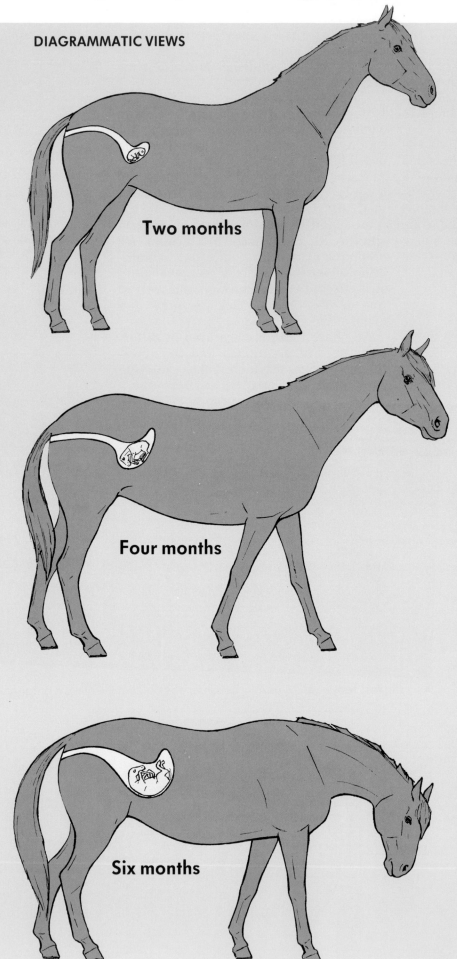

DIAGRAMMATIC VIEWS

Two months

Four months

Six months

In the first stages, the foal – known as the embryo at this stage – has little recognizable shape.

By 20 days after conception there are already millions of cells and the shape of the legs and head can be seen, although the embryo is only 2cm (about ¾in) long.

Once the limbs and internal organs have started to develop the tiny foal is called a foetus and this name applies up until birth.

At two months the foetus is clearly recognizable as a tiny horse and measures between 5 and 7cm (2–2½in) from head to tail. By three months the hooves have developed and the body is between 7 and 14cm (2½–5½in) long.

At four months hair begins to grow on the lips. Meanwhile the placenta develops and the umbilical cord forms. The foal's body is connected to the placenta by the umbilical cord. Blood circulates around the foal's body and then passes down the blood vessels in the umbilical cord to the placenta. Here it comes into contact with the mother's blood, picking up food and oxygen.

It is now possible to see the earliest change in the mare's waistline.

At six months, when the foal is 30–60cm (12–24in) long, small hairs are developing on the nostrils, the eyelashes and the eyebrows. At seven months the tail is beginning to form. A change in the mare's shape may be fairly obvious. However, the mare's behaviour can still be quite normal, showing no signs of pregnancy.

At **eight months** the foetus measures from 50–80cm (20–32in) and the mane is starting to form. The outer part of the ear develops and the limbs take shape.

By the **tenth month** the foal has reached about 60–90cm (24–36in) long and the body, except the abdomen and between the thighs, is covered with a thin layer of short hairs.

In the **last stages of pregnancy** the foal weighs between 30 and 60kg (66–132lbs) and is between 75 and 145cm (30–60in) long. Just before birth the foal moves into the birth position.

The pregnant mare

In many cases it is only in the last few weeks of pregnancy that the mare starts to get rather restless, often lying down and getting up again, seeming uneasy or being difficult with other horses. In these final weeks the mare must have plenty of peace and quiet and be kept away from horses which may bully her.

Light exercise is quite alright after the first six weeks of pregnancy, but the mare should be allowed to rest from seven months onward.

During pregnancy keep an eye open for changes in the mare's behaviour which can't be explained, and watch for loss of appetite or alteration in her general condition. Also, look for signs of colic and, in particular, for discharge from the mare's vulva.

If anything is worrying about the pregnancy call the vet. Even if nothing is wrong it is best to be reassured that the mare's pregnancy is progressing normally.

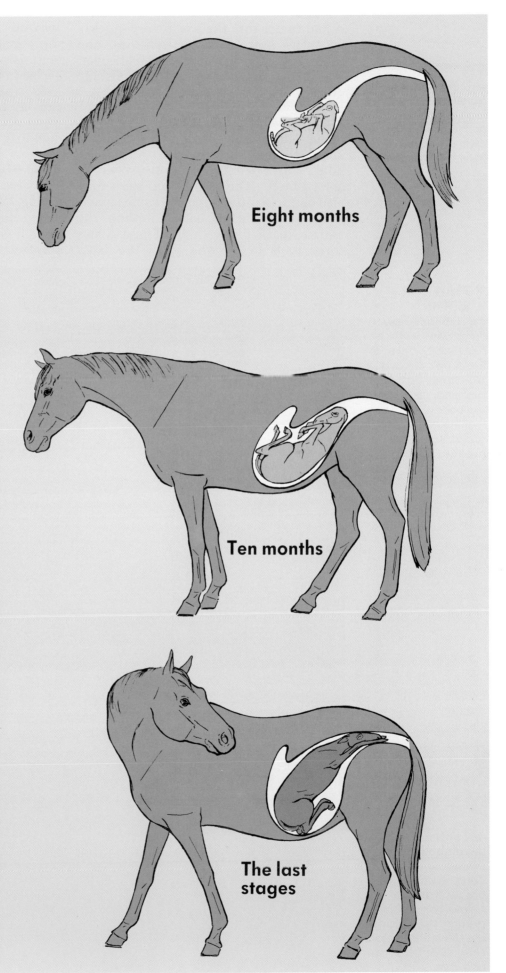

Eight months

Ten months

The last stages

The birth of a foal

A foal comes into the world very quickly once the process of birth begins and there are rarely any problems. However, it's important to have professional help quickly available in case of difficulties.

Before birth begins

Some mares show no sign that they are about to foal, but in most cases the udder starts to enlarge one or two weeks before birth. The mare's quarters may also begin to dip around the same time.

About five days before foaling the mare's teats fill with fluid and about three days before the birth the teats 'wax up' (they become coated in flakes of waxy material). Milk dripping from the teats is a sign that the foal is likely to arrive in the next 24 hours.

As well as these visible signs, tests can be carried out on a milk sample (from about ten days before the foal is due) to predict the time of the birth.

The stages of labour

The first stage of labour (the process of giving birth) varies. A mare in a field with other horses leaves the group and finds a corner of her own. A mare in a stable walks or trots around the box and

DID YOU KNOW?
Most horses have their foals during the night and nearly half of them are born between 10pm and 2am.

! TWIN BIRTHS
It is rare for horses to carry twins successfully, because the mare's uterus is not big enough to hold two embryos. If twins are born it is unlikely that they will both grow into strong, healthy adults.

► Foals are well developed at birth compared with many other mammals. They are soon able to follow their mothers around, staying close by. This mare keeps a close eye on her foal as it rests.

may roll, sweat and start to look at her abdomen. Sometimes this sort of behaviour is only a false alarm and it may happen a week or more before the actual birth.

The birth – the second stage of labour – is generally quick. There is little reason for people to take part in the process. However, any attempts to help the mare should be made with great care in case she kicks or rolls.

The birth process begins with the escape of the fluid which surrounds the foal in the womb. This is known as the 'waters breaking' and there may be up to a gallon (3.8 litres) of fluid.

Once the fluid has escaped, the foal must be delivered quickly – and within no more than three hours – or it will almost certainly die. The mare probably lies down for this part of labour and the foal's forelegs should appear within 20 minutes after her waters break. If this does not happen, and certainly if the hindlegs come first, call the vet.

The foal should be born from five to 30 minutes after the forelegs have appeared. It generally comes into the world covered in the amnion (the inner membrane covering it in the womb).

A foal is born

After delivery the foal frees itself from the amnion with a little help from the mother. If the foal appears weak and the membrane is not broken quickly it should be torn way. Any fluid from the foal's mouth and nostrils should be wiped away.

The mother usually licks and nuzzles the foal to dry it but, if she shows no interest in doing so, the task should be performed for her using straw or towels.

The mare gets to her feet within 40 minutes of the birth and, as she does so, the umbilical cord breaks. The placenta, (now called the afterbirth), is usually produced about 60 minutes after foaling. This process is the third stage of labour and is often referred to as 'cleansing'. If the complete afterbirth is not produced within three hours of foaling a vet must remove it from inside the mare.

Most foals are on their feet about one and a half hours after birth and they should take their first drink from the mother's teats within the next hour. This first milk contains a substance called colostrum which passes on antibodies, to protect the foal from infection.

The birth process

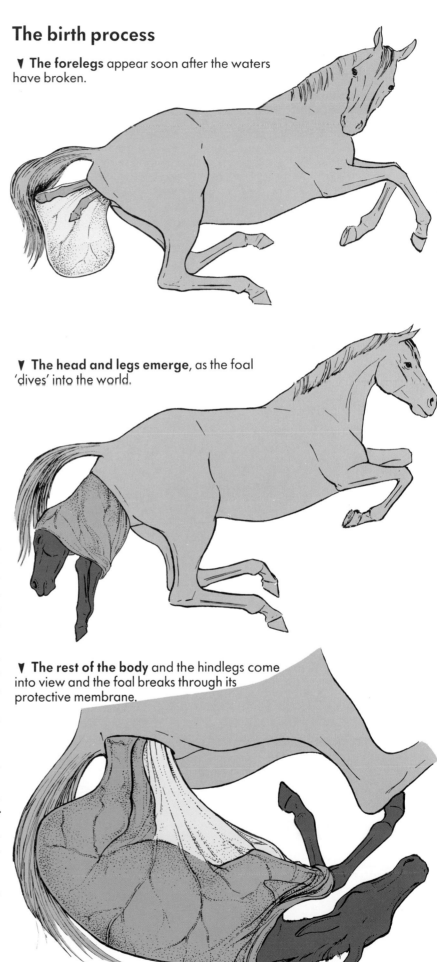

▼ **The forelegs** appear soon after the waters have broken.

▼ **The head and legs emerge**, as the foal 'dives' into the world.

▼ **The rest of the body** and the hindlegs come into view and the foal breaks through its protective membrane.

The first year

Unlike a newborn baby, a foal can stand and walk within a few hours of its birth. After a few days, it can run fast enough to keep up with its mother.

The need to escape

Nowadays, most horses are domesticated and have no fear of other animals. But, in the wild, they are just one link in nature's food chain and must protect themselves against predators like wild cats and dogs.

When foals are born their legs are already 90% of their adult length so that youngsters are instantly equipped for speed – and can escape from danger by running away.

Young horses are naturally inquisi-tive and eager to learn about their surroundings. They enjoy playing and charge around investigating all the new sights and smells and testing the strength of their legs. This helps to build up their muscles but they soon get tired. To make up for all their skittish activity, regular periods of sleep are essential. Plenty of rest helps 'recharge the batteries' and ensures that the foal is healthy and happy.

Rate of growth

For the first five years of life, one year for a horse equals five human years. So a six-month-old foal is at the same stage of development as a two-and-a-half-year-old child.

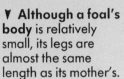

▼ **Although a foal's body** is relatively small, its legs are almost the same length as its mother's.

The long legs enable the foal to run quickly so that it can keep up with the herd and escape from any potential danger.

A mare gets to know her foal just after the birth. A new mother is usually very protective of her foal and, for the first few days, should be given as much peace and quiet as possible.

Like most youngsters, foals have bundles of energy. Exercise develops healthy muscles in the legs — which are always a bit wobbly at first!

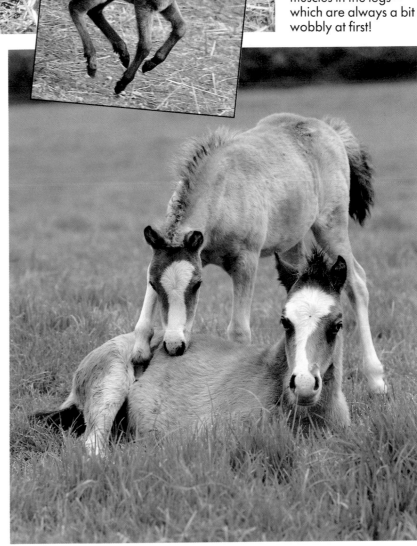

Unlike humans, however, a foal achieves about three quarters of its total growth in its first year. During the first four weeks, its height increases by about a third. Development slows slightly, then between six and 12 months the foal shoots up again. Its body fills out and its girth measurement increases.

You can estimate the mature height of a foal when it is three months old. Measure in inches from the point of the elbow to the ground. Halve the number of inches and you have the approximate height in hands. So, a foal which measures 28 inches will be about 14 hands high – as long as it doesn't have any setbacks. Foals who are deprived of exercise and good food, particularly during the first month of life, suffer from bad health and never achieve their full potential height or strength.

A hungry youngster looks tired and thin and stays close to its mother, constantly trying to feed. By contrast, a contented foal is well-rounded, has a shiny coat and spends its life feeding, sleeping and, of course, playing!

▶ **Friendship** is extremely important to ponies. These Welsh pony foals spend much of their time playing and resting together.

The second year

Although growth in yearlings – horses between 12 and 23 months old – is less dramatic than in foals, a one-year-old shows distinct changes in development and behaviour.

Growing up

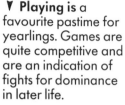

▼ **Playing** is a favourite pastime for yearlings. Games are quite competitive and are an indication of fights for dominance in later life.

From the age of one, a horse's body begins to fill out and starts to catch up with its long legs. The hindquarters, which provide drive and power, increase in strength and become more muscular. As this 'engine room' develops, yearlings can canter and gallop at a reasonable speed but still lack the strength and endurance of more mature horses.

In their first autumn, the youngsters lose their fluffy foal coats and the short, soft hair in their manes and tails is replaced by 'proper' hair. This more grown-up appearance can lead to quite dramatic changes and the new coat may be a completely different colour from the old one! A dun foal may, for example, become either bay or brown unless it is a true dun – with black legs, mane and tail and a dark stripe along the backbone. It is also quite common for a chestnut foal to turn grey if it has one grey parent.

Although horses are not sexually mature until the age of three, yearlings can serve (mate with) females and get them in foal. So yearlings should always be kept away from mares when turned out in a field.

Competition time

As they play together, yearlings are more boisterous and more competitive than foals. They are weaned from their dams (mothers) and usually have no adult horse among them to keep order: instead, they must establish their own pecking order and decide who is boss!

Croup high

In yearlings, the highest point of the hindquarters — the croup — is usually above the highest point of the forehand — the withers. This conformation (shown by the red line on the right) is called 'croup high', and is normal in youngsters.

The hindquarters develop earlier because, like an engine, they provide the power to drive a horse forward. This makes the yearling look out of proportion for a while.

The withers and croup usually even up at the age of three or four. But in some horses they never catch up. These mounts give their riders the feeling that they are going downhill all the time — not a very pleasant experience!

▲ **The body** begins to fill out and catch up with the long hindlegs, but the face still looks young.

▼ **Yearlings are** still developing their speed, although they may look full of energy. They are not yet strong enough to run for long periods of time.

The middle years

A horse is usually fully mature when he is six years old. By then, he has reached his full height and his bones are fully grown and 'hardened'.

Filling out

The main change you'll notice in a horse's appearance is a general filling out of his body. This is because his muscles have developed. He looks bigger and more imposing, but without getting any taller.

His adult life should be long and productive as long as he has been well looked after during his early years.

Strength and stamina

The speed a horse builds up as a youngster reaches its greatest point between the years of two and six. From then on, his actual speed lessens but is replaced by increased strength and stamina.

He *gets* fit more quickly than a young or old horse and *stays* fit longer without needing a rest or holiday.

The prime of life

A horse's 'teenage' years, in human terms, are from three to five. After he is six years old, you can reckon that one

▼ **Filling out:** As the horse gets older and does more work, his body becomes broader and more muscular. This makes him seem larger even though he's already reached his full adult height.

year to us equals three to a horse. So, from six to 14, he's at roughly the same stage as a person of 18 to 45.

A horse is at his peak, in the prime of life, between eight and 12-14. These middle years are often a horse's healthiest. He is no longer plagued so much by the health problems of the young – teething, strangles, jarred limbs, warts, breathing diseases. But he hasn't yet succumbed to the disorders of the elderly either.

Provided his work is sensibly balanced, it is difficult to overburden a fit, healthy and well-cared-for horse at this time of life.

Fully formed

Once the word 'teen' appears in a horse's age, some people feel he is getting past his best. But many horses continue to work eagerly and productively even after the age of 14.

Technically, a horse is said to be 'aged' when he is eight years old. Aged in this sense doesn't necessarily mean old, just that you can no longer tell his age accurately.

At the age of eight, a horse's character is fully developed and he knows about the world. His outlook on life – whether sensible, calm and wise or nervous, excitable and scatty – is unlikely to change much now.

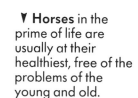

▲ **Speed gives way** to strength and stamina; a horse can work harder now than at any other time in his life.

◄ **Worldly wise:** By the age of eight, a horse has learnt a lot about life, and his character is formed.

▼ **Horses** in the prime of life are usually at their healthiest, free of the problems of the young and old.

The last years

Physically, horses in their 20's are past their best, but mentally they are often in better shape than their younger counterparts.

Schoolmasters

For many purposes, older horses are better than younger ones: they are experienced and usually sensible and unruffled by any situation.

They can make excellent 'schoolmaster' animals, being patient and steady enough for beginners to learn to ride on them. They show young horses the ropes when out hacking, giving a lead over tricky places and in traffic. And, when travelling, they have a calming influence on ponies who are nervous about being boxed.

Growing old

The average lifespan for a horse is 25 years, although it has been known for them to live much longer than this. A Cleveland cross-breed called 'Old Billy', born in 1760, is said to have lived to the remarkable age of 62!

Ponies tend to live longer than horses. A 20-year old pony is about equal to a 70-year old human, a 30-year old pony to a 100-year old human.

▼ **Just because a** horse gets old doesn't mean you can't ride him any more. Indeed, regular (almost daily), steady exercise is much better for him than little or no work.

Older horses cannot work as hard or for as long as young ones. But regular, light exercise keeps them healthier than occasional work or none at all.

Like all old animals, horses feel their age sooner or later. They become slower and stiffer as their joints lose mobility, and their limbs and body in general lose their youthful suppleness. Because of this it becomes increasingly difficult for horses to lie down and stand up again, so they often prefer to stand while resting.

Body matters

Older horses are likely to suffer from disorders such as arthritis and rheumatism, and the circulation and digestion begin to deteriorate. As the teeth begin to wear down, old horses commonly suffer from dental problems.

The horse's outward appearance also changes. Some old horses start to lose weight. Careful management of work and feeding is required to prevent them from losing condition, especially in the winter, when they feel the cold more.

The back may sink down a little, and the legs bend slightly forward at the knees and sink lower at the fetlocks.

The colour of the coat can change – for example, a grey pony lightens with age. Other colours may produce grey hairs in the coat, particularly on the head – giving a grizzled, slightly 'dusty' look.

▲ **Slightly bent knees** are a common feature of old age, as the leg joints stiffen up.

◄ **Just like humans,** some horses go grey as they get older.

▼ **It is often hard** to tell if a pony is old just by looking at him. A hollow (dipped) back is a good clue.

2 Getting started

Fitting tack

▼ **The saddle** must have a rider in it before the saddler sees how it fits the pony. It must also suit you, even when you change position for jumping (inset).

The basic tack you need when you've just bought a pony is a saddle, with girth, stirrup leathers and irons, a simple bridle, probably with a snaffle bit, and a headcollar.

General-purpose saddle

There are various sorts of saddles for specialized equestrian disciplines such as show jumping, dressage, showing, long-distance riding and racing. But the most useful to begin with is a general-purpose saddle.

These types are designed so that you can comfortably use different lengths of stirrup leather because the flap, on which your leg rests, extends slightly toward the shoulder.

When you raise your stirrups for jumping your knee comes forward, so you need a saddle which lets your leg move without your knee going off the flap. However, when your stirrups are the normal length for flatwork, there must be enough flap *behind* your leg.

Fitting the saddle

To check how it fits, the saddle must be on the horse with a rider on his back and someone experienced to hand. If the saddle does not fit your pony properly, it could make him very sore from pressure or rubbing.

Once you are in the saddle, you should be able to fit the width of your hand in front of your body without it going off the saddle, and the same at the back. The flap should allow for your different leg positions.

With the pommel in its normal position just over the back part of the withers, the cantle must be on the pony's back and not extending on to his

There should be no pressure points when you lean backward . . .

. . . or forward.

loin and kidney area. As for width, the saddle must not slip and rock from side to side (too wide) or pinch his withers and seem to perch above them (too narrow). You should just be able to slide the flat of your fingers under the saddle at the front on each side.

Ask your pony's heaviest rider to sit in the saddle, and ride around for about 15 minutes. This lets it settle on to the pony's back. You should now be able to fit three, and preferably four, fingers sideways between the withers and the pommel, and the cantle and backbone.

Looking down the gullet (from cantle to pommel) when the rider is mounted, you must be able to see a clear

Ponies with a good deal of Thoroughbred blood often have high withers which can make saddle-fitting a problem. In such cases, you may need to buy a saddle with a 'cut-back head'. The pommel is cut away backward to fit round the withers.

Ponies with flat withers and little shape in front, or those who are rather fat, cause the saddle to slip forward. They may need girths which are shaped behind the elbows to avoid chafing.

They may also need a crupper (a loop going under the tail and buckling to the back of the saddle) to hold the saddle back.

You should be able to fit a hand's width behind and in front of you.

The pommel must not press on or pinch the withers.

There must be a tunnel of daylight along the pony's backbone.

53

tunnel of daylight all the way down the pony's backbone. The tunnel should still be there when the rider leans forward and back. It is most important that the saddle does not press anywhere at all along the backbone.

The stuffing should be smoothly distributed inside the seat panels (the two built-in pads on the underside of the saddle), so that there is even pressure on the pony's back.

The saddle must be well balanced. You should be able to sit in the deepest part of the seat – the centre. It should not tip you forward or let you slide back when the pony moves.

Some saddles with high cantles are tricky to judge, and you may need your instructor to advise you, particularly if the saddle seems strange and uncomfortable at first.

The bridle

The bridle should fit so you can easily slide a finger under it all over the pony's head. If it is too tight, it will be most uncomfortable and could cause soreness.

The browband is not adjustable so you must get the right size. Most small ponies take pony-size and those of 14.2 hands high upward take cob size, but much depends on whether or not your pony has a big head! The browband should allow the headpiece to lie comfortably behind the ears without pulling it into the base of the ears; the browband itself should lie just below the base of

Numnahs

A numnah (saddle pad) is useful for absorbing sweat (unless it is nylon) and for giving the pony a softer, more comfortable feel on his back. However, it is not essential for your starting-off tack, and a thick numnah is not an excuse to use a badly fitting saddle. Numnahs do not remove pressure; they only lessen it.

If you do buy one, make certain you pull it up fully into the saddle gullet all the way along when saddling up. You should be able to pass your whip right down the pony's back from pommel to cantle. If the numnah is flat on the back, the saddle pushes it down further. Your weight causes quite firm pressure on the back, particularly the withers, and the pad can make your pony very sore.

Make sure, too, that the numnah is not creased or tucked up anywhere beneath the saddle; this creates uneven pressure and more soreness. The numnah should also be cleaned regularly to prevent chafing.

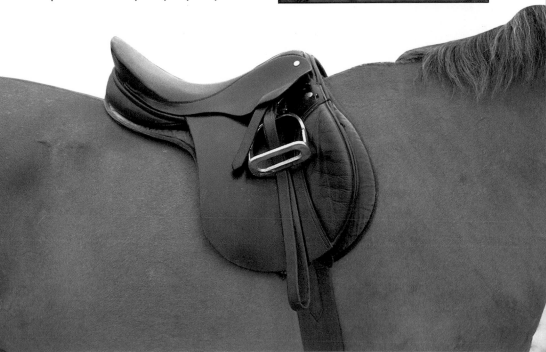

the ears so it does not cut into them. It should not be so long, however, that it flops about.

The other parts of the bridle are adjustable with buckles. You should be able to fit the width of four fingers between the throat-lash and the pony's round jawbones.

The bit itself should show about 7mm (¼in) each side of the pony's mouth. If it is wider it slides about and does not act properly or evenly; if it is narrower it pinches.

Adjust the bridle cheekpieces so that the bit *just* wrinkles the corners of the pony's mouth. If the bit is too low it could bang on his teeth or make it possible for him to get his tongue over the mouthpiece and evade its action; if it is too high it is uncomfortable and could make his lips sore at the corners.

With a well-schooled pony who goes nicely, you do not *have* to have a noseband. A plain cavesson noseband makes a pony look 'dressed', but do not buy any other kind unless your instructor advises it.

The headcollar

A headcollar is better than a rope or web halter, which is not as practical,

Oiling

Before using leather tack for the first time, give it extra protection by oiling or dressing it. You can use neatsfoot oil or a branded, lanolin based leather dressing, available from hardware stores.

Give two *thin* coats. Pour the dressing into a bowl or saucer and use a paintbrush about 2.5cm (1in) wide. Pay particular attention to the underside of your bridle, saddle flaps, girth tabs and stirrup leathers as these are the most absorbent. Don't over-oil or you'll make everything slimy. Re-dress the tack if it gets very wet so it remains in good condition and does not lose its suppleness.

strong or easy to use. The headcollar can be leather, or cotton or nylon webbing. The noseband is all in one with the rest.

The basic fit is the same as for bridles. You should be able to get the width of three fingers between the noseband and the pony's nose (most are much too big and loose). The noseband should come midway between the corners of the lips and the sharp face bones so it doesn't rub. If it is lower the pony might be able to push it off.

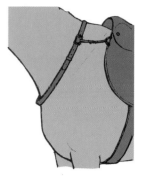

NECK STRAP
A neck strap is a useful piece of tack, even if you aren't a beginner. You can buy the leather 'collar', which fits round the base of your pony's neck and fastens with two leather loops to the front D-rings of the saddle.

Alternatively, you can improvise with a stirrup leather and binder twine. Buckle the leather round the pony's neck and put one loop of binder twine through the buckle. Attach this to the D-ring to stop the buckle slipping down to the breast and perhaps cutting into the pony.

On the opposite side, tie binder twine to the other D-ring and thread it through a hole in the stirrup leather to secure it.

◄ **A well-fitting** bridle leaves room for you to slide a finger under every part, and the width of four fingers between the throat-lash and the pony's jawbones.

Snaffle bits

The snaffle is usually thought of as the simplest and mildest bit. But in fact the name 'snaffle' covers a whole family of bits, which vary in their action on the pony's mouth. All, however, consist of a mouthpiece with rings at each end to which the reins and cheekpieces are attached.

How snaffles work

When correctly fitted, snaffles operate by exerting pressure on the bars of the pony's mouth – his gums, across the portion of the mouth where the bit rests – and on the corners of his lips. You can see this working to some extent if you stand alongside a pony's head while his

► **An egg-butt snaffle** is one of the kindest bits you can use. The rings are fixed so your pony's mouth does not get pinched, while the wide mouthpieces are comfortable for him. It is an ideal everyday bit.

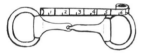

MEASURING UP
Snaffle bits are measured in inches between the two rings. As a rough guide, ponies usually take a 5in (12cm) jointed bit size, and a 4½in (11cm) unjointed mouthpiece, but ask an expert to help you fit a new bit.

DID YOU KNOW?
The jointed snaffle is believed to be one of the first bits invented for riding in prehistoric times.
   Archaeologists have found, preserved in peat bogs, pony-sized bits thousands of years old. They are almost identical to the jointed snaffles ponies wear today.

rider gives rein aids.

Inside the pony's mouth, the snaffle also puts pressure on the pony's tongue. How much pressure depends on the kind of snaffle used. Overall, the effect is to bring the pony's head up and in, helping you to regulate his pace, steer and stop him. Whatever bit you use, however, your body and legs should be doing most of the work of controlling the pony!

Kinds of snaffle

The mildest form of snaffle has a thick, unjointed, gently curved mouthpiece (often known as mullen mouth) made of rubber.

▼ **Many ponies** are bitted with a loose-ring, plain, jointed snaffle. It is simple and easy to use. The rings are rounded to stop them rubbing the pony's face.

The rubber or hardened rubber (vulcanite) makes it even easier on the pony's mouth. This is a good bit for a young pony, or for one with a tender, sensitive mouth; a pony which fidgets and gets upset in a stronger bit often goes quietly in a rubber snaffle.

The plain, jointed snaffle, usually made of uncovered metal, has a two-part mouthpiece with a joint in the middle. This gives the bit a 'nutcracker' action, with more pressure on the pony's tongue. It allows the rider greater control – in theory, at least!

Some snaffles are more severe than others. Harsher types may have a twisted, rather than a plain, jointed mouthpiece, or a series of rollers inside or fitted round the mouthpiece. Otherwise there may be two thin mouthpieces, each with a separate joint at a different point across the mouth, for a double nutcracker effect.

Harsher snaffles are used for ponies that 'lean' on your hands, pull or are hard to stop and steer. They are not beginners' bits! They should be bought, fitted in ponies' mouths, and used only with expert supervision.

The snaffle rings

The rings on a snaffle stop the bit sliding through the mouth. They may be loose – fitted through holes in each outer (butt) end of the mouthpiece – or fixed, as in the popular, eggbutt snaffle. The rings, however, can move sideways even with a fixed-ring snaffle.

Older, loose-ring snaffles usually had wide, flat rings. Nowadays, the rings are often rounded as these are less likely to rub the pony's face. And, as they only need small holes in the butts of the mouthpiece, there is less risk of pinching the pony's lips.

Snaffle bits in old-fashioned racing prints often had long 'cheeks' (vertical strips) set between mouthpiece and ring. These are a steering aid, as the cheek applies pressure against the side of the horse's face.

Buying the right bit

Snaffles today are usually made in stainless steel or vulcanite. They come in half-inch sizes. For safety and comfort, the mouthpiece of the bit must be the right width. If it is too narrow, it pinches the pony's lips; if it is too wide, the bit slips about in the mouth.

It's easy when you are buying a new snaffle for your pony, and know his old bit is the right fitting; just measure across the mouthpiece. If you are not sure, ask an expert to help, or explain your problem to the saddler. From your pony's size and breeding, he probably knows the bit size you need. Then have your expert make sure that the bit is fitted correctly on to the bridle and in the pony's mouth.

A bit can be fitted on to the bridle and reins with buckles or stud billets (like a hook and eye they are neat, but less easy to undo). It can be sewn permanently into place, although this is more appropriate for a showing bridle.

Whatever you choose, clean the bridle and bit thoroughly and regularly. Check for worn places on fastenings, straps, rings and mouthpiece – a bridle or bit that breaks is a frightening experience. Don't ask your pony to wear a rough, rusty old bit, or one covered with stale froth and grass – but don't give him a mouthful of metal polish, either!

▼ **The snaffle** is a versatile bit that can be used successfully to a fairly high standard of riding. It is only when you reach an advanced level of dressage work or serious showing that you need more precision for perfect collection and control.

Popular types of snaffle

For everyday riding — hacking, hunting, competition work or jumping — there is almost sure to be at least one among the family of snaffle bits which suits you and your pony.

Always ask an expert to help you fit the bit and advise you on what kind to choose. The snaffles shown here are the types most commonly found.

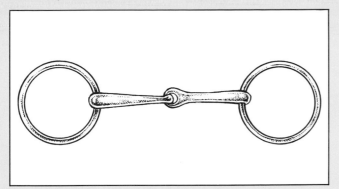

Plain, jointed snaffle
When you start riding, the pony you learn on is often bitted with the simplest bit, the plain, jointed snaffle. Usually made of stainless steel, it has two rounded bars linked in the centre, with rings at either end. The central join gives you more control than a straight bar.

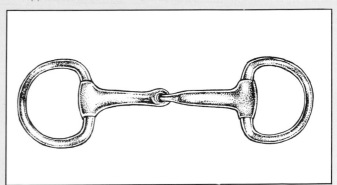

Eggbutt snaffle
Unlike the plain, jointed snaffle, the eggbutt snaffle has fixed rings. These help stop the rings sliding and pinching the pony's lips. It is a popuiar bit that suits many ponies, and is a good choice for a first buy.

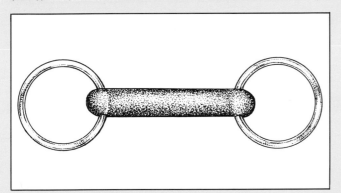

Unjointed, rubber snaffle
This is the mildest type of snaffle and it is good for young or very sensitive ponies that are nervous of bits. The rubber or hardened rubber (vulcanite) has a metal core for safety.

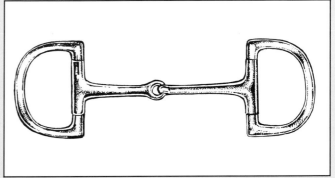

D-ring snaffle
Derived from cheek snaffles, the D-ring snaffle is sometimes used for racehorses. The straight side of the D, set against the horse's face, acts as a mini-cheek to help with steering. It is also an extra safeguard against the bit pinching the lips or slipping through the mouth.

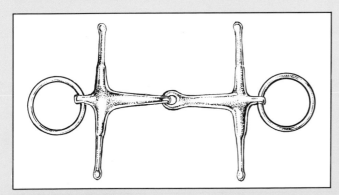

Fulmer cheek snaffle
So called from a famous English riding school where its use was brought to a fine art, this cheek snaffle has loose rings separate from the cheeks. Many ponies go well in this mild bit. It needs retaining straps for the top cheeks, attached to the bridle, to keep the bit in place.

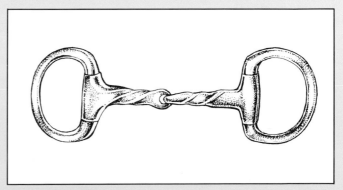

Twisted snaffle
This is a strong bit because the twisted mouthpiece is severe in action. It should only be used in expert hands and on a pony with a hard mouth. It can either have loose rings or fixed ones.

Saddling up

When you have built up your confidence by being around ponies and practising the basic paces, it's time to learn about tacking up – putting on the saddle and bridle.

Safety first

At the riding school, each pony has his own tack which fits well and comfortably (for both horse and rider) and is maintained in clean condition. No other pony uses his saddle and bridle.

Properly fitted tack is essential. Ill-fitting equipment can rub, causing sores which may become infected, harming the pony and keeping him off work until he's healed. Also, it is uncomfortable and irritating for the pony and potentially dangerous for you, as he may be frustrated into rearing or bolting as he

EGGBUTT SNAFFLE
A jointed eggbutt snaffle is one of the mildest forms of bit. It's likely that this will be the bit you use when you start to ride.

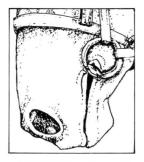

CHECKING THE BIT
When you've placed the bit inside the pony's mouth and before you fasten the buckles up, check that the bit fits correctly. The pony's mouth should be wrinkling a little at the corners.

► **Tacking up a pony** on your own makes you more independent and confident around the stables.

tries to get rid of the discomfort.

Hard, dry, uncared-for leather is a problem for the same reasons, and because it may break. If you help to clean the tack, check the leather for wear and the stitching for signs of weakness. Caring for tack is a basic safety precaution in riding. Well-fitting, regularly maintained tack is safe; anything else is not.

How to prepare

It's a good idea if a more experienced person stands by during your first attempt to tack up. You'll be concentrating on keeping control of the pony while juggling with saddle and bridle. You can prepare by being familiar with what the bridle looks like when it is on the pony. If you have ever cleaned the tack you'll be used to the various parts.

When you collect the bridle from the tack room you may find that the throat-lash has been crossed over the front of the bridle with the reins looped over it at the back. When you undo the throat-lash the reins will drop down quite easily. The noseband may also be outside the cheekpieces and this should be placed inside before putting the bridle on the pony.

Approaching the pony

When you leave the tack room you should have with you bridle, saddle – complete with stirrup leathers, irons and girth – plus headcollar and rope (this may be outside the pony's box).

Once at the stable, carefully put the tack down. Don't rest the saddle on the stable door. It may crash to the ground and it puts strain on the stable door hinges.

Walk confidently into the stable and bolt the door behind you. Standing on the near side, put the headcollar on the pony. Decide where you are going to tack up and secure him there with a quick-release knot. If you saddle up in the stable, remember to bolt the door behind you as you go in and out to pick up the tack.

Positioning the saddle

The saddle should sit comfortably just behind the withers. With fat, or naturally round ponies, this point might be difficult to distinguish, but there is usually a dip behind the withers.

Stand on the near side. With your left hand on the pommel and your right hand on the cantle, lift the saddle. Make sure the girth is over the seat of the ➤

▼ **Placing the saddle** has to be done carefully. By sliding it back into position from the withers, the hairs lie flat under the saddle and the pony feels comfortable.

Fitting the bridle

1 Stand on the pony's near side and refasten the headcollar round his neck so he remains secure.

2 Place the reins over his neck. Hold the bridle in your right hand and use your left hand to guide the bit in.

3 Once the bit is positioned, put the headpiece on — guide it over the pony's ears until it rests on the poll.

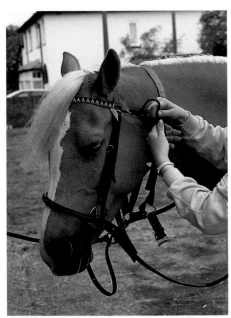

4 Before you fasten any straps up, check that the bit looks comfortable in the pony's mouth and that it is above the tongue. Then you can buckle up the throat-lash fairly loosely.

5 Fasten the noseband so that it fits snugly; remember it fits inside the cheekpieces. Check that the noseband and browband are level.

6 Pull the forelock out from under the browband and any mane from under the headpiece. Loop your arm through the rein nearest to you while you remove the headcollar. The pony is now fully tacked up.

Testing the fit

▲ **The noseband** fits properly if there is space for one finger's width.

▲ **The throat-lash** should be four fingers' width away from the pony's jaw.

❗ TAKING THE BIT
❗ Most ponies open their mouths ready to take the bit, but the odd one is more reluctant. If you are having problems getting the bit in, just slide your thumb — on the hand supporting the bit — into the side of the pony's mouth, two thirds of the way back. Here, a little before the corner of his mouth, he hasn't any teeth so you won't get nipped!

saddle. Place the saddle a little further up the withers than you would want to sit. Then just slide the saddle down until it comes to rest naturally on the pony's back. This ensures that the hair underneath lies flat.

The pommel and cantle should appear about level when the saddle is in the correct position. If it is not in the right place, your own position will be wrong. This makes riding uncomfortable and makes your aids ineffective.

When the saddle is correctly placed, walk around the front of the pony and drop the girth down, making sure the girth straps are not twisted. As you do this, try to keep a hand on the saddle for as long as possible. Come back again to the near side, reach underneath the pony for the girth and do it up gently. Keep the girth fairly loose at first and tighten it before you get on.

The bridle and the bit

If the bridle belongs to the pony it will already be adjusted correctly so you won't have to worry about that the first time. However, checking that the bridle looks about the right size is a good habit to acquire. Hold the bridle alongside the pony's face, sideways on, to make sure the bit will lie in the correct position in his mouth.

There are various methods of saddling up, but the basics remain the same. Watch other people tacking up and learn from them, but always maintain high safety standards and don't cut corners.

Alternative tack

Drop nosebands are quite common. They are used on headstrong ponies to increase the rider's control. Instead of fastening above the level of the bit, the drop noseband passes underneath the bit rings, fastening in the chin groove. It should not 'droop' too low on the nose or it interferes with the pony's breathing. But it must be tight enough to stop the pony from opening his mouth, without pinching him.

Cruppers go under the tail and fasten on to the saddle. They are used for small, round ponies to stop the saddle slipping forward. They are often lined with towelling to prevent rubbing. If the pony wears a crupper, this will already be attached to the back of the saddle, so simply pass the tail through the loop until the crupper rests at the top of the dock.

Removing the pony's tack

An important aspect of learning to ride is knowing what to do when a ride has finished. The pony must be made comfortable and the tack removed and stored safely.

The end of the ride

At the end of a lesson always make sure the pony arrives at his stable cool and relaxed. Make the transition from walk to halt; when the pony is standing still give him a pat on the neck to thank him. Still mounted, loosen your girth one or two holes.

Dismount and then take the reins over the pony's head. Keep your arm looped through the reins so you still have control.

The stirrups

Run the stirrups up the stirrup leathers so they are secure and not flapping and banging against the pony's sides: take the top of the stirrup leather into one hand to do this.

With your other hand run the stirrup iron up the underneath leather until it reaches the buckle end of the leather. Pass the remaining leather through the stirrup iron so that it is held in place and cannot slip back down.

Removing the saddle

Unbuckle the girth on the left side of the pony and lay it over the top of the seat. Be careful not to let the buckles of the girth bang against the saddle or scratch the leather.

With your left hand on the pommel (front of the saddle) and your right on the cantle (back of the saddle), lift the saddle off the pony's back and carefully put it on the ground. Lean it against the stable wall with the pommel on the ground and the cantle balanced against a wall so that the saddle cannot possibly fall over.

Never hang the saddle on the stable door as it could easily fall to the ground and be damaged. Even better than standing the saddle on the ground is having a small foldaway saddle rack just outside the stable door for the saddle to rest on until you have removed the bridle.

◄ **Always handle tack with care.** Prop the saddle against a wall while you take the bridle off. Never balance a saddle on the stable door where it could easily tip off and be damaged.

How to take off the saddle

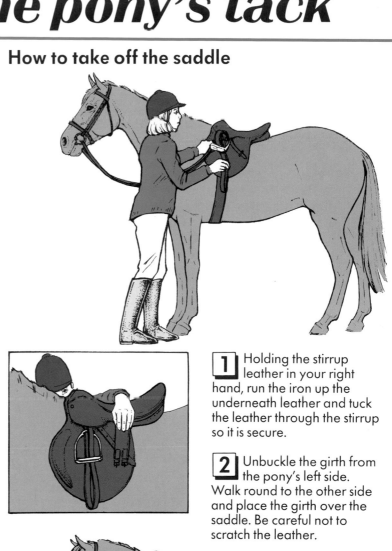

1 Holding the stirrup leather in your right hand, run the iron up the underneath leather and tuck the leather through the stirrup so it is secure.

2 Unbuckle the girth from the pony's left side. Walk round to the other side and place the girth over the saddle. Be careful not to scratch the leather.

3 Remove the saddle by placing your left hand on the pommel (front) and your right hand on the cantle (back) and lifting it off gently.

4 Put the saddle on the ground, pommel down, and with the cantle resting against a wall, until you can store it properly.

SADDLE HORSE
The safest place to store a saddle is on a rack specially designed for the purpose.

Removing the bridle

Before taking the bridle off, strap a headcollar round the pony's neck. This way you always have control.

To remove the bridle, undo the noseband and the throat-lash. Lift the headpiece and reins together over the pony's ears. If you can, use one hand to catch the bit as the bridle comes off.

Now you can fit the headcollar. Place the noseband over the pony's muzzle. With your right hand put the headpiece over his poll and just behind his ears. Do up the cheekpiece, allowing about four fingers' width between it and the pony. Tie him up with a quick-release knot while you put the tack away.

Carrying the tack

Always carry the tack properly to avoid scratching the leather or, worse, breaking the saddle.

Hold the bridle by the headpiece together with the reins in your left hand. If you're small, try not to let the reins drag along the ground. If you are tall you won't have difficulty with this – you can carry the bridle in your left hand at waist or shoulder level.

There are two ways to carry the saddle. One is on your right arm with the pommel in the crook of your elbow, the bridle remaining in your left hand.

The second method is easier if you are small. Put the headpiece of the bridle

BRIDLE PARTS

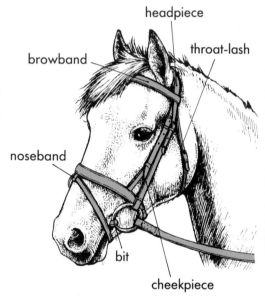

- headpiece
- throat-lash
- browband
- noseband
- bit
- cheekpiece

How to take off the bridle

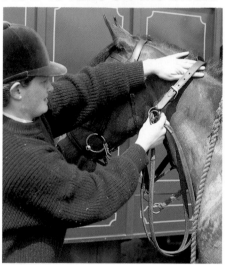

1 Strap the headcollar around the pony's neck before taking off the bridle and check it's not too tight.

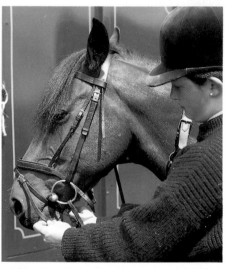

2 Gently undo the noseband. This pony is wearing a noseband called a flash.

3 Once the noseband is undone, unstrap the throat-lash. Then you can take the bridle off.

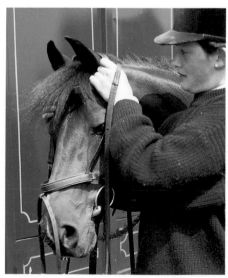

4 Gently slip the headpiece and reins over his head. The bit will drop from his mouth as you do this.

5 Fit the headcollar properly. When you do up the cheekpiece, allow about four fingers' width.

with the reins on to your left shoulder. This leaves both of your hands free to carry the saddle. The left hand holds the pommel, the right hand the cantle.

Storing the tack

Keep the tack in a safe place. At riding schools there is usually a special room called a tack room where you find hooks for the bridles and saddle racks to put the saddles on. If you have your own pony you will probably keep your saddlery at home. The bridle should be hung up and the saddle put on a saddle rack or a specially made rack called a saddle horse. If this isn't possible, store the saddle somewhere safe.

▲ **Loop the reins** through the throat-lash, so they don't fall to the ground and get dirty.

◄ **Carry the bridle** on your left shoulder – the reins don't trail and you can hold the saddle in both hands.

Tack tips

☐ Always take care of your saddlery and keep it clean.
☐ Never drop your saddle or bridle on the ground – it may crack the bit and will certainly damage the saddle.
☐ Never lead your pony with his stirrups dangling. They may bang his sides and hurt him.
☐ Always approach your pony from in front and speak to him so that he knows you are there.
☐ Never shout or hurry when moving in the stable, as you can frighten a pony and he may injure himself.
☐ Always bring your pony in cool from exercise and lead him to his stable.
☐ Never ride your pony into his stable: the door is too low.
☐ If you ride at a school, offer to help put the pony away.

Cleaning the tack

Dry, cracked tack is uncomfortable for the pony and dangerous for the rider. Cleaning it regularly keeps the leather supple and strong.

What you need

To clean the tack, you need a bucket of clean, lukewarm water; a bar of saddle soap (from a saddler's or leather store); and two thinnish sponges. One is for washing and one for soaping. Never mix them up or both become useless. Using different colours helps to keep them separate.

Other useful items are a matchstick for poking excess soap out of buckle holes; a coin or blunt knife for removing lumps of grease; and a chamois (pronounced *shammy*) leather – imitation is fine – for drying the leatherwork.

For polishing the stirrups, buckles and bit rings or cheeks, you need some

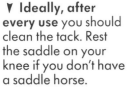

▼ **Ideally, after every use** you should clean the tack. Rest the saddle on your knee if you don't have a saddle horse.

metal polish and two cloths: one for applying and one for bringing up the shine. A stable rubber (or old tea towel) is handy for holding polished metalwork so you don't fingermark it.

Wash and dry the metal every time you clean the tack and polish it about once a month or before special occasions. Never put polish on the mouthpiece and clean off any that spills on to the leather.

You'll find it easier to clean the tack if you have a bridle hook suspended from the ceiling (but mind your head!) or a wall bracket, so you can hang up the bridle, and a saddle horse to rest your saddle on.

Try to clean tack after each use. If you don't have time, at least damp-sponge the underside, because the chemicals in sweat can rot leather.

How to clean the saddle

Strip the saddle – remove the girth and the stirrup leathers – and take the stirrup irons off their leathers.

Dampen the washing sponge, and wipe off the mud. Rinse the sponge and squeeze it out, then firmly rub off grease. If little lumps of black grease (called 'jockeys') cling, gently scrape them off with a handful of horse hair, a coin or blunt knife. Leave the saddle to dry or rub it with the chamois, and wash the stirrup leathers.

Never dunk your saddle in water to wash it. The panel stuffing could shrink and become hard and lumpy, altering the fit and making it uncomfortable. If your tack is very greasy, use warm – not hot – water with two or three drops – not squirts – of washing-up liquid. And never dry wet leather by artificial heat or in direct sunlight as it might crack.

Dip the bar of soap into the water and rub it on the other, soaping, sponge. *Don't* dip the sponge in the water and rub it on the soap as it will be too wet and foamy. The sponge should be barely damp and never rinsed.

Rub soap into the saddle with a circular motion. Pay particular attention underneath the flaps, and to the parts which touch the pony and to the girth straps. Frequently re-soap the sponge. When you've done the saddle, soap the stirrup leathers.

If your girth is leather, clean it the same way. Hang it in a loop by both sets of buckles to dry.

Washing the saddle

1 Start by taking off the girth and girth guards, and the stirrup leathers.

2 Wash the underside carefully, particularly if you don't use a numnah under the saddle.

3 Lift the saddle flap and take the grease off both sides of leather, remembering the straps.

4 Rinse your sponge and squeeze it. Now clean the top of the saddle and round the cantle.

5 Wash the parts you took off the saddle: the stirrup leathers, girth guard and the girth if it is made of leather. For a fabric girth, scrub it with baby soap (which is very pure and so doesn't irritate the pony's skin). Rinse the soap off thoroughly.
Leave the saddle to dry, or rub it with the chamois leather, before soaping it.

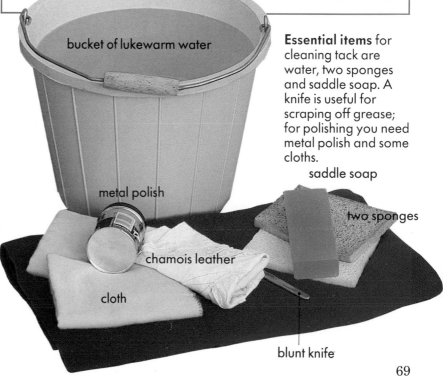

bucket of lukewarm water

metal polish

cloth

chamois leather

saddle soap

two sponges

blunt knife

Essential items for cleaning tack are water, two sponges and saddle soap. A knife is useful for scraping off grease; for polishing you need metal polish and some cloths.

OILING TACK
Regularly used tack cleaned with saddle soap stays supple. However, you should use a leather dressing to oil new tack.

After that, you can, if you wish, oil the leather parts that take the greatest strain (usually the straps) about once every three months.

▼ **At Pony Club camp,** you'll find that cleaning tack is a regular task. Your pony can watch you doing all the work while he relaxes with a hay net!

Soaping the saddle

1 Dip the bar of soap into the water. Never dip the *sponge* in water and rub it on the soap, as you will work up far too much lather.

2 Take your second sponge — *not* the one you used for washing. Rub soap on to the sponge, which should be barely damp.

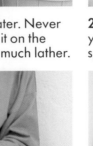

3 Rub soap into the saddle. Pay particular attention to the girth straps as these get a lot of wear from the buckles.

4 Do the girth if it is leather, making sure you work the soap into the individual strands so they are supple and don't rub the pony.

The bridle

It's most thorough to take the bridle to pieces. However, until you are confident that you can put it back together again, you may prefer to keep it in one piece! In this case, move all the buckles a hole or two so that the leather actually touched by metal (which wears and cracks most easily) is properly soaped.

If your bridle is very muddy, do what the army and police often do – dunk it in the bucket to rinse off the mud. But it then needs careful drying and plenty of soap. Preferably clean it on the bridle hook, bracket or table.

Rinse and squeeze out the sponge. Wrap it round each strap and wash off all the grease, most of which will be on the underside. Grip the sponge firmly and run it up and down each strap with one hand, while keeping the leather taut with the other.

Soap the bridle as you did the saddle, but use an up-and-down action. Remember to take extra care over the parts normally touched by metal.

The metalwork

1 Pull the treads out of the stirrup irons and wash the mud off both.

2 When dry, apply the metal polish. A towel on your lap stops you getting dirty.

3 Use a chamois leather or clean cloth to polish the irons, working up a good shine.

4 Put the irons together and thread them on to the leathers. Hook them on the stirrup bar.

Putting the bridle back together

1 Once you've cleaned and soaped the bridle, wash the bit but don't polish the mouthpiece.

2 Hold the headpiece with the throat-lash length on your left. Thread the browband through.

3 Buckle the bottom halves of the cheekpieces to their tops (attached to the headpiece).

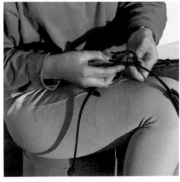

4 Fasten the bit to the cheekpiece hookstuds, making sure it's not upside down.

► If your pony's bit is a jointed snaffle, check that the flat sides are together.

5 Thread the noseband through the headpiece and do it up. Attach the reins to the bit.

 STIRRUP LEATHERS

☐ To re-assemble the stirrups, hold the leather with the buckle facing downward and toward you, pointed end away.

☐ Thread the point through the eye on top of the stirrup iron.

☐ Bring the leather up and back toward you, and fasten the buckle.

☐ Change over stirrup leathers so they take even stress. Otherwise the left one – which you mount by – stretches.

HOOKSTUDS AND BUCKLES

Hookstuds fold *in* toward the pony for neatness. Buckles face *outward* for comfort. Tuck strap ends inside their keepers and runners (the fixed and free loops on the straps).

And remember the noseband goes *inside* the cheekpieces.

Choosing foodstuffs

⭐ **CEREAL
TYPES**

Most cereals (such as oats, bran and maize) are treated before being fed to horses and ponies, to open or remove the husks (outer layer). Whole cereals are harder to digest.

Clipped: The grains are cracked open, allowing the inner part of the grain to be digested easily.

Rolled: The cereals are put through a roller and broken apart slightly.

Flaked: The grains are flattened and cooked.

Cut: The husk is cut.

Extruded: The cereals are put through a 'mincing' machine to break them down.

Cracked: The cereals are lightly rolled to crack the husks.

Crushed: The cereals are broken up completely.

Micronized: The process involves pre-cooking cereals in a similar method to microwaving (from the inside, out), except that micronizing uses rays of infra-red light. This makes the energy-giving starch inside the cereal more digestible.

For information on general feeding tips see pages 106–109.

The range of foodstuffs available can make your choice difficult. Knowing a little about what's on offer helps you make the right selection.

Which food?

A pony's food requirements depend on his age, temperament, type, the amount of work he does, whether he lives in or out, his health, likes and dislikes. As a general rule grass-fed ponies need less concentrated food than stabled horses.

Grass nuts (or meal) consist of dried grass. They vary in protein content. Choose the lowest protein form you can, as a high content is only necessary for pregnant mares and young foals. You can add grass nuts to a pony's concentrate ration, or use it to supplement poor hay or grazing.

If your pony is allergic to dust, grass nuts make an ideal alternative to hay. Mix them with chaff (chopped up straw or hay), or chaff with molasses, to dilute them. Grass nuts are also good for balancing vitamin and mineral intake when fed with cereals, such as oats.

Wheatfeed meal is a cereal by-product of flour milling and needs careful balancing with minerals. It is best left in the hands of experts.

Locust bean meal is a product of the carob bean or locust bean tree. It is sweet and often included in compounds.

Oats are fed whole, clipped, rolled, flaked, cut, micronized or extruded. They are a useful energy source but many ponies 'hot up' on them. Oats need to be balanced with non-cereals such as dried grass or sugar beet.

Soya bean meal is high in protein. It is unnecessary for ponies over two years, except for elderly ponies with digestive problems.

Maize (corn) is a cereal. Many compound feeds contain flaked or micronized maize. It is rich in energy but low in fibre (unless on the cob) and should be fed with chaff (chopped hay), grass meal or sugar beet. As with all new foodstuffs, introduce it gradually into the diet.

Sunflower seed is a protein and energy source used in compounds.

Oatfeed meal is a cereal by-product used mainly in horse and pony nuts.

Barley is fed rolled, flaked, cut, micronized, extruded or boiled, but *not* whole. It contains more digestible energy than oats – because it has less husk and less fibre – making it a good mix with non-cereals.

Linseed cake is poor quality protein but is used to make coarse mixes more tasty. The oil helps coat condition.

grass nuts

wheatfeed meal

locust bean meal

whole oats

soya bean meal

whole maize

sunflower seeds

whole barley

oatfeed meal

linseed cake

Storing foodstuffs

Hay and straw can be stored outside if necessary. Keep the bales raised off the ground on well-drained land and as sheltered as possible. Cover them with a large polythene sheet secured with a 'net' of binder twine. The cover can be weighted down by tying old tyres on to the net. On fine days remove the cover to let the hay 'breathe'.

▼ **Galvanized metal** feed bins are the most economical in the long term as they don't rust and are vermin proof. Plastic containers are easier to move around and are useful when going to a show.

Storing feed properly is essential to good hygiene. If you allow concentrated feed to become damp, it quickly rots – attracting mould and fungus. Your pony could become seriously ill if he eats feed in this condition. It's important, too, to make sure that your feed bins are protected against vermin, as rodents like rats can infect the feed itself with disease.

Careful storage of feedstuffs also saves money: hay exposed to rain can have some of the goodness washed from it and be quickly ruined.

Types of feedbins

The best sorts of storage bin for corn are made of galvanized metal. You can buy bins in all sizes and use them for any hard feed you wish. Those with two compartments mean you can fill each side in turn as you buy new feed.

Never buy more coarse mix or processed grain such as crushed barley or rolled oats than you can use within two weeks. Otherwise it could start to go bad. Cubes (nuts) and whole grain last for weeks or months if kept cool and dry. Molassed meal, sugar beet and chaff are best stored in a fridge in summer.

Always keep the bin lid down. Secure it with a small padlock to keep out ponies – and perhaps 'borrowers'!

Other materials such as sacks, plastic and fibreglass can all be chewed through by rats. Wood was used in the past and can be good if it's left natural and *not* treated with preservative which can taint the feed and cause poisoning.

Galvanized dustbins (refuse cans) are a safe compromise. You can tie down the lids even if you can't lock them.

All bins should be kept in cool, *dry* buildings – watch for leaky roofs dripping into them. Buildings made of metal or even wood heat up in summer unless well insulated.

Storing hay and straw

Hay and straw should be stored in *dry*, airy conditions. The building should be well ventilated – leave windows or top doors open. Old hay barns have ventilation bricks (bricks with drilled holes) installed.

It's best to stack bales off the ground, perhaps on wooden pallets. Leave enough space for a cat to squeeze underneath and root out rats and mice.

Don't store bales round the sides of indoor or outdoor riding arenas as they become covered in dust and unfit to feed. They should be stored downwind of the stables so any fungi and moulds present (even in good-quality fodder) blow away from the stables.

Plastic bins are a good temporary measure

Water containers

! BUCKETS
● If you use a bucket in a stable, don't leave the handle on. The pony could catch his headcollar on it when he drinks.

▼ **Field troughs** with a mains supply are best because your pony has a constant water supply.

Modern plumbing means that many fields have water supplies piped underground to troughs or taps. Piped water is a great advantage, as your pony has a permanent drinking supply and you don't have to carry large containers of water or use a hose pipe.

Troughs

Troughs are big enough to hold about as much water as a bath; automatic types have a reliable filling mechanism so they don't flood or dry up. Those with a plug hole make draining and cleaning easier.

There are two main sorts of filling mechanism. The first is the automatic ball-and-cock method. When the water is the correct height in the container the floating ball, which is attached to a metal arm, causes a cut-off device to stop water flowing. As the pony drinks, the level falls, the ball lowers and the water device opens allowing water in.

The other mechanism is a manually operated tap. You have to check the water level at least twice a day and turn on the tap to add water.

Whichever mechanism you have, it should be inside a strong cover at one end of the trough. This prevents the pony from injuring himself and stops him tampering with it.

Troughs are usually oblong, and made of galvanized metal, stone, heavy clay, plastic or glass-fibre. Plastic and glass-fibre troughs are safest because they cause less injury to ponies who collide with them. But these materials often crack if ponies chew them. Whichever type you choose there shouldn't be any sharp edges on which the pony could harm himself.

If you put the trough on a base to raise it off the ground, out of the mud, make sure the corners are rounded off to prevent leg injuries.

Drinking machines

Automatic drinking machines are quite common nowadays. Each stable has its own automatically filling container in the corner. It should be checked at least twice a day. Most 'auto-drinkers' hold about as much as a bucket.

Some are fitted with a meter so you can see how much the pony is drinking. The filling mechanism in each box is covered so that the horse or pony cannot fiddle with it.

Keep an eye on a pony who is not used to an auto-drinker. If he is reluctant to drink from it offer him water from a bucket until he becomes familiar with it.

To make sure the system is fitted properly it is best to get a plumber to do the job. If your stable is not fitted with an auto-drinker a water bucket, in a metal holder, is enough.

Salt and mineral licks

★ **SALT IN THE FEED**

If your pony won't use a lick — perhaps because it makes his tongue sore — add a little salt to his feed every day instead. You should also do this for very hard-working ponies who may not be able to obtain enough salt from a lick.

Check with your vet or a nutritionist about how much to add — a dessertspoonful a day for a pony and a tablespoonful a day for a horse should be enough. Don't add it all to the same feed, and beware of adding too much at one time— it may put the pony off his feed.

If you are feeding prepared foods such as nuts or coarse mixes, check with your vet, as the salt content may already be adequate.

► **Salt is a vital** part of the diet, and every horse should have a constant supply. Putting a salt or mineral lick in his stable is a convenient way of ensuring this.

A salt lick should always be available in your pony's stable or field as salt is an essential part of his diet. It is particularly important in hot weather, especially during hard work, when the pony loses a lot of salt in his sweat.

Types of lick

A plain, iodized lick (containing iodine) should be the basic source of salt for any horse or pony. Commercially produced licks are oblong brick-shapes. You can also get natural rock salt, which is greyish in colour and comes in irregularly shaped chunks.

Licks are also available in a variety of flavours, such as mint, clove, cinnamon and aniseed. These are intended to get the pony to lick them more, so ensuring his salt supply.

You may have to try several flavours before you find one your pony likes. Always have a plain, iodized lick available anyway and treat specially flavoured ones as an extra.

You can also get 'mineralised' licks, which contain a range of other trace elements and minerals, as well as salt.

Salt lick holders

Special holders are available to take salt licks. They are either metal, plastic, or plastic-coated metal. Holders are simply the same shape as the lick with an open top and

▲ **Ponies at grass** should have a salt lick in the field or field shelter, or a special field feeding block which contains salt.

turned-up sides and bottom. You fix them to the stable wall at the pony's head height, and slide the lick in from the top.

Metal holders need checking regularly. Salt causes metal to rust, and rust from the holder may soak into the salt lick and contaminate it. Also, you need to replace the salt lick straight away when it is finished, because the metal holders have sharp edges.

If you get a plastic-coated holder check regularly that the coating is not chipping or cracking and, if it is, get another one.

Some horses like licks so much they actually bite chunks off them. In case this happens, don't site the holder over the water container. If a lump of salt falls into the water and dissolves, it taints the water and your pony won't drink it. This is very unpleasant for the pony, and it is bad for him to go without water.

Some people leave the lick in the horse's manger instead of in a holder. However, this can result in food being left congealed round the lick, which is unhygienic. The manger and the lick must be cleaned thoroughly after every feed.

mineral lick

salt lick

metal holder

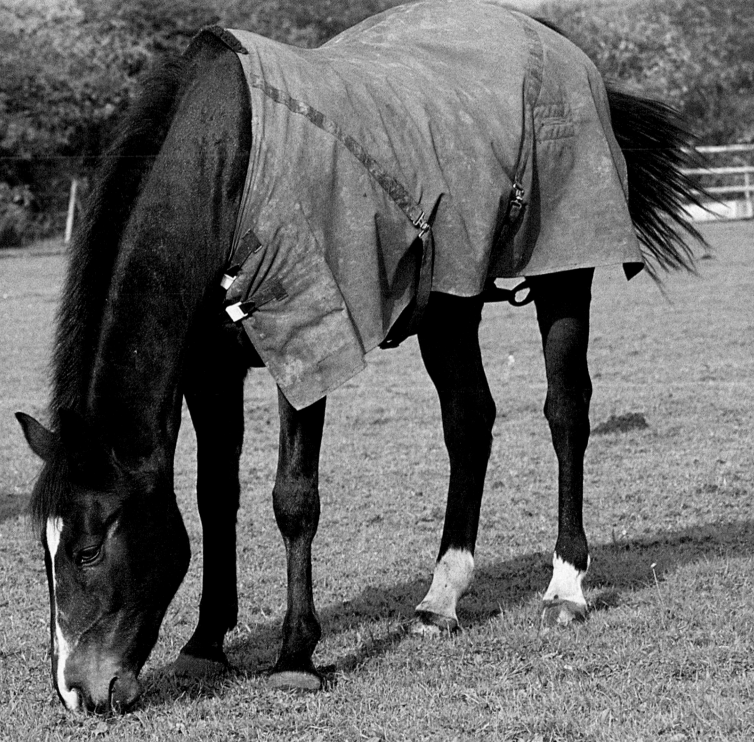

3 Grass-kept ponies

Maintaining a field or pasture

Ponies pick up and swallow worm larvae when grazing. The larvae travel through the body, causing damage and blockages, and end up as mature worms in the intestines, where they lay eggs.

These are passed out with the droppings on to the grass, hatch into larvae and the cycle begins again.

➤ **Droppings should** be removed from your pony's field at least once a week. This helps the grass to stay juicy and nutritious and keeps down the level of worms.

! GRASS
• CLIPPINGS
Many people imagine that grass clippings from a lawnmower are a treat for a pony.

This is only the case if they are *really* fresh. Clippings start to ferment within 15-20 minutes of the grass being cut. This fermentation process produces a build-up of gas in the pony's stomach which can be extremely harmful.

Whether they're from a garden next to your field, or on a grass verge beside a road, *don't* let your pony eat grass clippings.

Ponies enjoy living in a field because the outdoor life is natural to them. Make sure the pony in your care stays healthy and contented by frequently checking the field for hazards and looking after the grass.

Checking the field

Whenever you visit your pony, walk right round the field and check that everything is in good order.

Rubbish: Look over the ground carefully to make sure that there are no dangerous objects or litter lying around. Half-buried wire, rusty nails, glass or plastic bottles, empty crisp packets and sweet wrappers can all harm a pony.

Fencing: Look for weak spots or breaks in the fencing, so that you can get it repaired *before* the pony escapes. If the boundary is a hedge, check for gaps, particularly when the leaves have fallen in winter.

Shelter: Leafless trees and hedges also make less of a windbreak, and a field shed may be necessary for winter shelter. You need to watch out for changes *outside* the field as well – someone cutting down trees nearby can drastically alter the amount of wind through the field.

Wooden field shelters should be checked weekly for damage from kicks or general wear and tear. Loose, splintered boards weaken the structure and can cause injury.

Water: Every day, especially in summer, top up the water supply. Clean water troughs regularly and, if the trough is automatic, make sure it's refilling.

In winter, you can float a plastic football in the water. Its bobbing movement helps delay freezing. Use a neutral tone – a bright colour can frighten a timid pony. If ice still forms, break it morning and evening and remove it – otherwise the water will refreeze almost instantly. Pile the ice in a safe area *outside* the field to avoid accidents.

If a stream runs through the field, ask your vet how to have it checked for pollution. Do not use stagnant ponds as a water supply. The water is still, and more easily contaminated.

Removing droppings

Horses are fussy eaters – some grasses your pony will like and eat down to the soil; others he'll dislike and leave to grow long. Ponies also keep an area of

the field for their droppings and they won't eat the grass there, either.

When a field becomes patchy with some bare areas and long, lank grass in other places, it is called 'horse-sick'. Try not to let your field get into this state. The first way of preventing it is to remove the bulk of your pony's droppings at least once a week. This encourages even grazing. You may be able to sell the droppings to keen gardeners.

Removing droppings also reduces the level of worms. Horse-sick paddocks not only have poor, sour grass but are riddled with worms. Worms in ponies can be the cause of poor condition, colic and, in extreme cases, death. Regular worming keeps the horse healthy and helps to reverse the cycle by reducing the level of worms in his droppings.

►**To keep tabs** on which field chores you've done each week, why not make your own checklist?
□ Write or draw pictures of what needs checking across the top of a piece of card. List the days of the week down the side.
□ Rule out a grid on a sheet of paper and tape it to the card so you have a daily box for each chore.
□ At the end of the week, tear off the filled-in grid, ready to start again.

MY WEEKLY CHECKLIST	RUBBISH	HEDGE/FENCE	FIELD SHELTER	WATER	DROPPINGS	POISONOUS PLANTS
MONDAY						
TUESDAY	✓	✓		✓		
WEDNESDAY				✓	✓	
THURSDAY				✓		
FRIDAY				✓		
SATURDAY	✓			✓		
SUNDAY		✓	✓	✓	✓	✓

79

Keeping your pony secure

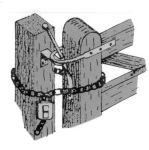

▲ **Padlocks:** Make life difficult for a potential thief by securing the gate to the stable yard or field with a padlock and heavy chain. To stop the gate being lifted off, either reverse the top hinge or have a metal disc welded on to the hinge. Padlock *both* ends for good measure.

Few moments can be more heart-breaking to a horse or pony owner than to have his or her much-loved animal stolen. Fortunately, there are several ways of deterring horse thieves. Whether your pony is stabled or at grass, the most effective is to have him freeze-marked.

What is freeze-marking?

Freeze-marking can be called 'cold branding'. Instead of a red-hot branding iron, super-chilled irons are used. This process is much more humane and pain-free than hot branding — but the results are just as permanent.

What happens during marking? First, the pony's coat is shaved around the marking area. The operator applies very cold irons to the coat and holds them on the skin for several seconds. This kills the pigmentation (colouring matter) in the skin. So when the hair regrows it is white, leaving a clearly visible code number in the coat. Your pony is the only one with this number.

Grey ponies have the irons left on longer so the hair is killed completely, leaving the number in bare skin.

The mark is usually placed on the back, in the saddle area. When the pony is tacked up and ridden the number cannot be seen. But should the pony be found wandering loose or in a sale yard, the number can be spotted at once and checked. Some companies sell sew-on patches for rugs to warn thieves that the animal is marked.

Who freeze-marks?

There are several companies who freeze-mark, operating slightly different systems. The best keep a register of horses and their owners.

This means that the papers given to you at the time of marking prove you are the owner, and the number marked on to the pony can be checked against

their register. If you sell the pony, the papers go with him and you inform the company of the change.

General security measures

As well as freeze-marking, you should take general precautions.

☐ Padlock the gate to the stable yard or field with a strong padlock and chain – at both ends if it can be lifted off its hinges.

☐ Ask local residents to tell you if strangers hang around the field. Give them your day and evening telephone numbers – and a 'thank-you' box of chocolates at Christmas!

☐ If you have a choice of field, opt for one with thick, prickly hedges around it. These are difficult for thieves to penetrate, while wooden and wire fencing can be taken down.

☐ Try not to leave a headcollar on your pony – it makes him easier to catch for other people as well as yourself.

Freeze-marking

This pain-free number marked on the back gives a horse permanent identification. If stolen, he can be easily traced. Avoid riding a pony for a few days after he's been marked, and use a numnah until the white hair has grown through. Freeze-marking makes no difference to a judge's decision when showing in-hand.

▼ **Having your pony stolen** leaves a hole in your life that nothing else can fill. So put off horse rustlers by getting your pony freeze-marked (cold branded).

You could also have a trip wire rigged up round the pony's field or stable. This is operated by battery, and sets off lights or an alarm if anyone intrudes.

Summer field care

▼ The pony's basic needs are the same summer and winter and you must check the field daily even when the weather is fine. The essentials are:

Long daylight hours make summer the most pleasant time for you to look after a grass-kept pony. But the pony himself can face problems – the main troubles created by sun, flies, hard ground and too much grass.

Rich pastures

Grass in summer can range from very rich to parched, dry and virtually useless. Surprisingly, the first kind is the most dangerous to ponies and cobs. These types are normally 'good doers', in other words, they do not need a lot of rich food and can become ill if they have access to it. They are better kept on poorish quality grazing – but they

still have to have *something* to eat!

If the grass is lush and your pony looks quite fat enough – or even just well covered – you are safest to restrict his grazing. If you don't have a stable, try to move the pony on to poorer grazing, or strip-graze his field by dividing it up with electric fencing or use a muzzle for part of the day.

For ponies and cobs the type of grazing used for sheep is quite good enough. That used for cows, particularly dairy cattle, is usually far too rich.

Parched grazing

On the other hand, if the grass in your field is very short and sparse or shrivelled up because of prolonged dry weather, the pony may not be getting enough food and roughage. This can cause health problems of its own – like

▲ Clean fresh water at all times

▲The right amount of quality food

▲ Overhead shelter from the sun

colic – apart from gradual weight loss.

If so, feed the pony hay, or a hay substitute such as one of the branded hayage products. Concentrates are not appropriate in this case.

If you are uncertain about how much hay to feed, give the pony the amount he would require if stabled, morning and night. Alternatively, check with your instructor or vet.

Feeding a field-kept pony in summer can be a fine balancing act. If you put him on an almost 'starvation diet' because you are frightened of him getting laminitis, you could find he gets so hungry he starts experimenting with poisonous plants and chewing the fences. If you feed him too much, he could contract laminitis after all. Always be ready to seek expert advice to get the balance right.

Water

Water sources must be checked at least twice daily in summer, particularly if they are not the self-filling type. In hot weather ponies can soon empty a large bin, or a trough if the filling mechanism has gone wrong.

Fresh clean water is vital to your pony's health and a careful eye must be kept on his supply.

Exercising the pony

If the pony is out all day, you do not *have* to exercise him yourself. But if you want him fit rather than just healthy, he needs ridden work and maybe a small feed of nuts. These give him extra energy and keep his muscles toned up for work as opposed to ambling about the field. His back muscles also need to be kept used to carrying your weight. ➤

★ **FIELD-SHARING**
If your pony is the only one receiving supplementary feeding in a field of several animals, you may have problems. Bring your pony out of the field at feeding times so that he gets his rations in peace without others stealing them. Then return him to the field when he has finished.

▼ **Summer sun** can reduce pasture to a mixture of scrub, thistles and dust with patches of grasses. In this case you should feed the pony hay morning and night.

Summer problems

The heat of summer brings out flies and other insects, and they cause some of the pony's worst problems.

Sweet itch: You can tell if your pony has sweet itch — caused by midges — because he will rub himself along the mane, shoulders, withers and tail. The condition can result in raw, infected skin which attracts flies even more, so do not think it will get better on its own. Call your vet as treatments are improving all the time.

The best preventive treatment is to stable the pony for two hours before and after dawn and sunset, when the midges are most active. If this is not possible, apply a fly repellant frequently.

Warble flies are much less common now than they used to be, but occasionally they crop up. If your pony develops hard, hot painful swellings in the saddle area, he could well have a warble maggot maturing in there. This is another task for your vet. He may need to get the maggot out and the pony will be off work until the wound heals — never ride a pony with such lumps on his back. Apart from the pain, you could kill the maggot which then rots under the pony's skin, setting up serious infection.

Bots: Pale-coloured eggs on your pony's legs and shoulders are bot eggs. If the pony licks them and swallows them he will have bots in his stomach all winter, unless you worm him in autumn with a medicine effective against them. You should give him a general wormer anyway, but if you see the eggs, scrape them off gently with a blunt knife or plastic spatula. Again a good fly repellant prevents the flies from landing to lay the eggs in the first place.

▼ **A rubbed tail** is often a sign of sweet itch, an irritating skin allergy caused by midges. Ask your vet for a lotion to alleviate the itching.

► **Fly fringes,** when used as well as a repellant, bring great relief to a pony.

▼ **Rich grazing** is hazardous as ponies can get the disease laminitis if they gorge themselves.

To keep a field-kept pony fit for weekend work such as shows, aim to ride him for about an hour or more on three weekdays. A lesson once a week reminds you about good riding techniques and keeps your pony working correctly and using the right muscles.

Shelter and shade

Do see that your pony has *proper* shelter and shade *overhead*. This means trees, high, overhanging hedges or a field shed to help him get away from too much sun.

However, the most effective way to protect him against flies is to apply a really good fly repellant (the type known as 'residual' is best because its effects last several days). This stops the flies landing on him to start with.

The daily check

Your daily check should include the pony, the ground, the water and the fencing.

The pony should show all the usual signs of good health – he should be alert, with a shiny coat. If he seems unusually quiet, dozy, perhaps unco-ordinated and standing on his own, he could be ill. In hot weather it is possible for animals with no proper shelter to get heatstroke. Check him for wounds and his feet for chipping horn if the ground is hard, and loose or missing shoes. Flies can cause ponies to gallop in desperation, jarring legs and feet.

Check the field for litter thrown in by passers-by, if they have access to the field, and remove everything you find. Take rubbish well away from the field and dispose of it properly — don't just dump it somewhere.

Check the water supply, which must be plentiful and clean, and finally check the fencing. Hedges, too, need to be looked at as leaves disguise gaps which the pony knows are there. You may need to fix rails across to close them up. Make sure the shelter is sound and remove droppings, which otherwise attract flies.

! VANDALISM
If you suspect your pony has been subject to vandalism — perhaps he has unexplained wounds, seems upset or tired, has had his mane or tail cut or your gate or field has been tampered with — tell the police at once.

▼ **Hosing down** after a sweaty ride is appreciated on a hot day! But don't let the horse become chilled afterwards.

Winter field care

▼ A clipped pony should be turned out in a New Zealand rug in winter. A neck and hood attachment keeps him extra warm.

Although many ponies are hardy, none can be left to fend for themselves in a field. In the wild, ponies roam over large areas of land and can shelter in woods and valleys or on hillsides. A domesticated pony is a 'prisoner' in a field which, left to itself, may offer no real shelter, little natural food, and may become badly poached.

Keeping a pony warm

The best way to keep your pony warm is to leave on his full winter coat, mane and tail, and provide plenty of shelter, overhead as well as side on. An unclipped, native-bred pony should not need a New Zealand rug but a finer-bred one or clipped pony does, and must have a proper field shed.

A New Zealand rug is waterproof, made from synthetic (probably nylon) fabric or canvas. It should be shaped to fit the pony, curving to fit his backbone, and darted at elbow and hip. Good makes have no surcingle, but fasten at the breast and with hindleg straps.

Put the rug on like a stable rug; fasten the leg straps then the breast straps. To remove, unfasten the breast strap and then the leg straps, and slide it off.

Take the rug off twice daily and check the pony for signs of chafing (rubbed hair or bald patches) or sore places, particularly at the withers, shoulders, hips and between the hindlegs. You really need two rugs so you can keep them fairly clean and dry in turn.

Grooming

Every day, pick out the feet and check the condition of legs, shoes and feet. Damp-sponge discharges and dirt from eyes, nostrils, sheath and dock and dry these areas with an old towel. Brush out the mane and tail to stop them becoming too tangled.

Do not body brush an outdoor pony. Unless you're riding, you don't even have to brush off mud every day as it protects against the wind. If the mud is wet, it won't brush off anyway, so if you want to ride, you have to dry the mud by thatching (covering the back in straw under a rug), then brush it off.

Feeding

The most important food is good hay because winter grass contains almost no nourishment. Buy hay from hay and

▼ **Breaking the ice:** In really cold weather, the water supply may freeze. You must break the ice and remove it from the trough to slow down re-freezing. Take it outside the field where the pony won't slip on it.

Check the water supply daily

► **Filling a hay net:**
Loosen the drawstring and open the neck. Shake the hay thoroughly to get rid of any dust, and pack it down into the net.

straw merchants or animal feed firms; your instructor can recommend a reputable firm.

Stress that you want *good* hay. Meadow or mixture hay is ideal for ponies and it contains varied grasses. Good hay should smell sweet, not musty.

There must be *no* mould (white, green or black powdery patches) or dust when you shake it out. Bad hay is dangerous to your pony's health. He may even

! IS YOUR PONY COLD?

A cold pony looks miserable, maybe hunched up, with his tail to whatever shelter there is. He may shiver, and his coat may stand up when it's dry.

Feel the lower half of his ears: if they are cold the pony's body is cold all over. He may even feel too unhappy to move about and warm himself up.

Don't let him stay like this or he could get hypothermia (a serious chill). Bring him into a stable or shed, dry him, put on a rug and stable bandages and give him hay and a feed.

Use a New Zealand rug on him in cold, wet, windy weather and have a field shelter erected.

Tying a hay net

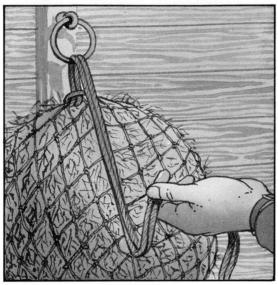

1 Lift the full hay net up to the height of the ring. Pull the drawstring tight and pass it through the ring. Loop the string through a square mesh low down in the net.

2 Pull it taut and hoist the net up tightly so that it doesn't lower too much as it empties. Pass the rope end round the back of the drawstring and pull a loop through. Tighten it. You now have a quick-release knot.

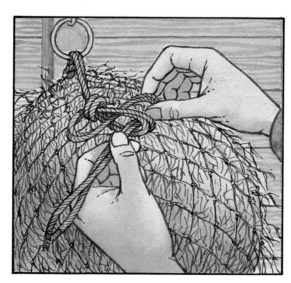

3 To stop the pony tugging the end and undoing the knot, make another loop with the end of the drawstring. Check that the net is high enough to stop the pony catching his feet in the mesh even when it empties. The knot may tighten as the pony eats from the net, but you can easily undo it by pulling the end.

MISTAKE!

Don't tie the hay net up loosely so that it sags down. The net must also be attached to a firm support so the pony has something to push against when he takes out the hay, and is best kept under shelter from the rain.

refuse to eat it although very hungry.

Ponies should have *ad lib* hay (as much as they will eat) in winter. Your pony needs about a third of a bale a day.

Feeding hay loose on the ground is wasteful, and cattle-type field hay-racks are dangerous for ponies. Use a hay net.

To fill a hay net, open up the neck, shake out the hay thoroughly and cram it down into the net. When full, pull the drawstring tight. Hang it at the pony's head height against the wall of the shelter (inside) or against a tree trunk, as he has to push it against something firm to get the hay out. You can also fasten a net to the top rail of wooden fencing, but it's better to keep the hay away from rain.

Extreme weather

You need to take extra special care of your pony when it's very cold or wet.

● In frost, break the ice on water supplies twice daily. Floating a plastic football in the trough helps delay freezing. Take all the ice out of the water otherwise it quickly re-freezes.

● If waterlogged areas of the field start to freeze over, cover them with a thick layer of used bedding, sand or grit, otherwise the pony could slip and fall over.

● You may need to give extra food during extreme weather, to help keep the pony warm and because what grass there is may be buried under snow.

● Check the hard ground is not breaking the hooves of unshod feet; if it is, call the farrier to put on light shoes. Prevent snow from balling in the hooves by smearing the soles with old cooking fat or oil (not axle grease or engine oil which can damage horn and skin).

● The pony's face can get chapped if his eyes water, especially in windy weather. Bathe with clear water containing a little antiseptic and apply a water-resistant antiseptic cream.

● It's safest to bring ponies into a stable or barn during storms or very severe weather.

● During heavy rain, ponies can become soaked to the skin and very cold. They must have proper overhead shelter; a steady downpour comes through trees, however dense. The ground becomes very muddy, particularly round gateways, troughs and shelter entrances. Spread thick layers of straw or used bedding here and top up regularly.

! LOSING WEIGHT
● A thick coat can hide a thin pony. Push your fingers right through the coat. If you can feel his ribs, increase his hay allowance, worm him and have his teeth checked by the vet.

▼ **When it snows,** make sure the pony has extra hay to eat as he can't easily get at what grass there is. He needs enough food to keep up his body heat as well as to give him energy.

Catching a pony

Most ponies are easy to catch but some play hard to get. Fortunately, it's a bad habit that can usually be changed with patience and persistence. And it's worth the effort because grass-kept ponies should be caught and checked over every day.

When all goes well

The right way to catch a well-behaved pony is to walk up quietly where he can see you. Hold a headcollar or halter in one hand and a titbit in the other (some really willing ponies don't even need a titbit). Don't approach from behind: if a pony can't see you and you startle him, you could get kicked.

Slide your leadrope over his neck behind his ears as you give him a titbit. Hold the rope together under his throat as you put on the headcollar or halter. You might feel as if you need three hands to begin with, but you'll soon get used to managing.

Attracting his attention

Handling a pony is much easier if he answers to his name – but most don't! Use his name whenever you approach him, before a command, to attract his

attention or to keep his concentration. Fuss him when he responds until it becomes second nature. Then when you enter his field and call, he'll probably come at once, especially if you have a titbit that he likes.

It helps if the titbit is something the pony can't resist. A pony who's just filled himself with grass won't find fresh food like carrot or apple appealing because it's too similar. Take something completely different – dried food like coarse mix or pony nuts, for example.

For those who really need tempting, such everyday feed may not be attractive enough. Find out what your pony has a weakness for and take that. Most have a sweet tooth and love sugar lumps or hard mints.

Turning him out

When you turn your pony out into the field, be calm and gentle. Don't surprise him, slap him on the bottom, shout and whoop or be rough. If the pony associates catching and turning out with excitement, rush and hassle, he'll expect this and become difficult. Remember the perfect combination – quiet, firm confidence and irresistible titbits!

▼ **Hard to get:** Many ponies know being caught means work and, understandably, they walk away as soon as you approach.

The trick is to turn catching into a treat – sometimes just make a fuss of the pony and let him go again. And remember the most vital ingredient – his favourite titbit!

When things go wrong

There are several ways to make catching a mischievous pony easier.

First, leave a headcollar on with a 15cm (6in) length of binder twine knotted to the bottom ring. This gives you something to take hold of. Offer the pony his favourite titbit with two hands and slip one under his chin to hold the twine. Do not use rope because it is dangerous – the twine must break if the pony puts his foot on it.

Many ponies don't really like work and know what's in store for them when they're caught. Break this pattern by catching the pony *without* working him. Give him a titbit, put his headcollar on and look him over for injury. Then let him go. Every now and then, go to the field just to inspect the fencing, water supply and so on, without going near him. He'll come to regard you as part of the scenery.

You can extend this idea by walking 'aimlessly' about the field, close to and away from him. Walk casually past him and catch the binder twine on his headcollar. Give him his titbit and leave it at that. He'll never know what to expect with this routine. The technique requires considerable patience, as running after the pony if he canters off undoes all your good work.

Sometimes, having a squeaky toy

Catching a willing pony

1 Approach the pony quietly from the front where he can see you. Hold the headcollar behind your back.

2 Offer him the titbit from the flat of your hand. A grass-fed pony is tempted by pony nuts or sugar lumps.

3 Slip the leadrope round his neck behind the ears. Use one hand to secure it under his throat.

4 Once you've put the noseband on, pull the main strap round behind his ears and buckle it up.

Finally, thank him with a pat.

Headgear

A headcollar that's made of leather looks like a heavy bridle with no bit or browband. But nowadays many are made of nylon webbing and come in bright colours. The leadrope clips to the ring under the jaw.

With a tricky pony, leave the headcollar on with a 15cm (6in) length of twine attached, giving you something to hold.

A halter (made of rope or webbing) is combined with its leadrope. Always use the special knot to stop the rope tightening.

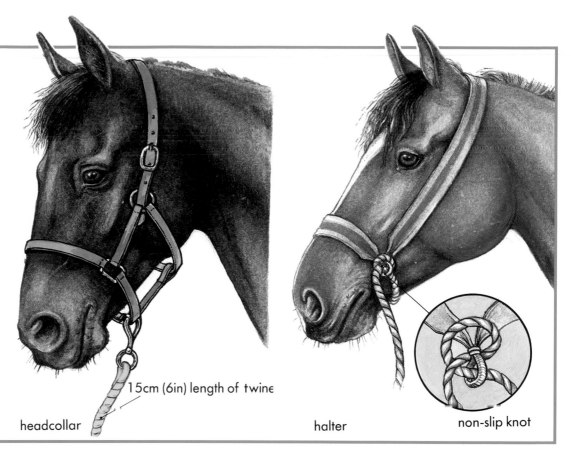

15cm (6in) length of twine

headcollar

halter

non-slip knot

helps – most ponies can't resist coming up to investigate the noise! Also, a large, rustly bag full of food that *you* are eating often works. Just stand still in the field and, when the pony comes for his share, wander towards the gate without giving him any – until he lets you catch him.

Drastic measures

If catching your pony turns into a real problem, you'll have to take more drastic action.

Herding a pony into a corner with several people holding a long rope occasionally works, as long as it is done quietly and craftily. The rope should be about 1m (3ft) off the ground, and kept in a straight line until he's cornered and caught. However, some ponies get wise to this trick and learn to charge, bite and kick, so only herd as a last resort.

One of a herd

With a pony that is a problem to catch you'll find it much easier to keep him on his own in a field. Having a companion is likely to excite him all the more, and there's nothing more exasperating than seeing two friends galloping gleefully to the other end of the field!

Other horses also get in the way, try to eat the titbits meant for your pony and may chase him if he is timid.

When you have no choice but to keep your pony with others, you may have to act bossily to make the unwanted ones stay away. However, loud, frantic behaviour may excite the herd into charging about, making your task totally impossible.

A sharp slap on the breast (never the head except for biting) with a firm growl – 'No!' – keeps most pushy ponies back. Behave calmly and confidently and, if the field contains a real bully, take a friend to help you cope.

Be particularly careful that other horses don't escape when you are leaving the field with your pony. A catching pen at the entrance (as in the picture below), with a second gate shutting off the escape route, helps to separate one pony from the rest.

Catching pen

A pen at the field entrance helps when you're singling out one pony from several. Instead of one gate, there are two which enclose a small space. Even if a pony escapes through the first gate his exit is blocked by the second.

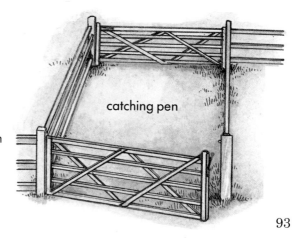

catching pen

Exercise plans for a...

▼ **Even when out hacking**, you can school your horse. Make sure he is concentrating and attentive to what you ask him to do. Practise smooth transitions and aim for rhythmical strides in all paces.

The fat, round sleekness of a pony at grass indicates perfect health but not physical fitness for work. Although you can never get a field-kept pony to the hard condition needed for regular hunting or competition work, you can make him fit enough for local shows and events, occasional hunting or limited endurance riding. Before you ask him to work, the pony needs a programme of exercise routines to build up his strength gradually.

...grass-kept pony

What is fitness?

Horses in the wild are nomadic, roaming widely over large areas where they gain natural exercise and variety of diet. In the confines of a field, a pony depends on you to recognize and correct any deficiencies that occur.

Exercising the pony means he can perform to the best of his ability without stress and strain. It strengthens his limbs and tendons, lowering the risk of sprains during exertion. It conditions and tones his muscles and reduces the amount of fat he carries. By decreasing the size of his belly, there's more room for his lungs – this eases the pony's breathing and lets him work more efficiently.

Feeding for fitness

It is unnatural for a horse to work and a diet of grass doesn't give him enough energy. Fitness is achieved by a combination of diet and exercise. The intake of energy foods must equal or slightly exceed the output of energy. A very rough guide is 450g of concentrated food for each 1.5km, or 1lb to each mile of ground covered. But you must also take into account the size of the pony and his character (high-spirited ponies need less concentrates).

The supply of concentrates, preferably balanced pony nuts, should be further increased for several days before a demanding occasion. Divide feeds into two a day and give them at the same times so that you establish a regular

SEASONAL CHANGES

The value of a pony's grass intake varies enormously according to the condition of his pasturage.

● **Early spring** may mean that you should restrict the area available to the pony so the grass can grow. Increase his hay ration accordingly.

● **Mid-summer:** On lush pasture, smaller ponies can become too fat. They should be switched to more sparse paddocks where they have to move around to get their food.

pattern. Allow at least 1-1½ hours for digestion before you saddle up the pony for exercise.

A pony – being much hardier than a horse – generally does better at grass and is more manageable. Keep a close watch on his appearance and behaviour. If the pony is excessively skittish too many oats are the likely cause. If he's lazy and sluggish, increase the energy foods. Fatness means the pony is eating too much and a poor and ribby appearance means you should increase the rations – but worm the pony regularly in case this is the cause of poor condition.

Recognizing his condition

In a 'soft' condition the pony's muscles are slack, he is fat with a gross belly and he cannot make a sustained effort without sweating and distress.

In a 'poor' condition the pony appears thin, has a 'staring' coat, is weak with a depressed expression and lacks energy.

The hard condition brought about by correct diet and exercise means he is free of extra fat and his muscles and tendons are toned up so that he can perform at the peak of his ability.

Changing the diet

A pony should always have the same daily weight of food, but the content of this depends on the work required of him. As you work him harder, so he needs more energy foods.

You must carry out all changes to the diet gradually. A 14-14.2-hand pony, weighing about 400kg (900lbs), needs about 9-10kg (20-22lbs) daily. For an unfit, grass-kept pony, this can consist entirely of bulk food: grass or grass and hay. A pony in full daily work needs two

The six-week exercise programme

At every stage of the programme, aim to encourage the pony into a free, forward movement with an even rhythm at all speeds. A good average is 9.5km/h (6mph). An irregular, jerky gait, and quick changes of pace over short intervals

make the pony lose concentration. The feeding amounts suggested are for a 14.2-hand pony weighing about 400kg (900lbs). If your pony is smaller, reduce the weight of the feed, but keep the proportions the same.

Week 1-2: Begin with walking only, initially for an hour, every day if possible and at least three times a week if not. Increase gradually up to 2½ hours' steady walking over sloping ground along varied routes.
Feeding: Morning and evening feeds – ½kg (1lb) of pony nuts or other concentrates to supplement his daily intake of 9kg (19lbs) of grass and hay according to season.

Week 2-3: After ten 'walking only' sessions, introduce increasing lengths of trotting into the rides. Always start out and finish with a ten-minute walk. This loosens up the pony at the beginning and cools him on return. Ride him on a long rein on the way back to relax him. Trotting up and down hills reduces the amount of fat a pony carries as well as conditioning and toning his muscles.
Feeding: Gradually increase the two feeds in quantity to ¾kg (1½lbs) each.

thirds bulk and one third concentrated food with an increased proportion of concentrates before a demanding event.

Which concentrates?

The concentrated part of the feed can consist of a variety of foodstuffs. The most suitable are balanced pony nuts. Check on the variety and content, and follow the manufacturer's instructions: these contain some bulk so you can reduce the hay ration. The bulk content also means the pony eats the feed slowly. However, pony nuts are the most expensive way of feeding your pony.

Other concentrates you can use are oats, which are best bruised and fed with bran; barley, which should be fed flaked or boiled and is less 'heating' than oats; flaked maize; cooked linseed fed as a mash; and sugar beet pulp which should be mixed with cereals or nuts as

it is unsuitable as a staple food on its own. You can add cut-up apples or carrots to feeds, give split peas and beans in small quantities and feed swedes and turnips whole.

Divide the daily ration of concentrates into two regular feeds, and three as the ration increases. Divide the daily hay ration into two and give it in a hay net morning and evening. The second ration should be the larger so the pony can munch through the night.

Preparing the pony

You may want your pony fit for sharp bursts of energy as in show jumping, for prolonged effort as in eventing or hunting or for slow, steady exertion like pulling a trap. Whatever your aims, there are several points to bear in mind when planning your fitness programme. □ Allow at least six weeks of prep-

● **Late summer:** Very dry conditions may mean the pasture becomes bare. Supplement the hay and keep a careful eye on the water supply.

● **Mid-winter** delay in supplementing the grass can cause loss of condition. The pony needs extra rations to keep warm, particularly if he is thin. It is now that the 'warming' foods like barley, maize (corn), split peas and beans, and turnips can be added to the diet.

Week 4: On suitably soft but not deep ground — never road surfaces, stony tracks or heavy mud — you can start gentle cantering during the fourth week of daily exercise. Make sure he has the correct bend on turns and a good, balanced carriage. He should be alert and responsive to your aids.
Feeding: Introduce a midday feed of ½kg (1lb) of concentrates.

Week 5-6: Start short gallops during the fifth or sixth week depending on the pony's condition.
Feeding: Gradually increase the size of each feed so that the pony has 3kg (6½lbs) of concentrated food per day — one third of his daily rations in high energy foods. This should be increased to half the ration (5kg/11lbs) for two days before a demanding event. If your pony is lazy, you could change very slowly from pony nuts to oats for energy build-up and go back to nuts or other less heating foods after the occasion.

aration before asking a pony in soft condition to make strenuous efforts.

□ The unfit pony must be shod before he can begin work on roads or hard ground.

□ The build-up should be a *gradual progression* – this is the aim in planning your exercise routine.

□ Girth galls and saddle sores are especially likely on soft, fat ponies. Make sure the pony is dry and mud-free in the saddle area before tacking up. Don't push the pony too fast or you may damage his legs, in which case you have to throw the whole programme out and rest him until he's recovered.

Varying the routine

To keep both your own and the pony's interest, vary the daily exercises within the general pattern of gradual development. Try to find several routes which offer long sections of firm grass track and ride over them in alternating direc-

▲ **As the pony gets fitter**, you can jump practice fences after schooling your pony or going out for a hack.

► **Schooling sessions** should be kept brief and if possible be followed by a ride out to stop the pony becoming bored.

If he has a very thick coat and sweats excessively when ridden, it is worth trace-clipping the pony and protecting him with a New Zealand rug in the winter months. Heavy sweating causes loss of condition.

tions. This avoids boredom and habits like 'we always gallop here' starting with a buck or two to show that he knows!

In the later stages of the exercise schedule, try spending the first half hour schooling your pony in the paddock. Practise bending and turning and keeping his attention on your aids.

If you can, put up several small but sturdy jumps at the side of the paddock. Pop the pony over these for practice after a schooling session or after a short ride when his fitness has improved. Take advantage of any suitable, natural obstacles to jump when you are out on rides. Always check the landing as well as the take-off side before attempting a jump.

Exercises in the school or over jumps should continue for 20 to 30 minutes – no longer. Always finish with a happy note of achievement, never after an unsuccessful tussle.

Carry out the daily rides and exercises sometimes alone and sometimes with others. Calm companions can be particularly useful for solving problems like traffic shyness or refusing to leave home. And going with friends adds to the fun and variety of the routines.

Keeping a pony fit

Daily exercise to maintain fitness is ideal to keep a pony prepared for special occasions but not essential otherwise. A minimum of three, two-hour sessions spaced through the week will keep up the pony's condition.

After a demanding day out – at a show or hunting – let the pony rest in his field for 24 hours. Just check him over for damage and lead him about for ten minutes to relieve stiffness and make sure he's sound. The next day you can go back to his normal routine.

CHOOSING YOUR TIME
Try to carry out your fitness programme during a long holiday period. This means that you can ride your pony daily, or almost every day. It also means you can give him a third feed at midday as the schedule progresses.

▼ **Place the feed** in a portable manger firmly hooked on to the top of the gate or fence where the pony may eat his rations undisturbed

4 Stabled ponies

Bedding

▲ **Tie up your pony** in a safe place away from the stable when mucking out.

★ **TYPES OF BEDDING**
Many materials make good bedding for horses, so be guided by what you can find easily in your area.

NON-ABSORBENT bedding needs to be mucked out every day. The most common is **straw**; wheat straw is best. **Bark** is also suitable, but takes several years to rot down into useful manure.

ABSORBENT materials need a full mucking out less often. They include:
Peat: Difficult to spot the dung! Good for horses with dust allergies and makes the best manure.
Fallen pine needles: Use the long, soft type.
Paper: Usually shredded. Avoid very long pieces which wrap round the legs.
Sawdust is good as long as it's not dusty.

◄ **Wood shavings** are a good choice. They are coarser than sawdust and therefore more dust free. Make sure they are safe for animals (not sprayed).

Bedding is important for two reasons: it provides a soft cushion for a pony to lie on and makes it easier to keep the stable clean.

How bedding helps

Horses are heavy and don't like lying on hard surfaces. If they do they may hurt their legs, and to avoid this, are more likely to remain standing up. This in turn causes stress. So make sure you give your pony a soft layer of bedding.

As well as warmth and comfort, bedding is important for hygiene. Stale, wet bedding can easily be removed and replaced with a fresh layer. Droppings are kept off the ground: where there is no bed the floor becomes slippery.

What to use

A wide range of materials makes suitable bedding. It should be dry, clean, easy to manage and not harmful to the pony. Sometimes horses are allergic to dust and react badly to fine materials like sawdust.

Some materials let urine pass right through and are called non-absorbent or draining. Other beds soak up wetness and are called absorbent or non-draining.

The list on the left gives you an idea of what products you can use. These vary from one area to another. If you live near a saw mill use wood shavings or sawdust; in other places peat or straw may be easily available.

Night and day beds

If your pony is stabled overnight, he needs a 'full' bed. The whole floor should be thickly covered with banks at the sides, because bare floors lose heat and chill the stable. A full bed is comfortable, shuts out draughts and keeps the horse warm. Pack it down well so the horse can walk about easily.

Leave gaps under the hay net, so the pony eats any spilled hay, and in front of the door, so the bed does not overflow into the yard when the door is opened.

For a pony that is only stabled during the day, a full bed is less important. A smaller 'day' bed does not need banks and occupies only half the floor – enough to lie on, but quick to tidy up!

SHOVEL AND FORK
When buying a shovel, choose one with a deep pan so you can clear away large amounts in one go.

The number of prongs required on the fork varies with the type of bedding. The finer the bedding the more you need: four is enough for straw, but eight is better when working with, say, sawdust.

Equipment for cleaning a stable. A bucket or laundry basket is a good substitute for the old-fashioned 'skep' and is for putting droppings in. Use a rubber glove or a pair of boards about 30cm (1ft) long for removing droppings by hand.

You also need a stiff broom, a fork with curved prongs and a shovel with a large pan and curved sides. Use lightweight tools with long handles so you don't get back ache. The barrow should be light, but large enough to avoid repeated trips to the muck heap.

Other useful items are a garden sheet to cover the barrow and to carry spare bedding and a rake for levelling the bed.

Cleaning up

There are three different routines for cleaning a stable, all part of the process of 'mucking out'.

Skipping out is a quick tidy up. You only remove the droppings. The name comes from the skip (or skep) – the traditional basket for the droppings. Nowadays, a laundry basket or plastic bucket serves the purpose just as well.

Setting fair means making the pony comfortable for the night. The bed is tidied up, and a few other chores done, such as refilling the water bucket and picking out the hooves.

A full muck out includes going right down to the floor and doing a complete clean-up job.

Skip out a deep litter of absorbent bedding, such as peat, several times during the day. You don't need to do a full muck out more than once a week. But muck out non-absorbent beds such as straw fully each day. Always set the bed fair in the evening.

A full muck out

Before starting to muck out, remove the feed bowl, water bucket and hay net from the stable. Put the pony in another stable or paddock, or tie him up in a safe place. Collect together all your tools. Park the barrow in the doorway and prop up the other tools against the wall or door where they are safe and convenient.

Skip out first, removing all the drop-

★ **WHEN TO BANK UP**
Normally you can leave gaps in the bedding under the hay net and by the door. But if your pony is ill, or you are looking after a mare that is about to foal, cover the floor completely and extend the banks to include the back of the door and keep out any draughts.

► **How often** you muck out varies according to the type of bedding. In this stable, wood shavings are used. Because they are absorbent, the box is given a full muck out once a week.

Every day, the stable is skipped out and tidied up, and the sides banked up.

Mucking out a stable

1 Most horses push the bedding toward the door during the night, so use the broom to sweep it back from the entrance.

2 With a rubber glove or two short planks of wood, pick up the droppings and put them in the bucket.

5 Let the floor air and dry out if possible. Shake up the clean bedding and level it out with the fork.

6 Wheel the dirty bedding off to the manure heap straightaway – don't leave it lying about in the barrow.

pings, and empty them into the barrow.

Take the dung fork and either pile all the clean bedding from one half of the box to the other half, or pile it from the middle to the sides. Leave behind any droppings you missed earlier, and the wet and dirty bedding. Sweep all this into a pile at the front of the box and shovel it into the barrow.

If you are working from one side to the other, put all the bedding to the clean half of the box. Finish the second half in the same way as the first.

Swill out the drain (if there is one) with a bucket of water. Check that it is draining.

Leave the stable to air for a while, and let the floor dry.

Bedding down

Use the dung fork or a pitch fork and shake up the clean bedding. Spread it evenly over the floor, piling it more thickly at the sides. Use the back of the fork to compress the banks of bedding against the walls. Level the surface of the bedding in the middle of the box, and check the depth with the fork — the bed should come up to at least the depth of the prongs.

Top up if necessary with extra bedding, shaking it well before you level everything off.

Refill and replace the water bucket and hay net. Try to allow about half an hour for any dust to settle before you return the pony to his clean box.

3 Fork the clean bedding to the sides of the box, leaving behind the hard wet shavings underneath.

4 Shift the dirty bedding into the wheelbarrow, then brush any clean bedding to the sides, so the floor is clean.

7 Collect more bedding if necessary. Tip out the new on top of the old — enough for a bed the depth of the fork prongs.

8 Mix all the bedding thoroughly, banking up the sides and leaving gaps around the door and under the hay net.

Feeding a stabled pony

A pony in a stable relies totally on people to care for him. After fresh air and water, the correct food is his most important need.

Nature and the horse

In the wild, ponies spend most of their time grazing. Often the grass is very poor and they need to eat plenty of it to get enough nourishment.

Nature has designed the digestive system to allow for this. The horse has a small stomach, suitable for always containing a little, but never too much at any one time. So try to imitate this feeding pattern for a stable-kept pony.

The pony needs plenty of bulk food – usually hay. The 'short', energy-giving, concentrated feeds like oats should be small and fed twice or even three times

◄ **Feed your horse** little and often because this is how he eats in the wild. Feeding from the floor is also natural, but can be wasteful if the bucket tips up.

a day so he eats little and often.

Aim to include something fresh each day, such as carrots or apples, because horses by nature eat fresh grass, not dry hay and short feeds.

When to feed

Feed your pony at regular intervals three or four times a day. Make sure he has water by him all the time. If you think he's thirsty, water him *before* you feed him. Drinking a lot after a feed can be harmful.

Avoid riding a pony for at least one hour after he has eaten to give the stomach time to empty. The horse may get colic if he is ridden immediately after feeding.

After riding, let the pony eat a little hay before a short feed. This takes the edge off his hunger and stops him gobbling the food too fast. Slow down a really greedy pony by putting a brick or some large stones in the manger so he has to work harder to find his meal.

▲ **Fresh food:** A stabled pony misses out on grass – his natural diet. Make up for this by giving him something succulent in his feed every day, such as apple.

sugar beet

oats

pony nuts

bran

◄ **Foodstuffs** suitable for a pony.
Oats are the traditional 'short' feed for horses. They are nutritious and easily digested but can over-excite ponies.

Sugar beet is sold dry. It gives the horse energy and is good roughage. Before feeding, soak it for 12–18 hours in about two and a half times as much water as beet.

Horse and pony nuts (cubes or pellets) contain concentrated ingredients, bulk feeds, vitamins and minerals. The exact mixture varies according to make.

Bran: Small amounts of bran can be used with oats. Alternatively, bran can be fed as a mash before a rest day or if the pony is ill.

![horse icon] **WATER ON TAP**

All ponies should have a constant supply of clean water. Refill the buckets with fresh water at least twice a day, even if the pony hasn't drunk it all.

Unless your stable is fitted with an 'auto-drinker' that refills automatically, two large buckets, or even a small dustbin of water, are ideal.

Remove the handles from buckets left in the stable, and secure them in a bucket holder or wedge them into a motor tyre for safety.

automatic drinker

★ **SALT**
This is the most important mineral for ponies. They need it every day because salt is lost in sweat and urine. Without salt, a pony may start chewing wood or eating his droppings.

Either provide a salt lick so the pony can help himself, or add one tablespoonful of salt to the evening feed.

➤ **Hay** should make up the bulk of your pony's diet. Fill up the hay net at least twice a day.

What to feed

Most ponies keep well on a diet almost entirely made up of hay. Make sure it is good quality – greenish, weed-free, succulent and sweet-smelling – and between 4–18 months old. If your pony is too fat, you can use clean feed straw rather than hay. Straw comes from cereals: choose oat or barley straw because wheat straw is not very tasty.

Short feeds of oats give most ponies too much energy, so usually just horse and pony nuts (cubes) are enough. Always give short feeds according to the work the pony is doing, his temperament and also his rider's ability. A fired-up pony is not a good idea for a novice rider.

How much to feed

The amount of food to give a horse depends on his size – the larger the pony, the more food he needs. In scientific terms, horses eat 2–2½% of their body weight a day. So a pony around 14 hands high, weighing about 300–400kg (660–880lbs), needs a total of 7½–10kg (16½–21lbs) food a day.

If the pony is healthy and not doing any work, all this food can be hay. As his exercise increases, so he needs some short feed. The hay should be reduced so he still gets the same *weight* of food – only the proportions change.

Give the hay in two lots and split the short feed. This gives four feeds a day which keeps any stabled pony happy.

Changing the diet

Sometimes you have to change a pony's feed, perhaps because he is working harder or you have decided to switch to a different make of food.

Introduce the change gradually, over a week. This gives the pony's digestive system time to adjust.

▶ **This chart** is a guide only: the *amounts* need to be lessened for a smaller, lighter pony and increased for a larger, heavier one. The *proportions* of hay to short feed, however, apply to all sizes.

Provide both the hay and the short feeds in two lots, giving most at night. For a horse doing hard work, divide the short feed into three portions.

Use dry weights, for example, weigh sugar beet before soaking it. Carrots and apples count as water so don't worry about including their weight in your calculations.

Feed chart for a 350-400 kg. (800-900 lb.) pony			
Amount of work	Proportion of hay	Proportion of short feed	Total weight
nil	all	none	7½-10 kg
Light: up to 1 hour a day	9/10	1/10	7½-10 kg
medium: up to 2 hours a day	4/5	1/5	7½-10 kg
hard: up to 3 hours a day	2/3	1/3	7½-10 kg
very hard: hunting, eventing	1/2	1/2	7½-10 kg

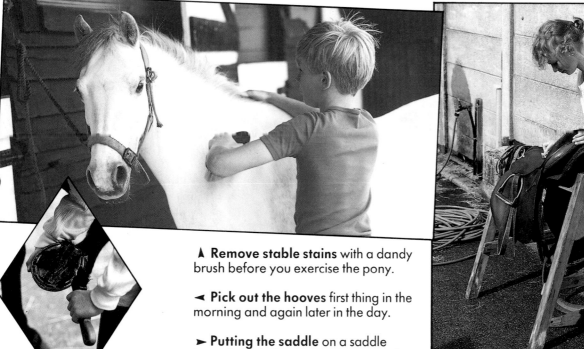

▲ **Remove stable stains** with a dandy brush before you exercise the pony.

◀ **Pick out the hooves** first thing in the morning and again later in the day.

▶ **Putting the saddle** on a saddle horse is the safest and easiest way of cleaning the tack.

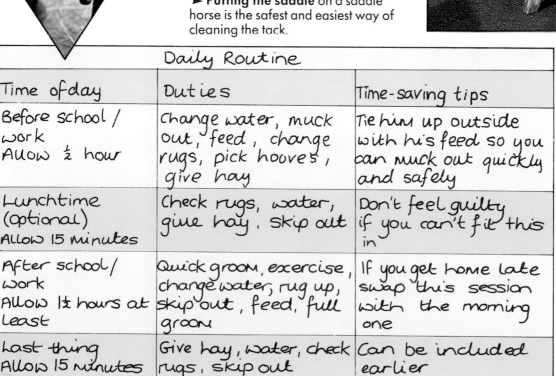

Daily Routine		
Time of day	Duties	Time-saving tips
Before school / work Allow ½ hour	Change water, muck out, feed, change rugs, pick hooves, give hay	Tie him up outside with his feed so you can muck out quickly and safely
Lunchtime (optional) Allow 15 minutes	Check rugs, water, give hay. skip out	Don't feel guilty if you can't fit this in
After school / work Allow 1½ hours at least	Quick groom, exercise, change water, rug up, skip out, feed, full groom	If you get home late swap this session with the morning one
Last thing Allow 15 minutes	Give hay, water, check rugs, skip out	Can be included earlier

◀ **This plan** suggests what chores to do when. Make sure you see to the pony first thing in the morning and in the evening.

The daytime tasks are more flexible, so arrange times that fit in with your other commitments.

Winter stable care

The winter care of a pony kept indoors is one of the most taxing parts of stable management. The pony must have enough exercise and food, and be kept warm, particularly if he is clipped.

Exercise

If you are out most days, the greatest problem is giving the horse enough exercise, as daylight hours are short. The pony must have exercise every day if he is to stay healthy and content, so do your best to get someone else to take him out if you cannot.

At night, if you ride on roads, it is a good idea to wear a stirrup light on your right stirrup. Reflective clothing for yourself and your pony is also safer. Choose the best-lit, quietest roads and avoid dark country lanes or busy main roads. If you have access to a floodlit outdoor arena or an indoor school, this is a great help.

Feeding

Exercise and feeding are closely linked because food supplies the fuel for energy and work. If you can only exercise your pony in the morning or evening, it is best to feed him as much hay as he wants. He may also be better off without any concentrates at all, as long as his bulk food is good quality.

Many ponies can be fed hay *ad lib* (permanently on supply). It is bad management to let ponies get very hungry, which they do when stabled and their hay runs out. This can lead to restlessness, anxiety and stable vices such as wood chewing and crib-biting.

Ponies fed *ad lib* hay do not usually gorge on it as do those only given it twice a day. But if the pony does become very fat, the supply must be restricted.

You can safely ride your pony immediately after he has been eating hay, provided that the exercise is no more demanding than a walk or steady trot. After all, ponies living out eat grass most of the time and move about all the while they are eating. However, if you are going to do faster work such as cantering or jumping, the pony should have no feed for an hour, or slightly longer, before work.

A pony also needs succulent foods in winter, like well-soaked sugar beet pulp, sliced or grated carrots or a whole turnip or mangold (if he likes them). These can be mixed with molassed chop (molasses and chaff) and fed in a bucket or manger, as if they were concentrates.

► **Early morning exercise** can be exhilarating on a crisp winter day and racehorses are galloped daily whatever the weather.

► **Finding time** to exercise a horse can be the most tricky part of winter stable management. You may have to ride at night, in which case make sure you wear light, bright clothing and reflective strips.

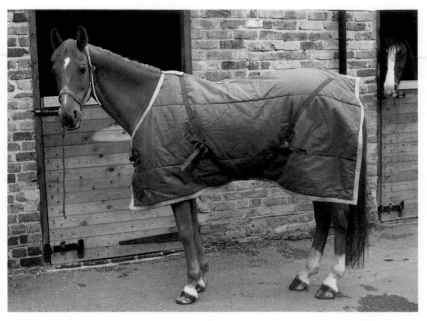

Clipped ponies

An unclipped pony rarely needs a rug —
and one with a breast-and-gullet clip
should only need clothing if he has a
very fine coat due to Arab or Thoroughbred blood. Any pony clipped more than
this needs a rug to help replace his coat.
And, if he has a blanket or hunter clip,
he could need one, or maybe two, under-
rugs or blankets as well.

To check if your pony is cold, feel his
ears, loins and belly in front of his
hindlegs with your bare hands. If he
feels chilly, he needs more clothing, but
don't overload him so that he is uncomfortable and hot.

Modern rugs with criss-cross surcingles are much more comfortable than
the old-fashioned types which are kept
on by a fairly tightly buckled surcingle
or roller round the pony's girth. Such
designs constrict the pony, particularly
when he lies down, and can press on the
spine, causing a sore back and maybe
putting the pony off work.

Unlike traditional jute or wool, modern fabrics are also easily washed. With
any type of rug, however, you really
need two so that you can keep each
properly clean.

Bedding

Bedding should be generous at all times,
but particularly in winter when it also
helps to keep the pony warm. The
warmest beddings are straw and shredded paper, the coldest is peat, and
wood shavings and sawdust come in
between.

Some owners leave a bare patch behind the door so the pony won't drag
bedding out with him, but this may also
leave a draught under the door in
winter. Keep the whole floor bedded

Measuring up for a rug

Any rug should fit from in *front* of the withers, not on top of them — and to the very root of the tail, so that the quarters are fully covered. It should come just past the elbow in depth, to ensure warmth and comfort.

To measure, take a tape measure and start in the *middle* of the pony's breast at the base of his neck. Run it, parallel to the ground, along his side to the back of his thigh. The number of centimetres/inches is the size he takes. You don't need to measure the depth as well: this automatically increases to suit the length.

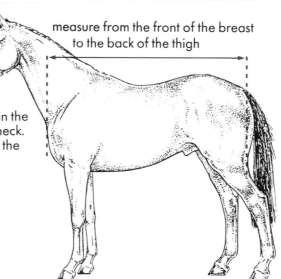

measure from the front of the breast to the back of the thigh

VENTILATION
Do all you can to improve the ventilation of your stable without causing draughts. Ridge roof ventilators or gable-end louvres are an excellent idea, as are windows combined with an open top door.

Always remember to fasten back the door securely so it cannot blow shut on to the pony.

gable-end louvre

ridge roof ventilator

down well and bank up the sides for extra warmth and comfort.

With a pony in all the time, you must remove droppings regularly to keep the bed clean. Even if you keep your pony on deep or semi-deep litter, never leave the yard with droppings in the box. If you possibly can, get someone to skip the stable out when you're not there.

Grooming

Your pony should have a full grooming every day. Because he is not exposed to the rain, which helps clean the coat of an outdoor pony, he has no means of removing the build-up of grease and dandruff in his coat, so you must do it for him.

If you genuinely do not have time, at least sponge his eyes, nostrils, lips, sheath/teats and dock, and under the tail. Dandy brush stable stains and dried mud and sweat, too. This freshens him up until you can do a thorough job.

The most important part of grooming is picking out the feet, particularly with a stabled pony who may often stand in his own droppings. Pick out the feet and check the shoes at least twice a day. Press the frog with the back of your hoof pick. If the pony flinches, it could mean he has thrush developing: this may occur on damp, dirty bedding. If there is also a nasty smell and maybe a dark discharge from the frog, call the vet at once.

Ventilation

Clean, fresh air is essential for ponies, who were born to live outside and cannot bear muggy, stuffy air — they can stand almost any amount of dry, still, cold air.

What they hate is wind and wet, particularly combined. Never shut the top door of your pony's stable unless the wind and rain are blowing directly in and, even then, leave the window open. Ideally, there should also be a window on the opposite side of the box, so you can leave that open when it is on the sheltered side in a lashing storm.

◄ **Picking out** the hooves every day is vital. Neglecting the feet can mean the pony develops unpleasant diseases such as thrush.

Exercise plans for a . . .

... stable-kept pony

A stabled pony doing up to 1½ hours' work four or five times a week can be described as half fit. This is enough for normal hacking, light schooling, a little jumping and the occasional dressage test or showing class. If you are planning to do more energetic work with your pony – such as hunting, long-distance riding or sponsored rides – you need to increase his level of fitness.

Stabling over grass

A grass-kept pony can only ever be half fit. This is because he spends much of the time with a full belly. A pony's stomach lies very close to his lungs, and a full stomach limits the lungs' ability to inflate during hard work. Eating a lot of bulk food means the pony requires more space in his abdomen, and slows him down in hard work.

A stable-kept pony can have his rations reduced before work so that his lungs can work fully. By reducing the amount of bulk he eats, the size of his belly can also be limited.

Remember, though, that a stabled pony is unable to walk about as much as the pony who is kept at grass. This lack of natural freedom must be compensated for by regular, controlled exercise. A whole day without going out of the stable will leave your pony feeling stiff, uncomfortable and probably explosive!

Exercise and work

Exercise and work are not always the same. A 'free' pony can 'exercise' himself as and when he feels in the mood. He moves about gently most of the time. Work, however, involves exercising, often strenuously, for *controlled* periods of time.

During training, certain groups of muscles are developed, lung and heart capacity is increased and limbs are toughened. *Exercise* is important for general circulation and well being. *Work* is important for the special demands made on riding ponies, so that they can do the job asked of them easily and without strain.

◄ **Hillwork** increases the pony's stamina. Remember to lean forward slightly so that you take the weight off the pony's back, and keep him to a steady pace.

Ponies and personality

In making a pony extra fit, allowances must be made for each pony's individual progress. A lively pony that has previously been fit, takes less time to bring to full fitness than a lazy pony. The longer a pony has been in light work only, the greater time you should allow for him to reach a peak.

It also depends on the rider: an athletic pony with a capable rider progresses better than a short-striding, heavily built pony with a novice rider.

With this in mind, the programme here is an approximate guide for an average pony of around 14 hands high.

Watchpoints

As you work toward fitness, watch these points.

● **Sweating:** A fit pony's sweat is clean and dries quickly. An unfit pony sheds a lot of grease and grime as he sweats. This makes him lather up, feel sticky and dry off slowly.

● **Fat or muscle:** Fat is flabby, soft and prone to dimples. Muscle is smoother, firmer to touch and can be seen to contract or extend as the pony moves.

● **Breathing:** Unfit ponies breathe with quick, shallow movements. After work, the rapid breathing may go on for some time. A fit pony takes deeper, more

◄ **Flatwork** can be increased in the fourth week. Trotting in circles, serpentines or figures of eight is good for balance and discipline.

▼ **Cantering** during schooling should be controlled and to a plan — you, and not the pony, must decide on the direction and speed.

rhythmical breaths and recovers in a few minutes after stopping work.

● **Skin and hair:** A fit pony is sleeker, shinier and cleaner than his unfit counterpart. He is also more sensitive during grooming, while the unfit pony enjoys a good scratch!

Nobody should know more about your pony than you who sees him every day. Take note of even the slightest change. It is better to hold up your programme by a week than to lose six months because your pony has gone lame. A steady improvement should be obvious and is your guide to move on to the next stage of the programme.

▲ **Jumping** logs across the path when out hacking stops your pony becoming stale from too much schooling.

➤ **Work at home** can include jumping as well as flatwork throughout the programme. Trotting poles and small fences are valuable for training at any level.

The fitness programme

Starting point: Walk, trot, canter, occasional short gallop, some jumping. One or two days off per week.
Feeding: Total of 2.7kg (6lbs) concentrates, 5.5kg (12lbs) hay split into two, the evening feed larger than the morning one. The concentrates can be made up from any of the following: pony nuts, bran (not more than ¼kg/½lb), flaked barley, sugar beet pulp, plus cut-up apple or carrot, for example. If you use a 'mix', check the ingredients to see what the proportion of oats is.

Week 1–2: Aim to work six days a week, for about 1–1½ hours per day. Increase walking to tone up muscles and harden limbs. Include some roadwork. Walk up and down hills without change of rhythm.
Feeding: Add ½kg (1lb) oats to evening feed after working days, plus ½kg other concentrates if the pony is losing condition. Remember that fat is a hindrance but food replaces lost energy.

Week 2–3: On two days a week, increase fast work. After a short gallop, continue in slow canter and follow with second short gallop. You are now working on heart and lung capacity.
Feeding: Gradually increase the oat ration unless the pony is already too lively. Boiled or flaked barley is then a good substitute. Reduce the hay by ½–1kg (1–2lbs).

Week 4–5: Continue with fast work twice a week, and with walking exercise. Increase time spent schooling at home, flat or jumping.
Feeding: Carefully increase oat ration, but only if it's justified by performance and condition. One day per week, a mash can be given. This should be the night before exercising – as opposed to working – only.

Week 5–6: If possible, increase time on slow days to 2½–3 hours including walking in and cooling off. Jumping performance should now be almost to competition level. Include sustained half-speed work – a moderately brisk canter for up to 3.2km (2 miles).
Feeding: Continue to increase as before. Total concentrates are now about 4.5kg (10lbs). If work is light on any day, or if the pony is too frisky, reduce the concentrate and replace with hay.

Week 7: Leave at least two days between fast, hard, training work and competition. 1½ hours' walking and steady trotting the day before keeps the pony fresh but not stiff.
Feeding: The pony should be eating the same amount of concentrated and bulk feed, about 10–11kg (20–22lbs) in all, depending on his weight and particular needs.

Waiting expectantly for his feed-time

The combined system

Keeping your pony on a combined system means he is partly stabled and partly turned out at grass. It is an excellent method that gives the pony the best of both worlds.

How the system works

The pony spends part of each 24 hours stabled and part at grass, although he may also have the occasional day entirely in or out. The system is very flexible, and you make of it exactly what you want. The time stabled or out depends entirely on what suits you and your pony's routine: there are no hard and fast rules.

Generally, the pony might spend the days out in winter and be stabled at night, so that when the temperature drops overnight he has the warmth and comfort of his stable. In the summer, he can be turned out in the cooler evening and be stabled during the day, away from the sun and the flies.

You can tailor the pony's hours in and out to your own requirements. If you are going to a summer show, for instance, you may want to keep him in the night beforehand so he stays clean.

When you do change the routine, make sure the pony has a daily supply of all his normal food – grass, hay and whatever else he usually has as well as water – so his digestion can cope. Where people go wrong with the combined system is in not keeping to the usual feeding routine, which thoroughly upsets the pony and can make him ill.

In winter, particularly if you tend to work your pony fairly hard at weekends and he is clipped, he can spend his days out wearing a New Zealand rug. You could go to the stables in the morning, ride or not as you wish, feed and brush him over, then turn him out for the day. He should have a good hay supply in the paddock to make up for the winter grass which has very little goodness in it.

◄ A comforting routine: These riding school ponies are usually kept in a field at night and stabled by day. They are so familiar with their daily schedule that they trot from field to stable every morning as soon as the gate is opened. Each pony knows that, once he is in the stable (inset), a feed is about to appear!

▼ For special occasions, you can wash a combined-system pony as long as you thoroughly rinse and dry him afterwards.

If you make a habit of washing him – before weekend shows, for example – do not body brush the pony during the week. Quartering with the dandy brush (inset) is enough. As the pony is out for much of the time, he needs the protection of some natural grease in his coat.

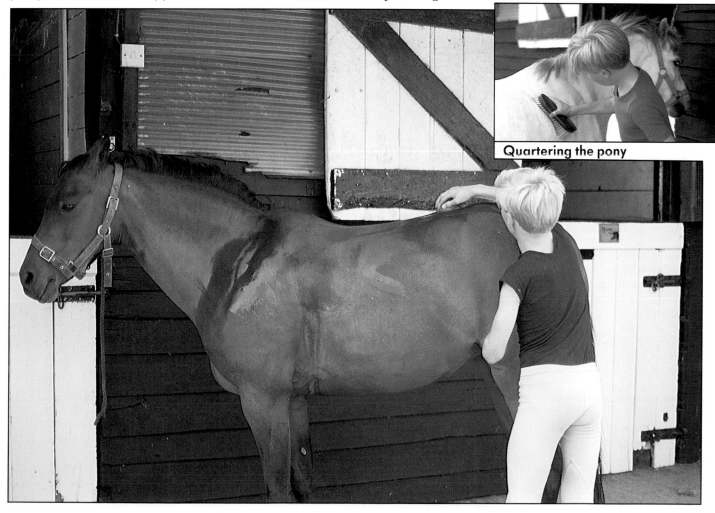

Quartering the pony

► **Feeding:** If several of you keep your ponies at DIY livery, you can arrange a rota to save time. Take it in turns to do morning chores such as mixing up the feeds.

Although the combined system is flexible, it is important to stick to a regular feeding pattern, or your pony may get colic.

▲ **Freedom to play:** A pony that's stabled for part of the time appreciates the open spaces of a field.

► **Mucking out:** One drawback of the combined system is that you have to do stable and field chores. As well as mucking out and keeping the yard tidy, you need to check the field regularly and remove droppings from the pasture.

But the good points outweigh the bad: the pony requires less exercising and leads a more natural life than a stabled horse.

Share with friends

If you keep the pony at a do-it-yourself livery yard, you can work out a rota with friends to share the chores so you do not have to go to the yard twice, or even once, every day.

However, you do all have to be trustworthy and knowledgeable enough so that, if one of you spots something wrong with a friend's pony, you can ring and tell the owner. You each have to treat the other ponies as if they were your own and look after them properly when it is your turn.

Obviously, one person cannot possibly exercise more than one pony early in the morning. But he or she could easily feed and turn out two friends' ponies, or bring them in if it is summer, and exercise their own pony. Exact rotas can be worked out and set down in a diary or on a wall chart, so everyone knows what they are supposed to be doing. If someone is sick, they ring up and someone else takes over their rota.

You have to use your common sense and co-operate with each other, but such systems work very well if everyone concerned is sensible and responsible and does the tasks allotted to them.

Day-to-day care

As far as grooming goes, combined system ponies can be groomed as for stabled ponies. But if they are going to be out *without* New Zealand rugs in winter, they should not be body brushed. This is because, when out for a lot of the time, horses need some natural grease in their coats for protection. And remember that the pony must have some sort of field shelter, even if only straw bales inside a framework.

It is still a good idea to use an effective fly repellant on a combined system pony in summer. Night-flying insects can be just as much of a nuisance as the daytime ones.

The advantages

From the pony's point of view, the combined system is ideal. He has the shelter and peace of his stable, if that is what he wants. Yet he also has freedom to play about as he wishes when out and, if he is kept with other ponies, the company of his friends in the field.

From your point of view, the beauty of this system is that you do not *have* to ride the pony if the weather is dreadful or you are busy. He exercises himself in the field, particularly if he has company and is warm and well fed.

Two such ponies, or more, out together, keep themselves half fit, so you only really have to ride them on two or maybe three days during the week, to ensure that they are toned up for work at weekends.

However, because both field and stable are involved, you do have the double job of checking the fencing and general condition of the field and also mucking out the stable and doing other indoor chores. But this is barely noticeable with the amount of time that you save on exercising.

Overall, the combined system is probably the best and most convenient form of management both for you and your pony. It allows you to keep him fitter and cleaner than a grass-kept pony yet still gives the pony freedom and a relatively natural lifestyle.

Yarding

Yarding is a system of keeping horses and ponies in a surfaced yard or enclosure. They are out in the open, if they want to be, yet are not at grass, so you can regulate their feeding.

The best yards have a covered area so the animals can wander in and out as they wish. Often a large barn-type building is used with a wide entrance. The ground surface of the covered area can be of normal bedding, as in a field shelter or stable. The pony should be fed with hay and succulents to compensate for the lack of grass. A water supply of some kind is essential.

The ground surface of the outside area must be safe and non-slip so the ponies can canter about and play around just as when in a field. Usually the materials are wood-chip based, perhaps with sand and salt added — rather like the materials used to floor indoor schools or outdoor arenas.

The fencing around the yard is ideally wooden post and rail. But any normal, safe fencing material recommended for horses — such as smooth, taut wire — is acceptable.

The pony should be treated like a combined system-kept animal. Although it may not be as carefree as a proper field, a yard is certainly more relaxing for a pony than being stabled for too long. Yards are particularly useful when the weather is so bad that turning out is impractical — in deep snow or if the paddock is waterlogged — and horses can happily live in such conditions all the year round.

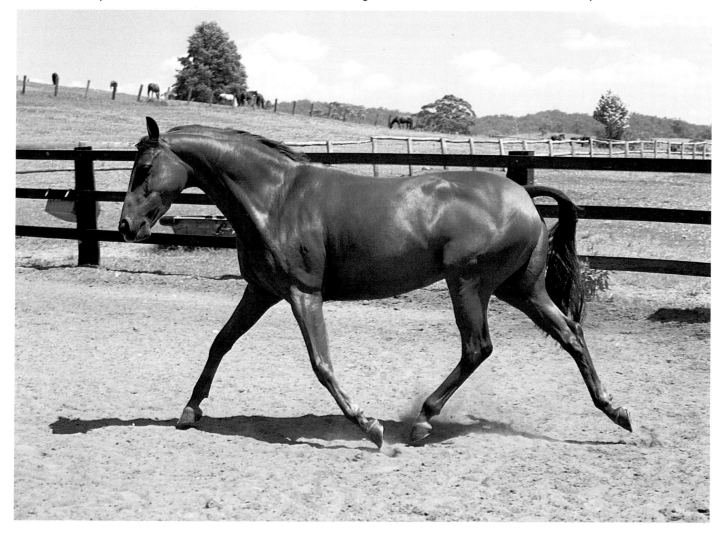

Rugs for the stable

▼ A modern stable rug is the most important choice for a stabled pony. If you are only buying one rug, this cosy quilted 'anorak' will keep any pony snug throughout the winter. Synthetic stable rugs are also washable.

You may wonder why ponies need rugs at all when they have natural fur coats to keep them warm. The answer is that unclipped ponies kept outside *are* less likely to need rugs.

But once a stabled pony is clipped – to stop him sweating too much during work and catching a chill afterwards – he feels the cold. When kept inside he is usually groomed to remove grease and can't trot about to keep warm. If ponies get cold, they need more food, catch more illnesses and feel miserable.

Indoor rugs

There are many different rugs for wearing in the stable, and all serve different purposes. The most important one, and the only one you need to begin with, is the stable rug.

Modern stable rugs are quilted and very warm and snug – like a pony anorak. They are made of easy-care, synthetic fabrics and so are quick to launder. Ponies can wear them night and day in winter – so a good stable rug is the basis of their wardrobe.

Anti-sweat rugs are like string vests. They are usually placed under an ordinary rug, where they trap air next to the coat, helping to dry off a pony wet from sweat or rain.

Day rugs are smart woollen rugs bound with cotton braid and often bearing your initials or the pony's name. They have to be dry cleaned and so are for daytime wear when the pony is unlikely to lie on a dirty bed.

Night rugs, of jute and often lined with wool, are worn at night when the pony might lie on his bedding.

Summer sheets are just to keep the dust and flies off a groomed, stabled pony in summer. They are made of cotton or linen, are fairly easy to launder, and can be worn night or day.

🐴 KEEP OUT THE COLD

Always keep a rug handy in case of sickness, when a pony can feel chilly even in summer. Although a healthy, unclipped pony can manage all year round without any, he may get soaking wet. When he's drenched, a rug helps to dry him off more quickly, so avoiding chills.

However, don't *over*-rug a pony – he'll be uncomfortable. Feel under the rug; if he's sweating he's too hot! But when his loins and the base of his ears are cold, he'll feel cold all over.

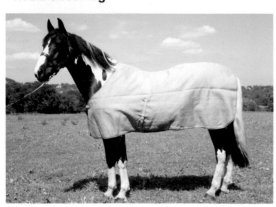

▲ Anti-sweat rug

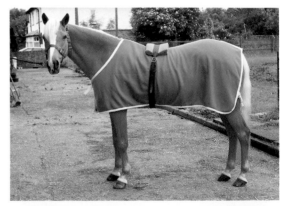

▲ Day rug

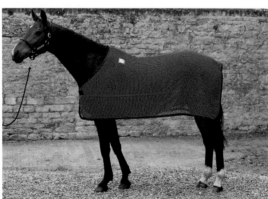

▲ Night rug

▲ Summer sheet

Rugging up

Before rugging up it is important to make sure that the pony's rug fits snugly. The best rugs have cross-surcingles (diagonal side-straps) which readjust as the pony moves, rather than a single belt around the pony's middle.

Fitting a rug

To work out what size rug a pony needs, measure him from the mid-point of his chest – where the front buckles fasten – to the furthest point on the back of his quarters – where the fillet string goes. Once you have this measurement, a good saddler can advise you on the correct-sized rug – 158cm (5ft 3in) is about right for a 13.2-hand pony.

A rug which is too large slips back behind the withers, making the pony's withers and shoulders sore. And if a rug is too small, it also rubs and leaves the quarters partly uncovered.

How to put a rug on

1 Fold the rug in half bringing the back over to the front. Approach the pony's near-side shoulder to let him know you are there and pat him gently. Quietly throw the rug over the pony with the front of it well forward from the withers.

2 Unfold the rug down the pony's back and over his quarters. Straighten it so that the centre seam runs down the spine. If the rug is too far forward pull it toward the pony's tail. Avoid moving the rug the other way – toward the withers – as this makes the hair lie in the wrong direction, and is uncomfortable.

3 Fasten the cross-surcingle around the pony's middle first. This ensures that the rug stays in place even if the pony moves off. If you do up the front fastenings first and the pony shifts position the rug can twist around and end up like a bib, over his front legs.

4 Move to the front of the rug and fasten the buckles across the breast. Check that the rug fits loosely in front of the shoulder so that the pony can move freely.

5 Standing to one side of the pony's quarters – the correct position to avoid being kicked – do up the buckle at the back of the rug under the pony's tail, and then the fillet string. If the string is too long when you fit the rug for the first time, cut off any excess. But make sure you leave enough to secure the rug properly.

6 Now your rug should be fitted comfortably and securely.

When taking it off, begin by undoing the buckle at the back (if there is one), then undo the front, and finally the cross-surcingle. You can leave the fillet string done up. By working in this order, the rug stays safely in place if the pony moves.

5 Grooming

Grooming a grass-kept pony

The great bonus about a grass-kept pony is that you don't have much grooming to do. In fact, 'outdoor' ponies must not be kept as clean as stabled ones because they need some natural grease to help protect them against the weather.

! WET PONIES

● In wet weather there may always be some powdery mud left in the coat. This doesn't matter and you can't do anything about it except wash the pony (not advised in winter).

Never brush wet mud as you'll just push it through to the skin. Dry the pony first by thatching him (see illustration opposite).

Why groom?

Why do ponies need grooming? After all, those running wild aren't groomed. No, but the dirt in their coats often attracts lice and ticks which suck blood and cause sore skin.

As well as helping a pony to look nice and feel better – grooming is like a form of massage – brushing the coat also removes most of the dust and dirt. This means you can check for parasites and wounds which could become infected if left.

You need to remove mud from the pony's coat, prevent his mane and tail from becoming tangled, pick out dirt from his hooves and sponge sensitive parts such as eyes and dock (under the tail).

The basic kit

The basic grooming kit for a grass-kept pony includes a hoof pick (a metal hook to remove dirt from the underside of the hooves), a dandy brush (which has longish, stiff bristles for brushing off dried mud and loose hairs), a rubber or plastic curry comb (for removing caked-on mud), two sponges (one for his head and the other for his back end) and a bucket of water. Use differently coloured sponges so that you don't muddle them.

Useful extras are a body brush and a water brush. Body brushes have short, close bristles for getting through a summer coat to the skin, but don't use them in winter. A water brush is a smaller version of a dandy brush, with soft bristles for use on the mane, forelock and tail.

How to groom

You should groom a grass-kept pony *before* riding to make him look respectable and to stop mud on the saddle and bridle areas chafing the skin. Go through the basic routine every day if possible, winter and summer, and always before working him. It takes about half an hour, less as you get used to it. If you haven't time for a full groom, at least pick out the feet and sponge daily.

Tie your pony up with a quick-release knot. If you're outdoors, face him to the wind so dirt doesn't blow back on to cleaned parts or in your face.

First pick out the hooves, paying special attention to the sides and cleft (middle groove) of the frog. With the

The equipment you need

The essentials for grooming a grass-kept pony are a hoof pick; *either* a rubber curry comb *or* a plastic one; a dandy brush; two sponges (different colours help you to keep them separate); and a bucket full of clean water.

Useful but not essential are a body brush and water brush for the head, mane and tail. Never use the body brush on a winter coat – you remove all the natural grease that protects a grass-kept pony from cold, wet weather.

bucket

dandy brush

body brush

two sponges

hoof pick

rubber curry comb

water brush

plastic curry comb

curry comb, carefully scrub off all dirt that's caked on your pony's body. Take the dandy brush and, working in the direction the hair grows, brush the pony firmly but not roughly. Start at the front and work back and down so you don't brush dirt on to parts already done. Be gentle on the head, where it is advisable to use the softer body brush.

Try this routine so you don't miss anywhere: head, left side of the neck, under the neck, the breast and between forelegs, shoulder, foreleg, back, quarters, side, flank, under the girth area and belly and lastly the hindleg. Repeat on the right side. Remove all dried-on mud and sweat from the saddle and bridle area before tacking up.

Forelock, mane and tail

These are done with the body brush, if you have one or, gently, to avoid breaking the hairs, with the dandy brush or dry water brush. Use your fingers to untangle knots.

To groom the tail, put your hand round all the hair at the end of the dock and hold it straight out toward you. Letting a few hairs fall down, brush them out starting at the bottom and working up to the roots. Gradually let down all the long strands, then separate the shorter hair at the top of the dock to get at the roots.

Lift the forelock with one hand, and brush out from the roots a few hairs at a time. Now push the mane over to the 'wrong' side of the neck and, starting behind the ears, brush it back over, lock by lock, from the roots.

Thatching

Before grooming a wet pony you need to dry him off by 'thatching' him. Pile a thick layer of straw on his back, fasten on a rug (inside out so you don't get straw on the lining) and leave him tied up, preferably in a stable, until he's dry. This could take up to two hours with a long winter coat.

If you have no straw, use an anti-sweat rug or an old cotton-mesh bed blanket instead.

Sponging

Take your 'head' sponge and wet it, squeezing it well until just damp. Gently sponge dirt and discharge from the eyes, inside the nostrils and the lips, steadying the pony's head with your hand.

Damp the 'back end' sponge and clean the sheath (if the pony is a gelding) or udder (if a mare), under the tail and between the buttocks. In cold weather, dry sponged parts with an old towel as the pony could get chapped skin if they are left damp.

And that's it!

Tying up

Tie the pony in a safe place — stable, yard or field.

Use a quick-release knot which can be undone, in emergency, with one tug on the free end. It is safest to tie up to a string loop which breaks if the pony pulls back in fright. The tying point should be as high as his head, if possible, to prevent him getting his legs caught up in the rope.

1 Loop the rope through the safety string.

2 Use the end of the loop to form a bow.

3 Pull the bow tight to fasten the pony securely.

4 Pass the loose end through the bow so it can't be undone.

1 Pick any stones, dirt and mud out of the hooves, always working methodically from heel to toe.

2 Make sure the pony is facing into the wind before using a plastic (or rubber) curry comb to remove caked mud.

5 Use a body brush to comb the tail, working through a few strands at a time.

6 Push the mane to the other side and brush it back over, starting behind the ears.

7 Dampen one sponge, wring out excess water, and remove dirt and discharge from the nostrils, eyes and lips.

8 Clean the dock with the other sponge. In cold weather, dry sponged parts with a towel to prevent chapped skin.

3 Finish cleaning the coat with the dandy brush, working from the front down toward the back.

4 Move calmly behind the pony to untangle the worst tail knots with your fingers.

Now you're ready to ride!

Grooming a stabled pony

Nowadays most people use a leather massage pad for wisping. But grooms used to wisp with hay.

To make a wisp, twist damp hay tightly into a 'rope' 2m (6½ft) long.

Form two loops at one end and twist the rest tightly round them.

Tuck the loose end firmly under the last twist.

17·5cm (7in)

body brush

metal curry combs

The basic grooming routine for grass-kept ponies is also used for stabled ponies, but for these there are two other parts of the process. The first, body brushing, is essential; the second, wisping (toning the muscles), is a matter of choice.

A full grooming

Stabled ponies need a full daily grooming unless some emergency prevents it. As they do not stand out in the rain, they have no need of their natural grease for protection. So body brushing keeps them clean.

Grass-kept ponies often roll to stimulate their skin and to massage their muscles. Stabled ponies are more restricted, so wisping helps to replace the benefits of rolling.

Equipment

You need all the basics used for a grass-kept pony – hoof pick, dandy brush, rubber or plastic curry comb, two sponges and a bucket of water – plus a few more.

The body brush is essential now. You also need a metal curry comb to clean it. Use a stable rubber (like a tea towel) or sponge for a final polish, and a hay wisp or a leather massage pad for wisping.

Don't use mane combs in grooming because they break the hairs. They are for trimming the mane (shortening and thinning it).

Hoof oils only do the pony any good if they contain hoof conditioner and/or antiseptic, but they do give a smart and shiny appearance. Ask your farrier for advice on this.

Quartering

After the pony's morning feed he is quartered. This means you fold his rugs back off the front of his body and dandy brush over both sides to remove stable stains. Fold the rugs forward and do the back half so all four 'quarters' of the body are tidied ready for work.

Quickly brush the mane and tail with the body brush so there is no bedding in them, and pick out the feet. Quartering takes about ten minutes.

Strapping

After work you should groom the pony fully (called strapping) while his skin is warm but dry and easier to clean. First, pick out his feet again, then dandy brush him all over as for a grass-kept pony to remove dirt.

Now take your body brush in one hand and your metal curry comb in the other. Slot your hand through the wide loop on the back of the brush with your thumb on the outside to hold it firm. If doing the left side use your left arm for the brush, and vice versa.

Hold your arm stiff but slightly bent, and run the brush along the pony's neck by leaning your *weight* on to it to push the bristles through to the skin. Make long, curved strokes.

If you push with your *arm* rather than letting your weight do the work you get

▼ **A full grooming kit:** As well as the basic equipment you need a body brush and a metal curry comb. Use a stable rubber for polishing and a wisp or leather massage pad for toning the muscles.

dandy brush

stable rubber

leather massage pad

water brush

rubber curry comb

hoof pick

tired before the pony is finished and end up only half doing the job. If your arm does get tired, use the other one for a while. Six brush strokes in one place should be enough.

After two or three strokes, hold the bristles downward on top of the teeth of the curry comb and drag them firmly across it to clean them. Every now and then, tap the curry comb on its side on the floor (near the door if you're inside the stable) to dislodge the dirt.

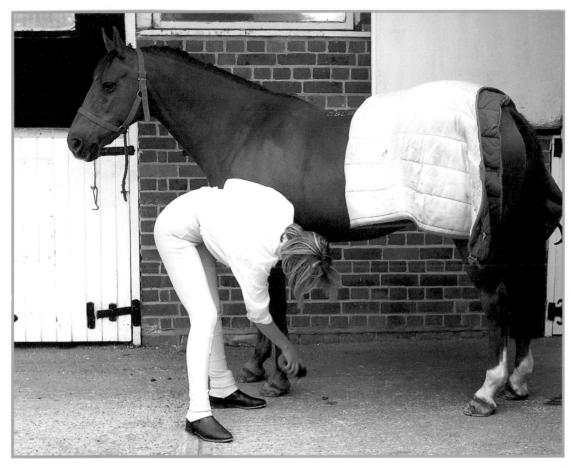

◄ **Quartering** is a ten-minute clean-up done in the morning after 'breakfast' and before exercise. Go over the pony's coat with the dandy brush to get rid of stable stains. Keep the pony's rug folded over the half you are *not* brushing so he stays warm.

When you've brushed the coat, switch to the body brush and remove any bedding from mane and tail, then pick out the feet.

◄ **Strapping** requires plenty of hard work. You should use the body brush after exercise when the pony is warm to clean the coat and massage the skin. Go gently on the legs and head.

▲ **Clean the brush** every few strokes by dragging the bristles through the teeth of the curry comb. *Never* use a metal curry comb on a pony – its *only* use is to remove dirt from the brush.

▲ **Remove dirt** from the curry comb by tapping it on the ground. Do this down wind of the pony so dirt doesn't blow back over him, and well away from his legs so you don't get kicked.

Brush thoroughly all over the coat.

On delicate parts (like head and legs) do not lean with your weight or use long strokes; just press on and brush in the direction of the hair. If your pony dislikes having his head brushed, use the stable rubber.

Body brushing is hard work and, if you're not used to it, could well take you half an hour.

After body brushing, do the forelock, mane and tail as for a grass-kept pony, and 'lay' them with the damp water brush. Sponge the eyes, nostrils, lips and dock and, finally, damp the stable rubber slightly, bundle it up and wipe over the coat.

Now the pony is finished – and you're exhausted!

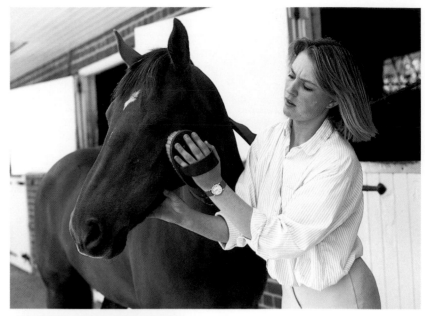

▲ **Brush the head very gently.** Take the headcollar off and strap it round the pony's neck so you can reach every part. Some ponies object to having their heads brushed – if so, use a stable rubber instead.

◄ **Flattening the mane:** After brushing the mane with the body brush, take the water brush and dip the ends of the bristles in water. Shake them hard downward and brush the hair flat.

▼ **Polishing** finishes the grooming session. Damp a stable rubber (either a clean tea towel or a sponge does the job if you don't have one). Scrunch it up into a bundle and wipe lightly all over the coat.

Do's and don'ts

☐ DON'T brush wet mud – it won't come off and you'll make the pony sore. Either hose it off or wait until the pony is dry, then brush it off.

☐ DON'T tug the brush through tangles in the mane or tail because you'll break the hair. Use your fingers.

☐ DON'T be rough or knock the pony with your tools while you groom.

☐ DO be considerate so the pony enjoys being groomed.

☐ DO pick out the feet at least twice daily for a stabled pony.

☐ DO speak kindly to the pony while grooming – then he'll respond to you.

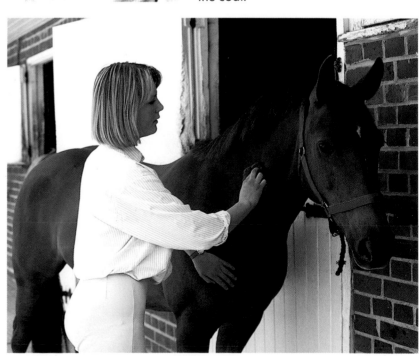

To keep a stable-kept pony in tip-top condition, give him a full daily grooming. He can enjoy the massage while you make him clean and trim.

areas to wisp

Setting fair and wisping

In the evening, go quickly over the pony with the body brush (known as brushing over or setting fair), and perhaps wisp him. Alternatively, you can wisp in the morning after body brushing. Most ponies enjoy having their muscles toned.

To wisp, use your weight in long strokes as in body brushing, and slap the wisp or massage pad firmly — but not *too* hard! — on to the top half of the neck, shoulders and quarters.

Don't wisp other parts, especially the loins (behind the saddle area) or legs as you could cause injury.

The idea is that the pony, expecting the slap, flinches his muscles to brace himself against the force. This helps to develop his muscles. Ten minutes each side is plenty.

Hoof care

Whether a pony is kept at grass or in a stable, his feet need daily attention to keep them clean and healthy.

Picking up the feet

Before checking your pony's feet, tie him up securely so that he can't move around. Always attend to him quietly as this relaxes him. Make sure he is standing square with his weight evenly distributed on all four feet.

Starting with the near fore (left foreleg), stand facing the pony's tail. Run your left hand down his leg so he realizes you are going to do something to him. If you suddenly grab his foot you could frighten him.

Most ponies lift their foot as soon as your hand reaches the pastern (just above the hoof and below the fetlock joint). If yours doesn't respond, firmly pinch his pastern with your thumb and index finger.

Picking out

You should pick out your pony's feet at least once and preferably twice a day. When you've lifted the near fore, rest it in your left hand and hold the hoof pick in your right. You'll have to bend or crouch down but *never* kneel or sit. You must be able to get out of the way quickly if the pony is unexpectedly startled.

Gently pick out any mud, rubbish and grit. Always work from the heel toward the toe – never the other direction. This way, there is no possibility of pushing a piece of grit into the sensitive part of the frog by the bars.

Pick out each foot in turn, near fore, near hind, off fore and off hind.

Washing the feet

To wash away all traces of dirt from the hoof use a water brush dipped into a bucket of water. Shake off any excess water. If your hoof pick has a brush attachment, you can use that instead.

Wash out the underside of the foot in the same direction as you use the hoof pick – working from heel to toe. Don't let water run into his heel as this can cause 'cracked heels' – like chapped hands for us. Place your thumb across the heel if you're splashing water, and never use a drenched, soaking brush.

Put your pony's foot down and wash the wall of the hoof. Take care not to go above the hoof wall.

Hoof oil

When the feet are dry, you can put on a thin coating of hoof oil. There are special brushes for this, but a small, clean 2–2.5cm (1in) paint brush does the job just as well. Oil the whole of the hoof, inside and out, including the bulbs of the heel. Do the inside first so *you* don't get smothered in oil.

Whether hoof oil does the feet good is a matter of dispute. But it makes the hooves gleam, and is generally beneficial for ponies with broken or brittle feet. Some also contain antiseptic, which helps ward off infections.

◄ **Gleaming shiny hooves** add greatly to a smart appearance.

Pick out your pony's hooves every day to get rid of manure, mud and stones. Washing and oiling can be done less often.

Know the foot

The frog is 'V'-shaped and provides the foot with a natural non-slip shock absorber.

The sole protects the underside of the foot. This is fairly thin, more so with some ponies than others, which is why you should take care when riding over a stony surface.

The wall is the most visible part of the hoof. Although it is continually growing it is insensitive. Compare it with our own finger or toe nails which have no feeling but still grow.

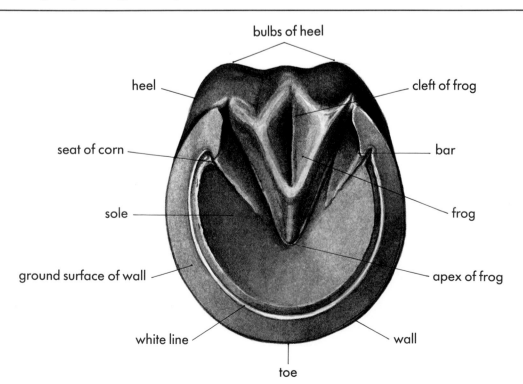

bulbs of heel

heel

cleft of frog

seat of corn

bar

sole

frog

ground surface of wall

apex of frog

white line

wall

toe

hoof oil

hoof oil brush

water brush

hoof picks

Regular check-ups

Remember to get your pony's feet regularly attended to by a farrier. A horse should have his shoes checked every three to five weeks, depending on the amount of road work you are doing and how often you ride.

Even an unshod horse needs five-weekly check-ups because the hoof wall grows non-stop – he needs his nails cut!

Causes of lameness

Ponies often become lame if a stone lodges between the shoe and the frog. This usually happens while you are riding – you suddenly feel your pony falter. Dismount immediately and pick out his foot gently. You can buy portable folding hoof picks; otherwise use your finger or a strong stick.

Nails in the feet are also common.

The complete treatment

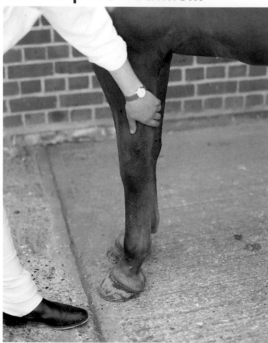

1 Facing the tail, run your left hand smoothly down the pony's leg to warn him you're going to pick his foot up.

2 Hold the hoof in your left hand and, with the hoof pick in your right hand, remove dirt and grit. Work from heel to toe.

▲ Your hoof-care kit should contain a hoof pick, water brush for washing (an old dandy brush will do), hoof oil and a brush.

5 Oil the inside of the hoof thoroughly, working it well in to the sole, frog and heel and all the crevices.

6 Put a light coat of oil on the hoof wall, starting at the top and taking care to avoid dirtying the hair above.

Before you remove a nail note whereabouts it is, what angle it is at and how deeply it has gone in. The nail may be penetrating a vital structure if it is in the back third of the foot or frog, in which case call the vet.

Thrush is a fungus and also needs the attention of a vet. It appears in the cleft of the hoof and gives off a foul smell like bad cheese. Its discharge is easily seen and occurs if you do not clean the pony's feet regularly or you leave him standing in a dirty stable.

Laminitis has many known causes, one of which is eating too much lush grass. Typically, the pony is in considerable pain, unable to walk properly and his feet feel hot to the touch. It is very serious and should always receive prompt veterinary action.

! HORSE CHESTNUT
If a pony is really stubborn and won't lift his foot up even when you pinch his pastern, there's a last resort.

Twist his chestnut (the horny piece just above the knee) with one hand while holding on to his foot with the other.

This is painful for the pony so don't do it unless you are absolutely desperate.

3 Dampen the water brush and use it to get rid of the last traces of dirt, but don't slosh water over the heel!

4 Put the hoof down and crouch to brush any mud off the outside of the hoof wall, keeping water away from the hair.

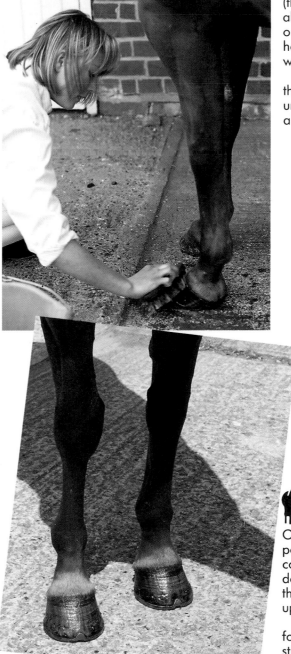

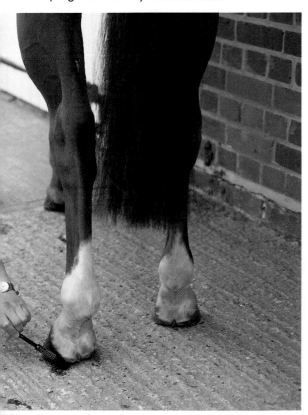

7 The reward of your daily foot treatment is knowing that the pony in your care has four hooves glistening with health and strength!

THE NEAR SIDE
Once you and your pony have confidence, you can do all the hooves from the near side to speed up hoof care.

To reach the off fore and off hind, you stretch underneath the pony and just run your left hand down his leg and quietly pick it up.

137

Shoeing

To protect your pony's feet and stop them becoming sore and broken when you ride him, you need to have him shod.

What are shoes?

Shoes are made up from lengths of iron or from steel. These vary in width and depth depending on the size of the horse and what kind of work he does.

Your pony will probably be fitted with a lightweight shoe, unless he has a foot problem – in which case the farrier may use a special shoe to try to remedy the fault.

An ordinary front shoe has a front toe clip, which helps to hold the shoe in place, and usually seven nail holes. There is often a groove which runs round the centre of the shoe. This is called fullering and gives the shoe better grip when it comes into contact with the ground. A hind shoe is similar except that it has two toe clips placed either side of the toe of the shoe.

The farrier

You may have heard the terms farrier and blacksmith used. Both shoe horses and deal with diseases of the hoof. But a blacksmith also carries out welding and other metalwork, which is useful if you need any stable fittings made or mended. Their apprenticeships are four and five years respectively.

The work a farrier does is very skilled, and its important to get a good recommendation before making a choice. Your vet may be able to suggest the name of a good farrier.

Nowadays most farriers have mobile forges, so if you live far away they can come to you. However, it's cheaper if you go to their premises – you don't have to pay their travelling fee on top of the price of fitting a set of shoes.

Do make sure you book regular appointments. Arrive on time at the forge or have the pony caught up ready when the farrier arrives. Have the legs as clean and dry as possible.

Remember that day-to-day foot care is your responsibility – the farrier can't make good feet from bad at one shoeing. Pick the feet out daily, oiling them if necessary, and feed the pony properly so as to build good horn.

What the farrier does

There are two main methods of shoeing: 'hot' and 'cold'.

Hot shoeing is when the shoe is placed into a furnace or fire until it is red hot. The farrier then holds the shoe on to the hoof wall for a few seconds. When he takes it away he can see whether it fits and make the necessary adjustments. This looks rather horrifying and smells dreadful, but it is quite painless because the wall of the hoof is virtually dead

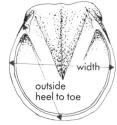

◄ **A traditional forge** where hot shoeing takes place on the premises.

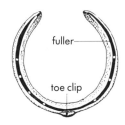

MEASURING THE FOOT
The farrier will measure the pony's foot for a new shoe but it's useful to know how to do it.

Pick up the foot and measure with a ruler from the outside heel edge to the toe; then across the widest part of the foot from the outside to the inside.

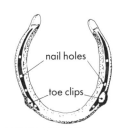

FRONT SHOE
A typical front shoe has one toe clip and seven nail holes. The groove (fullering) gives the shoe grip.

HIND SHOE
This has two toe clips on either side of the shoe toe.

When to shoe

There are several pointers that tell you when your horse needs shoeing:

● If the shoe has worn thin or become loose. The pony will be uncomfortable and a loose shoe could twist and make him lame.

● If the clenches (tips of the nails) have risen and stand out of the wall of the hoof. Instead of lying flat against the hoof, they stick out and could cut the pony.

● If the foot grows too long and out of shape. The hoof looks as though it has grown over the back of the shoe, but in fact what happens is that the foot draws the shoe forward as it grows longer.

● If the shoe has fallen off (been 'cast').

● If it is five weeks since the farrier last came. The shoes may still look fine, but you should have them taken off and the pony's feet pared (cut back) before the shoes are put back on. This is known as 'removes'.

▲ **The clenches have risen,** making the shoe loose and causing the hoof wall to crack.

The hot-shoeing method

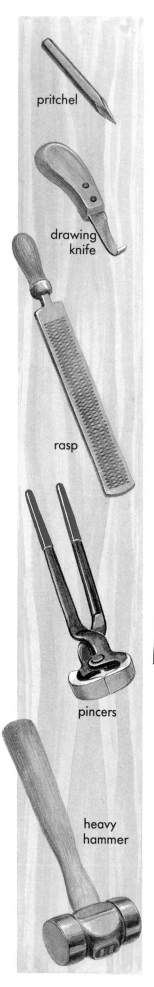

pritchel

drawing knife

rasp

pincers

heavy hammer

1 The farrier starts by taking off the old shoe. He uses the buffer and driving hammer to bring up the nail heads.

2 When the shoe is loose, he uses pincers to prize it away from the horse's foot.

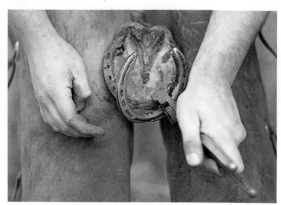

5 Meanwhile, the shoe heats up in the furnace (inset). The farrier shapes the shoe on the anvil, using the heavy hammer.

6 The shoe is held by a nail hole with the pritchel (shaped like a pencil) while it is tried on the foot. The farrier has the drawing knife in his other hand.

tissue, like our nails.

Once the farrier is satisfied that the shoe fits correctly, he submerges it in a bucket of cold water until it has cooled down. When he's prepared shoes for each foot, he nails them on, making sure that the nails only go into the hoof wall and not into the sensitive laminae.

The farrier turns the nail tips and twists them off, leaving enough to form a clench (a small 'hook', which helps to hold the shoe on). Finally, he rasps a small groove for the clench to lie in against the wall of the hoof.

Cold shoeing is when the farrier puts on a machine-made shoe: he may adjust the shoe beforehand or (to a limited extent) on the day.

The well-shod pony

It is most important that your pony is well shod. Look out for the following indicators.

☐ The shoe must fit the foot, not the other way round – the hoof wall should not be rasped away to meet the iron.

☐ The pony must be comfortable, with a shoe suitable for the work he has to do, neither too light or too heavy.

☐ The hoof wall should be trimmed to remove excess horn growth.

☐ The nails should appear at roughly the same height up the hoof. They should be the correct size so that the heads sit neatly in the holes of the shoe.

☐ There should be no daylight between the hoof and the shoe.

3 The farrier prepares the foot by trimming off the overgrown horn. He also tidies up the sole and frog by cutting away ragged bits.

4 He rasps the sole to make it level. At the same time, he can look at the condition and shape of the foot.

7 When the shoe is cool, the driving hammer is used to nail it on, starting at the toe. The right-sized nails must be chosen.

8 With pincers, the ends of the nails are drawn down to make clenches (hooks) and the shoe is tightened.

9 Finally, the clenches are rasped and embedded in the wall, and the rasp is used to smooth the outside of the wall where it meets the shoe. This helps stop the wall cracking.

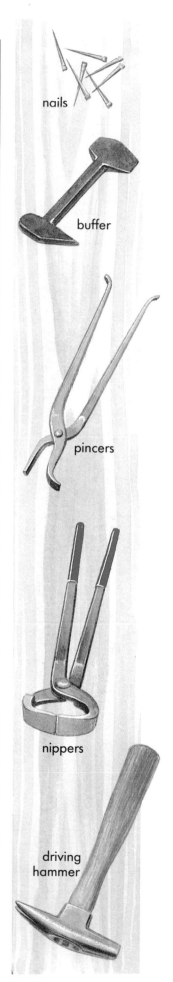

nails

buffer

pincers

nippers

driving hammer

141

Tail bandaging

Tail bandages have two purposes: they improve appearance by flattening the hair on the dock (top of the tail), and they protect the tail from rubbing when travelling.

Putting the bandage on

Tail bandages are made of stockinette or crêpe. Both these fabrics are stretchy, so dampen the hair before bandaging. (If you are bandaging for appearance's sake you have probably washed the tail first anyway.) Do not dampen the bandage in case it shrinks while on the tail and becomes too tight.

With bandage in hand, move behind the pony, putting a warning hand on his hindquarters to let him know where you are. Put the dock over your shoulder if the pony tries to clamp his tail down between his hindlegs.

Unroll the loose end of the bandage and leave a short strip to spare. Roll once round the top of the tail. Bring the spare end down over your turn and cover it with another roll to anchor the bandage. Carry on bandaging to two thirds of the way down the dock.

Once you reach the tapes, tie them in a bow on the outside (toward you). Tuck

▼ **Practise bandaging** the tail until you get the feel of just how tight to make it. The horse can enjoy a snooze in the sun while you work! Here the bandage is being used to improve appearance.

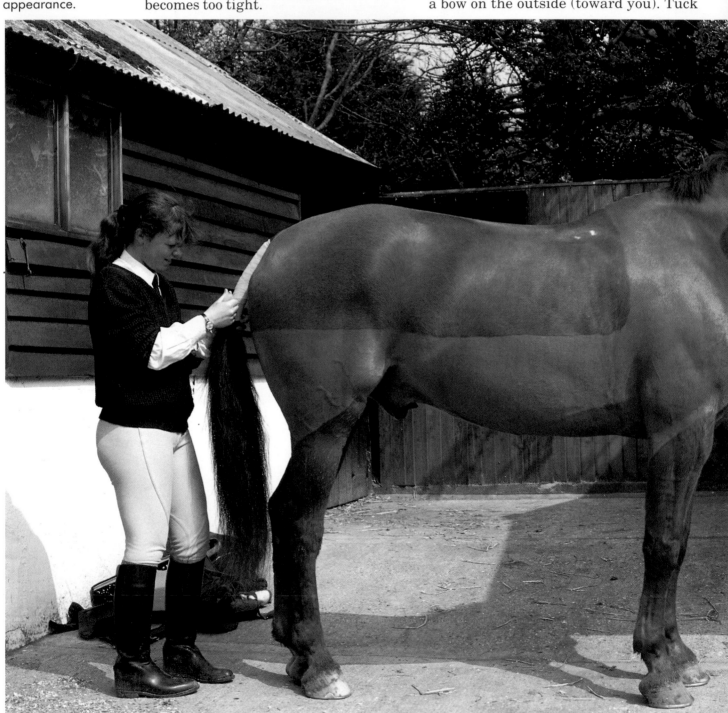

in the tapes neatly underneath the bandage. Bend the dock back into a comfortable, natural curve – the process of bandaging pulls it out of shape.

Of all the tack and clothing you put on a pony, bandages are probably the trickiest to do correctly. If they are too tight, the hair at the roots dies, falls out and regrows white. Wavy hair on the dock is a sign of a tail bandage that's been put on too tightly.

If it is too loose, however, the bandage can trail off and trip up the pony. Aim to bandage firmly but without cramping the tail.

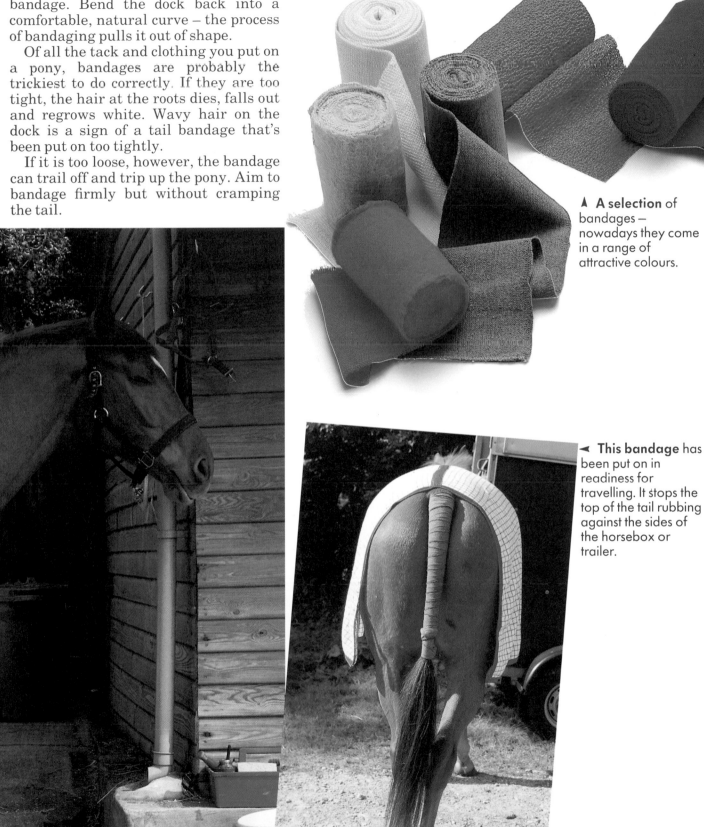

▲ **A selection** of bandages – nowadays they come in a range of attractive colours.

◄ **This bandage** has been put on in readiness for travelling. It stops the top of the tail rubbing against the sides of the horsebox or trailer.

143

How to put on a tail bandage

1 After dampening the top of the tail with a water brush, unroll the straight edge leaving about 15cm (6in) to spare.

2 Bandage once round under the tail, holding the spare edge out of the way. This is easier if you put the tail over your shoulder.

★ **MIX AND MATCH**

With the range of colours available now, you can give your pony a really smart appearance by matching his accessories.

If you have a nylon headcollar, use that as your base colour. Every time you get a new piece of equipment, choose the same colour. So, for instance, you could end up with a blue headcollar, blue tail and leg bandages, blue numnah and rug.

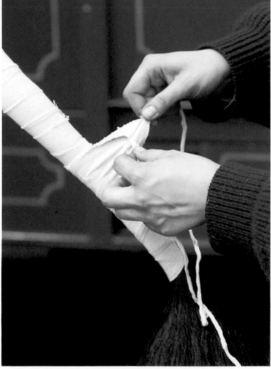

5 Roll back up again if you haven't yet reached the tapes at the end of the bandage. When you've used up the entire length, pull the tapes apart.

6 Wind the tapes around the bandage. Tie them on the outside (nearest to you) with a double bow so that the fastening doesn't come undone. Don't tie them *too* tightly or you could kill the hair at the roots.

3 Bring the flap down and secure it with another turn. This stage is crucial — if you work too loosely the bandage falls off.

4 Continue bandaging to two thirds of the way down the dock. Try to keep the bandage flat and the overlaps even.

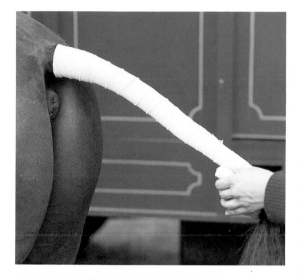

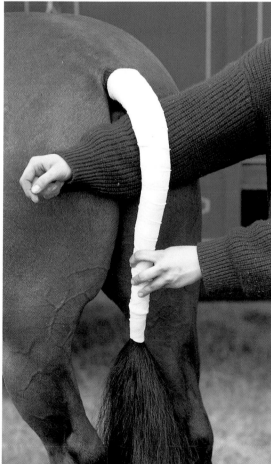

7 Tuck the tapes in for security and so there are no loose, untidy ends. Put your arm under the dock to bend the tail back into its smooth, natural curve. You now have a neat, well-fitting tail bandage.

Taking off the bandage

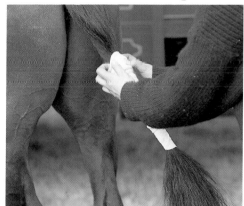

◄ **To remove**, grip around the top of the tail and simply slide the bandage off. Leave tail bandages on for a maximum of two hours or for the time the journey takes if travelling.

Rolling up the bandage

Once you have taken off the bandage, always roll it up. When you can, iron it first. But if you've just transported your pony to a show, that has to wait until you get home.

1 Hold the bandage at the tape end, sewn side up. Pull the tapes clear.

2 Wind the tapes around your fingers as if you are rolling up a ball of wool.

3 Fold them neatly across the triangular end of the bandage so the tapes form a 'core'.

4 Roll the bandage, keeping the sewn side inward until you end with the straight edge outside.

Leg bandaging

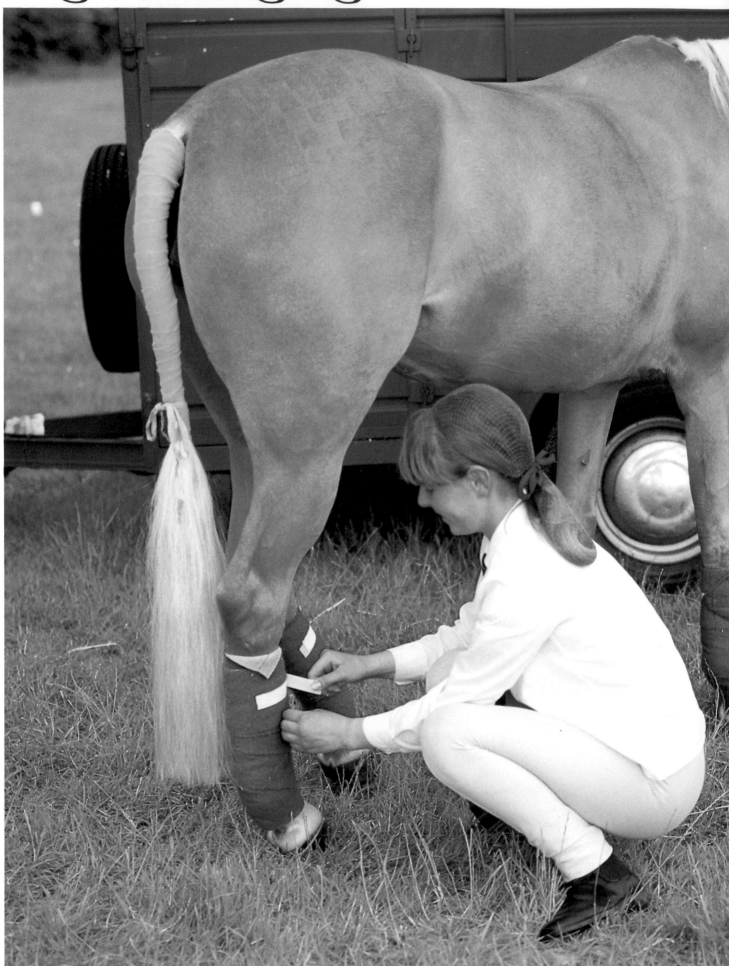

Leg bandages can go on all four of the horse's legs. There are two types: stable bandages for warmth and drying off legs in cold weather and for protection when travelling; and exercise bandages to guard against knocks when riding.

Exercise bandages

Also called work bandages, these are usually made of stretchy fabric or knitted cotton stockinette. One end is straight and the other pointed, with tapes sewn on.

They go on over padding (gamgee tissue, special leg padding from a saddler or, not so good, plastic foam). The padding helps lessen any uneven pressure, as the bandage must be firm but not too tight.

Exercise bandages act as a buffer if the horse knocks his leg and, to some extent, prevent jarring. However, they do not support tendons. To do that, they would have to be put on around a joint, such as the fetlock, and restrict its movement to reduce strain on the tendons. But this would also hamper the free leg action needed during work.

So exercise bandages go from just below the hocks (on the hindlegs) or knees (on the forelegs) to just above the broad part of the fetlock. Some saddlers stock different lengths of bandage: pony, cob or full sizes.

Stable bandages

Stable (also described as 'travelling') bandages are longer and wider than exercise bandages. The easiest to use are of fine-knitted wool which moulds to the leg. They cushion the leg from knocks when travelling and keep stabled horses' legs warm and dry in winter.

Stable bandages go on just the same as exercise bandages but usually have Velcro fastenings rather than tapes. Instead of stopping at the fetlock, these bandages, plus their padding, go right over the fetlock and pastern to the heels and coronet (top of the hoof). Unfortunately, many are rather short and you may need to sew two together to make a good long bandage.

◄ **Stable bandages** (main picture) go right down over the fetlocks and pasterns and protect the legs when travelling. Exercise bandages (inset) go down to just above the fetlock and stop the legs jarring during work.

TRAVELLING PADS
Travelling pads are quick to put on if you haven't the time to leg bandage, but should *only* be used for travelling — not for exercise or in the stable.

They are usually made of plastic on the outside, and always padded on the inside. They fasten with strips of Velcro and are sometimes shaped with darts. The padding shields all four legs from knocks, but does not support the legs.

Starting to bandage

So that you get the feel of just how tight to work, it's best to practise on a drainpipe or young tree trunk before trying out bandaging on the pony.

You should be able to get your fingertip in a turn of the bandage and pull it away from the leg, but not too easily. Stable bandages should be slightly looser than exercise ones.

Cut the padding so it goes a little above and below the finished bandage and wrap it round the leg. You'll soon learn the knack of keeping it on while starting the bandage, and of keeping it smooth during bandaging. The padding stays put better if you damp the leg hair first.

Start with the near foreleg. Crouch down beside it. Never kneel because you can't get up quickly enough for safety should the pony play up at all.

Dressed for exercise

Hold the rolled bandage in your right hand with the loose straight end furthest from you opening to the left. Unroll about 20cm (8in) and place it diagonally across the leg, end uppermost, with the roll just below the knee.

Putting on a stable bandage

1 Cut the padding generously to come slightly above and below the bandage. Wrap it round the leg.

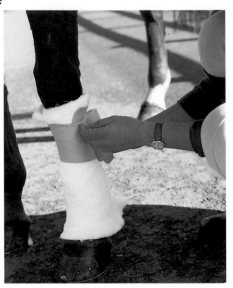

2 Keeping the padding smooth and secure, wind one roll of the bandage, leaving a flap at the end.

3 Fold the flap over the bandage and make another turn to cover the flap and anchor it.

► **Once you have completed** bandaging all four legs, the pony is ready for travel or for keeping warm in the stable. But because the bandages go right over the fetlock they restrict movement and cannot be used when exercising.

Most stable bandages now fasten with Velcro. Velcro has two advantages over tapes: it is quicker and easier to do up, and the pressure is even all the way round the leg. With tapes, it is all too easy to make pressure points where you tie the fastening.

Do one turn anti-clockwise right round the leg. Let the loose end drop down the outside of the leg and do another turn over it to anchor it. Keep rolling down to the fetlock covering half the bandage's width at each turn.

At the broadest part of the fetlock, turn upward and roll up to the knee. Roll firmly but do *not* stretch the material as it has a self-tightening effect anyway.

Finishing off

Try to finish with the pointed end toward the tail (so twigs don't catch in it if the pony brushes through undergrowth). Make sure the tapes aren't twisted, and tie them round the leg, one to the left and one to the right and back facing you again. Finish with a firm bow.

Tie the tapes *the same* tightness as the bandage itself, no tighter. You may want to cut the tapes if they are very long. Tuck the ends of the bow into a turn of the bandage so they don't get caught – and you've finished.

Always tie the tapes at the side of the leg and on the outside. If you tie them on the front bone or back tendons, you will create a lumpy pressure point, and on the inside the pony could kick the tapes undone.

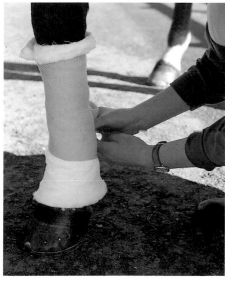

4 Roll down over the fetlock and pastern to the heel, overlapping about half the width every time.

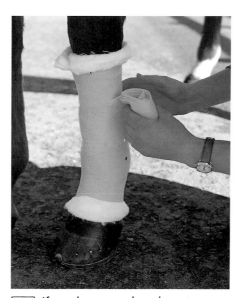

5 If you have any bandage to spare, roll back up, remembering to keep an even tension all the way.

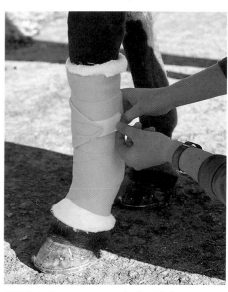

6 When you reach the Velcro, press the two strips together so that the bandage is held firmly in position.

Taking off a bandage

Peel the Velcro apart and unravel the bandage, passing it from hand to hand.

Run your hand briskly down the leg several times to restore circulation.

Clipping your pony

All horses grow a new coat for the winter, although moorland-type ponies grow denser, more furry coats, and cob-types grow longer, shaggier coats than Thoroughbreds, Arabs and other fine breeds. So, in early autumn, you must decide how you plan to keep and use your pony through the winter, and whether or not to have him clipped.

An unclipped pony

Unclipped, with his natural fur coat on, your pony should be able to live out, day and night all winter through – although fine-bred and very old ponies may need a New Zealand rug for extra protection.

But make sure your pony has as much good quality hay, fresh every day, as he will eat. He may also need concentrates – such as pony cubes – to keep him plump, cheerful and lively throughout the winter. A pony who is not getting enough food to keep his system stoked up quickly loses condition, particularly toward the end of winter. So keep checking, and adjust his feed as necessary; a thick coat may well be hiding a thin pony.

An unclipped pony looks shaggy rather than smart. You should not attempt to groom him deep down with a body brush. He needs the grease in his coat as protection against cold and wet.

Provided you feed him properly, he will be well up to quiet riding. If you ride him regularly, you can get him fit enough for a short day out – to compete in the odd class or at an indoor show. But do not expect too much.

Winter fitness

You cannot get an unclipped pony really fit. With his heavy coat on, fast work ▶

▼ Shaggy ponies quickly become hot and exhausted if they are exercised too much without being clipped.

A trace clip like this is a good compromise for a hardy pony; you can get him fit enough for competitions and jumping while still wintering him in a field.

Types of clip

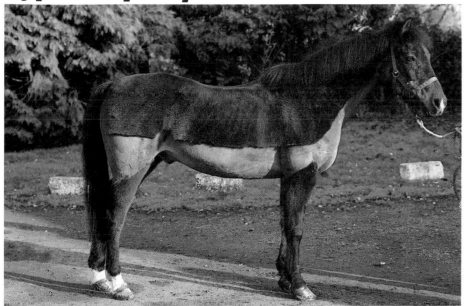

◄ **The trace clip** follows the line of the harness horse's traces — halfway up the pony's sides. This useful, practical style dates from the days of horse-drawn transport. The line of the clip continues up the pony's neck. Traditionally, his head is clipped, but modern variations may leave the head wholly unclipped. Alternatively, long, woolly hair under a pony's jaw may be clipped while the face is left alone.

This is a good clip for an owner who has stabling and wants the pony fit, but cannot exercise him every day. Unless he is very delicate, a trace-clipped pony, made fit in autumn, can be turned out in a New Zealand rug to exercise himself on most winter days when he cannot be ridden.

➤ **Blanket clip:** The horse's head, neck and body are clipped, except for the area an exercise sheet would cover — the back, loins and quarters. The leg hair is left on.

Gullet clip: If you only have a field to keep your pony in but he becomes hot, wet and unhappy whenever you ride him, a gullet clip may be the answer. Hair is removed on the pony's belly and between his forelegs. The clipped portion tapers upward in a V-shape to a point halfway up the underside of the pony's neck.

A gullet-clipped pony does not look as if he is clipped, but he stands work better, without losing the benefit of his winter coat. Use your common sense, however, about the work you give him. No pony in winter — indeed no pony at all — should be pulled out of his field, unfit, for hours of galloping.

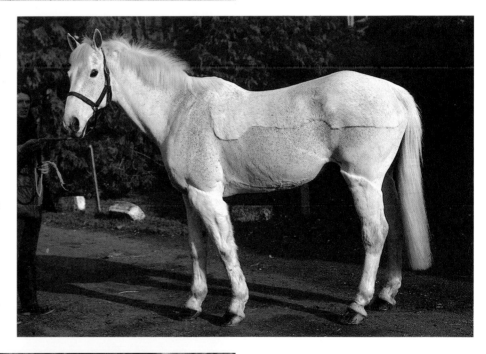

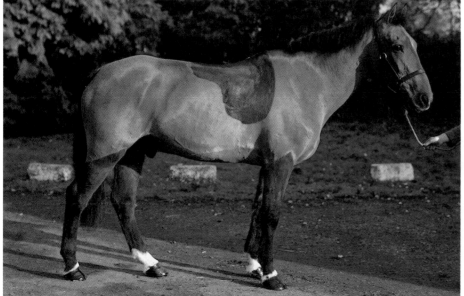

◄ **Hunter clip:** The horse's head, neck and body (except for a saddle patch) are clipped. The hair is left on the legs for protection against cold and thorns.

Full clip: The coat is taken off from nose to toe. This is also known as 'clipping a horse right out'.

Either a full or a hunter clip means you must keep your horse stabled for the whole of the winter. You must decide whether you have the time and facilities to keep your pony in this way: daily mucking out and grooming, giving hay, water and feed at least twice a day and exercising the horse for at least an hour, six days out of seven.

makes a pony sweat heavily, just as a person would if he went for a cross-country run wearing several sweaters and a thick jacket.

Your pony becomes wet, hot, tired and distressed if you ride him hard when he is not clipped. And, after riding, he may become chilled before you can get him dry. He will lose weight and condition. If you want your pony fully fit for winter work, you need to have him clipped.

The clipped pony

Clipping involves shaving off a horse's coat, over all or part of his body. It is usually done with electrically operated clippers and is not a job for the inexperienced pony-keeper to tackle.

A local stable-owner may provide a clipping service. Otherwise, the nearest Pony Club branch or riding club should be able to advise you.

The clipped pony needs stable cloth-

Soothing the pony: Stand by the pony's head and talk to him so you keep him occupied while he is clipped. At the same time you can watch the expert at work.

You can help by stretching the front leg forward when the pony's girth and elbows are clipped. This helps to avoid nipping any loose folds of skin.

ing to wear in place of his natural coat when he is not working. Modern stable rugs – like duvets, with built-in surcingles and/or leg straps – give warmth without weight, and need no roller.

When to clip

A pony's winter coat starts growing in early autumn. He should be clipped for the first time in mid-autumn, before his coat becomes too long. The coat goes on growing afterwards, so he'll need a second clip early in winter.

By mid to late winter, the summer coat starts to grow. If you want to do competition work in spring, clip again in mid-winter. But if you want to turn the pony out again when the weather is warm enough, avoid a third clip. Just remove the long 'cat' hairs that develop along the line of the neck and hindquarters to smarten him up.

Getting your pony ready

Before clipping, your pony should be stabled and ridden regularly for a week or so if possible. After riding, sponge him down with warm water to remove grease that may clog the clippers – but dry him well so he doesn't get chilled.

The pony should be clean and dry on the day. And remember to wear something that horse hair does not stick to! Handle him in a calm, matter-of-fact way so he is quite happy to be clipped. In any case, clipping seldom takes more than an hour.

You can ride your pony home after he is clipped, but bring an exercise sheet to save him from catching cold. Rug him up if you are boxing him home – never leave a clipped pony standing in the stable without clothing. Use the body brush rather than the dandy brush to groom him once he is clipped.

▼ **Chaser clip before and after:** This is a high-cut, modern variation of the trace clip. The chaser clip is so called because it can be used on steeplechasers to keep their backs warm.

It is an excellent choice for ponies who are stabled but sometimes turned out during the day.

Trimming your pony

Unless your pony is a native breed, trimming makes him look much smarter, particularly for showing.

Before you start

Before you start trimming, groom the pony to remove any excess dirt and mud. There's no need to wash him first, but it is a good idea to give him a thorough bath with horse shampoo afterwards to remove any loose hair. Choose a warm day so he doesn't get chilled.

For trimming you need round-ended scissors and a mane comb. If you have them, electric or hand clippers are also useful.

The legs

The feather, which grows at the back of the fetlock joints, can be cut back with either clippers or scissors. When using clippers make sure that you don't go too close, as you do not want a skinned look.

Start with the forelegs. Remove the long hair from below the pony's knee right down to his pastern. When using scissors, lift the hair with the mane comb and pull it taut so you cut evenly and don't leave the pony looking 'chewed' — work as if you are cutting a person's hair. Either cut downward or upward but not across, so you get a smooth finish.

When trimming the hindlegs be wary of your pony kicking. Crouch down — don't kneel — beside (not behind) the leg.

You can also cut carefully round the top of the foot with the scissors to remove long hairs growing over the hoof wall.

Some experts believe that you should not trim your pony's feather in winter. They feel that feather helps to keep the pony's legs warm and protect them from mud fever or cracked heels. However, if you don't trim the legs it is difficult to spot the first signs of trouble. If you are not sure about winter trimming, ask ▶

▼ **While ponies** do not *have* to be trimmed, removing stray hairs and levelling the mane and tail neatens their appearance.

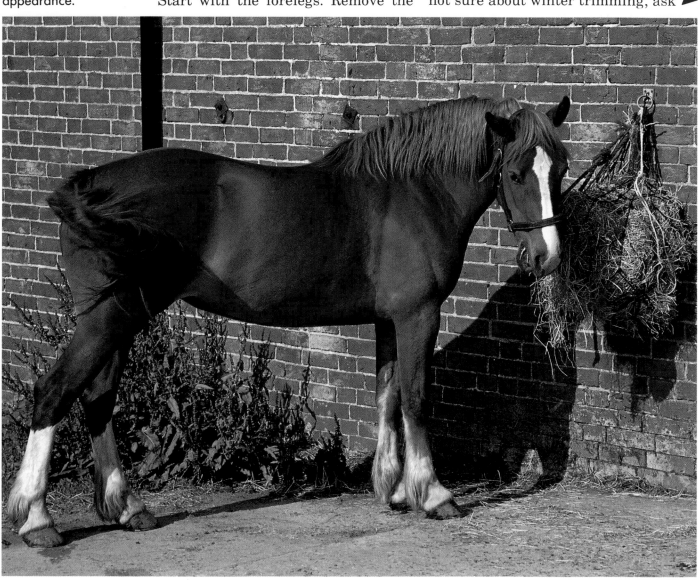

Trimming checklist – what to remember

● DO tie the pony up with a quick-release knot in case the clippers scare him.

● DO groom the pony thoroughly before you start.

● DO choose a warm day if you're going to wash the pony afterwards, otherwise he might get chilled.

● DO use round-ended scissors to reduce the risk of accidental cuts.

● DO make sure that your clippers are in perfect working order.

● DON'T kneel down when you trim the hindlegs.

● DON'T cut the eyelashes.

● DON'T let any hair fall into the ear.

● DON'T use electric clippers on the head of a nervous pony.

● DON'T cut the feather straight across.

▲ **Tie the pony up** with a quick-release knot and give him a thorough groom before you start trimming.

The legs and feet

1 Lift the feather away from the leg with the mane comb. Cut the hair jutting through the teeth of the comb on a *slope*, not across, or you will end up with a series of jagged layers.

2 Cut evenly around the coronet so that the hair meets the hoof wall in a clear line.

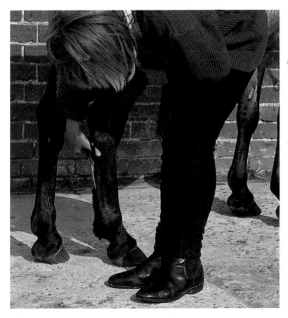

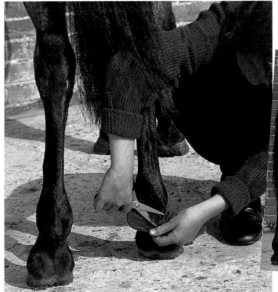

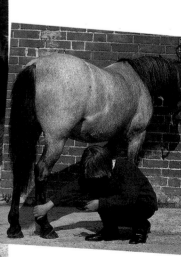

3 Snip off any stray hairs growing down the back of the leg. Hold the tail out of the way so you can see what you're doing.

4 Trim the hindleg feather as you did the forelegs. Crouch close to the pony's side just in case he kicks out.

▲ **Check** you haven't missed out any hairs. All four legs should feel smooth and even.

the advice of your vet or instructor – someone who knows your pony.

The head and ears

To make your pony's head look well-defined, you can remove the facial whiskers – which it is thought horses do not need for feeling as, say, a cat does. Snip off the long hairs around his chin and muzzle, between his cheek bones and down the underside of his head. *Never* cut the eyelashes.

The whiskery hair that comes out of the ears and the excess hair growing round the edge of the ears can also be trimmed to neaten the pony's head. Work extremely carefully as *no* hair must drop into the ear – this causes considerable discomfort and distress.

To trim the outer edge, hold the ear so

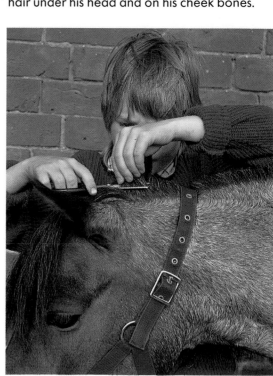

Trimming the ears and muzzle

1 Hold the pony's head still with your free hand. Very carefully, snip off the whiskers round the muzzle and chin.

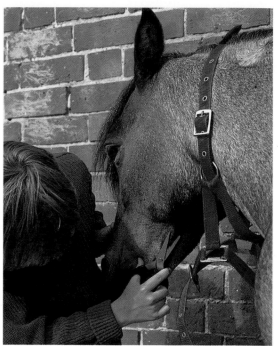

2 Undo the headcollar and tie it round the pony's neck. As long as he is quiet, trim the hair under his head and on his cheek bones.

3 Gently press the sides of the ear together so no hair can fall in. Cut the hairs sticking out along the edges.

4 With the comb, part the mane in a straight line about 5cm (2in) behind the ears. Cut a path for the headpiece to lie on.

TRIMMING THE TAIL

Most pony's tails are too long. When the tail is 'carried' (when the pony is moving and holding his tail up), a practical length is to have the end in line with the hocks.

It's much easier to work out the length if a friend lifts the tail up to the position it is in when carried. Cut it across with clippers or scissors.

The pony's tail should be pulled, unless you plait it, so that it lies neatly against the quarters. For more information on trimming, pulling and plaiting the tail, see pages 158–161.

To stop the mane becoming long and straggly it should also be pulled. This is described on page 163.

that the sides are together and there are no gaps for hair to drop in. Use either scissors or clippers – although some horses won't tolerate electric clippers near their heads – and cut along the edges, taking great care not to cut the ear itself.

The pony looks neater if you trim away the mane where the headpiece of the bridle lies, just behind the ears. Use the mane comb to separate a straight line of about 3-5cm (1½-2in) from the rest of the mane, and cut it off at the base with the scissors.

You can also trim the mane over the withers. But if the pony often wears a rug you may prefer to leave the mane intact so that it can help protect the withers from getting rubbed by the rug and becoming sore.

When *not* to trim

Certain breeds, such as Arabs, Welsh ponies and Fells, always keep their manes and tails long. The Mountain and Moorland breeds do not have their feather trimmed.

Heavy horses like Shires and Clydesdales have beautiful long manes and feather, but their tails are trimmed in a special style if they are going to be shown.

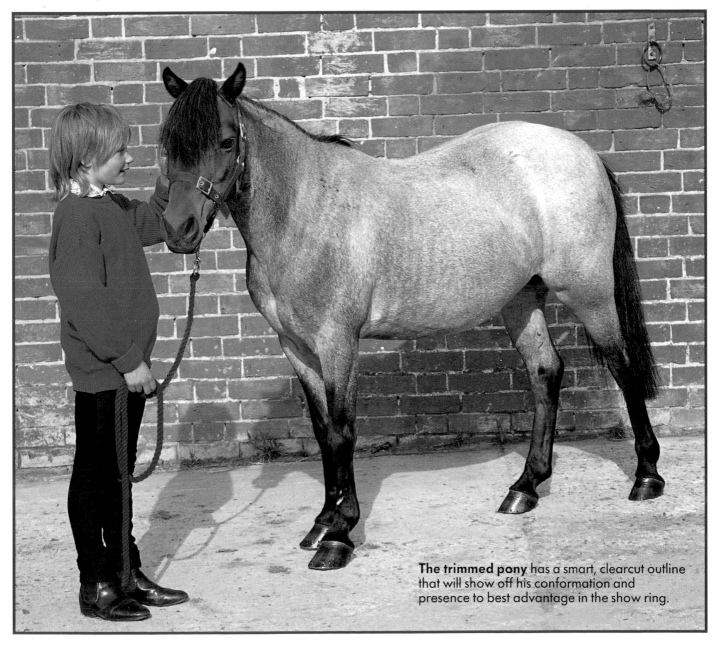

The trimmed pony has a smart, clearcut outline that will show off his conformation and presence to best advantage in the show ring.

Plaiting the tail

Plaiting your pony's tail smartens up his appearance when you go to a show or competition. It's easy to do once you've got the knack. Alternatively, you can pull (layer) the tail.

Getting the pony ready

Before you start plaiting, the tail needs to be well-brushed, clean and damp. Start by washing it. Sometimes a tail that's just been washed is so 'squeaky' clean it's difficult to handle. In this case, wash the tail a week before the day and dampen it just before plaiting.

Always use a specially prepared horse shampoo or pure soap, never a detergent which can irritate the skin. You'll also need a bucket with warm soapy water and one with warm rinsing water, two sponges and an old towel.

Plaiting equipment

The tail has to be tangle-free for plaiting, so have handy a water brush and tail comb (which is exactly the same as a mane comb).

Once you've plaited the tail you sew it up. For this you need strong thread, a needle, and scissors to cut the thread. The thread should be about 60cm (2ft) long, doubled and knotted at the end. Choose the same colour as the pony's tail so it doesn't show. But so *you* don't lose sight of it while you are plaiting, carefully pin the needle on to your jacket or jersey.

◄ **The confidence** you feel from knowing your pony is groomed and plaited to perfection means you're already halfway to gaining first prize!

Washing the tail

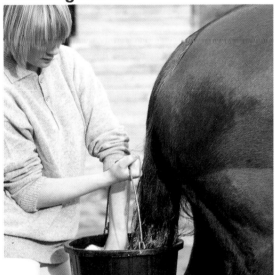

1 If your pony is quiet, you can stand behind him. Otherwise, work from beside his quarters. Put the tail in the soapy water.

2 Put the bucket on the ground to wash the top of the tail. Run your hands down the tail, squeezing it to get rid of excess water.

3 Rub the tail either between your hands or with the sponge. Keep dipping the tail into the soapy water until it feels clean.

4 Switch to the bucket of warm rinsing water. With the tail in the bucket, rinse the top down using your clean sponge.

▲ Pull the hairs apart to check you've removed all the soap.

★ **RINSING AND DRYING**
You may need several buckets of rinsing water, as you must get all the soap out of the tail.

For a placid pony, you can dry the tail by swinging it round like a helicopter propeller. If your pony doesn't like you doing this, use an old towel to rub it so that it is just damp.

Brush the hair with the water brush, and the tail is ready to plait.

How to plait

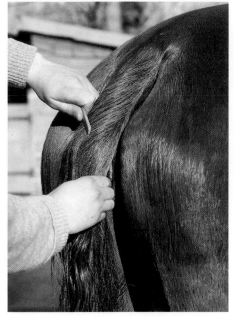 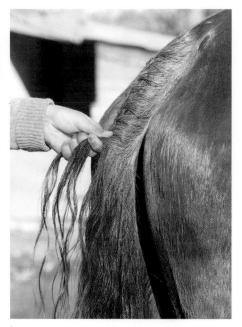 

1 Thoroughly comb the hair with the tail comb, particularly the sides, which you will join in to the top of the plait. Work down to about 10-15cm (4-6in) from the end of the dock.

2 Take a small amount of long tail hair from either side edge and the same amount from the middle and start to plait. Every second or third plait, join in more hair from the side edges.

3 Plait as tightly as possible and continue down the tail to about 10-15cm (4-6in) from the end of the dock. Go on plaiting without taking hair from the sides.

Pulling the tail

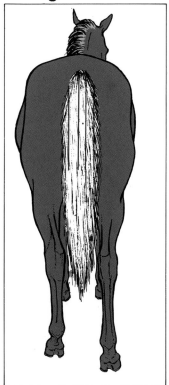 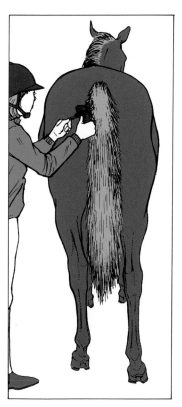 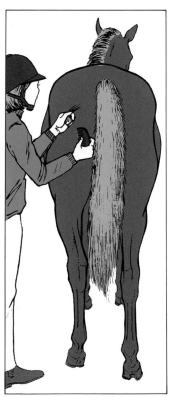 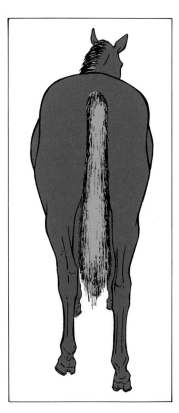

1 Imagine four or five lines running from the top of the tail down to about 7.5cm (3in) below the point of the buttock. These help you pull the tail evenly.

2 Take a few hairs at a time from each section between the lines: one on either side of the tail and several in the centre. Wrap the hairs round the tail comb.

3 Pull quickly downward so that the hair comes away with the comb. Only do a little at a time, and don't carry on too long or the pony will become bored, restive and sore.

4 The tail should be levelly pulled, and sit neatly against the hindquarters. It may take several days to complete. Wash the tail thoroughly and bandage it afterwards.

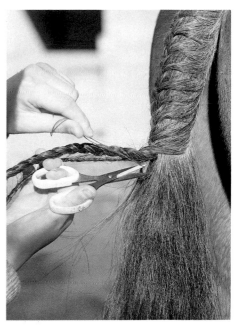

4 When you reach the end of the hair, secure the plait with the needle and thread. Sew through the end, and wrap the thread round it a few times. Sew through the plait again.

5 Fold the long plait up in one big loop. Secure it to the underside of the base of the French plait by sewing through the middle of both plaits. Be as neat as possible.

6 Fasten off by winding the thread round the loop to stop it coming undone. Cut off any thread left over with the scissors. The thread should hardly be visible.

The techniques

When you plait the tail you use two techniques. Both methods use three strands of hair to make the plait. But in the first (called French plaiting) you join in more hair from the sides as you go along. The plait stands out from the tail if you bring the side hair in from *underneath*; if you add the hair to the *top* of your strands, the plait appears flat.

The second method is just a normal plait without any hair taken from the sides. Combine both techniques – with a French plait to the bottom of the dock, and a normal plait to the end of the tail hair.

To hold the plait in place, dampen the tail again – it will probably have dried out – and put on a tail bandage. Remember when removing the tail bandage to unroll it and not pull it off – or all your hard work could be wasted.

If your pony's tail is not thick enough to plait and you want it to look smart, you can pull it. This means pulling hair out of the upper part of the tail so the hair is thinned out – similar to layering your own hair.

Do not be tempted to use clippers or thinning scissors – when the hair grows again the top of the tail could resemble a scrubbing brush.

Trimming the tail

The length of the tail should be about 10-15cm (4-6in) below the point of hock. You can either leave the tail uneven at the bottom (a 'swish' tail), or cut it straight across with the scissors or clippers (a 'bang' tail).

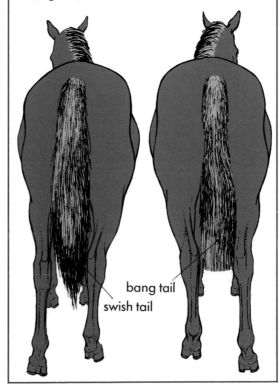

bang tail
swish tail

▲ **It's smartest** to sew the halves of the loop together all the way down so the plait lies flat. When you've finished sewing, the plait should be secure, with no sign of the end of the tail.

Plaiting the mane

▼ **Practice makes perfect:** It takes an expert touch to produce a turn-out like this champion Polish Arab stallion at the Canberra Show in Australia.

When you go to a show, dressage competition or any special occasion, it adds to your confidence to know your pony is well turned out. Plaiting the mane neatly is an art that improves with practice, so you may need a few trial runs at home first.

Pulling the mane

It is virtually impossible to plait a mane or forelock in the traditional way if it is very long and thick. Before attempting to plait, you need to pull both the mane and forelock to about 10cm (4in) in length.

As the mane should always hang down to the right, stand on the off side of the pony. Start by brushing the pony's mane with the water brush. When it is tangle-free, take the mane comb and thoroughly comb the hair.

It is easiest to work down the neck from behind the pony's ears to his withers. Pull out the longest pieces of hair first. To get the correct amount of hair, hold a small amount in your left hand. With your mane comb in your right hand, push the comb up the hair toward the pony's crest, so that you are left with a few strands of hair in your hand.

Repeat the action, then wrap the remaining strands round the mane comb and pull downward firmly, or just tweak the hair out with your left hand. Pull the forelock in the same fashion as the mane.

If you are left-handed, reverse the instructions.

Getting ready

The mane should be clean before you plait it, so wash it with mild shampoo. Do this a few days before, as immediately after the wash the hair is more difficult to handle. Be careful not to get any water in the pony's ears or eyes.

Gather together the equipment you'll

! KEEP IT SHORT

It is easiest to pull the pony's mane after exercise when the pony is warm and his pores are open. Only pull a little at a time, or the pony becomes bored and sore and you get blisters.

Avoid the temptation to give up using your mane comb for a pair of thinning or ordinary scissors — your pony's mane will look terrible and be extremely difficult to plait.

How to pull the mane

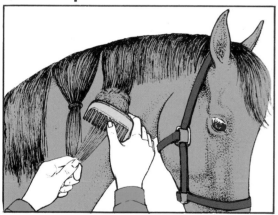

1 Take a small section of hair, hold it taut and push the mane comb up it.

2 Repeat, so you are left with fewer strands, and wrap the hair that's left round the comb.

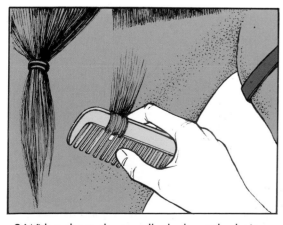

3 With a short, sharp pull, pluck out the hair.

► The mane should be an even 10cm (4in) in length.

HOW MANY PLAITS?

Use the mane comb to work out how many plaits you need. Hold it at the top of the mane, and turn it over and over down to the withers, counting one plait for each comb's width.

You should plait an odd number so, if you end on an even number, do one more or less. Flatter your pony's shape by making it one less if his neck is long and thin; one more if it is a bit stubby.

It is fashionable in some sports, notably show jumping, to do a large number of much smaller plaits.

★ THE FORELOCK

You plait the forelock slightly differently from the mane. Start off in the same way as you plait the tail — incorporating hair from either side as well as from the middle. This means you can pick up wispy pieces of hair that grow round the poll.

Work down until you come to the main part of the forelock, then plait as for the mane.

need: water brush, mane comb, plaiting or strong button thread or elastic bands (the colour of the mane and forelock), a bodkin-type needle, scissors and water. Cut about 150cm (5ft) of thread and thread the needle. Double it and tie a knot at the end. Pin the needle into your jacket so you don't lose it.

Use the mane comb to calculate how many plaits you are going to do. Hold the comb in your right hand, and place it at the top of the mane behind the ears. Turn the comb lengthwise down the crest, keeping a count of the number of times you do it as this is how many plaits you need. It is traditional to make an odd number of plaits, so you may need to take slightly less or more than a mane comb's width per plait.

How to plait

Beginning at the top of the pony's neck behind the ears, gather your comb's width of mane. Divide the hair into three equal parts and plait as you would do for a person. Make it as tight as

How to plait with needle and thread

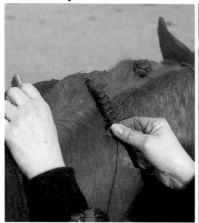

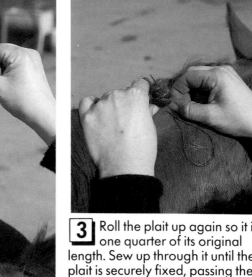

1 Plait as far down as you can. Sew up through the end of the plait several times, passing the needle to right and left alternately.

2 Fold the plait up and sew through the centre of it close to the crest.

3 Roll the plait up again so it is one quarter of its original length. Sew up through it until the plait is securely fixed, passing the needle from right to left as before. Fasten off on the underside.

If you are using elastic bands instead of thread, twist them round the plait at each stage. The band must be tightly stretched at the end to keep the plait secure.

Plaiting equipment:
Shampoo the mane about a week before. You need special horse shampoo, a sponge and water for washing, and plenty of clean water for rinsing. Dry the mane with a towel.

Before you plait, damp down the mane and brush it on to the off side and also comb it. To fasten the plaits, use a blunt needle and thread, or elastic bands.

warm rinsing water

warm soapy water

rubber bands

sponge

horse shampoo

needle and plaiting thread

water brush

possible without hurting the pony. Plait close to the neck, not out toward yourself, and go down as far as you can.

Take your needle and thread and sew through the end of the plait, wrap the thread round the hair and sew through it again to stop it unravelling. Fold the plait under so your knot can't be seen. Bring the needle up through the middle of the plait so it comes out on the top side. Fold the plait again and sew through it once more, so you have quartered the length of the plait.

Fasten it securely as if you are sewing on a button: pull the thread round one side of the plait and up the middle, then round the other side and up the middle, and so on. Finish with the needle facing down and cut off the remaining thread.

Continue until you have plaited all the mane. The plaits should lie as tight as possible to the neck and stay firm even if you tug them.

Instead of using a needle and thread you can use elastic bands. This is quick but the plaits may come undone.

UNRULY MANES

Some ponies' manes are so unruly that they won't stay on one side of the neck, let alone on the off side where they are meant to be!

Try dampening the mane well and plaiting it on the off side, but without rolling the plaits up. Leave them in for a couple of days.

When you unplait the mane it should stay on one side, even if it is a bit wavy. Keep brushing it regularly and dampening it with your water brush.

◄ **A well-plaited mane** creates a good impression with the judges.

An alternative – high plaits

▲ **Hold the hair upward** as you plait, secure the end as normal, then thread the plait through the hair near the roots.

▲ **Coil the plait** round the loop, and secure with elastic bands or thread. These plaits sit on top of the crest and give more height.

The finishing touches

If you are showing your pony, his presentation is as important as his manners and action. A smartly turned-out pony 'takes the judge's eye' and gives you a better chance of winning.

The day before

Wash and shampoo the pony the day before the show, particularly if he spends time in a field. Use a horse shampoo or mild soap, never a detergent.

Check that the chestnuts and ergots are not protruding too much. If they are, gently pick them back with your fingers. Sometimes the ergots need cutting back. If you are worried about doing this, your farrier will help and can do it with his pincers.

Clean the tack thoroughly. If you have a coloured browband, you can put

that on for show pony classes, but not for show hunter pony or working pony classes. Try to use a girth that is a similar colour to your pony: a white girth on a dark bay, black or chestnut spoils his outline.

In the morning

On the morning of the show, groom your pony thoroughly. Plait his mane, unless you are going in for a breed class that

has specific requirements for presentation. In general, show ponies have pulled, not plaited, tails.

When you dampen the mane and forelock, put a little baby oil in the water. This makes the hair shine and helps to keep in any unruly strands.

Wash and dry round your pony's eyes, nose, muzzle and dock – in that order – and put baby oil gently on these and on the chestnuts. Baby oil defines the head

▼ **When the time comes** to line up for the judge's inspection, the most impressive pony will be correctly presented and in the peak of health.

Putting on quarter marks

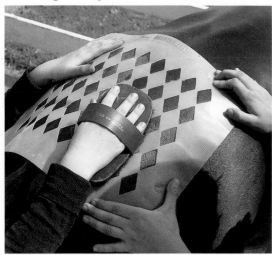

1 Damp the quarters and place the stencil on top. It's easier to stop it shifting if a friend helps to hold it firmly in position.

2 When you have brushed the hair downward, carefully lift off the stencil, taking care not to rub the marks as you do so.

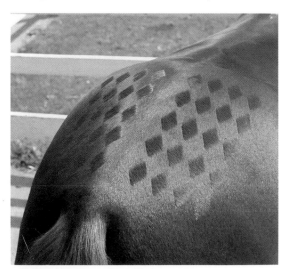

3 To keep the diamond pattern of marks in perfect formation, spray them with hair spray and don't touch them!

and makes it look prettier. You can use Vaseline or petroleum jelly instead of baby oil, but they sometimes become lumpy and don't give such a smooth finish.

If the pony has white socks, you can rub saddler's chalk on them to make them look even whiter.

Wipe the coat with the stable rubber, putting on coat polish (show gloss) if you have some. This makes the coat glow and keeps it free of dust.

The pony's feet should be smart, well-shod and perfectly clean. Put hoof oil on the underside of the hoof and on the outside. Be careful not to get any on his coronet band or hair.

Decorative patterns

When you have arrived at the show and taken your pony out of the box, go over the morning's finishing touches again.

You can now add quarter markings (a 'draught board' pattern of squares on the hindquarters) and shark's teeth (zigzags lower down the quarters), depending on what class you are entering the pony for.

For riding pony, best pony, leading-rein pony, hacks and riding horse classes, you can use both types of decoration. In show hunter pony and working pony classes just apply shark's teeth and maybe large blocks high up on the hindquarters.

Quarter markings

You can put quarter marks on with a comb or with a stencil. Practise at home until your work is perfect.

★ **WHITENING THE TAIL**
If your pony has a white tail, you may find the hairs at the end tend to go yellow. To make them gleaming white, try putting household fabric conditioner in the rinsing water when you wash the tail.

▲ **Rubbing chalk** on socks and feather — after washing them — makes them look as white as snow. You can buy chalk from a saddler.

Making quarter markings with a comb

Damp the coat and comb downward in alternate squares, starting each at the corner of the one above. The squares should all be the same size, and placed in the shape of a triangle pointing up or down.

168

In the comb method, buy a cheap plastic comb and break it to the size of square you want – the smaller the pony, the smaller the squares. Moisten the coat, and comb downward to make one square. From its bottom-left corner, comb downward again to make another square, then do the same from its bottom-right corner, and so on. Work in reverse if you prefer the point of the triangle facing down.

You can buy stencils with various sizes and styles of quarter marks. Damp the hair on the quarters with a flannel. Place the stencil on the quarter and brush the hair that shows through in a downward path. Remove the stencil.

To keep the quarter marks neat, spray them with hair spray. If your pony doesn't like the noise, use hair gel. In this case, damp the hair, put on the gel and smooth the hair in the correct direction *before* making the pattern.

Shark's teeth

Shark's teeth go on your pony's flanks and are made with a damp body brush. Stand behind the pony and brush triangles of hair toward you, against the grain. Work down to the thigh area, leaving intersecting diagonals of hair brushed with the grain, so you end with several 'teeth'. Use hair gel or spray as for quarter markings.

Remember that it is no use making these patterns unless your pony is fit and healthy with a naturally shiny coat.

Arab plaiting

An alternative to normal plaits is Arab plaiting, used on Arabs and on ponies with long manes such as palominos.

Brush the hair flat. Starting at the poll, divide the first mane comb's width of hair into three. Plait as normal, but add in a new strand from the left after every section of the plait. Make sure you keep the hair tight. When you reach the withers, sew up with thread.

◄ **Shark's teeth** and quarter markings are not merely a decoration: they improve the look and outline of the horse's quarters.

◄ **Quarter markings** complete the turn-out of a show pony that is glowing from health and thorough grooming.

169

The annual check up

You should always consult a vet if your pony becomes ill or lame. But you also need to call the vet in for routine procedures that keep the horse healthy and *prevent* disease.

A yearly visit

Your horse needs to be vaccinated against serious diseases such as tetanus and flu. He has booster vaccinations each year. The vet has to come to give your pony his injection, so it's a good time to make sure the horse is in tip-top shape all over.

The vet examines the pony's teeth thoroughly. He also studies the feet and skin to make sure there are no lumps or bumps or other problems.

An annual check up gives someone else – who hasn't seen the pony for a while – the chance to have a good look at him. Sometimes it's easier for another person to notice signs of, for example, stiffness or loss of condition, than for the person who sees the animal every day.

◄ **The vet feels the pony's legs** for any heat, lumps or swellings that may indicate splints or tendon trouble.

Making a note

A yearly visit is also the ideal time to ask the vet's advice on any aspects of your pony's health that are worrying you. These might include his body condition, feed, worming programme, the state of his feet or any shoeing problems. Similarly, if you have found any specific trouble areas, such as a skin growth or irritation, now is the time to ask the vet about it.

Sometimes you only remember what you wanted to ask just after the vet has driven away! So it is a sensible precaution to make a list of questions on a piece of paper beforehand. Then nothing gets forgotten.

Before the check up

Any time of year is suitable for the check up. However, you shouldn't work your pony hard for four or five days after a vaccination, in case he has side effects such as a stiff neck.

There are no specific preparations to make before the vet arrives. However, although he will be happy to spend time checking over the horse and answering your questions – he will not be happy to waste time waiting around while you

VACCINATION CERTIFICATES

Many authorities who organize equestrian events have made flu vaccinations compulsory for all horses entering their events. You need a vaccination certificate, on which the horse is identified and the date when boosters have been given is recorded.

Boosters given at the wrong interval can not only make the horse ineligible to compete, but could also prove expensive – as the vaccination programme may have to be started all over again.

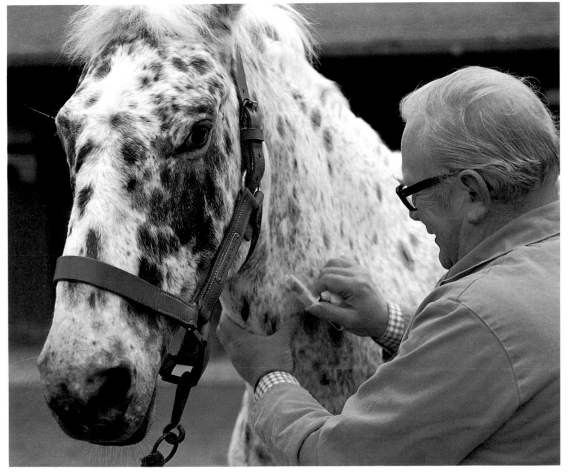

◄ **Combined flu and tetanus vaccines** are available. Giving your horse a dose against both diseases forms the most essential part of the annual check up.

catch the pony, or to examine a horse that's covered in mud.

Catch a grass-kept pony an hour or so before the appointment. Give him a thorough grooming and pick out his feet. While you do so, study his skin, feet and legs yourself – then you can ask the vet about them if need be.

It's tricky to examine a horse's mouth if he has recently been eating. Keep him away from grass and hay, and give him his feed, at least an hour beforehand.

Tetanus vaccination

This is a major part of the annual check up. Vaccination – against the serious disease tetanus particularly – is one of the most important contributions you can make toward keeping your pony healthy.

Horses can easily pick up tetanus when wounds become contaminated with the tetanus organism which lives in the soil. Horses are particularly at risk because this organism sometimes lives inside their bowels. If the bowel wall becomes damaged in any way, the organism within the gut could enter the horse's body and cause tetanus.

The horse should be permanently vaccinated against tetanus. This means two initial injections of tetanus vaccine a month apart, and a booster one year later. Afterwards, the pony needs a booster at least every two to three years.

A pony that's not permanently vaccinated needs an injection of tetanus antitoxin *every* time he receives a cut or a puncture wound (such as when a shoe nail from a loose shoe punctures the foot). The tetanus antitoxin works immediately, but its protection *only* lasts for three to four weeks.

Equine flu

This is another nasty disease which spreads rapidly from horse to horse in epidemics. It can also give the pony a nasty cough which lasts for several months.

The horse needs two primary vaccinations 21 days to 92 days apart, and a booster six months later. Afterwards, boosters must be given regularly every year.

The teeth

The second most important annual task is to check your pony's teeth. Ideally, the horse's upper and lower cheek teeth

▲ **The vet** listens to the pony's heart beat with a stethoscope.

► **He studies the eyes** to make sure there are no cataracts or other disorders that affect the pony's sight.

▼ **He may do a 'spavin test':** He holds the leg up high and then watches the pony being trotted away. Any stiffness or lameness shows up immediately.

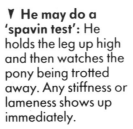

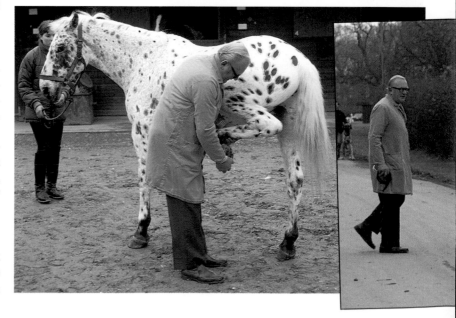

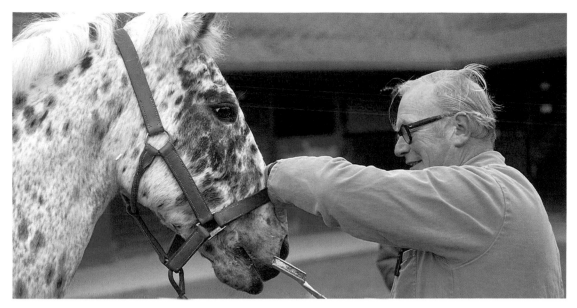

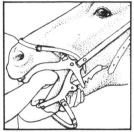

USING A GAG
Usually, a headcollar is enough to restrain the pony when the vet rasps the teeth.

Sometimes, however, he may insert a metal instrument known as a 'gag' into the horse's mouth to hold the jaws open. This helps him to get a better look at the back teeth. A 'gag' is also helpful for ponies that try to bite the rasp.

(molars and premolars) should meet exactly, and should be worn evenly by the constant grinding action of the jaw.

In practice, the upper teeth usually lie slightly outside those in the lower jaw. This means that the inner edge of the upper teeth, and the outer edge of the lower teeth, tend to be worn more. The unworn outer edges of the upper teeth remain sharp and cut the cheeks, while the unworn inner edges of the lower teeth cut the tongue.

You must have your pony's teeth checked once a year to make sure that they are not sharp or worn irregularly. The vet can rasp off any sharp points and level the grinding surface of the teeth. This prevents a cut tongue or cheeks, and enables the pony to grind his food properly.

If he can't chew his food thoroughly, it passes through his system only partly digested or just drops out of his mouth. To absorb nutrients, your pony must be able to digest his food normally.

Old and young teeth

Young horses lose their temporary (milk) teeth between two and four years of age. The new permanent teeth can be sharp, and you may need to have them looked at more often – every six months – during this period.

Older horses, too, often have irregular teeth which don't meet properly. The teeth may have become loose, or even be missing. In this case, the tooth opposite the missing one is not worn down. It becomes long and sharp and may cut the pony's mouth. So more frequent attention is also required to keep older horses' teeth in good shape. Animals of this age (20 years and over) may need their teeth checked over at least twice a year.

▼ **Routine health** procedures can get overlooked. Why not keep a calendar in the tack room, specially as a health planner for your pony?

Trotting the pony up

OCTOBER

Annual check up vet 10 a.m.

M	3	⑩	17	24	31
T	4	11	18	25	
W	5	12	19	26	
T	6	13	20	27	
F	⑦	14	21	28	
S	1	8	15	22	㉙
S	2	9	16	23	30

Farrier 11 a.m.　　　　Worming

Worms and worming

▼ Ponies at grass must be wormed about every six weeks. You must dose ponies in the same field at the same time to have any effect. Be doubly sure to worm frequently in early and mid-summer, when the immature worms are most active.

Ask your vet how big a dose to give — and how often: the amount must be worked out by the pony's body weight and not by his height.

In the wild, horses graze over large areas and are rarely troubled by worms. Worms are a problem we have inflicted on horses by domesticating them and confining them to small areas of grazing. Regular worm treatment is probably the most important contribution you can make to keeping your pony healthy.

Why treat for worms?

The worms that live inside all horses are parasites — they feed off the tissues of other animals. Although it's difficult — if not impossible — to wipe out worm infection altogether, you can go a long way toward reducing the health problems that worms cause.

Treating your pony regularly (every six weeks) for worms has two benefits. You improve the horse's health by ridding him of harmful adult worms, and possibly immature worms (larvae) too (depending on which wormer you use). Equally important, you reduce the pasture contamination — lessening the risk of further infection to your pony and to others sharing the field.

Giving a worm medicine forms only part of a worm-control programme. Horses also have their own built-in worm defence mechanism — they are reluctant to eat grass near their drop-

176

pings (which contains most larvae).

Forcing them to do so, by over-grazing or keeping too many ponies on the same piece of ground, can have serious health consequences. Resting the grazing, picking up droppings at least once a week, and grazing with other farm stock (which eat horse worms but are not affected by them), all help reduce the risk to horses.

How to treat for worms

Worm treatments come in the form of powders or granules given in the food, or as pastes squirted into the horse's mouth. You can buy them from your vet or saddler.

You can give them yourself – there's no need to call the vet. Only in a few cases, where the horse is ill because of worm damage, may the vet have to give a more powerful drug, or larger doses of a suitable drug, by stomach tube.

Ponies are very clever at detecting 'doctored' food, so it's worth trying to disguise the taste of a wormer. Mix it with a small amount of bran mash, or add a sweetener like molasses. Most ponies also like bread. Sandwiching a powder between two slices often works.

Worm pastes, in a ready-loaded syringe, make sure the pony receives a full dose. Take trouble to give it properly, or the horse may spit it out.

How to give a worm paste

1 If you are right handed, it is much easier to give the paste from the pony's right (off) side. If you're left handed, reverse the sides. Put a headcollar on your pony and ask a friend to stand by the left (near) shoulder and hold him. Make sure the pony has no food in his mouth.

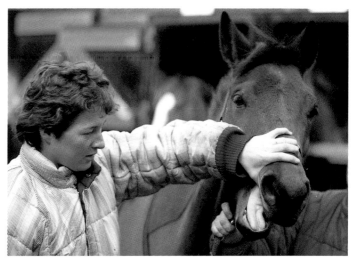

2 Hold the tube in your right hand. To open the pony's mouth, put your left hand on the bridge of his nose, just above the nostrils. Push your left thumb under the lip into the space behind the front teeth, and press the tip of your thumb against the roof of the mouth.

3 Keep your left hand in place and insert the tip of the tube to the back of the horse's mouth with your right hand. Squirt the contents on to the back of the tongue.

4 Withdraw the syringe quickly and close the mouth. Lift the pony's head in the air by holding a hand under his lower jaw. Wait until the pony swallows.

The different worms

There are many different varieties of worms that damage horses, and some are more serious than others. Most of them affect the digestive system, so the horse can't get enough nourishment to keep him healthy.

It's hard to identify which worms your horse is suffering from by his symptoms, so ask your vet which wormer he thinks is most suitable. The newer types kill worms at all stages of development.

Strongyloides attack the small intestine. They are only a problem in foals and yearlings and, in very young foals, may cause enteritis (inflamed intestines).

Roundworms, like strongyloides, mainly affect the small intestines of foals. They can have serious effects, including coughing and enteritis.

Bots are the larvae of the *Gastrophilus* fly. They affect the stomach and, in large numbers, can cause gastric ulcers.

Hairworms attack the stomach, resulting in a general loss of condition.

Pinworms (sometimes called seatworms) affect the large intestine. They irritate the rectum and the horse will seem to have an itchy tail.

Small redworms live in the large intestine and can cause severe disease. Grazing horses can pick up huge numbers of these parasites if not regularly wormed. The horse may have a pot belly, dull coat, anaemia, diarrhoea or colic.

Large redworms: Adult worms live in the large intestine, but the migrating larvae damage the horse's internal organs. Blood vessels supplying the bowels are most often affected. Large redworms are the commonest cause of colic.

small intestine   right kidney   spleen   stomach

Tapeworms are rare but can affect the large intestine, giving the horse colic.

large intestine   liver

Lungworms, as their name suggests, affect the lungs and make horses cough. They are often acquired from donkeys.

ungs

Threadworms affect the neck, causing skin sores and a stiff neck.

heart

Life cycle of the large redworm

The large redworm (called in Latin *Strongylus vulgaris*) is the most damaging of all. Its total life cycle takes between eight and 11 months.

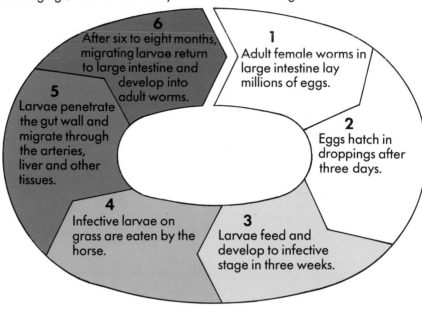

6 After six to eight months, migrating larvae return to large intestine and develop into adult worms.

5 Larvae penetrate the gut wall and migrate through the arteries, liver and other tissues.

1 Adult female worms in large intestine lay millions of eggs.

2 Eggs hatch in droppings after three days.

4 Infective larvae on grass are eaten by the horse.

3 Larvae feed and develop to infective stage in three weeks.

How horses are infected

Adult female worms living in the horse's intestines lay large numbers of eggs which are passed out in the droppings. In the warmth of the droppings, these eggs hatch to release tiny larvae which are too small to be seen with the naked eye. These move by wriggling, leaving the droppings to seek the moisture on the surface of the grass.

Within three to four weeks they develop into 'infective' larvae. These are swallowed by the horse. What then happens to the larvae depends on the species of worm. Some develop inside the wall of the bowel; others migrate through different organs.

Most adult horse worms live in the digestive system of their host, where they either suck blood, or live off digestive juices. The damage they do stops the horse being able to absorb nutrients from his food properly. Some worms penetrate the lining of the intestines, enter other internal organs and damage them. In large numbers, they can rupture the intestines.

Although horses acquire worms when they are grazing, the parasites can live inside the pony's body for several years and may not all be killed by worm treatment. Even horses that have been stabled for two or three years continually, with no access to grazing, may still have a few worms – in spite of being regularly treated.

WHAT THE LARGE REDWORM DOES

Large redworm larvae are particularly attracted to the blood vessels which supply the horse's bowels and intestines. The damage they cause in these vessels often severely affects the blood supply to the gut.

Over 90% of cases of colic are probably due to the effects of past or present infection with this particular parasite.

! WHEN TO WORM

If you have a new pony, worm him 24 hours before turning him out. A horse that is stabled through the winter should be wormed when he first comes in, and again when he goes out in the spring.

But if a pony is turned out to graze for part of the day, he will need worming at more frequent intervals – every six to eight weeks – even in winter.

Types of colic

To prevent colic – abdominal pain – you should worm regularly, feed top-quality food, and not let your pony become so hungry that he gorges himself. Colic, however, has a number of causes and, if you suspect your pony is suffering from this distressing condition, you should ring the vet immediately, whatever time of day or night.

Types of colic

Some types of colic are more serious than others but the symptoms are simi-

lar – the pony looks fretfully at his sides, perhaps trying to bite at them. He paws the ground, maybe groaning, and patchy sweating breaks out. He rolls repeatedly, but without shaking when he gets up (which ponies do when healthy). In very painful cases the pony may throw himself around the box.

The first action the vet takes is to decide what might be the cause.

Spasmodic colic is the most common form. This is caused by a spasm (contraction) of the bowel or by over-active movements of the bowel. If you give

▼ **Rolling** is generally a healthy sign. But a pony who keeps rolling, and doesn't shake himself when he gets up, may have colic – particularly if he shows other symptoms of distress.

unsuitable food, allow your horse to over-eat, or give cold water without taking the chill off it, this type of colic may develop.

Flatulent colic is due to a build up of gas in the bowel and is particularly common after eating foods which produce large amounts of gas by fermenting in the bowel. Too much of the wrong kinds of concentrates, particularly sugar beet pulp, may cause this kind of colic.

Impaction occurs when material which the horse cannot digest collects and blocks the bowel. It usually develops more slowly than other types of colic, often taking several days. Foods which have a very high content of woody material, or badly prepared foods containing sand or grit, may cause this condition.

Obstruction happens when the bowel becomes twisted on itself (called torsion or volvulus), telescopes into itself (intussusception), or something similar happens.

Obstruction may follow on from other types of colic, or from other diseases, or

► **Prevention** is much better than cure. Feed your pony little and often and make any changes in his diet *gradual.* An incorrect feeding regime is one of the major causes of colic.

▼ **A thirsty,** hot horse should be offered water with the chill taken off. Never work a horse hard immediately after he has had a long drink.

may develop by itself. This is a very serious type of colic and surgery is often necessary. In a few cases the damage to the bowel may be so great that surgery cannot save the horse.

Thromboembolism is one of the most complicated causes of colic. It is caused by worm larvae which have found their way into the blood vessels of the bowel. The larvae cause damage to the walls of the blood vessels, and blood clots develop which block the supply of blood. This results in severe damage to a section of bowel.

Treatment of this condition with drugs is often unsuccessful and the damage may well be too great for surgery to be possible. But prevention is easy – worm your pony regularly to ensure that this type of colic is very rare.

There are also cases of colic where no cause for the pain can be found.

Diagnosis and treatment

As soon as you have called the vet, think carefully about your horse's behaviour,

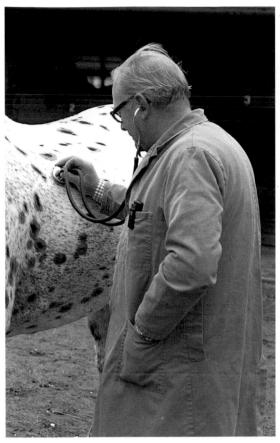

▲ **The vet** may listen to the horse's stomach to help him find the cause of colic.

► **Taking a blood** sample is another method the vet uses to make his diagnosis.

▲ **A tube** is passed down the nostril to the stomach. The vet uses it to put back fluids the horse may have lost through dehydration.

▼ **An injection** of antibiotics can speed up the horse's recovery.

feeding and dunging over the last few days. The vet needs as much information as possible to help diagnosis.

He also examines the horse, maybe taking blood or fluid samples from the belly to find the answers. The vet may pass a tube down the nostril to the stomach, or examine the rectum.

The diagnosis depends to some extent on the response to the first stages of treatment. Early treatment usually consists of the vet injecting a pain killer either into the horse's muscles or directly into the bloodstream, using the jugular vein (the main vein in the neck). He may also give sedatives or antibiotics.

He uses the same methods to pass fluids into the body, as the horse may have become dehydrated. If the vet suspects impaction, he may also use a stomach tube to administer a laxative.

It is important that the vet can decide which sort of colic the pony has as soon as possible. If surgery is needed, the sooner the decision to operate on the pony is made, the better the chance of success.

All about laminitis

Laminitis is one of the commonest causes of lameness in ponies. The disease occurs when things go wrong within the structure of the hoof – and it's very painful.

★ **WHAT HAPPENS?**

In the hoof, 'sensitive' laminae (which have nerves) interlace with a second set of 'insensitive' laminae (with no nerve supply).

In laminitis, the blood flow to the sensitive laminae changes. This alters their blood supply, depriving the laminae cells of oxygen, and they then die.

★ **RARER CAUSES**

Occasionally, laminitis can be a complication to an infection or disease elsewhere in the body, such as a pituitary tumour. It could even be an unwelcome side-effect when drugs, such as cortisone, are used to treat the horse.

Laminitis can also be a result of poor foot dressing – maybe from bad shoeing – allowing a long toe conformation.

What is laminitis?

Laminitis literally means an inflammation of the sensitive laminae within a horse's foot. The hoof becomes loosened from its attachment to the rest of the foot and, worse, the whole weight of the animal presses down on the sore area.

There is no human equivalent to laminitis, so it is hard for us to realize just how painful this disease is for a pony. However, think how sore a damaged fingernail can be when you knock it. Then imagine what it would be like if you had to support your bodyweight by balancing on sore fingernails!

What causes the disease?

Laminitis cannot be caught from other horses, and it rarely happens because of any foot problem. It develops because of toxins (poisons) released elsewhere in the horse's body which affect the circulation in its feet. There are several possible sources of toxins, but by far the most frequent is the bowels – where poisons originate because of feeding too much protein.

Many pony breeds have changed little over thousands of years. Their digestive systems evolved to deal with a sparse supply of a relatively coarse and indigestible material – grass. Ponies are not designed to cope with large amounts of lush protein-rich spring grass or concentrates.

Larger horses have been much more selectively bred by man, not only for their size, but to grow quickly and mature early. They can cope much better with a richer food supply.

So the commonest cause of laminitis is turning ponies out in lush grazing during late spring and early summer, particularly if the ground has been treated with fertilizer. Laminitis can strike at other times of the year, too, if you feed your pony too many rich concentrates for any length of time. It could also occur if your pony broke into the feed-store and gorged himself!

What are the signs?

Laminitis affects both front feet, and may well affect all four hooves. The pony is in severe pain and usually refuses to stand up or walk.

If he does stand, it is in a peculiar way – with his hindlegs well under his body to support its weight and with the front feet forward to leave as much weight on the heels as possible. When he has to move, it is with a pottering action, walking on his heels. The feet feel warm to the touch and the pony looks very sorry for himself.

He probably also has a temperature and a bounding pulse in the digital artery at the back of the pastern.

A pony who has had laminitis for a

long time is likely to have abnormal hooves – a 'dropped' sole from the bone pressing down, and laminitic rings because of differing hoof growth (a lot of heel growth and very little horn at the toe). The hoof wall may separate from the sole at the toe, with rotten horn in between – called 'seedy toe'.

Treating laminitis

You must call in the vet to treat the pony without delay, before foot changes go too far.

First, he will advise you to remove the cause of the trouble. This usually means taking the pony away from his grazing. It may also involve cutting out the concentrate ration, and feeding hay and water only.

Second, he will give a pain-killing injection as soon as possible. This works immediately, and he normally leaves more powders (to be given in the feed) to continue pain relief for several days.

Applying water from a hose or standing the feet in a running stream also helps, although hot water may be better to improve the circulation.

You need to relieve the pain so the animal can walk – which stimulates the

▼ **Horses** are much less likely to get laminitis than ponies because they have been carefully bred by humans and can cope with richer food.

▲ **Hosing down** the legs can bring some relief to laminitis sufferers. However, some vets believe that warm water is better than cold because it improves the circulation.

circulation in the feet. The pain becomes less as the pony moves. About 10 minutes of leading at a walk, six times a day, should be enough.

Longer-term treatment
With long-term laminitis, you'll need both the vet and the farrier to correct hoof problems.

They have to remove any long or rotten horn at the toe to restore a more normal foot shape. Sometimes they have to cut away large amounts of the hoof wall at the front to allow healthy horn to grow down in its place.

The vet may take an X-ray to see how the foot can best be re-shaped. He may put on a special shoe to provide support and stop the bone moving downward.

Any horse that has suffered an attack of laminitis must be given a suitable vitamin, mineral and amino-acid feed supplement afterwards. This stimulates a good growth of new and healthy horn to replace the old, crumbling layers.

Preventing the disease
Ponies in general are prone to laminitis, and some individuals are highly susceptible. But in nearly every case, laminitis can be prevented with a little care and forethought.

This means never over-feeding your pony with concentrates. And don't let him on to lush grazing in early summer. If your pony gets fat on very little, be extra careful and try to keep his weight down. Laminitis is always worse in ponies that are overweight.

Some ponies may get laminitis even when on relatively poor grazing. In this case, you must remove the animal from grazing altogether during the summer months and just feed him on hay and water. Try to keep the pony in a large yard where he can move about, rather then confining him to a stable for long periods of time.

You must always be aware of the danger of laminitis and seek help the moment you notice any suspicious signs.

Characteristic posture

A horse with a severe attack of laminitis appears rooted to the spot and is unwilling to move. The hindfeet are tucked under the body to take the weight off the forelegs. The forelegs are extended forward to keep the weight on the heels.

The condition is very painful and the horse may appear to be in distress.

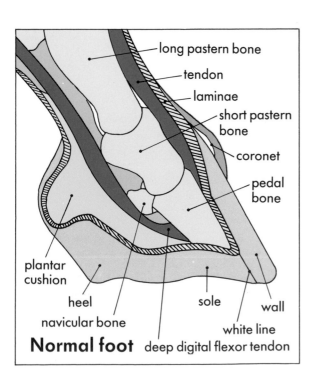

- long pastern bone
- tendon
- laminae
- short pastern bone
- coronet
- pedal bone
- plantar cushion
- heel
- navicular bone
- sole
- wall
- white line
- deep digital flexor tendon

Normal foot

Golden rules – laminitis do's and don'ts

DO always look for signs of laminitis when you check your horse each day. If he is reluctant to get up or move, feel his front feet for signs of heat.

DO call the vet without delay if you suspect your pony may be developing laminitis.

DO be extra careful if you know your pony has ever had laminitis before. He is likely to get it again.

DO be sure to bolt the feed-store door so that it is impossible for a pony to break in and gorge himself.

DO get a farrier to attend to your pony's feet regularly and keep shoes on him all the time if he suffers from chronic laminitis.

DO ask your vet to recommend a suitable mineral, vitamin and amino-acid feed supplement if your pony has hoof problems from chronic laminitis, or has recently sufffered an attack. The supplement stimulates new growth of healthy hoof horn.

DON'T turn ponies out into lush grazing in spring and early summer.

DON'T treat grazing used by ponies with nitrogen fertilizers.

DON'T let your pony get fat. Laminitis is always more of a problem in overweight horses.

DON'T over-feed your pony on concentrates at any time of the year.

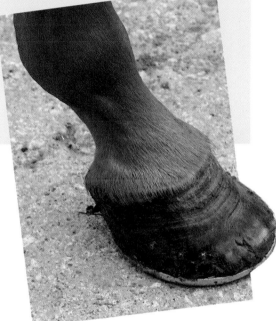

▲ Signs of laminitis are long toes, flat soles and worn heels. Because the toes have little wear, the horn there hardly grows at all, while the heels keep producing it. This unevenness causes 'rings' around the hoof wall.

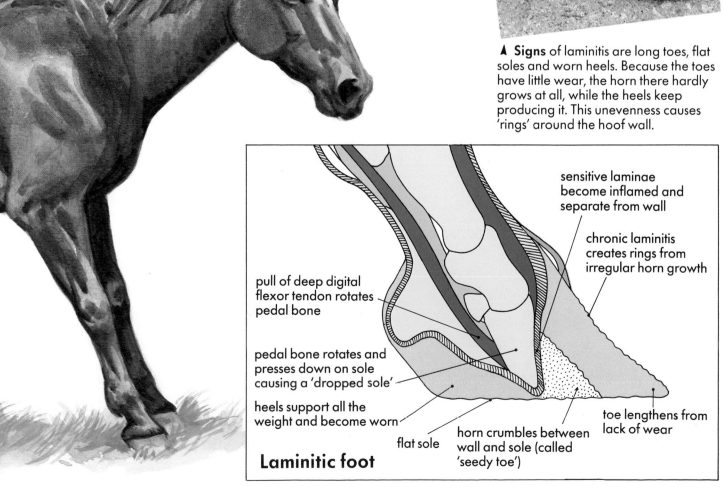

sensitive laminae become inflamed and separate from wall

chronic laminitis creates rings from irregular horn growth

pull of deep digital flexor tendon rotates pedal bone

pedal bone rotates and presses down on sole causing a 'dropped sole'

heels support all the weight and become worn

flat sole

horn crumbles between wall and sole (called 'seedy toe')

toe lengthens from lack of wear

Laminitic foot

Strains and splints

Pushing your horse on over stony ground, and particularly down hills, can be a cause of strains. Always make sure your horse is properly warmed up before strenuous exercise.

As a horse is an athlete, injury to the legs is very common. Working a pony too hard when he is not properly fit can lead to problems and lameness.

The tendons

Strains happen when the horse's movement is at its most strenuous. If you make a horse gallop when he is unfit or force him on in heavy going, or when he's tired, the muscles can no longer use their elasticity to cushion the shock.

The shock is then thrown upon the tendons. As these have very little elasticity – unlike the rubbery muscles – they strain or even rupture. The foreleg muscles take the most weight and are more quickly fatigued than the larger ones in the hindlegs, so strains occur most frequently in the front legs.

They are also more likely to affect the *flexor* tendons which are responsible for lifting the leg off the ground. The *extensor* tendons carry the leg forward after it has left the ground. They have less work to do and so take less strain.

The best way to prevent your horse from straining his legs is never to gallop him when he's unfit, and never to push him on when he is tired.

Treating a strain

Once a tendon has become stretched beyond its limit – strained – the horse is usually lame with considerable swelling and pain if you press the area. In severe cases the back tendon area 'bows' outward. Call the vet as surgical treatment may be necessary.

Luckily, lameness because of tendon trouble is not usually so severe – the severity depends on the number of fibres ruptured. But even with mild strains, rest the horse in a stable, bandage the leg and call the vet.

The ligaments

Strains can occur to the ligaments. Ligaments hold the bones together and are made of fibres like tendons, but they are even less elastic.

Shock from fast work on hard ground or general overwork in an old horse can produce strains. If the horse slips and the legs splay outward at an unnatural angle this may well wrench a ligament.

Try *not* to work your horse at swift paces on hard, stony surfaces. As he gets older, reduce his jumping work.

▲ **Racehorses** are prone to leg injuries, and working over heavy going doesn't help. To cut down the risk of strains and splints, they are trained gradually to a peak of fitness – like all athletes.

★ STRAIN OR SPRAIN?
You may hear the word 'sprain' used instead of 'strain'. Strictly speaking, however, a strain describes *stretching* which causes injury, while a sprain describes an injury caused by a *knock or compression*.

► **Jumping,**
particularly landing,
puts great stress on
the horse's forelegs.

▲ **If you suspect**
your horse is lame,
call the vet. He will
diagnose the cause by
feeling the legs for
swelling, splints or
other problems.

Tendons and muscles

The tendons connect
the muscles to the
bones in the leg.
Imagine the muscles in
the upper leg as large
rubber straps and the
tendons below them
as wires.

When the muscles
contract, they pull the
tendon 'wires' up. As
these are attached to
the bones in the hoof,
the foot is pulled off
the ground and
forward.

But, if the 'wiry'
tendons are over-
stretched, they
become strained —
the fibres tear apart.

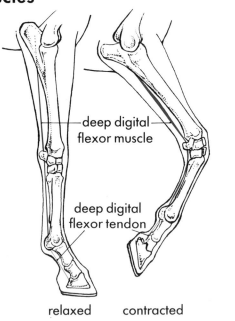

deep digital
flexor muscle

deep digital
flexor tendon

relaxed   contracted

Resting

All 'cures' depend on helping the body's
natural mechanism for repair of damaged tissue. Rest is the most important
factor in healing any injury. It lets the
body right itself naturally. However,
most horses need gentle exercise after a
few days – walking for short periods
several times a day – to pump away
unwanted fluid from the injury. Ask
your vet for advice.

After the pain and swelling have gone
down, you can turn the horse out into a
small, level paddock where he cannot
gallop about. Do not return him to hard
work too soon but bring him back to
fitness in easy stages. Strains can take
up to 18 months to heal.

Splints

A splint is a layman's term for a firm
swelling found on the splint bone where

it connects to the cannon bone. Splints mostly occur in the foreleg – you can feel a hard lump on the inside of the leg. If they occur in the hindleg, they are generally on the *outside*.

There are two splint bones: one on either side of the cannon bone in each leg. They are held to the cannon bone by ligaments. In young horses these ligaments may become inflamed.

After the age of four the splint bones are fused to the cannon bone. Splints occur as a result of concussion (shock), for example, when an immature horse is given excessive work on hard ground. Faulty shoeing can also be a factor as it throws an uneven strain on the leg.

The swelling can be any size. The horse may or may not be lame, depending on the position of the swelling and the extent of the injury.

When they are forming, splints feel spongy with some heat and are painful when pressed. To examine for splints, lift the leg and run your finger and thumb along the groove at the back of the cannon. Do not mistake the nodules at the lower end for splints as there are natural 'buttons' at the bottom of the splint bone.

Rest and reduced work is all that is generally needed with a young animal. With a mature horse, splints that feel cool and are not high up do not cause lameness and don't much matter. Call the vet to make sure there is not a fracture of the splint bone.

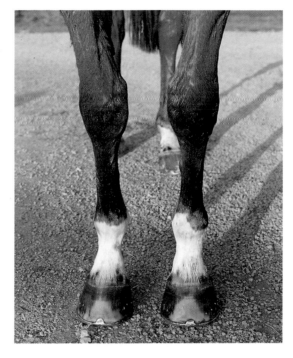

How to tell if a horse is lame

Most lameness occurs below the knee of the foreleg and from the hock down in the hindleg. A lame horse is one that does not move freely, or moves with an unnatural gait. He may step 'short' at the walk, so that the front legs look as if they are pottering. Or the hindlegs may not 'track up' – one doesn't reach as far forward as its opposite number.

At the trot, a lame horse 'drops' on one side and throws up his head as the lame front leg comes to the ground. If it is a hindleg that is lame, the quarters are carried higher on one side.

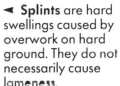

◄ **Splints** are hard swellings caused by overwork on hard ground. They do not necessarily cause lameness.

❗ **RACEHORSE WARNING**
'Breakdowns' in the lower legs of young racehorses are fairly common. This is partly due to the fact that these horses are made to work too hard for their immature physique.

If you have any part in the care of a horse under the age of four or five, take care to bring him on slowly. Have the vet check that the joints, ligaments and tendons can stand up to it before you ask the horse to perform really strenuous work. Then he will have much less trouble from sprains and splints.

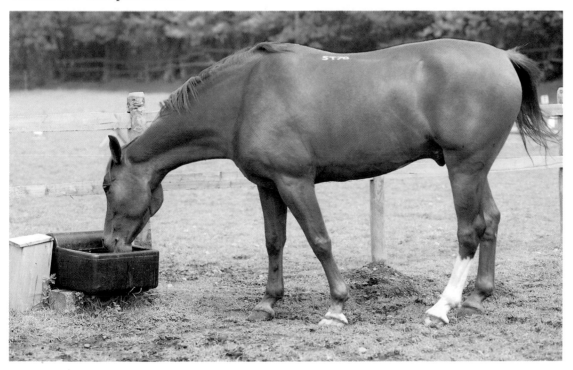

◄ **Rest cures:** Horses recovering from lameness should be confined to a small paddock so that they cannot gallop about.

Treating cuts and bruises

One of the reasons for checking a pony at least once a day is to look for wounds. Even small cuts need treatment and, if you find one, you should apply first aid.

Types of wounds

How you reduce risk of injury and treat a horse wound depends on what type it is.

Clean-cut (incised) wounds are straight edged. They are usually clean with no surrounding tissue damage or bruising. However, they may cut into joints such as tendons and so can be serious. Make sure you clear sharp objects like glass from the box, yard or paddock. When setting up practice fences, check the ground around them as the pony is most likely to fall while jumping.

Torn (lacerated) wounds: The skin is torn apart, leaving irregular edges. The muscles underneath may be damaged or torn, depending on where your pony is

◄ **Cross-country jumps:** Protect the pony's legs in case he hits one of the fences. Check him over carefully afterwards for cuts, bruises or splinters of wood.

wounded and how fast he or the object was travelling at the time.

Barbed wire is the most likely cause. A startled pony can run into the fence and the wire tangles around his legs. As the pony pulls the wire tightens, and the barbs tear the flesh, causing deep and serious wounds. Any type of wire fence can be dangerous, so use wooden railing if possible.

Puncture wounds are caused by an object like a nail driving through the skin and passing into the body. They can be very misleading. A tiny wound can look like nothing but, if caused by a fork prong, there may be a lot of damage under the skin. Worse, a wooden object could leave splinters inside the wound. Always mend broken fencing immediately. Never take your pony through a narrow gap where twigs or other pointed objects protrude. Put your fork away safely – don't leave it lying around the yard.

Bruised wounds (contusions): The force of the blow breaks the skin and bruises the tissue underneath, causing swelling under the skin. The legs are most commonly affected – the pony may bruise himself by overreaching or brushing, or by kicking a jump or crashing over it. Boots or exercise bandages help protect the pony's legs while jumping.

Treatment

Wounds are usually quite easy to see, except for small punctures. Always check your pony every day so you are familiar with how he looks and feels normally. Then, when a small wound occurs, you notice the swelling or small patch of blood. Finding the wound early means you can treat it promptly and the pony recovers quickly.

First you must stop the bleeding. Press firmly on the wound with a clean cloth or wad of cotton wool. If the wound is on the leg, wrap a crêpe bandage fairly tightly over the cotton wool to keep the pressure on. You can apply a simple circular bandage to most areas but a figure-of-eight bandage over fetlock, knee and hock joints gives better contact. If you can't stop the bleeding, call the vet.

Once the bleeding has stopped, the wound needs a good wash with antiseptic and water. Remove all the grit and mud, but try not to disturb the clots as the wound may start bleeding again. A clean-cut wound with little bruising or complications is best left uncovered. The dry air helps form a clean scar quickly, and the cut heals rapidly.

However, all lower leg wounds should be bandaged to prevent further contami-

> ► **Exercise bandages,** which run from just below the hocks or knees to just above the fetlocks, guard the legs from jumping injuries.

▲ **Glass:** Sharp edges cause 'clean-cut' wounds which can be severe if on a joint. Broken glass may be left inside the wound and is hard to see.

▲ **Wire** can cause tear wounds if the pony panics and gets tangled up in it. Barbed wire is most dangerous.

▲ **Sharp prongs** puncture the skin, leaving deep wounds that can result in serious infection. Never leave pitchforks lying around.

HOCKS
AND KNEES
Normally if your pony has a cut or graze which needs bandaging, you can put on a crêpe or self-adhesive bandage over a non-stick dressing. But with hocks, knees and fetlocks, the bandage has to be flexible enough to let the pony move.

You can either buy special contour bandages, which are stretchy and fasten with zips, or put on an exercise bandage in the shape of a figure of eight.

nation. And any wound that is getting dirty should be covered with a piece of Melolin or paraffin gauze under a bandage. Change the bandage daily and check for weeping from the wound. If yellow discharges of pus, excessive swelling or lameness appear call the vet before they get worse.

Large clean-cut and torn wounds may need stitching to repair the damaged tissue underneath. Puncture wounds and large ones are best treated with antibiotic, both topically (on the wound) and systemically (injected). Bruised wounds, particularly if they are very swollen, need cold compresses to stop haemorrhage for the first hour. Then Lasonil ointment should be applied.

Finally, don't panic. If you are unsure of what to do, call the vet.

Putting on a figure-of-eight bandage

1 Cut gamgee to fit the area around the hock and place it around the leg — not too tightly or you restrict the pony's movement. Wrap the bandage round once above the hock.

2 Pass the bandage down in a diagonal round the front of the hock, and wrap it round the leg. Do another diagonal turn to above the hock and repeat until secure.

▲ **Get expert help** especially with lower leg wounds which must always be bandaged.

3 When you reach the end of the bandage, pull the tapes apart so that they are straight and flat. Wind them round the leg and tie them on the outside in a bow.

4 Tuck the tapes in so they don't get in the way. There should be no pressure on any part of the joint and no bandage around the point of the hock or the pony can't move.

The medicine chest

It is essential for all horse owners to have at least a basic first-aid kit in case of accidents and emergencies.

Most items are readily available from good chemists. Otherwise your vet can advise you on what to buy and where to get it from.

The basic kit

The first thing you need is a container. Use a clean box, cupboard or drawer for storing the first-aid items. Keep it in the house or tack room. A portable box or strong bag is also useful for taking a kit to shows. Your medicine chest should contain the following:

A mild antiseptic solution for bathing wounds.

Antiseptic or antibiotic cream to ward off infection.

Moist pads for cleaning wounds, when clean water is not available.

Melolin non-adhesive dressing pads.

A small clean bucket kept only for bathing wounds.

Some kind of poultice dressing such as 'Animalintex'. A poultice is applied to a wound either to draw 'poison' from an abscess, or to reduce swelling – on a sprained tendon for example. Another

product that you can use for this purpose is Kaolin.

Gamgee tissue for bathing wounds and for padding and protecting them under bandages. Gamgee is cotton wool covered with gauze to stop 'fluff' sticking to wounds.

Clean elasticated bandages for keeping dressings in place. Crêpe exercise bandages are effective. Keep two clean ones in your kit. Non-stretch gauze bandages are little use as they nearly always come off, while stretchy ones mould to the leg and stay on better.

A pair of curved scissors for cutting dressings.

Optrex for bathing eyes.

A clinical thermometer to take a horse's temperature.

Maintaining your kit

It is important to keep the container clean. A dirty container is unhygienic. Also, keep equipment like scissors clean. Always wipe and replace tops of bottles, tubes and jars after use.

Keep gamgee and other dressings well wrapped up and wash bandages in hot, soapy water after each use. Rinse them in clear water containing a little antiseptic liquid.

First-aid kits should be on hand when needed and contain all their basic items. When you start getting low on a particular item, put it on a special list and get the replacement *before* you run out.

Keep a permanent list of what should be in the kit and check it regularly. If any item has run out you can then replace it in plenty of time.

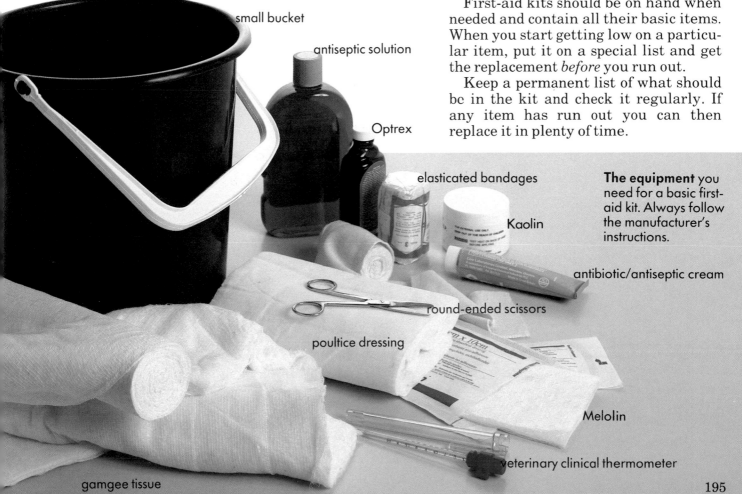

small bucket

antiseptic solution

Optrex

elasticated bandages

Kaolin

The equipment you need for a basic first-aid kit. Always follow the manufacturer's instructions.

antibiotic/antiseptic cream

round-ended scissors

poultice dressing

Melolin

veterinary clinical thermometer

gamgee tissue

Looking after a foal: 1

A foal of your own! It's an appealing idea for anybody – especially if you have a favourite mare as the prospective mother. But, while the basics of foal care are worth learning, the best advice for the novice owner is to follow expert advice.

Think things through

Even with an experienced horse breeder in charge, things can go wrong. The mare may have difficulties during foaling, her youngster may be born with a weakness or disability or could even have an accident while in the paddock.

It's important to think about these unpleasant possibilities beforehand. More important, though, you must think about the young foal's growing years and plan five, six or 10 years ahead.

You may want to keep your youngster. But suppose he grows up to have a bad fault of conformation or a difficult temperament? Or what if he is too small – or big – for you to ride?

Then again, your lifestyle could change. You might not be able to keep horses or might find it difficult to feed and look after both a mare and her

▼ **At grass:** Foals can be turned out with their mothers or with other youngsters. Make sure the field is well fenced and contains no hazardous wire or litter.

rapidly growing young foal.

Even if you plan to sell the foal, you must be prepared to care for him until he is old enough to be backed and schooled for riding. Trying to take short cuts by selling too soon is potentially fatal for the youngster: few new owners want to take on an unproven foal and the most likely buyer could be someone from a local slaughterhouse.

Pony buyers

Pony buyers today can be choosers. For a foal to have any chance of finding a good, lasting home, he should be *out of* (have as his mother) a pony whose own conformation, performance record and temperament are well above average. For preference, the mare should have the prizes to prove it – from good-class shows, trials or other competitions.

The stallion should be selected to produce a good foal from your particular mare, countering in his conformation any flaws in her shape. The foal must also be *well done* (fed and looked after) and well handled by knowledgeable people throughout his babyhood and young life so that he does not acquire any bad habits.

▼ **A young foal** may be adorable but he grows up! Breeding is a responsible job and should only be undertaken by experts.

Looking after a foal: 2

As well as getting a foal used to human handling, breeding from a mare means you are responsible for the health of mother and baby.

The newborn foal

Most foals are born at night, and mares prefer to deal with the birth in peace, though a watchful eye should be kept on them. The birth is near when the mare's udder swells, wax shows on her teats, and the muscles around the root of her tail relax as her body prepares for the foal to be born.

A pony mare may foal out of doors – as she would in the wild – but this has dangers in a small, crowded paddock, where she cannot escape from other horses to have her foal in peace. A refined breed of mare, on a stud, is brought into a special foaling box.

A normal birth comes front feet first. The foal 'dives' out into the world and, in the process, breaks the protective membrane surrounding it. After the foal is born, the mare also delivers the afterbirth (placenta), in which the foal has grown in her womb. This usually comes away cleanly within an hour or so. If the afterbirth, or parts of it, remain inside the mare, this could cause blood poisoning and very acute laminitis. The vet must be called in quickly because this is an emergency.

▼ **After a healthy birth,** this Dartmoor mare and her one-day old foal are soon out at grass. While its mother enjoys her grazing, the foal takes a first bewildering glimpse at the outside world.

After a normal birth, mare and foal are soon on their feet. The mare licks and nudges the foal, cleaning and warming it. Humans may long to help as the foal totters about seeking the mare's udder (often between her forelegs, first try!) but mother and baby are best left on their own to tackle this early problem naturally.

A foal's vital first feed is not ordinary milk but a rich substance called colostrum. This helps the foal resist disease and pass the hard black dung accumulated in his gut while in the womb; the digestive system can then work normally. It is critical that the foal receives his colostrum.

▲ **Newly born:** The mother nudges the foal and licks its coat to clean and warm it up. The foal should be on its feet and trying to suckle within the first two hours of its life.

★ **TIMING DEVICE**
Racehorse breeders like mares to 'foal down' as near January 1 as possible. This is the official birthday of all Thoroughbreds. A colt born at the natural time, around midsummer, would be only 18 months old when asked to compete in two-year-old races, a big disadvantage.

► **Suckling** is the foal's main source of food for the first four to six months of its life. When it reaches this age, it should be gradually weaned away from its mother.

▼ **Tetanus vaccinations** are essential. A course of injections for the first 15 months protects a foal from this horrible disease.

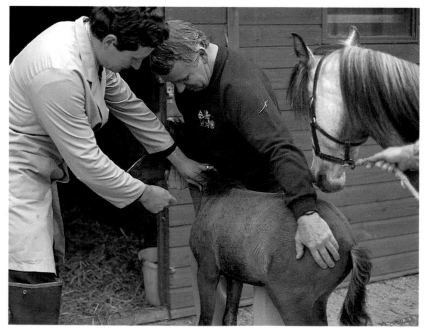

Weaning

Weaning means separating a foal from its mother, both to set the youngster on its way to becoming an adult, independent horse, and to stop the drain on the mare of feeding her fast-growing colt or filly. The foal will have been given solid food well before it is weaned, to avoid too much shock to its system. Afterwards, it needs a high protein diet to build its strength during the vital years of fast growth to four years old. A youngster stunted and starved in the 'weanling' stage seldom recovers fully.

Foals are ready for weaning at four to six months old. Exactly when depends on their date of birth. Pony mares are generally best covered (mated) so they foal down – about 11 months later – at the natural season in early summer. It is warm, there is plenty of grass, and the foal has every chance to thrive.

Weaning involves taking the mare out of earshot of her foal. The foal may be left behind in the stable one morning when the mare goes out to the paddock. It helps if the foal can see another youngster next door. Alternatively, if several mares and foals share a paddock, the mare may be taken out while the foal stays with its friends. Either way, youngsters – and their mothers – soon settle, given good food and good handling, plus another pony for company.

Medical matters

In-foal mares, like all ponies, need regular worming. A worm dose a month before the mare is due to foal reduces the risk of her newborn foal picking up worms from his dam's droppings. The newly weaned youngster also needs worming.

All horses should be injected against

▼ **By the time** they are yearlings, most colt foals have been gelded (neutered). Allowed to recover at grass, geldings are much calmer and easier to manage than stallions.

tetanus, a horrible and usually fatal disease. An in-foal mare given a 'booster tetanus jab' a month before foaling passes on protection to her foal in the colostrum – vital, since foals are careless of their own safety! A course of injections over its first 15 months should then give the young pony protection.

Colt foals, except those to be kept for breeding, must also be gelded (neutered). The testicles are surgically removed, under anaesthetic. This can be done when the youngster is a foal, provided he is strong and well grown, and that the testicles have both 'come down' from inside his body into the skin bag that holds them (the scrotum). Alternatively, gelding can be left until he is a yearling.

Usually, the operation is carried out in either autumn or spring, when flies are not a bother but the weather is fine enough to let the newly gelded pony out for plenty of exercise, to work off any swelling.

He soon recovers, and his quieter ways as a gelding are a relief both to any mares he has been trying to woo, and to the humans who are handling him! Entire (ungelded) colts can become difficult to manage from as young as nine or 10 months old – one more reason why owning a foal is not for the novice!

Looking after an old horse

▼ **Having an old horse** in your care is a rewarding responsibility. Look after him well and he'll repay you with years of faithful service.

The care of an old horse depends upon his condition and circumstances rather than on his actual age. While horses in heavy work are usually retired between the ages of 12 and 15, a gently used pony can continue to lead an active life well into his 20s.

At grass

The work required of an older pony should be less frequent and not too vigorous, so it is usually best to keep him at grass where he can take his own exercise. If he has always been stabled in the past, let him get used to life outside gradually.

Even more than most, old horses appreciate the protection of good thick hedges or an open shed in the field. Bring your pony in at night during the colder months. Put him in a New Zealand rug if he's newly turned out in bad weather or if he has not yet re-grown a full coat after clipping.

One of the values of an old horse is as a calming friend to a younger, excitable pony. All horses, being herd animals, are naturally happier in company. But watch out that your old pony is not bullied by a number of younger animals – you have to separate them if this happens.

Feeding

To maintain his body heat and condition, an older pony needs more food than a middle-aged one. But the proportion of concentrated to bulk food (hay and grass) changes. Carry out any adjustments in diet gradually. The total quantity of food needed each day by a 14-hand pony is about 9kg (20lbs) and for a horse doing no work this can be entirely bulk. But, to build up condition in a neglected older animal or for one carrying out a modest amount of work, give a proportion of concentrates.

If the pony is still being gently ridden by young riders, pony nuts or cubes are most suitable. Barley adds variety to the food and helps to condition an old horse in poor shape without exciting him.

If your pony is at grass, fresh water, grass and hay should ideally be unlimited because most ponies adjust their intake to their needs. The only time to restrict grazing is when the pony is first turned out on to lush spring paddocks, fertilized pastures or clover fields.

Exercise

Daily exercise is essential for the horse at any age. While an older, grass-kept pony can exercise himself, even an old, sick horse benefits from being led out for half an hour. And a stabled pony who is fairly fit can cope with an hour or more of gentle hacking including modest jumping, a canter and hillwork.

However, galloping about at gymkhanas, hunting or eventing is unsuitable. Whatever is asked of an old pony should be built up slowly and in ▶

▼ **At grass:** Old ponies are often most content in a field. The hollow back is a typical sign of ageing and does not interfere with the pony's ability to exercise himself.

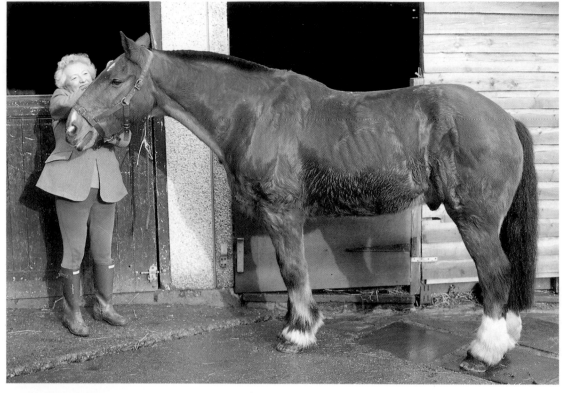

► **Take particular care** to check an old horse every day for wounds, lameness, coughing and skin problems.

▼ ► **Exercise:** Even if your horse isn't up to being ridden, lead him round lanes or through fields to stop him getting stiff.

A daily half-hour 'walk' is especially important if he's kept in a stable.

keeping with his former capabilities.

Health problems

You must take extra care to keep to all the routines of good horse management with an older animal. The daily check for problems is particularly important.

Teeth should be filed at least once a year. The outer edges of the upper molars and the inner edges of the lower molars get less wear and become very sharp. This can cause an old pony to refuse food and fight shy of the bit. He may even get attacks of colic (bad stomach ache) from poor chewing.

Feet: The pony only needs to be shod if he is doing roadwork. But even unshod, his feet must be regularly checked and filed to keep the soles level, and trimmed to prevent hooves splitting.

Brushing (striking the inner side of the opposite leg) can be the result of age or overwork. Protective boots are available and the blacksmith can help with special shoeing techniques.

Ponies frequently rest a hindleg on the tip of the hoof. But if this 'pointing' occurs with a front leg it is usually a sign of trouble. There are many causes of lameness in the older pony and you should always seek your vet's advice.

Coughs and colds: Old ponies catch coughs and colds readily. They can have chest problems which cause breathing difficulties. Provide rest and extra warmth and call the vet if you're not sure what to do.

Lumps, bumps and tumours frequently appear on old ponies. Although unsightly, they may be harmless – but leave that decision to the vet.

Worming: Do this at least every three months, especially for an old pony in a field used by a number of other horses. Worms are often the reason for a pony's condition failing to improve and for his harsh, staring coat.

Skin problems like mange, ringworm, lice, ticks and warts tend to arise more often on the older horse. All are curable with the correct treatment, so ask your vet. Remember to separate a pony with a skin disease or problem from other horses, as some are catching.

This may seem like a long list of ailments but, provided you cultivate a good local vet and are methodical with the daily check, most problems can be nipped in the bud.

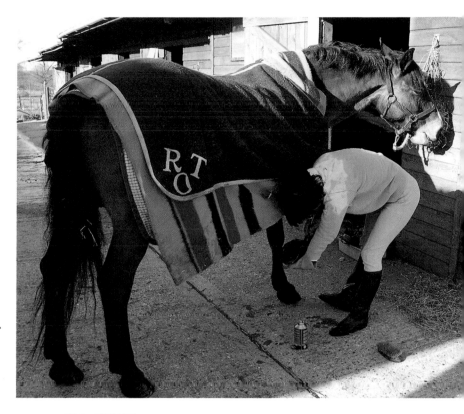

▲ **Keeping warm:** The sun may be shining, but the chill of winter quickly penetrates old horses' bones. A horse that's tied up can't move around to keep warm, so make sure he has plenty of rugs on while you attend to stable chores.

◄ **Young riders** and old horses are an excellent match: mature ponies are tolerant and kind to novices going through their paces. This pony is 28 years old and still giving hours of pleasure.

Index

ACKNOWLEDGEMENTS

Photographers: A.G.E. Fotostock 40, 43(t); Animal Photography 47(t), 184–5, (R. Wilbie) 26(tr), 43(c); Aquila Photographics (R. Maier) 26(bl), 36, 45(c), 47(b), 120(c), 180–1, (J.F. Preedy) 35(b); Simon Butcher/ Eaglemoss 195; Bruce Coleman/Eric Crichton 75(t); Robert Estall 24(c); Mary Evans Picture Library 12; Harry Hall 58; Robert Harding Picture Library 73(b); Kit Houghton 6–7, 31, 33, 34(b), 37, 45(t,b), 56–57, 87(inset), 110–111, 138, 151, 182(t), 186(t), 197(inset), 199(t); Kit Houghton/Eaglemoss 52–53, 55; Bob Langrish 27(t), 29(t), 43(b), 47(c), 49(b), 68, 70(b), 139, 150, 164(t), 165(c), 166–167, 169(b), 172–173, 174, 175(t,b), 182(b), 183(t,c), 187(t), 188–190, 190(l), 191(t); Lavenham Rugs 54(cr), 122(cl); National Motor Museum 19; NHPA (B. Chaumeton) 35(tr), (P. Fagot) 35(tl); Octopus Books (C. Linton) 72; Nick Rains/ Eaglemoss 194(bl); Mike Roberts 82(t), 120(t), 200(t), 201(b); Peter Roberts Collection 74, 82(c,b), 84(cl), 89, 122(bl), 168(l), 183(b); The Slide File 25(br); Sporting Pictures 190(t); Tony Stone Worldwide 2–3, 42, 46; John Suett/Projekt Photography/Eaglemoss 29(b), 75(b), 107(b), 126, 130, 136(l), 143; Survival Anglia Picture Library (L&T Bomford) 28(b); Shona Wood/ Eaglemoss front cover, 4–5, 24(bl,r), 25(t,c), 28(t), 48, 49(t,c), 50–51, 54(b), 57(inset), 60–64, 66–67, 69, 70(t), 71, 73(inset), 76–83, 84(cr,b), 85–87, 88(tc), 90–92, 94–106, 107(t), 108–109, 112–119, 120(b), 121, 122(tc,br), 123–125, 128–129, 131–134, 136– 137, 140–149, 152–163, 164(b), 165(b), 168(br,cr), 169(tr,tc), 170–171, 175(br), 176–177, 191(b), 192– 193, 194(t,br), 196–197, 200(b), 201(t), 202–205; Zefa Picture Library 27(b), 44, 198–199, (R. Sponlein) 34(t).

Illustrators: Catherine Constable 18–23, 30, 32–33, 178–179, 186–187; Michael Cooke/Eaglemoss 81, 108, 130, 139; Denys Ovenden 31, 81, 113(r), 127, 140–141, 193; Maggie Raynor 8–11, 13–17, 24–25, 37–39, 41, 59, 63, 65, 93, 113(t), 135, 160–161, 163–164, 190.

The World Aflame

The World Aflame

A NEW HISTORY OF
WAR AND REVOLUTION:
1914-1945

Dan Jones
&
Marina Amaral

with Mark Hawkins-Dady

PEGASUS BOOKS
NEW YORK LONDON

THE WORLD AFLAME

Pegasus Books, Ltd.
148 West 37th Street, 13th Floor
New York, NY 10018

Designed by Isambard Thomas / CORVO

First Pegasus Books hardcover edition August 2020

ISBN: 978-1-64313-222-8

10 9 8 7 6 5 4 3 2 1

Printed in the United States of America
Distributed by Simon & Schuster

Previous page
French soldiers in a trench on the Western Front, during the First World War

Overleaf
Children in Kent take cover during the Battle of Britain, summer 1940

PICTURE CREDITS

All images © Getty Images, except
p.102: Siege of Kut © Alamy; p.148–9 POWs © US National Archives;
p.172–3 Anna Coleman Ladd © Library of Congress;
p.338–9 Czeslawa Kwoka © Auschwitz Memorial and Museum

ACKNOWLEDGMENTS

The authors would like to thank Anthony and Nic Cheetham, Richard Milbank,
Clémence Jacquinet, Dan Groenewald and all the team at Head of Zeus.

Thank you also to Paul Reed.

Special thanks to Mark Hawkins-Dady.

Introduction

n the northern French town of Bar-le-Duc, on 28 July 1946, the French general and statesman Charles de Gaulle reflected on the troubled history of his times. Bar-le-Duc was in the region (or *département*) of France known as Meuse, and that made it a poignant place for de Gaulle to give a speech in which he collected his thoughts about the recent past.

A generation previously, men had dug deep, wet, muddy, diseased, and miserable trenches through the ground of Meuse, and monstrous armies equipped with hellish new weapons fought a battle nearly a year in duration, which produced around three-quarters of a million casualties. Then, two years before de Gaulle gave his speech, troops had once again torn through the same, barely recovered countryside, bludgeoning out the endgame of another appalling conflict, slaughtering each other and massacring villagers – ordinary civilians who had done nothing more than be in the wrong place at a terrible time.

De Gaulle spoke of these things with grim, heroic reverence: they were 'the greatest events in our history', he said, which had required the people who suffered through them 'to guard intact the force of their souls'. More than that, he argued, the events that had torn apart Meuse amounted to a tragic 'war of thirty years'. In other words, they were flare-ups in a single great conflagration, which had raged during the first half of the twentieth century. Just as seventeenth-century Europe had endured one Thirty Years War, suggested de Gaulle, so the modern world had suffered again. Two years later, Britain's wartime prime minister Winston Churchill would toy with the same idea in the first volume of his historical memoirs, where he announced his intention to describe 'another Thirty Years War'.

Today, historians dislike the 'Second Thirty Years War' theory. They are much more comfortable in thinking about the First World War of 1914–18 and the Second World War of 1939–45: the two conflicts close but separate, best kept on different shelves. Perhaps this is wise. But whichever terms we prefer, and however we choose to arrange our historical bookends, most people would agree with Churchill's judgement that the events of 1914–45 amounted to 'the two supreme cataclysms of recorded history'.

This book is a journey through those deadly but fascinating wartime years. It is a history in colour. It contains 200 photographs, all of which were originally shot in black and white, and each of which has been colourized here. Each picture is paired with a short explanatory text to give context to the image, and the book proceeds in more or less chronological sequence, so that it can be studied piecemeal or read from cover to cover. It is not an attempt to impose (or reimpose) a grand new historical shape on the events it describes. Rather, it is a book that asks you to look at a story that has been told many times over in a brand new light, and perhaps to think – as de Gaulle did at Bar-le-Duc in 1946 – *all this happened here.*

Colourizing historical photos is not an exact science. It is a delicate and technical process that requires, on the one hand, diligent historical research and, on the other, the use of what can be called – without apology – artistic licence. Colourization does not – cannot – 'restore' anything to a black-and-white photograph, for such an image has no hidden colours to hunt for. Instead, it adds them, based on known facts and responsible guesswork. It is an interpretive tool, whose limitations must never be brushed over or forgotten.

Yet this does not mean that colourization is frivolous or 'fake'. It is self-evident that as members of the species *Homo sapiens* we respond to colour instinctively, and in deep, primal ways. It stirs our hearts as well as our heads. Colourization at its best is an emotional enhancing agent: it magnifies empathy and horror, pity and disgust. It challenges us to respond to history not simply as accountants and analysts, but as human beings, capable of the same fear, confusion, passion, ambition, anger and love as those whose images we see. It asks us to ask more. It nudges us to go off and hunt for the truth behind these extraordinary scenes. That is its purpose. That is its power.

Assembling 200 photographs that do justice to the history of the First and Second World Wars was a hard and sometimes harrowing process. The selection you see here is only that – a selection. We hope it tells a story that honours the times it narrates, but present it knowing that it can only ever be partial. Miles upon miles of books have been written on the topics we mention; in many cases, a single photograph and caption here has an entire scholarship devoted to its study. We offer in advance our apologies for any omissions and errors, all of which are our own. But we hope that this book will inspire new readers to the topic to delve deeper into the history, and encourage older heads to reconsider what they think they know.

In the two years we spent working on this book, we passed the centenary of the end of the First World War, and the eightieth anniversary of the start of the Second World War. We heard all too often of the deaths of veterans of the latter conflict, now a sadly dwindling group. Some time in the next decade or so, the last of the wartime generation will be lost to the world, and their deeds and experiences will become solely the preserve of history, and not living memory. We offer this book in part as a tribute to those men and women – some of them heroes, some of them victims, and others just ordinary people who lived their lives through terrifying times.

We also offer this book as a warning. As we write, fascism, nationalism, populism, anti-Semitism, hatred, bigotry, racism and the politics of exclusion, division and isolation are on the march once more all over the world. Let what you see here be a reminder of where this leads. The world is fragile. It takes less than we think to set it aflame.

Marina Amaral *&* Dan Jones
Belo Horizonte *and* Staines-upon-Thames

1900–1914

End of an Era

The lamps are going out all over Europe;
we shall not see them lit again in our lifetime.

Sir Edward Grey, British foreign secretary,
to editor of the *Westminster Gazette*
(3 August 1914)

On 20 May 1910, London glittered with royalty. No fewer than nine kings and emperors, augmented by myriad princes, princesses and potentates, gathered to mourn a man to whom many of them were related. Edward VII was known as the 'Uncle of Europe'. He had less flattering names, too, including 'Tum Tum', in reference to his colossal waistline, and 'Edward the Caresser', a tribute to his expertise in the art of adultery. His formal title, though, was all gravitas: 'By the Grace of God, of the United Kingdom of Great Britain and Ireland and the British Dominions beyond the Seas, King, Defender of the Faith, Emperor of India.' It was almost as expansive as the territories over which he had reigned for nine years: an empire whose lustre seemed to shine as brightly as ever.

First among equals at the funeral ceremonies was Edward's only surviving son and successor, King George V. Apart from a shared love of shooting animals, the temperaments of father and son were very different. Disciplined, upright, obsessed with punctuality, George (*pictured centre, previous pages*) would pick up where his grandparents Victoria and Albert had left off, resetting the constitutional monarchy along a trajectory of probity and duty.

By George's side, pride of place as a chief mourner went to his first cousin, a man whose sense of duty that day probably outweighed personal sentiment. Prickly, complex and impetuous, Kaiser Wilhelm II of Germany can be seen in this photograph – taken as the procession neared London's Paddington Station, from where it would travel by train to Windsor – gripping the reins of his horse with his 'withered' arm, the legacy of a difficult birth. He had little love left for his late Uncle Edward; now, in London, he found himself in the heart of an empire he envied, whose navy outclassed his own, and whose diplomatic relations with France seemed (to him)

to be aimed at boxing in Germany.

The king these illustrious mourners came to bury had exceeded expectations. During his long tenure as Prince of Wales and heir to the throne, 'Bertie' (as he was then known) had indulged his appetites so freely that his mother, Victoria, had despaired. His reign as Edward, which began in 1901 when he was nearly sixty, was expected to be neither long nor glorious.

Yet Edward managed to surprise everyone. He played to his strengths: charm, an international outlook and some adroit diplomacy. These qualities came together when Edward's personal efforts helped to secure the Anglo-French agreement of 1904 known as the Entente Cordiale. With this understanding, historic enmities and some more recent imperial frictions were put to one side in favour of a new spirit of cooperation.

The 'Edwardian age' (often extended by historians to the summer of 1914) would be the last time a British monarch's name defined an era. In the backward-shining light that history throws, it is often presented as a time of optimism, promise and the casting off of Victorian primness. Yet it was also a time of turbulence in a not-so-United Kingdom. Trade unionists flexed their muscles. The Labour Party made electoral advances. Women vociferously demanded the vote, and the suffragist and suffragette movements provided, respectively, outlets for those who wanted to pursue the campaign peacefully or militantly. The polarizing question of Home Rule in Ireland threatened to explode, as Irish nationalist and loyalist paramilitaries began arming themselves.

Edwardian Britain also had to engage with a continental Europe that, by the end of the nineteenth century, had slipped into confrontational blocs. Since the Battle of Waterloo in 1815, Britain had pursued imperial and economic expansion while avoiding European

---

17 December 1903

The Wright brothers make the first machine-powered flight outside Kitty Hawk, North Carolina; within 8 years, aeroplanes are dropping bombs.

8 April 1904

The signing of the Anglo-French Entente cordiale signals a new era of Franco-British co-operation after decades of intense imperial competition.

January–October 1905

Russia experiences a naval mutiny at Odessa, a revolution (in which Tsar Nicholas II is forced to permit a parliament, the Duma) and defeat in the Russo-Japanese War.

10 February 1906

King Edward VII launches the Royal Navy's HMS *Dreadnought*, to the envy of Germany's Kaiser Wilhelm II: a 6-year Anglo-German race to build battleships follows.

6 October 1908

The Austro-Hungarian Empire formally annexes the one-time Ottoman province of Bosnia-Herzegovina, angering Bosnia's nationalists as well as neighbouring Serbia and Russia.

entanglements – a stratagem described by the contemporary cliché 'splendid isolation'. Britain's wars between 1815 and 1914 were, with the arguable exception of the Crimean War, colonial rather than European matters. Now things were changing.

Most palpable among the new European realities was the fact of a united, Prussian-dominated Germany at Europe's heart, bitterly opposed by a France still all too aware of the prestige and territory lost during the Franco-Prussian War of 1870–71. By 1910, Germany's industrial output pipped Britain's and far exceeded France's. (In a different sign of the times, the United States' thrusting economy dwarfed any in Europe, though America was still a sleeping giant militarily.) Yet as the German economy expanded, German democratic institutions remained relatively weak – which meant the Kaiser and his military still exerted disproportionate power over the state. Since his imperial accession in 1888, Wilhelm II had abandoned the strategic caution of his grandfather Wilhelm I, dispensed with the services of the elderly master-statesman Otto von Bismarck, and allowed a carefully calibrated German relationship with Russia to lapse in favour of consolidating relations with Austria-Hungary.

In 1894, to counter the new German–Austrian partnership, a French–Russian entente was agreed. This was effectively a mutual defence pact, which Germany inevitably interpreted as a threatening encirclement. Britain's Entente Cordiale with France fell short of this sort of defensive alliance. Nevertheless, Germany could see that Britain had chosen sides in the great geopolitical game. During Edward's reign, the two countries embarked on a frantic race to build more powerful battleships. Hostility was out in the open.

As alliances shifted among the Western powers, further east lay the 'sick man of Europe':
the Ottoman Empire. As it was steadily dispossessed of its European provinces, the retreating empire spat out newly independent nations – and new risks for the international system. In 1903, Serbians (fully independent from 1878) assassinated their pro-Austrian king and embarked on a pan-Slavic and pro-Russian course. Austro-Russian regional tensions grew ever more acute. 'The Balkans' became a byword for instability.

None of this should suggest that the rest of the world was a haven of calm. Bloody revolutions gripped Mexico and China in 1910 and 1911 respectively – and their effects on global stability would become grimly apparent in time. Still, the most immediate dangers plainly lay in Europe, where a system of formal alliances and competing imperial interests meant that one misstep could – and would – yield catastrophic consequences.

Against that background, as almost the entire monarchy of Europe gathered in London to pay their respects to Edward VII, they were unwittingly marking the end of an era. Within less than a decade, many of these kings would have no thrones to occupy. For millions of their subjects, an even worse fate was in store.

---

27 April 1909

Mehmed V replaces his brother as the Ottoman Empire's sultan, although real power has passed to the 'Young Turk' nationalists in government, including Enver Pasha.

20 November 1910

Discontent spurs rebellion against ageing autocrat Porfirio Díaz in Mexico; the next year, China experiences revolution too, leading to the abdication of child-emperor Puyi.

April–November 1911

In the Agadir Crisis (or Second Moroccan Crisis), French and German imperial ambitions clash dangerously over Morocco; tensions are defused, but Britain backs France.

April–May 1912

The prospect of Home Rule for Ireland (with a parliament in Dublin) threatens armed rebellion by Protestant paramilitaries and a counter-reaction from Irish nationalists.

10 August 1913

The Treaty of Bucharest formally ends the second of two Balkan Wars, fought over borders in these former Ottoman states; the region lives up to its reputation as a 'tinderbox'.

The Belle Époque

As Edward VII discovered during his apprenticeship as Prince of Wales, Paris was Europe's playground, full of the louche delights of the 'Belle Époque' – the near half-century of relative stability before 1914, when the arts, progressive thought and good living flourished in Europe's leading cities. No corner of Paris exemplified *joie de vivre* as well as the Moulin Rouge in Montmartre – known for the high-kicking, flesh-and-bloomers-revealing can-can. Depicted here is the Moulin's rear 'garden', with dancers and tutus, assorted clientele – and an extraordinary hollow elephant; its recreational uses were said to have included a hideaway for opium-smoking.

There was, however, another, darker side to these years of gaiety and pleasure. Fractures in French society were starkly exposed by the protracted Dreyfus affair (1894–1906), in which an innocent French-Jewish army officer was scapegoated for espionage by a conservative, Catholic, anti-Semitic establishment, while liberal voices – notably the writer Émile Zola – spoke up passionately in his defence.

The Dreyfus case began with accusations of military secrets revealed to Germany – which spoke volumes about French insecurities of the time. France had been humiliated by the Prussian Army in 1871, when a newly unified German Empire was proclaimed on French soil, at Versailles. With wings clipped, territory lost, a declining population – and now a large, industrially vibrant and militarily dynamic German power as a neighbour – the French, and especially their politicians and military chiefs, had plenty to worry about.

New Americans

A world away from Old Europe and its global empires lay the optimistic and energetic United States. During the nineteenth century, the USA had managed to feed its own imperial appetites through westward expansion, with native peoples cleared from the land in order to satisfy a continental conquest given the pious title 'Manifest Destiny'.

Many of the new Americans fanning out towards the Pacific Ocean were poorer European migrants, tempted by the promise of land, absence of persecution and the opportunity to make (or remake) themselves. In the 1910 census, nearly 12 million Americans reported having been born in Europe; this photograph captures one small, wide-eyed group of recent arrivals, enjoying a first Christmas dinner in their adopted home.

The relationships these new Americans retained with their native countries were complex. Although immigrants brought their varied languages and heritages, the USA traditionally adhered to a policy of separateness, avoiding Old World conflicts and preoccupations – one pillar of the so-called Monroe Doctrine (1823), articulating America's military and diplomatic place in the world.

Yet America's capacity to absorb and employ so many immigrants meant that it could not remain alone and aloof forever. By 1910, US industrial production was equivalent to that of Britain, Germany and France put together. This bald statistic, combined with the generations-old and constantly refreshed ties between the Old and New Worlds, meant that when Europe descended into war, the USA's manifest destiny proved in fact to lie on battlefields across the Atlantic.

The Machine Age

In a rapidly industrializing world, few inventions symbolized the new, mechanized era better than the Ford Model T (pictured here) – not merely a car, but a phenomenon, which confirmed that the era of the automobile had truly arrived. The Model T was not at all glamorous, but it became an icon of modernity in a country that was perfectly primed for motor cars – with virgin land being everywhere transformed into neat, gridlined suburbs. By the First World War, four-fifths of the world's cars were made in America.

Henry Ford's genius as an industrialist lay less in pure innovation – the motor car was invented in Europe – but in adaptation and clever production techniques, which drove down costs. When his first Model Ts came to market in 1908, aimed at farmers on America's rough-hewn roads (hence the distinctive high chassis), they cost a sizeable $825. Within five years, the price had shrunk by nearly a third, as Ford's new plant in Michigan mass-produced vehicles on an assembly line – a new concept. When the last of the 15 million Model Ts rolled off the assembly line in 1927, its price was a mere $290. It was the archetypal 'people's car'.

Mechanization of the sort that Ford embraced changed the lives of travellers, workers, businesspeople and consumers. Yet its contribution to human ease and economic efficiency soon had to be weighed against something much grimmer: a global conflict defined by the mass production of weapons and the spectre of mechanized killing.

The Era of Flight

While Henry Ford accelerated the era of the motor car, other entrepreneurs were looking to innovation in the skies. In 1903, the American brothers Orville and Wilbur Wright made the first major machine-powered flight. An 'air race' soon began, and in 1908 the *Daily Mail*'s owner Lord Northcliffe put up a prize of £1,000 for a successful flight across the English Channel. An obsessive French aviator, Louis Blériot, eventually made this extraordinary journey on 25 July 1909, spending about 38 minutes aloft – and the public celebrated another feat of the modern age.

Aircraft manufacture now proliferated in Europe and the United States. Also in 1909, in the USA, Glenn Curtiss's Manufacturing Company diversified into aircraft production, creating a classic design: the Curtiss 'pusher'. In these fragile assemblages of metal, canvas, rope and wood – like a tricycle with wings – the pilot sat exposed, pushed along by the propeller to his rear.

Military minds soon began co-opting the technology. In this photograph (1912), Thomas DeWitt Milling tests out a Curtiss pusher for the US Army at College Park, Maryland; by the time it was taken, Curtiss pushers had already made their first take-offs and landings on naval vessels. Far away, meanwhile, over the deserts of Libya, Italian airmen conducted the first operations in which bombs were dropped from an aircraft.

By 1917, Milling was supervising the training of US Army pilots for Europe's war zone. Air power's age of innocence had lasted little more than a decade.

A Naval Arms Race

The invention of aeroplanes suggested that Britain's traditional line of defence against invasion – the sea – might not be the bulwark it once was. All the same, few doubted that the British Empire's security still rested fundamentally with the Royal Navy, whose global pre-eminence seemed to be confirmed by the launch, in 1906, of HMS *Dreadnought*, pictured here. The most advanced warship in the world, she was powered by turbine engines, boasted a fearsome array of guns with advanced targeting capabilities, and could speed through the seas at up to 21 knots. *Dreadnought* was such an extraordinary vessel that she lent her name to an entire class of battleship.

Among those who took envious note was Kaiser Wilhelm II, a man drawn to all things naval as a means of projecting Germany's influence well beyond her coastal waters, and thereby of enhancing her imperial grandeur and world-power status. To that end, the Kaiser had a willing accomplice in Admiral Alfred von Tirpitz, his naval chief, whom he tasked with expanding the strength of the German imperial navy, the Kaiserliche Marine.

When Germany sought to manufacture her own dreadnoughts, a full-blown Anglo-German naval arms race commenced. Between 1906 and 1912, both nations threw money and resources into shipbuilding, and soon even *Dreadnought*'s design was outclassed by successors. This competition proved to be a popular patriotic effort, and despite British anxieties, the Royal Navy retained its superiority. Fatefully, however, after accepting that they could not outmuscle the British in shipbuilding, German strategists began looking to a different sort of vessel to make up the difference: submarines.

Mexico at War

In the years before 1914, the British Empire, of which Churchill was an ardent champion, remained the most vigorous and extensive in the world. By contrast, Spain's empire had shrunk to virtually nothing. Mexico, one of the former jewels in its crown, had long ago wrenched itself free (1823). However, independence had done little to create an enduring political or social settlement in Mexico, and violent discontent simmered. In 1910 this boiled over into rebellion and revolution, when Mexico's long-standing but ageing autocrat Porfirio Díaz tried to cling on to power through a rigged election. For years Díaz had pursued an agenda that modernized and enriched the country, but at the cost of extreme inequality and rampant corruption. He was, his critics also asserted, too much in thrall to foreign and particularly US interests.

One of the key figures in the many-stranded conflict that comprised the Mexican Revolution and civil war was the colourful, radical figure of Emiliano Zapata Salazar. His campaigning for villagers' rights in his home state of Morelos evolved into an armed peasants' revolt. His calls for land redistribution spawned a manifesto (*Plan de Ayala*) and an eponymous movement ('Zapatismo'); his followers naturally were known as the 'Zapatistas'. Zapata (*front row, fifth from left, in dark jacket*) cultivated an appropriate image of a typical Mexican *charro* (literally 'horseman').

The Zapatistas helped to topple Díaz in 1911, only to find themselves embroiled in armed conflict and later guerrilla resistance, during many subsequent years of civil war. Zapata's life would end violently too, in a 1919 ambush; but his legend and inspiration lived on.

Young Winston

As First Lord of the Admiralty from 1911, Winston Churchill was in his element, propelling the British naval expansion to contain the German threat. Here, clear-eyed and fresh-faced, the young Winston exudes the self-confidence that became both his greatest strength and, sometimes, his siren weakness.

By his thirties, Churchill had already trained as a cavalry officer, worked as a war reporter in South Africa, escaped from a Boer prison camp, become a Conservative MP (1900), crossed the floor to join the Liberal Party (1904) – thereby enraging his former colleagues – and then, in government, pursued social reform as President of the Board of Trade. A tenure as Home Secretary followed (1910–11), during which he struggled with tensions in Ireland and the perplexing challenge (to much of the male political class) of the campaign for women's suffrage, which was taking a militant turn. In 1911, Churchill exhibited his lifelong love of being at the centre of things by joining police and soldiers on London's Sidney Street, where a gang of suspected anarchists, who had already murdered three policemen, were holed up. MPs criticized the Home Secretary for his rashness in courting personal danger; but the man himself pronounced the experience 'such fun'.

For many a politician and statesman, Churchill's career to date would have already represented a life's work. In fact, he had barely begun.

The End of Imperial China

While Mexico was consumed by internal conflict, across the Pacific Ocean violent uprisings reverberated through China's provinces in 1911. The bloody results are evident in the beheadings (*shown here*) by which the authorities sought to intimidate potential rebels.

China had no long-in-the-tooth strongman to overthrow, but rather an enfeebled court government and a child-emperor, Puyi – the eleventh ruler of the Qing dynasty and, as it transpired, the last. On ascending to the throne shortly before his third birthday, Puyi understandably preferred running around the palace firing his airgun at eunuchs to the business of ruling an empire. Some hasty and overdue reforms to overhaul the antiquated imperial administration in his name proved to be too little, too late.

On 10 October 1911, troops mutinied, in the Wuchang insurrection, which in turn sparked the much wider Xinhai uprising, under the leadership of veteran revolutionary Sun Yat-sen. On 12 February 1912, Puyi abdicated, and two millennia of Chinese imperial rule reached an end. In their place came a delicate provisional government, under the experienced politician Yuan Shikai.

Enormous in size and rich in tradition, but poor, internally fragmented, industrially backward and inward-looking, China could not be transformed at a stroke by a transition to republican government; indeed, the future held only more turbulence and suffering. Sun, for his part, founded the profoundly influential Guomindang (Kuomintang) political movement, while thousands of Chinese would make their own often overlooked contribution to the coming world war, mainly as labourers for the French.

The Balkan Tinderbox

The dissolution of another imperial entity, the Ottoman Empire, had begun in the nineteenth century. As Ottoman control over the mountainous Balkans receded, it left behind uncertain borders, vying nationalist interests and fragile new states, which seemed to offer easy prey for two neighbouring regional powers, Austria-Hungary and Russia.

First, though, there was unfinished business with the old empire. In 1912, Serbia, Bulgaria, Greece and Montenegro put internal arguments to one side and formed a 'Balkan League' against Ottoman Turkey. In October 1912 they went to war, during which time this photo – showing League troops pausing to rest along the Serbian–Bulgarian border – was taken.

The First Balkan War was a short, sharp affair, over within two months. It pushed back the Ottoman Empire's European border all the way to Constantinople (Istanbul) and eastern Thrace, while Albania achieved independence, and the League allies carved up the province of Macedonia among themselves.

Scarcely was the fighting over, however, than Bulgaria, unhappy with its share of the spoils, attacked its erstwhile allies, prompting a Second Balkan War (1913). In this conflict, Bulgaria lost most of what she had gained in the First Balkan War, while stoking anti-Serbian and anti-Romanian resentment that would erupt again during the First World War.

The Balkans were often described as a 'tinderbox', and the events of 1912–13 seemed to bear out the cliché. Just as worrying, these Balkan wars presented a dangerous illusion: that modern wars could be managed to deliver quick results. The hazards of such thinking soon became apparent.

Gothaische
Kohlensäure-Werke
(Sondra - Quelle)

Max Sperling

Descent to War

There is blissful joy in every victory won for the
sake of this beautiful German land.

Eduard Schmieder,
a German student-turned-soldier, in a letter
(23 August 1914)

verything changed in Europe on 28 June 1914. That morning, a pro-Serbian assassin named Gavrilo Princip killed Archduke Franz Ferdinand, heir to the Austro-Hungarian imperial throne. A few weeks later, all across Europe, millions of people were mobilizing for war; Franz Ferdinand's death had sent the continent spiralling towards a major conflict. Duty called, and young men were bidding what they hoped would be a temporary farewell to sweethearts, families and friends.

As troops signed up and moved out, there was plenty of bravado. Drums beat a rhythm as infantry regiments marched through provincial towns. Crowds cheered. Backs were slapped. Hats were tossed in the air and handkerchiefs were waved as trains pulled out of stations, soldiers leaning out of the windows. Many in Germany took their leave to the sound of military bands playing 'Die Wacht am Rhein', a song that had become a sort of unofficial anthem of German mobilization. 'Dear Fatherland, put your mind at rest!' went the chorus. 'Fast and true stands the watch on the Rhine.'

Ernst Jünger, twentieth-century Germany's most famous war diarist, recalled departing 'in a rain of flowers, in a drunken atmosphere of blood and roses. Surely the war had to supply us with what we wanted; the great, the overwhelming, the hallowed experience… Anything to participate, not to have to stay at home!' He volunteered as an infantryman on 1 August, when he was just nineteen years old.

Yet for all this heady, jut-jawed triumphalism – which was by no means confined to Germany – every individual parting, when it came, would also have embraced all the quieter emotions: fear, a nervous excitement, anxiety, uncertainty. Would they come home? And if so, when?

It is hard to escape the sense that it might all have been averted. For a while during July, the leaders of Europe's great powers had a chance to escape the conflagration many of them had long feared. Had the crisis caused by the assassination of Franz Ferdinand been confined to the Balkans, there might have been a localized, punitive war – a Third Balkan War, targeting Serbia.

Instead, the complex and delicate networks of allegiance that bound together Europe's most populous and powerful nations (and their empires) had all been activated at once. In place of containment came escalation. Rather than mutually assured peace, the world was now threatened with an early form of mutually assured destruction.

The process by which the shooting of the archduke became a world war was both simple and dizzyingly complex. In the end, it boiled down to a few stark events. On 28 July, Austria-Hungary declared war on Serbia, confident of German backing. In response, Russia vowed to defend Serbia, a position that France was treaty-bound to support. On 1 August, Germany therefore declared war on Russia, and, two days later, on France as well. By 4 August, Britain and its empire, including Canada, Australia, New Zealand and South Africa, had entered the fray, and the foreign secretary, Sir Edward Grey, had uttered his famous, prophetic remark concerning the historical significance of the moment: 'The lamps are going out all over Europe; we shall not see them lit again in our lifetime.'

Yet beneath that short timetable of belligerence lay a huge range of imperial interests, national preoccupations, diplomatic rivalries, personal predilections and short-term ambitions, all of which seemed to collide at once. At least

28 June 1914	28 July	1–3 August	4 August	7 August–6 September
Archduke Franz Ferdinand, heir to the Austro-Hungarian throne, is assassinated in Sarajevo. Austria-Hungary, supported by Germany, blames Serbia – which is backed by Russia (allied with France).	Austria-Hungary declares war on Serbia, hoping to limit war to the Balkans region.	After reciprocal declarations, Germany is at war with Belgium, France and Russia. The First World War has begun, pitting the Allies against the Central Powers	Germany invades Belgium, prompting Britain to declare war on Germany.	In the Battle of the Frontiers, French troops swarm across the German border but are repulsed, as the German Army surges across the Franco-Belgian border.

as well known as Grey's elegiac prediction was its precise opposite: the jaunty forecast popular in many quarters during August 1914 that the war would 'all be over by Christmas'.

This confidence relied on war being as easy to end as it was to begin. As the lamps went out, they were replaced by the roar of engines, the smoking stacks of steam trains, and the hiss of ship's turbines to speed men and machines to where they needed to be. Germany's war plan was almost a railway timetable in itself: all aboard for Belgium, and onward into France for, it was hoped, a quick victory. The Belgians put up a struggle before, inevitably, being knocked down, their forts bombed into piles of concrete.

As Germans poured into Belgium and France, Russians poured – surprisingly quickly – into Germany, as did the French. A British Expeditionary Force landed in France, not to invade but to help, but it was painfully small in number. Austro-Hungarian armies penetrated Serbia three times, but Serbia stood firm, for the time being.

Invasions were not limited to Europe, for this was a conflict of empires. Germany's colonies across Africa came under attack, especially where there were important communications sites to neutralize. Much further east, Japan piled in as well, beginning to realize her own imperial dreams, while in British India volunteer soldiers headed up the gangplanks on to ships, bound for unknown destinations. Amid all this war-making, there were voices in the neutral United States pleading for peace. But they were drowned out.

Two battles were game-changers. At Tannenberg – a name that conjured up conflicts of centuries ago in the days of the Teutonic knights – a Russian army was wiped out and a German general called Hindenburg became his nation's saviour. Near France's River Marne, a 'miracle' was said to have taken place, when a mainly French counter-attack finally disrupted the German steamroller and saved Paris. The German Army began digging trenches, so as not to be pushed further back. Little did they know what a trend they were setting.

Within weeks, the declarations of war had led to death and destruction on an industrial scale. By the start of the winter of 1914–15, the list of casualties – dead, wounded, missing or captured – suffered on all sides had already reached two million. Historic centres such as Louvain, as well as scores of rural towns and villages across north-eastern France and Belgium, lay in ruins.

So the war was not 'over by Christmas'. But by December 1914, it *was* over for hundreds of thousands of young servicemen who had taken their leave of loved ones less than five months previously. For them, the promise of reunion contained in *auf Wiedersehen* had been overtaken by the finality of 'goodbye'.

23–24 August

The British Expeditionary Force fights the Battle of Mons in Belgium, its first bruising encounter with German troops. Far away, Japan enters war on side of the Allies.

27–30 August

A Russian army that has invaded Germany is destroyed at the Battle of Tannenberg, in East Prussia.

6–12 September

In the Battle of the Marne, a Franco-British counter-attack saves Paris and pushes the German Army back northeast, to the River Aisne.

19 October– 22 November

British imperial, French and Belgian troops narrowly prevent a German breakthrough towards the English Channel, at the First Battle of Ypres. Both sides dig trenchlines.

1 November

The Ottoman Empire joins the Central Powers, having attacked Russian Black Sea ports. Days later, an Indian Expeditionary Force lands in Ottoman Mesopotamia (Iraq).

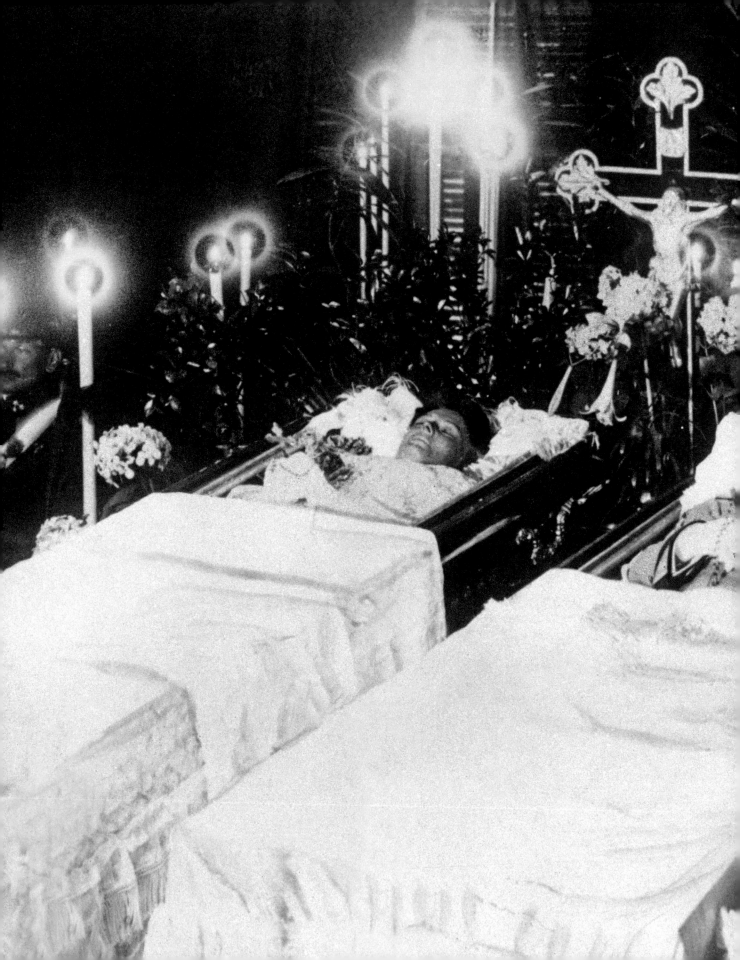

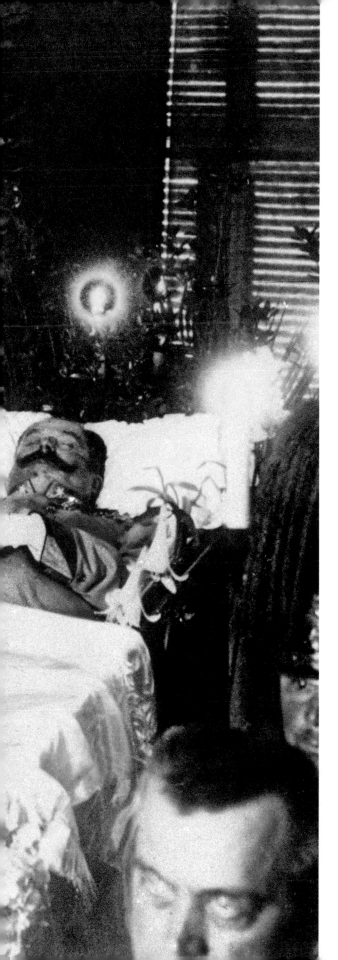

Franz Ferdinand

On the morning of 28 June 1914, Archduke Franz Ferdinand, heir presumptive to the imperial throne of Austria-Hungary, and his wife, Sophie Chotek, were riding in a motorcade through Sarajevo. The city was the capital of the province of Bosnia-Herzegovina, a troubled territory that had been controversially annexed by Austria six years previously, and which contained many Serbs who dreamed of living independent of imperial rule.

As the couple were driven through the city, they were attacked by assassins associated with the secret military society known as the 'Black Hand'. One assassin tossed a bomb at their vehicle, but it bounced off, damaging the car behind. Despite the shock, the archduke continued on his way and gave a speech at Sarajevo's town hall. After leaving, his car took a wrong turning and was forced to stop momentarily outside a café where one of the would-be assassins, Gavrilo Princip, happened to be waiting. Princip fired his pistol at close range.

Both Franz Ferdinand and his wife were fatally wounded – this photograph shows them lying in repose before their funeral. But their deaths were more than a personal tragedy. They sparked the diplomatic and military manoeuvres that became the First World War. Austria-Hungary – supported by Germany – immediately blamed and threatened Serbia; Russia, allied with France, took the opposing side. Neither would back down, and so the spiral to war began. The archduke's murder proved enough not only to light the Balkan tinderbox, but to set Europe ablaze.

The Tsar Declares War

In the summer of 1914, mass displays of patriotism erupted across Europe. Yet national leaders and crowned heads were, in varying degrees, considerably more apprehensive. The first cousins Tsar Nicholas II and Kaiser Wilhelm II exchanged telegrams – signed 'Nicky' and 'Willy' – each pleading with the other to avert a catastrophe. It came to nothing. Germany declared war on 1 August.

On 2 August the Tsar attended a religious service at the Winter Palace in St Petersburg, his capital – very soon to be renamed Petrograd. Later, he strode onto the palace balcony to read out Russia's own declaration of war on Germany. When this photograph was taken, thousands of his subjects were thronging the vast space of the palace square below him, some waving Russian tricolour flags. They cheered as Nicholas spoke of Slav brotherhood in the face of Austrian aggression and attacked Germany's failure to understand that Russian mobilization was merely a defensive measure. Now, he said, the time had come to uphold Russia's status and honour. Russians should cast aside their differences, reaffirm their bond with their Tsar and prepare for self-sacrifice.

The previous month, Russia had been rocked by protests and strikes. But at midnight on 3 August, Colonel Alfred Knox, the British military attaché to St Petersburg, wrote that: 'The spirit of the people is excellent… There is no doubt that the war is a popular one.' The coming clash of arms would test Russians' enthusiasm for conflict – and royal rule – to breaking point.

To War, By Train

Germany declared war on France on 3 August 1914, claiming that French aviators had entered German airspace and dropped bombs. Later the same afternoon, France made its own declaration of war. Although many in Paris and beyond harboured considerable doubts about the wisdom of fighting, this was not the view of President Raymond Poincaré, who demanded a *union sacrée* (sacred union) of French people and politicians.

Although France lagged behind Germany in wealth, population, technology and resources (especially iron, steel and coal), she at least had a well-developed rail network. It was now pressed into action as the French conscript army – nearly two million men, representing a much higher proportion (around 10 per cent) of the male French population than Germany's men in uniform – was moved to defend the borders, an operation that demanded more than 20,000 rail journeys.

The reservists of the 6th Territorial Infantry Regiment, pictured here boarding at Dunkirk in August 1914, are wearing the blue greatcoats, red kepis and red trousers that symbolized French military pride. Before 1914, a desire to blend into the environment had influenced the dress of the German, British and Russian armies, but to French diehards and patriotic politicians such utilitarian drabness was unacceptable. In particular, the bright red trousers, the *pantalon rouge*, were totemic. They denoted French fearlessness, which informed a strand of French military belief in *l'attaque à outrance* – relentless offensive action. To tinker with that tradition, the thinking went, would be tantamount to undermining the French fighting spirit.

The Schlieffen Plan

German mobilization in the west demanded its own colossal rail effort. At the outbreak of war, troops commenced what would be more than 40,000 train journeys from Cologne's Hauptbahnhof, from where they were transported across Europe. Moving manpower on this epic scale was no mean feat, but it was essential to fulfil the strategic aims of the so-called Schlieffen Plan, named after the late German chief-of-staff, Alfred von Schlieffen (1833–1913).

First formulated in the 1890s, the Schlieffen Plan suggested that the best way for Germany to win a European war against a Franco-Russian alliance would be to launch a lightning, six-week attack to knock out France in the west before tackling Russia in the east. To that end, Schlieffen suggested routing invasion forces through Luxembourg and neutral Belgium, bypassing heavy French border fortifications.

On 4 August 1914, a revised Schlieffen Plan was put into action. Belgium's modest, largely reservist army was no match for Germany's. Outdated forts such as those defending Liège, the 'gateway' to Belgium, and along the River Meuse, crumpled as they were pounded by massive howitzer guns. On 17 August the Belgian government abandoned Brussels; all over the country German troops poured in. By the end of November, virtually the entire country was under foreign control. The invading forces pictured here in the aftermath of Belgium's capitulation are enjoying a meal from a field kitchen. German troops would continue to occupy Belgian cities for the following four years.

Fear and Flight

As German troops invaded and the Belgian Army was thrown into a fighting retreat, thousands of ordinary Belgians were also on the move, fleeing to safety. Those pictured here were lucky enough to have motor transport, which took them to the cobbled streets of Paris, where they aroused much fascination. Others were less lucky, having to trudge for miles along the roads and fields, carrying only their most precious possessions.

As they retreated, Belgians enraged their attackers by destroying bridges and railway lines, slowing the German advance – and imperilling the timetable of the Schlieffen Plan. In response, German military chiefs chose to regard a whole raft of defensive Belgian actions as illegal warfare – or terrorism. German propaganda warned inexperienced servicemen to beware civilian snipers, ready to pick them off around any corner.

Within days of the invasion of Belgium, reports began to circulate of an uncompromising German policy of mass punishment executions and the razing of whole villages. When news spread of the wanton destruction of the university town of Louvain (Leuven) in the last week of August 1914, the Allies began to use a new phrase: 'the rape of Belgium'.

Events in Belgium shocked the world and turned minds against Germany, including in the United States. German brutality brought about the deaths of some 6,000 Belgians under occupation, but it was also a powerful propaganda tool for the Allies, whose recruitment messages for the rest of the war would be morally as well as patriotically charged.

Prince Edward and the BEF

Many Germans hoped that Britain would keep out of the war, but the Entente Cordiale with France was taken seriously across the Channel, as was Britain's long-standing treaty commitment to guarantee Belgian neutrality. The German chancellor, Theobald von Bethmann-Hollweg, could not believe Britain would send her young men to face death for the eighty-five-year-old 'scrap of paper' that guaranteed support for Belgium. He was wrong. Britain declared war on 4 August 1914.

A week later, one eager new lieutenant began his officer training. In this photograph, the twenty-year-old Edward, Prince of Wales, parades in London, dwarfed by the older and more seasoned men of the 1st Battalion Grenadier Guards, to which he was attached.

New recruits were indeed in great demand. About half of the functioning professional British Army was outside Europe, policing the Empire, and the British Expeditionary Force (BEF) that began crossing the Channel on 7 August 1914 numbered a mere 100,000 men. 'Contemptible!' declared the Kaiser, inadvertently providing a nickname they proudly bore. The BEF's baptism of fire came near the Belgian town of Mons on 23 August, where, despite wreaking havoc with their rifles and artillery, they had to fall back with their French allies, having suffered 1,600 casualties (including wounded).

By this time, men were flocking in their thousands to the recruiting stations, answering War Secretary Lord Kitchener's exhortations for 'New Armies'. Kitchener also approved Prince Edward's pleas to be allowed over to France. King George's anxieties meant Edward was kept out of firefights, but, seconded to BEF headquarters, he threw himself into his duties and earned the respect of those under his command.

Aggression in Africa

In 1885, during the 'Scramble for Africa', European statesmen had tried to ensure that their colonies on the African continent could claim neutrality in any future European conflict. Within days of the outbreak of war, those hopes had been roundly squashed.

Germany's colonies in Africa were weak and exposed from the start, being bordered by the more numerous colonies of their enemies. So it was that two weeks before any soldier of the BEF fired at the enemy in Belgium, the Allies had captured their first capital – in West Africa. From the British colony of Gold Coast (now Ghana) and then from French West Africa, small forces converged on German Togoland (now Togo), reaching the city of Lomé on 7/8 August. In fact, the very first British rifle shot of the entire war is credited to an African recruit of the Gold Coast Regiment, some of whose members are shown here, during rifle inspection.

The British troops' real goal in Togoland was a radio station at Kamina that was a key node of German imperial communications throughout Africa and across the Atlantic. But they failed to secure it, for the Kamina station's operators blew up their transmitter before it could be captured. Nevertheless, on 26 August, Togoland unconditionally surrendered. First blood had been drawn in a theatre of war that would expand rapidly, bringing fighting across the length and breadth of the African continent for the next four years.

The Battle of Tannenberg

While the BEF and the French Army fell back before the German advance through western Europe, the citizens of East Prussia, at Germany's north-eastern edge, were reeling in the face of a terrifying shock.

Ever since 1795, Prussia, Russia and Austria had shared substantial borders, and Germany's military chiefs had been able to comfort themselves with the conventional wisdom that Russia's conscript army, though massive, was badly led and poorly equipped, so would spend weeks preparing itself for war. They were therefore deeply alarmed when, in mid-August 1914, two Russian armies marched into East Prussia, sending the German Eighth Army into retreat and threatening the East Prussian capital at Königsberg. Germany was suddenly an invaded nation. A replacement general, Paul von Hindenburg, was now scrambled into place to defend the Reich.

This photograph shows Russian prisoners being transported by rail in the aftermath of an engagement that became known as the Battle of Tannenberg – in reference to a medieval conflict fought in similar territory in the year 1410. Then, the Germanic warrior-monks known as the Teutonic Order had been convincingly defeated by a coalition of Slavic forces. In 1914, the humiliation was to be reversed.

Despite the shock of the Russian advance into German territory, between 26/27 and 30 August a resurgent and reinforced German Eighth Army managed to encircle and annihilate the Russian Second Army. Estimates of the Russian dead and wounded were 50,000 (including the Russian general, Alexander Samsonov, who shot himself) but twice that number formed an ocean of 100,000 prisoners, a bare few of whom are seen here.

The Miracle of the Marne

While Russians armies were being mauled at Tannenberg, in France Marshal Joseph Joffre, the French chief-of-staff, was demanding assistance from the battered BEF for a grand if desperate counter-attack against rampant German forces, along the River Marne. The threat to France was rapidly becoming existential. To that end, Joffre sacked commanders, reconfigured his armies, and took advantage of every mode of transport, including Parisian taxis, to rush men and machines into a position to resist.

From 5 September, the Allies attacked German positions between Paris and the fortress city of Verdun. The assault was dubbed a 'miracle', since it forced the Germans back to fixed defences along the River Aisne. But this photograph makes plain the terrible price that was paid. Here, in the normally quiet commune of Maurupt-le-Montois, lay lines of shattered bodies. They added to the carpets of death already visible across north-eastern France.

German casualties were mounting, but for ordinary French servicemen – the *poilus* – no phase of the war was as deadly as its first weeks. In August 1914, French generals had sent soldiers surging into German-occupied Alsace and Lorraine, until German counter-attacks had devastated the *poilus*, conspicuous in their red and blue uniforms. The nadir of the doleful slaughter known as the 'Battle of the Frontiers' came on the 22nd, when 27,000 French soldiers were killed – more than on any other day in the war. They were but a few of the quarter of a million French casualties suffered by 31 August.

The Seventy-Five

The 'Miracle of the Marne' in September 1914 saved Paris and averted an Allied catastrophe. It also left the Schlieffen Plan in tatters. Indeed, the defeat was so ruinous to German strategy that the chief-of-staff, Helmuth von Moltke the Younger, suffered a nervous breakdown.

An essential component of the Marne victory – and of later French battles – was the 75mm field gun, seen here during French Army exercises in 1909. First developed in 1897, it was a revolutionary weapon. Its sophisticated mechanism removed the need to reposition and resight the gun between each round fired, because, although the barrel's recoil whipped back well over a metre, it stayed aligned on the target; the gun carriage did not move. The result was a much more rapid rate of fire than anything invented before it.

Other armies adopted their own versions of the 75mm. The British had the 18-pounder, the Germans a 77mm gun. But the *soixante-quinze*, as it was known, bested them all.

However, while the French had the best type of light gun, they lacked the diversity of artillery of their enemies. True, the French defenders didn't need monster howitzers, pulled by thirty-six horses, of the kind with which Germany had pulverized the forts of Belgium during the early days of the war. But the struggle in the west was about to develop in a way that would call for many, many more – and larger – guns.

Nursing the Wounded

Although in earlier times soldiers wounded on the battlefield had been left to fend for themselves, by the early twentieth century care for those injured in the line of combat was part of the basic expectations of warfare. And the appallingly bloody first weeks of the war in 1914 confirmed the need for medical operations of unprecedented proportions. Nursing was not just fundamental to maintaining morale and discipline among the troops; commanders were also keen to return to active service as many of the sick and wounded as they could.

Military nursing care had made great strides since the days of Florence Nightingale in the Crimean War of the 1850s and it provided a way for women to contribute directly to the war effort. Women's voluntary organizations sprang up across the warring nations, such as the Voluntary Aid Detachments (VADs) of the British Red Cross, who worked in casualty clearing stations and hospitals, and accompanied wounded men being ferried home for treatment.

Such volunteers were often discreet, unattached young women of respectable backgrounds, who did not need to earn a living. Less respectable, certainly less discreet, but much more famous (at least in Paris and Moscow) was the avant-garde Russian-born dancer Ida Rubinstein, pictured here. In taking up nursing duties in Paris, she swapped the exotic and risqué costumes of roles such as Salomé and Cleopatra for a nurse's 'uniform' – in her case, this striking flowing garment, designed for her by the artist Léon Bakst.

Ypres and the Indian Army

The British Expeditionary Force needed nurses just as much as any of its allies and enemies. Following the severe setback on the Marne, Germany's new military goal was to seize France's Channel ports – which would cripple the Franco-British alliance. Both sides therefore embarked on a 'race to the sea'. As new troops poured into the fighting on both sides, a desperate, chaotic battle took place around Ypres, in which British forces very narrowly prevented a breakthrough, but at a cost of 54,000 casualties.

Although the war had been under way for less than three months, the ranks of the regular BEF were shredded. So into Europe there now arrived contingents of the largest volunteer army in the world: the Indian Army. Shipped from the far reaches of the British Empire, and landing at Marseilles in late September, the Indian divisions reached the theatre of conflict in north-east France and Belgium by travelling the entire length of France overland – on foot, on horseback, by train and in fleets of requisitioned London buses. From 22 October, they joined battle.

Immediately, members of the Indian Army were dying and nursing wounds, like this group being visited by King George V. Marking the arrival of Indian troops on the Western Front, the king had sent an official welcome message: 'I look to all my Indian soldiers to uphold the British Raj against an aggressive and relentless enemy.' During the course of the war, eleven Indian soldiers would be awarded the Victoria Cross.

The Masurian Lakes

On the Eastern Front, Germany's triumph at the Battle of Tannenberg had smashed the Russian Second Army. (It had also turned General Hindenburg and his chief-of-staff, Erich Ludendorff, into national heroes, whose power in Germany was destined to grow and grow.) Despite this, however, the Russian First Army, under its commander Paul von Rennenkampf, remained on East Prussian soil, where it menaced the state capital, Königsberg (now Kaliningrad).

To deal with this threat, Hindenburg and Ludendorff gathered their forces to move against the Russians around the waterways and forests known collectively as the Masurian Lakes. They could not repeat their military coup de théâtre in this longer running affair, fought over the second week of September 1914; but, outnumbering the Russians, they forced Rennenkampf into a retreat towards the border. The Russians suffered another 100,000 dead, wounded and captured. Although the East Prussian adventure was not the end of Russian designs on Germany, the echo of these heavy defeats rang in Russian ears for a long time.

In this photograph, German machine-gunners are manning a position near the East Prussian town of Darkehmen (now Ozyorsk, Russia). Infantrymen on all sides in this war feared their vulnerability in an attack against heavy machine-gun positions. In raw statistics, machine guns did not kill as many men as did artillery, but they instilled their own form of terror as the scythe of the battlefield, often aimed low to cut men down at the knees.

The Christmas Truce

On the Western Front, nothing was quick. The First Battle of Ypres continued into mid-November, when a miserable Flanders winter set in. The fallacy of the idea that the war would be won in months was sinking in. Zigzag lines of trenchworks were beginning to appear along a front that would stretch from the North Sea to the Swiss border.

Yet before the era of trench warfare truly began, a wholly unexpected interlude reminded combatants of their shared humanity. In stretches of the British and French sectors, for a few short hours the firing stopped for Christmas. The slaughter that had already claimed hundreds of thousands of lives paused – briefly, but memorably – as soldiers remembered what they had in common.

The 'truce' started late on 24 December, the traditional day of celebration for Germans, as carols were sung and a few German Christmas trees were posted on the trench parapets. On Christmas Day, with their hands raised just in case, soldiers from both sides ventured into no-man's land between their trenches. With imperfect understanding of each other's languages, they communicated by gesture, by drinking together, with more singing, by exchanging gifts and mementoes, by acts of kindness, and in some places by impromptu games of football. They swapped items of uniform, as seen here among this mingled group from the 104th and 106th Saxon regiments and the London Rifle Brigade at Ploegsteert in Belgium. Senior commanders hated it.

Had the war truly been 'over by Christmas' as the optimists had proclaimed, it would have been a beautiful ending.

A Widening War

'Murdered by the Huns – Enlist in the 99th
and help stop such atrocities.'

Recruitment poster for the Canadian Expeditionary Force,
featuring the face of Edith Cavell

n the closing months of 1915, the British writer William Thomson Hill published a slim, fifty-five-page volume entitled *The Martyrdom of Nurse Cavell*. Its subtitle was unambiguous: *The Life Story of the Victim of Germany's Most Barbarous Crime*.

This was a bold claim, to say the least. After everything 1915 had thrown up – from poison gas at Ypres to Zeppelin raids on civilians, from the sinking of the passenger liners RMS *Lusitania* and SS *Arabic* to the murders and rapes in Belgium – there was no lack of competition for the title of Most Atrocious Deed committed in the name of the Kaiser. Yet somehow, amid all this, a vicar's daughter from a village in Norfolk achieved a form of secular sainthood, her life and fate coming to epitomize what the British, in particular, told themselves they were fighting for.

Edith Cavell's background and demeanour were blamelessly middle class. Born in Swardeston, near Norwich, in December 1865, she enjoyed a happy if rigorously evangelical childhood and grew up to demonstrate a heartfelt desire to help those in the parish who had fallen on tough times. After boarding school, she found work as a governess in Essex, and later in Belgium, then in 1896 gravitated towards nursing.

Cavell trained for two years in London and rose in the profession's ranks. This photograph shows her in 1903, when she was assistant matron at Shoreditch Infirmary (now St Leonard's Hospital, Hackney). By the outbreak of the First World War, she was back in Belgium, working in Brussels, where she was the matron in charge of a landmark training school for new nurses, the École Belge d'Infirmières Diplômées.

At the outbreak of war, Cavell happened to be visiting her mother in Norfolk, but she soon returned to Brussels, expecting – not unreasonably – that war would make plenty of work for the nurses whose training she was overseeing.

The rapid German advance through Belgium at the start of the war meant that by 20 August Brussels was already behind the lines. So were plenty of Allied servicemen, and, in the weeks following the Battle of Mons (23 August), Cavell's humanitarian activities began to follow a risky course. Her nursing school became a discreet refuge for Allied soldiers and Belgians evading the occupation authorities – part of a covert network that provided them with hiding places, false documentation and a route over the Belgian border to safety in the neutral Netherlands.

Cavell and her nurses continued this subterfuge for several months. But she inevitably took risks – and the German authorities in occupied Brussels soon noticed her. Eventually, on 8 August 1915, she was arrested. In prison for ten weeks, she refused to lie about her activities and signed a statement that served as an admission of guilt. While she was in solitary confinement, the US and Spanish ministers to Belgium attempted to intercede on her behalf, but to no avail. Cavell was court-martialled on charges relating to undermining the German war effort and sentenced to death for 'war treason'. Within forty-eight hours, early on 12 October 1915, she donned her matron's uniform one last time to face the firing squad.

Uproar followed. Britain's foreign secretary, Sir Edward Grey, felt her death would be received 'with horror and disgust not only in the Allied States but throughout the civilized world'. The European edition of the *New York Herald* duly excoriated 'one of the blackest chapters in Germany's black war history'. The reputed last words of the principled nurse, as carved into her post-war

19 February	22 April	25 April	Early May	7 May
British and French warships begin bombarding the Dardanelles strait, in a plan to capture Constantinople and knock the Ottoman Empire out of the war.	At the start of the Second Battle of Ypres, the German Army deploys poison gas (chlorine) – its first use on the Western Front.	In the Dardanelles, British (including ANZACs – Australians and New Zealanders) and French troops land on the Gallipoli peninsula. In eight months, they make little progress.	Ethnic cleansing begins, as Ottoman authorities 'relocate' millions of ethnic Armenians accused of being pro-Russian. Hundreds of thousands of men, women and children die.	The British passenger liner RMS *Lusitania* is torpedoed by a German U-boat off the Irish coast, killing nearly 1,200 (including 128 Americans).

London monument, embodied a Christ-like meekness that only made her posthumous power greater: 'Patriotism is not enough. I must have no hatred or bitterness for anyone.'

Cavell's execution was immediately exploited by the British propaganda machine to incite hatred and bitterness towards the Germans. Not that Kaiser Wilhelm's army or navy did anything in 1915 to help their reputations. After the commander of the German High Seas Fleet announced, in February, that 'every enemy merchant vessel encountered in [the waters around Great Britain and Ireland] will be destroyed', U-boats went on the prowl, looking for Allied prey. Torpedoing merchant ships without warning was bad enough, but when the passenger liner RMS *Lusitania* was sunk off Ireland, there was an international furore. In the air, too, Germany went beyond the pale in the deliberate bombing of civilian targets using bloated airships, such as Zeppelins.

In 1915, the trenches begun the previous year continued to expand, and fast came to be seen as the defining feature of the Western Front. As soldiers on both sides adapted to subterranean lives worsened by boredom, squalor, noise and danger, their commanders puzzled over how to break the deadlock. Ever more artillery seemed the answer, but, as the British found, their factories struggled to produce enough shells for the sheer scale of bombardment demanded. Thousands of new women workers, the 'munitionettes', came to the rescue as the government rushed to invest in arms manufacturing.

Other deadly weapons soon arrived. At the Second Battle of Ypres, German troops used poison gas for the first time. The outcry following this flagrant breach of the rules of war was loud but brief, as all the armies started to produce and deploy their own gas weapons.

The boundaries of war spread, too. In 1915, Italy abandoned past commitments to Germany and Austria-Hungary, threw in her lot with the Allies, and rushed into an attack against Austria, beginning an icy mountain war. Meanwhile, further east, Austrians tried, in vain, to forestall an invasion by Russia.

In November 1914 the Ottoman Empire joined the Central Powers, and between February and October 1915 proceeded to fend off an Allied assault on the Gallipoli peninsula, despite heroic efforts by troops from Australia and New Zealand. But elsewhere, Ottoman defeat by the Russians in the Caucasus mountains led to a genocidal massacre of ethnic Armenians, who were made scapegoats for the defeat.

As the First World War widened and deepened, so the mood of the world darkened. The courageous efforts of people like Edith Cavell provided rare, beautiful points of light.

23 June	5 September	25 September	9 October	12 October
Having declared war on Austria-Hungary in April, Italy begins the first of 12 battles along the Isonzo River and the unforgiving landscape of the Dolomites.	After a wholesale Russian retreat along the Eastern Front, Tsar Nicholas II makes himself commander-in-chief of the Russian Army.	On the Western Front, British and French offensives at Loos and in the Champagne begin; they last until November with little to show except more casualties.	Belgrade falls, beginning the conquest of Serbia by armies from Germany, Austria-Hungary and their new ally Bulgaria. The Serbian Army makes a desperate escape.	British nurse Edith Cavell, arrested in occupied Belgium for aiding Allied soldiers to escape, is tried and executed, prompting international condemnation of Germany.

U-boats

Britain's position as a world superpower owed much to the Royal Navy. But British ships were not invincible, and the hazard naval commanders feared the most were the Kaiser's submarines, or U-boats (from *Unterseeboot*, literally 'undersea boat'). Experiments with building U-boats had taken place in Germany since the 1850s and manufacturing them had become a key element of Kaiser Wilhelm II's pre-war naval strategy. As a result, at the outbreak of the First World War the German navy had more than thirty U-boats active or under construction, and during the course of the war, ten times as many would be put into active service.

Fighting aboard U-boats was hard work. Sailors had to deal with the cramped, hot, dangerous and claustrophobic nature of life below the waves, as this image of submariners doing checks in a U-boat's oil-powered engine room suggests. But submarines were potent weapons of war. On 22 September 1914 the U-boat *U-9* torpedoed and sank three British cruisers in the North Sea. These were the first of several dozen warships and thousands of merchant vessels that would fall victim to U-boat attacks during the next four years. Between 1914 and 1918, around 2,600 vessels were sunk by underwater attacks. Germany's most successful U-boat commander of the war, Lothar von Arnauld de la Perière, was singlehandedly responsible for destroying nearly half a million tons of shipping. Figures like these represented a menace pitched perfectly to excite the fears of an island nation.

War in Mesopotamia

As war spread below the seas, so it entered new lands, including those of the Ottoman Empire, whose territory extended from Constantinople across Anatolia and into the Arabian Peninsula, and whose sultan claimed spiritual supremacy over the Sunni Muslim world.

Ottoman Turkey was an empire in search of friends. Historically hostile to Russia, by 1914 relations with Britain had also turned chilly. Yet at the same time, the Ottomans had forged closer links with Germany, based on a mutual interest in the (incomplete) Berlin–Baghdad railway, a section of which is shown in this photograph.

Although the Ottoman government pretended neutrality at the outbreak of war, in August 1914 members of the pro-war 'Young Turk' faction, including the minister for war, Enver Pasha, made a secret promise to support Germany and her allies against Russia. This alliance became public knowledge on 4 November 1914, when Ottoman ships bombarded Russia's port of Odessa, on the Black Sea. Two days later, British ships in the Arabian Gulf responded, by firing into the Shatt-al-Arab waterway in southern Mesopotamia (Iraq). They were preparing the way for the landing of an Indian Expeditionary Force on Ottoman soil.

By November 1915, British imperial troops were within 20 miles (32km) of Baghdad. However, by this point the invaders were overstretched, and Ottoman troops were able to use completed portions of the Berlin–Baghdad railway to resupply themselves and prepare for counter-attack.

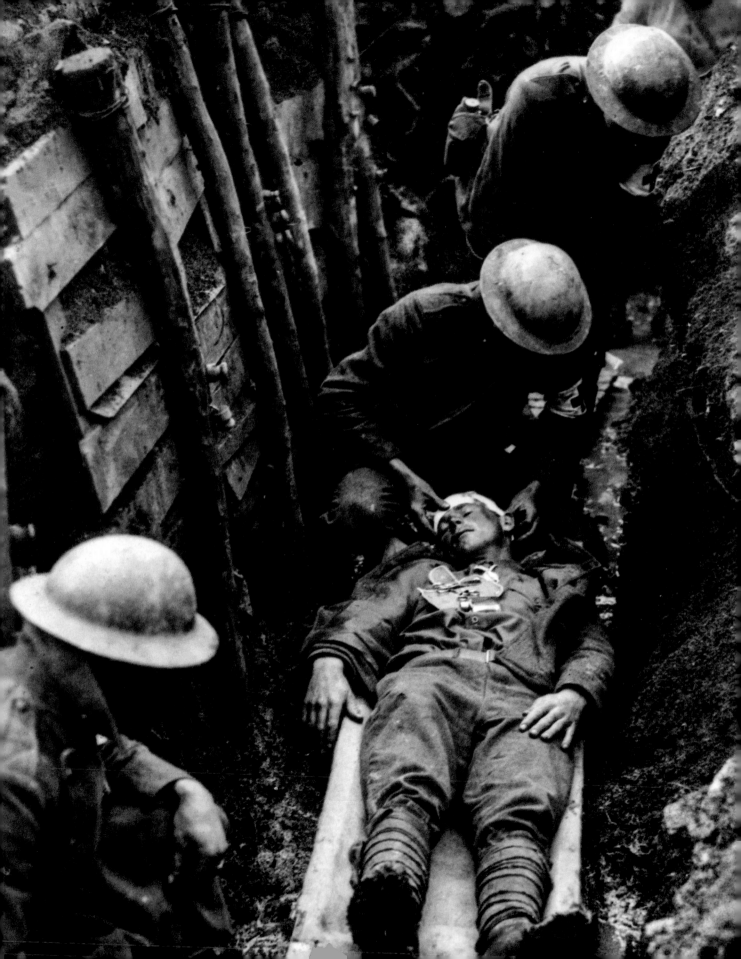

Life in the Trenches

By the beginning of 1915, the Western Front was dominated by trench warfare. Trenches varied with the landscape, but in general they were dug deep into the ground, with their walls shored up with boards and stakes. German trenches tended to be better positioned, more elaborate and more durable than those dug by the Allies.

Although Allied and German forward trenches could be just a few dozen metres from one another, both sides also created intricate secondary and tertiary networks of trenches stretching far behind the front line, connected by mazes of communication trenches. Beyond these lay heavy artillery and huge, evolving hinterlands of infrastructure to support the men, machines and horses.

As the reality of this grim industrialized war began to bite, some long-held military traditions were abandoned. The French Army abandoned the *pantalon rouge* in favour of the more discreet *horizon bleu* uniform, designed to merge into the skyline. Armies also adopted metal helmets, such as the French Adrian and the British Brodie. Both can be seen in this photograph, which shows a Red Cross team tending a head wound.

Life in the trenches was frequently soggy and unhygienic. Men suffered with lice and rats, 'trench foot' and 'trench fever' and were fed on bland, repetitive rations including tinned or 'bully' beef. To try to alleviate the tedium and discomfort, troops were regularly rotated between trench lines and allowed breaks 'out of the line', when they could get deloused and even share a bottle of *vin rouge*.

The Artillery War

By 1915, twenty-five years of rapid military innovation had transformed the relationship between humans and artillery. By the outbreak of the First World War, massive guns could be deployed with previously unimaginable lethality, blasting out a relentless barrage of shrapnel shells, high explosives and even gas shells.

As well as long-barrelled guns, battlefields were now plagued by howitzers – snub-nosed weapons whose history went back to siege warfare in the seventeenth century. Howitzers sent shells arcing high into the air before plummeting onto enemy gunnery, fortifications or trenches. A direct hit would obliterate virtually everything within a large radius.

The example shown here is a German 15cm *schwere Feldhaubitze*, or 'heavy field howitzer', concealed in a camouflaged placement to hide it from the prying eyes of enemy spotter planes. Despite the 'heavy' tag, this howitzer was a versatile and manoeuvrable workhorse of a weapon, which elicited a grudging respect in Allied trenches.

The artillerymen here are covering their ears, presumably in preparation to fire. Few soldiers on the Western Front ever forgot the cacophony of artillery bombardments, whose effects were a major cause of the post-traumatic stress disorder colloquially known as 'shell shock'. Artillery also contributed significantly to another burgeoning category of war casualties: the 'missing', a term used to accommodate all those warriors who ended their days reduced to unidentifiable pieces of flesh and bone.

The Shell Crisis

On 9 May 1915 a British attack on the Western Front, known as the Battle of Aubers Ridge, ended in unmitigated failure, with no territory or advantage won, and 23,000 casualties suffered. In the aftermath, Sir John French, commander-in-chief of the British Expeditionary Force, complained bitterly to a journalist of *The Times* about the lack of high-explosive shells available to his artillery. When newspaper reports to that effect duly appeared, the 'shell crisis' became a national scandal. In response, a new Ministry of Munitions was created, headed by the effervescent Welshman David Lloyd George. Its mandate was to oversee a massive increase in shell production.

Since making more shells meant building new arms factories, it took some time for this policy to translate to the battlefield. However, the shell crisis had a profound impact on British society, as large numbers of women were called upon to produce the required ammunition. Thanks to the mass enlistment of men into the armed services, women's work in Britain had already been diversifying; and now the 'munitionettes' flowed into the new arms factories.

They were paid less than men, worked long hours, and some, particularly the shell-fillers, took their chances with toxic substances and accidental explosions. But their jobs provided income, welfare, food, sometimes housing, and a sense of community that many welcomed. Women's work during this war played an important role in the struggle for women's suffrage.

The Sinking of the *Lusitania*

On 1 May 1915, RMS *Lusitania*, a luxurious British passenger liner, departed New York bound for Britain with nearly 2,000 people aboard and a quantity of arms and ammunition in the cargo hold. Thanks to German attempts to blockade British shipping, and the presence of U-boats beneath the waves, the waters around Europe were hardly a haven of calm. But the rules of war held that passenger liners should never be targeted by military vessels.

On 7 May, protocol was abandoned. The *Lusitania* was in waters off the southern coast of Ireland when the German submarine *U-20* fired a torpedo. It found its mark in her hull, ripping a hole below the waterline and causing an internal explosion. As the liner listed, most of her lifeboats became unusable. *Lusitania* sank within twenty minutes of the attack, with the loss of 1,198 lives. Only one in five of the children aboard survived. Those few bodies that were recovered – numbering around three hundred – were buried in Ireland (as shown here), at mass funerals attended by hundreds of mourners.

Although a tragic loss of civilian life, the sinking of the *Lusitania* was a major victory for Allied propaganda, which emphasized German viciousness and the illegality of the Kaiser's war. In the United States, public opinion was outraged at the killing of all but a handful of the 139 Americans on board. How long could the USA avoid entry into a war that now manifestly endangered American lives?

Gallipoli

This beach on the Gallipoli peninsula in Turkey, now known as Anzac Cove, was the starting point of one of the most ignominious Allied operations of the First World War.

The Gallipoli campaign was initially meant to be a naval affair. The aim was to send warships into the Dardanelles strait, which would restore Russian access to the Mediterranean via the Black Sea, and pave the way for attacks on Constantinople (Istanbul) to cripple the Ottoman Empire. The campaign began on 19 February 1915. However, within weeks, British and French vessels had been battered by Ottoman artillery batteries and sea mines. It became clear that amphibious landings were needed to clear the threat from the shore.

At first light on Sunday 25 April 1915, therefore, thousands of troops, largely of the Australian and New Zealand Army Corps (ANZAC), disembarked on the sand to begin a campaign to take the peninsula. They were in for months of attritional uphill fighting. The Allies were tormented by daytime heat and night-time cold, flies and floodings, dysentery and malaria. In November, Lord Kitchener visited and decided to abandon the campaign. Allied troops were extracted by 9 January 1916.

Britain's First Lord of the Admiralty, Winston Churchill, lost his job as a result of Gallipoli. By contrast, the Turkish divisional commander Mustafa Kemal, later to be known as Atatürk, emerged as an Ottoman hero. In Australia and New Zealand, Gallipoli remains central to modern ideas about nationhood and remembrance.

Austria's Soldiers

Archduke Joseph Ferdinand of Austria (*right*), who also enjoyed the historic title of Duke of Tuscany, was a man steeped in Austrian military tradition. In 1915, he led the Austrian Fourth Army. But in an Austro-Hungarian Empire riven by competing nationalisms, multiple languages and superficial loyalties, it was an uphill struggle to imbue troops with a sense of cohesion and to maintain morale. In this propaganda photograph, the archduke is posing alongside thirteen-year-old Josef Kaswurm, from the Tyrol: the youngest soldier in imperial service.

Propaganda was needed, because as 1915 opened, Austria-Hungary's problems were multiplying. In launching weak attacks on both Serbia and Russia, the empire's armies had suffered more than 950,000 casualties. They had been driven out of Serbia, and Russia had counter-invaded Galicia (on the modern-day border between Poland and Ukraine), where the archduke was serving. Meanwhile, behind Russian lines, isolated and besieged, in the immense fortress complex of Przemyśl, more than 130,000 soldiers and civilians had become stranded and trapped. (An attempt ordered by the Austrian chief of the general staff, Conrad von Hötzendorf, to relieve the fortress in the first three months of 1915 ended in ignominy, with around 790,000 more casualties accrued before Przemyśl finally surrendered in March.)

Despite his empire's ailing fortunes during the First World War, the archduke survived. He eventually died in 1942, having endured a brief period in a Nazi concentration camp. Kaswurm's fate is unknown.

The Armenian Genocide

'An Armenian child lies dead in the fields within sight of help and safety at Aleppo.' This simple, awful caption written in faded typescript accompanies the original black-and-white version of this photograph, which has been reproduced thousands of times to illustrate the horrors of a cycle of violence widely known as the Armenian genocide.

Tensions between Turks and Armenian Christians in eastern Anatolia had existed since the days of the medieval crusades. The poisonous circumstances of the First World War ensured that in 1915 hundreds of years of ill feeling now boiled over. Early in that year, the Ottoman Third Army was routed by Russian troops in the southern Caucasus. Many attributed the defeat to ethnic Armenians fighting – treacherously, in Turkish eyes – with the Russians. This blame narrative fed into jihadist sentiment and the nationalist politics of the Young Turk movement – with deadly consequences.

In May 1915, an Ottoman government decree was issued ordering the forcible removal of Turkey's Armenian population to Syria. During the course of the deportations that followed, as many as one million Armenians died, from starvation, disease, violence, deprivation, neglect and exposure. This massive loss of civilian life, the direct consequence of targeted Ottoman policy, has unsurprisingly been called a genocide. The designation is still hotly denied in Turkey. But the photographic legacy – including many appalling images captured by the German soldier and medical officer Armin T. Wegner – tells its own story.

Italy Enters the War

Italian mountain troops, known as the *Alpini*, had a long and distinguished history of service inside and outside Italy. The *Alpini* had fought in Abyssinia (Ethiopia and Eritrea) during Italy's attempts at colonial conquest in the 1880s and 1890s, and later in the Libyan desert. In 1915, however, they fought in one of the most punishing terrains of the First World War – the high-altitude *fronte alpino* (Alpine Front) on the border with Austria-Hungary.

Despite being a member of the Triple Alliance, with Germany and Austria-Hungary, the Italian government declined to join the fighting in the autumn of 1914, instead claiming neutrality as it waited to see which way the war would go. It was not until May 1915 that Italy was persuaded to enter the fray – on the Allied side, having been tempted by generous British war loans and the prospect of regaining territory around the north-eastern Adriatic known as *Italia irredenta* ('unredeemed Italy').

Belatedly called into service, the *Alpini* were soon busy doing what they did best: gouging out ice tunnels, climbing sheer rock faces, and risking falls and avalanches. They took part in a series of battles fought along the Isonzo River and the border with what is now Slovenia. In the first four of these, in 1915, Italy traded around 300,000 casualties for a few miles of Austrian territory. There would be eight more battles of the Isonzo during the following two years.

Flight from Serbia

Austro-Hungarian armies had invaded Serbia three times in 1914 and on each occasion they had been beaten back. A year later, however, the situation was reversed. Faced by a joint assault of German, Austro-Hungarian and Bulgarian forces, in late November 1915, the Serbian Army, together with its king, Peter I, and retinues of civilian followers, was forced to embark on a long winter march through the mountain passes of Montenegro and Albania, heading for the Adriatic coast, where survivors were to be evacuated by the Allies to Corfu.

In the gruelling expedition, sometimes called the Albanian Golgotha, men, women and children starved or sickened, and one in ten of the 140,000-odd refugees died. Some died of hunger and thirst, others of exposure or epidemic influenza. The marchers were also at the mercy of Albanian tribal attacks: there was little love for Serbians in the Albanian countryside, where memories of the ferocious Balkan wars fought earlier in the decade remained strong.

A moment during the Serbian escape is captured in this photograph. Serbian soldiers, with a flag bearing the double eagle that has symbolized Serb national identity since the medieval Nemanjić dynasty, march past what appears to be a shoe shop, watched by curious onlookers.

Serbian forces who survived the march to the coast were often shipped on to the so-called Salonika Front, in Macedonia. Meanwhile, the Serbian population faced a terrible wartime occupation. In relative terms, more Serbs died in this war than did citizens of any other fighting nation.

Poison Gas

Military scientists experimented with using poison gas against enemy troops on the Eastern Front; but its first major use on the battlefield came on 22 April 1915, when the Germans released more than 5,700 canisters of chlorine gas against French and French North African troops during the Second Battle of Ypres. Airborne chlorine scorched the lungs of those who inhaled it, causing panic as well as terrible internal injuries.

Using gas in warfare was officially considered an affront to humanity – the Hague Convention of 1899 had prohibited the 'diffusion of asphyxiating or deleterious gases' on the battlefield. But very quickly the efficiency of poison gas at disabling its victims led to its widespread use by all sides, and troops on the front line were given protective equipment as a matter of course.

At first, anti-gas kits consisted of goggles and face pads soaked in bicarbonate of soda – or urine. But by autumn 1915, prototypes of the respirator gas mask became available, as modelled by these German soldiers. Their donkey is wearing a human mask, but specialized equine masks became available too.

Soon new types of gas were developed, such as 'mustard gas', which burnt the skin. Gas shells replaced canisters for more reliable dispersion. And poets recorded the hateful nature of gas for later generations. In 'Dulce et Decorum Est', the British soldier Wilfred Owen described blood 'gargling from the froth-corrupted lungs, / Obscene as cancer, bitter as the cud'. Only 2 per cent of deaths in the war were caused by gas, but it retained throughout the dark power of nightmare.

Airship Attacks

In the first year of the Great War it seemed as though all the nineteenth-century rules of conflict had been abandoned. A grisly new era of warfare had emerged, in which mass death and assaults on civilians were becoming normalized. Even mainland Britain, which had hardly ever experienced the direct impact of European conflict, was not safe.

The first bombardments of British civilians came from opportunistic battlecruisers, which shelled Great Yarmouth on 3 November 1914. But two months later, on 19 January 1915, the same Norfolk town (as well as nearby King's Lynn) became the first in Britain to be targeted by a new danger: airships.

Airship attacks were part of a deliberate German attempt to sap British civilian morale. By night, hydrogen-filled dirigibles – mainly aluminium-framed Zeppelins, but sometimes wooden-framed Schütte-Lanzes – would release payloads of up to 1,360kg (3,000lb) of explosives on to towns below. On 31 May 1915, London was hit for the first time, when bombs dropped across the East End and the north of the city killed or injured forty people.

Scenes of destruction, like the one photographed here, drew curious crowds, eager for a taste of 'real' war. But public outrage also spurred the organization of air defences. By autumn 1916 Britain's Royal Flying Corps were able to destroy dirigibles. Their 'kills' were cheered by civilians below. Yet within a few months, airship attacks were old news. A more efficient aerial killer was emerging: bomber planes.

1916

Attrition

I found his head and shoulders lying some
distance outside the trench, and his legs inside;
all else of the poor fellow had
entirely disappeared.

Captain R. P. Perrin, on the fate of his orderly
during the Somme campaign
(14 July 1916)

At 7.00 a.m. on 1 July 1916, in a narrow British support trench opposite the little village of Beaumont Hamel in Picardy, northern France, a handful of men attempted a last few minutes of rest under cover. Around them all, the landscape had a wintry appearance. Although it was high summer, this was chalk country, and trench-digging had dispersed a white layer across the ground. As the men waited, John Warwick Brooke, a photographer attached to the Royal Engineers, caught a look in the eyes of one man – perhaps of trepidation, perhaps resignation or just plain weariness.

During the past week, 1,400 Allied guns had rained artillery shells on the German lines opposite. At 7.20 a.m. something even more dramatic shook the earth. Beneath Hawthorn Ridge – a German-occupied high point outside Beaumont Hamel – 40,600lb (18,416kg) of 'ammonal' (an explosive compound of ammonium nitrate and aluminium powder) was detonated. During the next ten minutes. more gigantic mines also blew before finally, at 7.30 a.m. – Zero Hour – British and French infantry clambered out of their trenches to commence the assault.

For many of the British Tommies, this was their introduction to war. They had signed up in 'pals battalions', recruited from the same localities and workplaces. Now, they were on the Somme.

The men advanced slowly together, as they had been instructed: rifles shouldered and 60lb (27kg) of kit on their backs. They had been told by their officers that enemy trenches would present little threat, since they would already have been obliterated by the artillery. This soon proved to be untrue. In fact, the bombardment had failed to destroy barbed wire or penetrate German bunkers. Thus, in the north of the sector, which included Beaumont Hamel, two waves of British soldiers were caught in the wire and massacred by machine guns. Survivors crawled back under German artillery fire. The attack was more successful further south, particularly for the French, but the British story was of unprecedented loss. On the first day of the Somme, 57,470 British died, went missing and or were wounded: the worst toll of casualties for any day in the British Army's history, before or since. Four more months of bloody, grinding attrition lay ahead.

The Somme offensive was the product of long planning. In December 1915, Allied commanders agreed to coordinate simultaneous attacks against German positions. Two months later, the British commander-in-chief on the Western Front, Sir Douglas Haig, agreed that the British contribution would take place around the Somme and Ancre rivers. However, on 21 February 1916, thousands of German shells pounded the forests and forts around the French citadel of Verdun, beginning a titanic ten-month Franco-German struggle there, and Allied plans were thrown into disarray.

As a result of the need to defend Verdun, the Somme offensive was brought nearer, then delayed, then temporarily shelved. Eventually, Haig and his political masters agreed to launch it at the end of June, in the hope of drawing German troops away from Verdun. The British now agreed to shoulder the bulk of the fighting, using 'New Armies' composed of men recruited since 1914. In many ways, they were unfit and unready for battle, and Haig knew it.

The Somme campaign lasted until November, the Verdun campaign until December. There were dizzying death tolls on all sides – the British and imperial forces suffered the loss of more than 21,000 lives for every mile

21 February 1916	24–29 April 1916	31 May–1 June 1916	4 June 1916	1 July 1916
Allied offensive plans are thrown into disarray by a massive German attack against the French fortress city of Verdun: the concentrated, bloody battle lasts until December.	In Ireland's Easter Rising, armed nationalists, mainly in Dublin, fight with British troops before surrendering; the rebel leaders are swiftly tried and executed.	The British and German navies clash inconclusively in the First World War's only large-scale sea battle, called 'Jutland' (or 'Skagerrak'), fought off the coast of Denmark.	Russia's General Alexei Brusilov launches a surprise offensive on the Eastern Front, almost leading to Austro-Hungarian collapse; but Russian success is temporary.	The British Army sustains nearly 60,000 casualties at the start of the Anglo-French offensive on the River Somme. By its end (November) 5 miles (8km) of territory has been won.

they advanced. The arrival of tanks on the Allied side, in September 1916, threw the German defenders into panic, but brought no decisive breakthroughs. One growth industry was treating the wounded, reflected in the burgeoning women's voluntary organizations operating behind the front lines.

Looking back on the Somme in a dispatch of 23 December, Haig described the campaign as having been worth it 'to wear down the strength of the forces opposed to us'. In a very narrow sense he was correct, for by early 1917 the German quartermaster-general Erich Ludendorff was ordering the German troops' withdrawal to a better defended line. But the victory – if that was what it was – had come at the most appalling cost, and the mere name of the Somme has since become a byword for misery, agony and a needless waste of human life.

Beyond the Western Front, in 1916–17 the British war effort waxed and waned. A clash of naval fleets in the Battle of Jutland cost thousands of lives, and it was followed in early June 1916 by the death at sea of a national hero – Earl Kitchener himself, the field marshal whose call to arms had been answered by so many young men now en route to the Somme. A new but much more unorthodox national hero was emerging in the sands of the Middle East: T.E. Lawrence 'of Arabia', but at Kut, on the other side of the Arabian peninsula, besieged Indian troops faced starvation and disease. The war fuelled violence in Ireland, where militant republicans tried to stage a revolution. And in August 1917, Haig began a Flanders offensive: a campaign that included the atrocious rain- and mud-filled Battle of Passchendaele, and which left hundreds of thousands more British, imperial and German soldiers dead.

In Germany, general shock at the casualties caused by the Kaiser's war steadily increased. It was true that in many places the war had gone rather well for Germany in 1916–17: Italian defeat at Caporetto, the occupation of Romania, and revolutionary spirit sweeping Russia were all good news for the Central Powers. Yet the Western Front remained stubbornly mired.

At the Somme, the German general Otto von Below had called for immoveable defence, demanding that his troops ensure that 'Only over corpses may the enemy find his way forward.' The cost of this attitude, which prevailed on all sides, was captured by Wilfred Owen, who served at the Somme and distilled its horror in his poem 'Anthem for Doomed Youth'. 'What passing-bells for these who die as cattle?' he wrote. 'Only the monstrous anger of the guns.'

8–14 March 1917

A week of revolutionary turmoil in Russia, reflecting discontent at shortages and war failures, brings in a new Provisional Government and forces the Tsar to abdicate.

6 April 1917

Angered by German U-boat actions and other provocations, the USA enters the First World War as an 'Associated' power.

9–12 April 1917

The difficult and skilful capture of Vimy Ridge, during the Battle of Arras, becomes the most celebrated achievement of Canada's troops in the First World War.

31 July 1917

British, ANZAC and Canadian troops launch the Third Battle of Ypres (to 10 November): the battle for Passchendaele becomes notorious for casualties and boggy conditions.

24 October 1917

After 11 wearying battles on the Isonzo River, in the 12th, also called 'Caporetto', German and Austro-Hungarian forces send the Italian Army into a deep, frantic retreat.

Verdun

The city of Verdun, on the River Meuse in north-eastern France, had long experience of German aggression: it had been attacked by Prussian forces in both Napoleonic times and during the Franco-Prussian War of 1870–71. As a result, by the time of the First World War it was staunchly and massively defended, with a ring of nineteen fortresses to protect it from assault. Unfortunately, in 1916 its symbolism as a bulwark of French defence helped turn the land around Verdun into a slaughterhouse.

The Battle of Verdun began at 4 a.m. on 21 February 1916, when shells from 1,200 German guns exploded along a 25-mile (40km) front, before infantry surged in. Within four days, Verdun's largest fort, Douaumont, surrendered. Shock waves rippled throughout France, and Allied troops were flung headlong into the region to attempt to hold the German advance at bay.

For the next nine months, until November 1916 when the French retook Douaumont, both sides approached the Battle of Verdun as a grim applied example of warfare by attrition. The German aim, asserted by their chief-of-staff, Erich von Falkenhayn, was to try to bleed the French Army 'to death'. The French, for their part, adopted a strategy summarized by General Robert Nivelle, who stated: *'Ils ne passeront pas!'* ('They shall not pass!'). Verdun became the longest battle of the war, producing roughly 700,000 casualties, including a quarter of a million dead or missing. This picture shows a lifeless German serviceman – just one of that grotesque number.

The Easter Rising

Britain's commitments to the world war had diverted attention from serious problems on the home front. In April 1916 these erupted, with a rebellion in Dublin against British rule in Ireland, which became known as the Easter Rising.

In 1914 the British government had been wrestling with the problems of granting Ireland Home Rule. Then, it had been agreed that the full implementation of Home Rule would have to wait until the fight against the Kaiser was over. But not everyone was happy: particularly members of the Irish Republican Brotherhood (IRB), who (with German backing) viewed the First World War not as an interval in the struggle for independence, but as an opportunity.

On Easter Monday, 24 April 1916, armed IRB revolutionaries gathered in central Dublin and marched on locations around the city. They established their headquarters at the General Post Office (GPO), and began a five-day battle with British forces. When the fighting was over, parts of Dublin lay in rubble and the GPO was a pockmarked, burnt-out shell. This photo shows children clambering over a shattered street, which has been ruined by fighting that involved shells, machine-gun fire and grenades.

More than 450 people died in the Easter Rising and fierce reprisals followed, in which the British executed fifteen rebel leaders by firing squad. But revenge would prove to be very unhelpful, serving to harden popular support for the Irish nationalist movement. Trouble between Britain and Ireland was a very long way from being over.

The Siege of Kut

Nearly 6,000km away from Dublin, in Mesopotamia, the spring of 1916 brought very different problems for Britain. Thousands of British and Indian troops were besieged by the Ottoman Army in the town of Kut, a little way south of Baghdad.

The siege of Kut began in December 1915, when British imperial troops falling back from a bloody battle at Ctesiphon were ordered by their commander, Major-General Sir Charles Townshend, to take refuge in the town. There they were pinned down by forces under the command of the notoriously brutal Turkish commander Halil Pasha and an elderly Prussian field marshal named Colmar Freiherr von der Goltz.

Attempts to relieve Kut proved futile, and a series of military expeditions to break the siege cost the British more than 20,000 casualties. Meanwhile, inside Kut, food and supplies failed. Men ate their horses and malnutrition caused disease to spread. Eventually, on 29 April 1916, Townshend surrendered. He spent the rest of the war under house arrest, but his emaciated troops, like the Indian soldier photographed here, suffered far grimmer fates. Around four thousand men died in captivity, some from disease and others from exhaustion, as they were sent on forced marches through the Iraqi desert in unbearable heat.

For the Ottomans, this was a triumph. For the British, the siege of Kut was a debacle to compare with Gallipoli – and it was judged by many as the most abject Allied defeat of the entire war.

☞ The Brusilov Offensive

On the Eastern Front in Europe, 1916 brought one of the deadliest and most dramatic military campaigns ever fought. It was carried out on the orders of Tsar Nicholas II, who had taken personal command of the Russian war effort the previous September, but named after his most brilliant general, Aleksei Brusilov.

The aims of the Brusilov Offensive were to respond to a series of demoralizing Russian defeats in the first year of the war, to inflict catastrophic damage on the Austro-Hungarian army and to relieve pressure on Russia's allies on the Western and Italian fronts. Rather than relying on attrition, Brusilov planned fast, targeted strikes of overwhelming force against weak points in enemy lines, followed up by lightning advances of massive numbers of troops. He would concentrate on territory around Kovel and Lviv (modern Ukraine).

The offensive began on 4 June 1916. It was a huge success. Hundreds of thousands of prisoners were taken within the first week, and by the end of summer Brusilov had pushed all the way to the Carpathian mountains. Casualties were appalling on both sides, but the damage to the Austro-Hungarian Empire was ultimately fatal.

In this image, Tsar Nicholas is inspecting some of the troops destined for the Brusilov Offensive. Typically, they wear peaked caps – few Russian soldiers had helmets. To face the rigours of climate and terrain, the men carry greatcoats rolled up around their torsos, and wear high-quality black leather boots.

Kitchener's Farewell

On 1 June 1916, the, sixty-five-year-old Field Marshal Lord (Horatio Herbert) Kitchener was photographed striding purposefully down the steps of Britain's War Office. Four days later, he was dead. Kitchener was aboard the cruiser HMS *Hampshire*, on his way to a summit in Russia, when his ship collided with a German sea mine near Scapa Flow and sank. His body was never found.

Kitchener's death shocked the nation, for he was one of the British Empire's greatest celebrities. At the turn of the century he had made his reputation fighting in Sudan and South Africa; in August 1914 he had been appointed as Secretary of State for War, and had rightly judged that Britain was destined for a war of far greater length and severity than most around him realized.

In light of this, Kitchener had urged a major military recruitment drive – lending his distinctive moustachioed countenance to posters calling on patriotic young Britons to sign up for service. He had literally become the face of the war effort. King George V called his death 'a heavy blow to me and a great loss to the nation and the allies'.

The impact of Kitchener's death was worsened by the fact that it coincided with another major naval shock: the Battle of Jutland. Fought off the coast of Denmark between 31 May and 1 June, Jutland was the largest naval contest of the war and the only major clash of British and German battleships. Nearly 10,000 sailors died, and the combined losses of warships amounted to a total of twenty-five ships (almost 200,000 tonnes).

Guns of the Somme

Although the Battle of the Somme officially began a month after Kitchener's death, on 1 July 1916, it was preceded by an Allied artillery barrage that lasted for seven days and rained around 1.7 million shells on German lines. Yet despite this monstrous battering, when British troops began their marches on enemy positions, they were mown down in their thousands by machine-gun fire from defenders who had been untouched by the shelling of the previous week.

This was the paradox of artillery on the Western Front. Despite the terror and the carnage that heavy shelling could cause, it was a blunt instrument that often failed in its purpose, generally serving as an alert to the enemy that an attack was imminent.

The British Army's largest guns were handled by the Royal Garrison Artillery (RGA). This photograph, taken in August 1916 during the Somme offensive, shows the RGA's 39th Siege Battery in action on the chalky terrain of the Fricourt–Mametz valley. They are firing 8-inch heavy howitzers: these were considered a reliable workhorse gun, and were often used to try to knock out enemy artillery, fortified positions and infrastructure.

The RGA also operated lighter and more mobile 6-inch howitzers, 9.2-inch howitzers that weighed over 40 tons and huge 12-inch howitzers, which were sometimes mounted on rail undercarriages for transport. Even larger were the RGA's 15-inch howitzers: spectacularly massive, these were so unwieldy that relatively few were deployed.

Romania's Conqueror

One of the most striking and experienced officers in the German army, Field Marshal August von Mackensen was a veteran of wars stretching back to the 1870s, and despite being of non-noble birth, he enjoyed the confidence and friendship of Kaiser Wilhelm himself. Aged sixty-four at the outbreak of war, much of Mackensen's vast military experience had been earned in Prussian Hussars regiments, which earned him the right to wear the black *Totenkopf* (death's head) uniform, complete with fur busby, in which he is photographed here.

In 1914 and 1915 Mackensen had commanded armies with great distinction on the Eastern Front and against Serbia, earning the admiration of his staff, who knew him as a 'hands-on commander with the instinct of a hunter'. In 1916, he had a new prey in his sights: Romania.

Romania declared war against Austria-Hungary in August 1916, marching troops into Transylvania. In response, Mackensen was sent into Romania from the south with a multinational army including German, Ottoman, Austro-Hungarian and Bulgarian units. By December he had captured Bucharest. He was handsomely rewarded for another stunning success: the Kaiser awarded him the highest class of the Iron Cross and named a new battleship class after him.

In 1917, Mackensen was appointed as the military governor of occupied Romania and survived long beyond the end of the First World War. He lived until 1945, when he was ninety-five. His life and public career had stretched from the Franco-Prussian War to the rise and fall of the Third Reich.

Tanks

While Mackensen was in Romania, the Somme continued to devour lives, money and military attention. As it did so, new technologies were deployed to try to break the deadlock. On 15 September 1916, at the Battle of Flers-Courcelette, the British Army unleashed tanks onto the battlefield for the first time.

Tanks were developed under the sponsorship of Winston Churchill, in his capacity as First Lord of the Admiralty: they were initially conceived as 'land ships'. The fifty 'Mark I' tanks that arrived at the Somme were equipped with caterpillar tracks that could crush barbed wire and machine guns and were crewed by eight men. Some ('male' tanks, as opposed to 'female' variants) also boasted 6-pounder cannon.

Fighting in these early tanks was difficult and dangerous. To begin with, crews rode next to the engine and fuel tank – which was only moved outside the body of the vehicle with the development of the Mark IV tank, seen here crossing an old trench in 1917. Tanks could be damaged by heavy machine-gun fire and artillery, were difficult to steer, moved at a crawl, often broke down and relied (at least at first) on semaphore or even carrier pigeon for communications. But they offered the British commander Field Marshal Sir Douglas Haig significant psychological advantage on the battlefield, striking fear into the enemy and earning a reputation on the German side as 'devil's coaches'.

Lawrence of Arabia

In 1909, while studying history at Oxford University, Thomas Edward Lawrence – now known as T.E. Lawrence, or Lawrence of Arabia – embarked on a three-month, 1,000-mile walking tour of the medieval crusader castles of Syria. After graduating, he returned east, learned Arabic and became an archaeologist. Bright, tough and with a working knowledge of the Ottoman-ruled Middle East, when war broke out he was readily co-opted by British military intelligence and tasked with mapping the Negev desert.

By 1916 Lawrence was in Arabia. There he built a friendship with Faisal, a son of the grand Sharif of Mecca (who in October declared himself king of the Arabs), and was closely involved in fomenting the Arab Revolt against Ottoman rule. During his time in the deserts, Lawrence adopted the typical Arab dress in which he is photographed here. Before long, Lawrence was more than just a British military liaison: he was effectively a guerrilla leader, and during the following two years his irregular forces attacked Ottoman railways and bridges and participated in the campaign to take Damascus. He ended the war with rank of full colonel, and with considerable scars, some of them physical, after he was captured in October 1917 and (so he later claimed) beaten and sexually abused.

After the war, Lawrence became a celebrity, famous for his lectures, writing and exotic tales of derring-do in foreign costume. He joined the Royal Air Force in the 1920s, but died in a motorcycle accident in 1935.

The February Revolution

On the Western Front, the winter of 1916–17 finally brought to an end the bloody battles at the Somme and Verdun. In the east, however, it ushered in a revolution that would change Russia forever.

Russian success in the east stalled after the Brusilov Offensive, and as it did so a sense of despondency and futility deepened among ordinary Russians. Food and fuel were in short supply, inflation was rampant and casualties on the Eastern Front were appalling. The army was growing mutinous, as were workers in Russian factories. Their anger was aimed at the man who had taken personal command of the war effort in 1915: Tsar Nicholas.

This photograph, taken in Petrograd, shows workers from the Putilov metal plant protesting during pay strikes, which began on 22 February 1917 (Julian calendar; 7 March New Style). Strikes led to demonstrations in the streets. Within a week the tsarist government had lost control, and troops ordered to quell the unrest were in open mutiny. Workers and soldiers began forming their own authorities (known as soviets), and the Russian parliament, the Duma, ignored the Tsar's instructions to disband.

On 2 March (15 March NS), Nicholas abdicated. When his brother, Grand Duke Mikhail, refused the throne, it spelled the end of both the Romanov dynasty and centuries of Tsarist rule. A Provisional Government was formed to try and save the empire and continue the war. But Russia's revolution was far from over.

The Air War

The Prussian aristocrat Manfred von Richthofen, known as The Red Baron (*centre*), was one of the most famous warriors produced by any side in the First World War. Handsome and deadly, he was all the more alluring because his weapon of choice was one that had been created by the war itself: the fighter plane.

At the start of the war, planes were primarily used for spying. Aerial cameras and advances in mapping meant that pilots could provide accurate information to allow generals on the ground to plot their manouevres and position their artillery. However, the effectiveness of air reconnaissance prompted the invention of aircraft that could disrupt it by shooting down enemy planes. In 1915, when German engineers developed machine guns that could be synchronized with frontal propellers, the battle for the skies was truly joined. From this point on, men like von Richthofen, standing here with fellow fighter pilots in front of a Fokker biplane, gripped the public's imagination, partly because their task was so dangerous; life expectancy for the average airman was around three weeks.

The Red Baron was the British Royal Flying Corps' nemesis during a British offensive at Arras in 1917. During 'Bloody April', as that month was known, the British lost more than 200 planes to superior German tactics and technology. Von Richthofen survived the battle and was not killed for another year, when he was shot down in Vaux-sur-Somme and died muttering the word '*kaputt*'.

The Women's Reserve Ambulance

The general and widespread carnage of the First World War made plenty of work for women's volunteer organizations, whose members could be found on both the fighting and home fronts. One of these, active between 1915 and 1919, was the Women's Reserve Ambulance (WRA) Corps, also known as the Green Cross Corps.

The WRA adopted khaki, battlefield-style clothing, wore felt hats and carried military ranks. They had mascots too: in this photograph, taken in June 1916, that role is played by a bulldog. Much of WRA's work took place around Victoria Station in London, where its members met wounded soldiers coming home by train, as well as thousands of men on leave, whom they helped to find places to stay. Often part-timers, juggling family commitments, the women of the WRA took on a huge range of tasks: assisting in the aftermath of airship raids, working as orderlies in hospitals, and transporting munitions.

The WRA was an offshoot of the Women's Volunteer Reserve, which had been founded in 1914 by Evelina Haverfield, an aristocratic suffragette from a military family. Haverfield had originally wanted to create a kind of women's home guard, armed with rifles to tackle potential German invaders. She led the WRA for a short while, before her taste for adventure took her abroad, first to Serbia and then to Romania and Russia, where she worked, in sometimes dire conditions, alongside her counterpart, the doctor Elsie Inglis, founder of the Scottish Women's Hospitals.

Caporetto

The autumn of 1917 was a decisive time on the Italian front, since it brought to an end the long series of twelve battles along the Isonzo, which had raged ever since Italy entered the war more than two years previously. This photograph, which shows dead Italian soldiers carpeting the rocky hillside near Cividale, illustrates the ferocity with which those engagements were fought.

By the late summer of 1917, it had become clear that both the Italian and Austro-Hungarian forces fighting along the Isonzo were exhausted and in many cases close to mutiny. The Italians were suffering under the leadership of Luigi Cadorna, who combined cruelty with stubborn tactical incompetence; most notoriously, he favoured random executions to try to scare his own troops into action. Kaiser Wilhelm approved the transfer of German divisions, armed with weapons including poison gas, to join the fight against the demoralized Italians.

On 24 October, a gas attack and artillery bombardment at Caporetto (now Kobarid, in Slovenia) announced the beginning of the final battle of the Isonzo. Behind this came German 'stormtroopers' with machine guns and flamethrowers. As further German and Austro-Hungarian troops poured forward, their attacks produced a collapse in the whole Italian line and a chaotic retreat to a line along the River Piave, 20 miles (32km) north of Venice. Italian soldiers threw away their uniforms and deserted, while hundreds of thousands of others simply surrendered. It was a bloody, humiliating disaster that would live long and bitter in Italian national memory.

Passchendaele

While Italian forces were crushed at Caporetto, another notorious battle was taking place on the Western Front. There was fighting around the Belgian city of Ypres throughout the First World War, but it was never more miserable than during the phase known as the Battle of Passchendaele.

The effort to take Passchendaele ridge from the German forces holding it was part of a broader British strategy devised by Field Marshal Haig to extend British lines, disrupt enemy railways and destroy U-boat bases on the Flanders coast. Yet what would be remembered was not grand military planning but basic human suffering.

In mid-July 1917, British guns fired four million shells towards German lines in preparation for an infantry attack. All this did was plough the clay soil of these Flanders fields; and when torrential rain began in August, the ground became a thick, cold, sapping quagmire. This British stretcher party (photographed near Boesinghe, a few miles from Passchendaele) was already knee-deep on 1 August.

The British and imperial soldiers, many of them from Australia, New Zealand and Canada, who took part in the three-month offensive in this foul marsh remembered hideous privations: men and horses drowning in mud; troops caught in barbed wire and machine-gunned to death; men dying mad from the horror. Haig ultimately gained five miles (8km) of territory at the cost of a total 475,000 casualties across all sides. 'I died in hell', wrote the poet Siegfried Sassoon. 'They called it Passchendaele.'

The Ruins of Ypres

The three great battles of Ypres, of which the third encompassed Passchendaele, left the city devastated, as this aerial photograph taken after the worst of the fighting shows. The roofless buildings are testament to month upon month of artillery fire – jagged monuments to the shattering of Belgium and so much of Europe beyond it by the First World War.

At the centre of this picture are the ruins of the medieval St Martin's Church. To the right is the burnt-out Cloth Hall, another great Gothic construction dating to the Middle Ages. Towards the top of the image is the so-called Plaine d'Amour or Minneplein, a grassy area that was redeployed as a cemetery.

British servicemen called Ypres 'Wipers' (Tommy slang had also rechristened the nearby village of Ploegsteert as 'Plugstreet'). Soldiers around Ypres published a satirical newspaper, *The Wipers Times*, produced on a printing press that had been abandoned by a fleeing Belgian publisher. The first issue of this newssheet, dated 12 February 1916, compared Ypres' 'jagged spires' to 'the fingers of ghosts' that 'seem to point to heaven, crying for vengeance'. One writer concluded that 'tomorrow she will have a nobler fame' for 'men will speak of her as the home of the British soldier'.

After the end of the war, Ypres was rebuilt, with the great medieval buildings returned as closely as possible to their former splendour. Ypres is today the location of the Menin Gate memorial, which commemorates the graveless British and imperial dead.

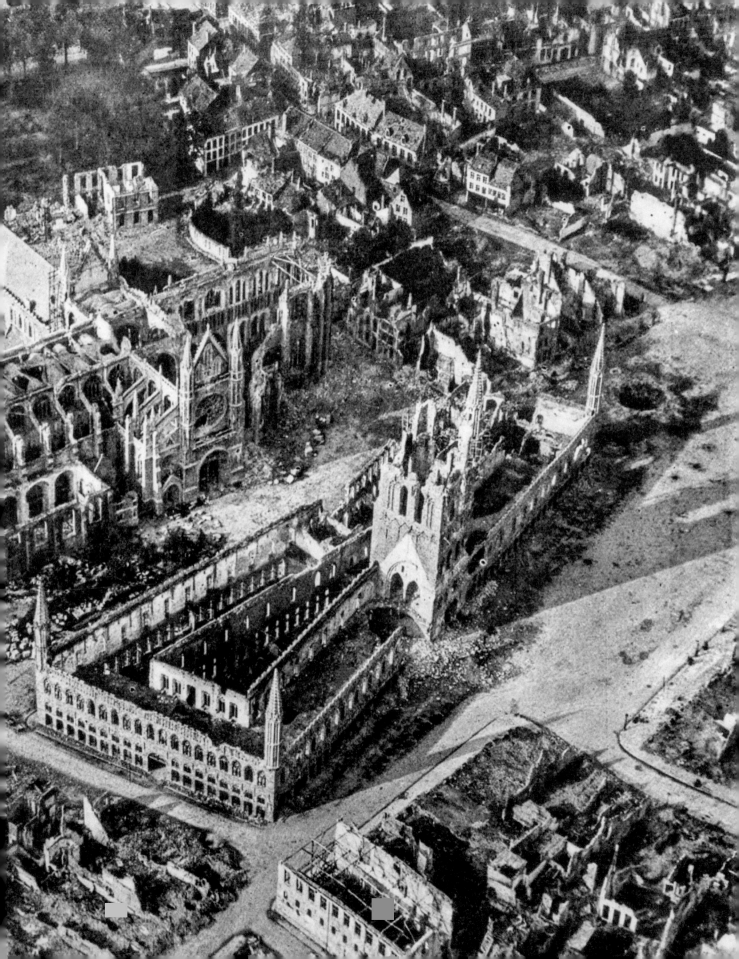

1917– 1918

Breakthrough

All aboard for home sweet home
Again to the girl I left behind
I'll go sailing 'cross the foam again
What a welcome there I'll find

American song lyric (1918) by Addison Burckhardt,
sung by Arthur Fields

Corporal Fred McIntyre (*previous page*) served in the First World War with the 369th Infantry Regiment of the United States Army – a highly decorated African-American regiment better known by their nickname, the 'Harlem Hellfighters'. To his fellow Hellfighters, McIntyre was known as 'Devil's Man'. But there was nothing diabolical about the appearance in Europe of the Hellfighters and their countrymen. Indeed, the arrival of the United States of America into the war in 1917 was viewed by many on the Allied side as a moment of deliverance: a decisive intervention that could swing the course of the war towards inevitable German defeat.

At the outbreak of war three years previously, the US government had been reluctant to engage – reflecting a strong strain of American public opinion favouring pacifism and neutrality. Although US banks lent to the British and French governments, the notion of sending America's sons to die in the trenches of the Western Front remained politically divisive. In November 1916, Woodrow Wilson had been able to win re-election as president on the slogan 'He Kept Us Out of War'.

Nevertheless, even as the USA clung to neutrality, stories of German atrocities and the 'rape of Belgium' became harder to discount. So too were German attacks on American ships in the Atlantic. In 1915, more than a hundred US citizens drowned when a U-boat sunk the British ocean liner RMS *Lusitania* (see pages 78–79). Shortly after this disaster, the German high command suspended 'unrestricted' U-boat warfare (that is, instructions that submarines were to sink merchant ships without warning, as well as enemy naval vessels). But on 1 February 1917 unrestricted U-boat attacks began again, once more putting American civilians in the Atlantic and

North Sea at mortal risk. Then, at the end of the month, President Wilson learned of the so-called Zimmermann Telegram: a cable sent by the German foreign ministry to the German minister in Mexico, authorizing him to propose an alliance that included 'an understanding on our part that Mexico is to reconquer her lost territory in Texas, New Mexico and Arizona'. Public outrage now overtook isolationism. On 6 April President Wilson declared war on Germany, stating that the USA would make 'the world safe for democracy'.

So it was that at the end of the year, 'Devil's Man' McIntyre and the rest of the Hellfighters embarked for France, part of an American military surge that would send around two million men across the Atlantic before the war was over.

The Hellfighters, formed from members of the New York National Guard, were remarkable for several reasons: their uncommon valour; their exceptional, ragtime-influenced regimental band; and their blackness. Only 10 per cent of US servicemen were African-Americans, and just two 'Colored' divisions were permitted to bear arms – a consequence of the enduring, wretched racism of American society and a deep fear on the part of white America at the notion of militarily trained descendants of former slaves.

Nevertheless, the 369th was among the first American units to see action. By July 1918 they were fighting alongside the French on the River Marne. Indeed, for military purposes they had actually become French, since, along with other African-American regiments, they had been seconded to the French Army, wearing hybrid uniforms (including French Adrian helmets), carrying French rifles and drinking French wine rations.

The Hellfighters suffered more casualties on the

7–8 November 1917

In Russia, anti-war Bolsheviks under Lenin and Trotsky topple the Provisional Government. On 5 December, the Bolshevik regime agrees armistice with Germany.

20 November–7 December 1917

A British offensive at Cambrai, on the Western Front, achieves a dazzling breakthrough with massed tanks, until a German counter-attack.

3 March 1918

In the Treaty of Brest-Litovsk, Russia accepts harsh peace terms dictated by Germany, in order to exit the war.

21 March 1918

Germany sends Allied armies reeling in the first of its 'spring offensives', hoping for victory before the American Expeditionary Forces become truly significant.

21 April 1918

The war's most illustrious and deadly flying ace, Germany's Baron Manfred von Richthofen, is shot down and receives a military funeral from the Royal Air Force.

Western Front than any other American regiment, but they were highly decorated for their bravery. One of their number, Henry 'Black Death' Porter, was the first American to be awarded the prestigious French Croix de Guerre – an award subsequently bestowed on the whole 369th Regiment.

In this photograph, taken when the Hellfighters were leaving Europe in 1919 aboard the USS *Stockholm*, McIntyre is holding a picture of the Kaiser, framed with bullets, which he took from a German soldier and thereafter carried for good luck. And indeed, it was McIntyre's good fortune that he survived to see his home again. The Hellfighters were welcomed back to New York as local heroes. They had fought for longer than any other US regiment in the First World War.

As the USA entered the war in 1917, another major belligerent and future superpower was leaving it. In late 1917, Russia was overtaken by the Bolshevik Revolution, led by Vladimir Ilyich Ulyanov 'Lenin' and Leon Trotsky. The revolution also prompted a vicious civil war in neighbouring Finland, as it broke off from the Russian Empire. In March 1918, following negotiations led by Trotsky, Russia signed the Treaty of Brest-Litovsk, and quit the war on terms harshly and heavily favourable to Germany and the other Central Powers. In July 1918, the deposed and exiled Russian royal family were murdered in Yekaterinberg.

Russia's retreat from world war into internal conflict ought to have been a boon to the Ottoman Empire. Yet the Turks ended 1917 in disarray and retreat, having lost much ground to a combination of British imperial forces and Arab irregulars. In December, British forces captured Jerusalem, and General Edmund Allenby entered the city on foot, an event that was celebrated in some quarters

– despite official British disapproval – as the culmination of a 'new crusade'.

For Germany, Russia's collapse and America's arrival into the war demanded a final major push for victory. The Spring Offensive, or *Kaiserschlacht,* of early 1918 gained more territory on the Western Front than had been taken by any side since the first months of the war. But German efforts ultimately proved futile. By the summer of 1918, American troops were pouring into France. The Allied counter-attack, known as the Hundred Days Offensive, began with a major battle at Amiens and succeeded in reversing all Germany's springtime gains. By October, the war had been decided. The only serious question left was how German surrender would be framed.

That question was answered with the Armistice, which came into force at 11 a.m. on 11 November 1918. The last serviceman on the Allied side to die in action was US Sergeant Henry Gunther, gunned down charging enemy lines one minute before peace was officially declared. He was one of around 54,000 US soldiers killed during their brief involvement in the most terrible war the world had ever known.

16/17 July 1918

The former Tsar Nicholas II and his family are executed while under Bolshevik house arrest.

8 August 1918

An Allied offensive at Amiens inflicts the 'Black Day of the German Army' and heralds 100 days of rolling Allied attacks.

29 September 1918

The Allies sign an armistice with the Ottoman Empire; they will sign an armistice with the disintegrating Austro-Hungarian Empire on 3 November.

9 November 1918

As the Allies advance, Kaiser Wilhelm II is forced to abdicate amid a German naval mutiny and revolutionary tumult.

11 November 1918

At 11 a.m., an armistice dictated by the Allies ends fighting on the Western Front. The First World War is formally over.

Liberty Loans

Roscoe 'Fatty' Arbuckle was a popular and highly paid Hollywood star of comic 'two-reeler' movies. Here, he is pasting up a poster in New York's Times Square, rallying the American public for the 'Second Liberty Loan of 1917'. Arbuckle was not alone in lending his weight to this campaign: fellow stars Charlie Chaplin, Douglas Fairbanks and Mary Pickford also encouraged Americans to help their government bankroll Allied efforts in the First World War.

Between April 1917 and September 1918, the US Treasury issued four series of war bonds, initially aimed at big investors but later at ordinary people. In theory, these bonds paid out a guaranteed interest rate, beginning at 3.5 per cent, and buyers would be able to redeem them after fifteen years. To whip up enthusiasm for the scheme, the euphemistically titled Committee on Public Information was charged with mobilizing public opinion and cultivating a general sense of patriotic obligation. The slogan of one typical poster left no ambiguity: 'Your Duty – Buy United States Government Bonds'.

Given long-standing American reluctance for warfare across the Atlantic, US propagandists had their work cut out. One reliable trope – recycled from earlier British propaganda – relied on crude imagery of the barbarous and beastly Hun. But alongside this, the vocabulary of 'liberty' was weaponized as the war's defining aim. Restaurants rechristened sauerkraut as 'liberty cabbage'. And war bonds were branded, irresistibly, as 'Liberty Bonds' or 'Liberty Loans'.

'London's Mighty Welcome'

On 15 August 1917, London witnessed an extraordinary scene. Hundreds of fresh-faced young American soldiers poured out from Wellington Barracks in Hyde Park behind a military band of the Coldstream Guards. In their trademark 'Montana Peak' campaign hats, they marched, four abreast, through St James's Park, past the US Embassy, where they gave a salute, and on to Buckingham Palace. There King George V, accompanied by Queen Alexandra and Prime Minister David Lloyd George, took another salute. Around the snaking column thronged thousands of joyful, fascinated Londoners, including this small child, who joined hands with one of the 'Doughboys', as American infantrymen were known. Government newsreels called the parade 'London's Mighty Welcome'.

And welcome they were. US entry into the war promised money, resources, ammunition, and an enormous supply of fresh manpower for a conflict in which brute force and sheer numbers mattered so much. Yet in 1917 the US Army was one of the smallest of all the 'belligerents'; a mass draft was introduced to provide numbers, but not ready-made military experience. For the soldiers photographed here, therefore, months of training and acclimatization to the conditions on the Western Front lay ahead. Although the first members of the American Expeditionary Forces (AEF) arrived in Europe in June 1917, they did not meet any actual combat until October; and most of the AEF would not join the fighting until the last three months of the war.

Trotsky

Leon Trotsky – a Ukrainian whose real name was Lev Davidovich Bronstein – was an experienced revolutionary. By early 1917, his CV included leftist agitation, Siberian imprisonment, escape, leadership of the Saint Petersburg soviet in the 1905 Revolution, a book of revolutionary theory, and war journalism in the Balkans.

Like all Russia's Marxist-inspired 'Social Democrats', Trotsky opposed the First World War and Russia's involvement in it. During the first three years of the war, he led a nomadic existence: first in neutral Switzerland, before expulsion from various European countries took him to the United States. After the February Revolution of 1917, Trotsky saw an opportunity to return home. By May he was back in Russia, and before long he was encouraging the Petrograd soviet to challenge the shaky Provisional Government, led by Alexander Kerensky.

By the summer, the Russian Army was mutinying on a massive scale, yet the government staggered on. Trotsky found himself in jail again following a series of violent demonstrations in Petrograd known as the 'July Days'. However, in prison Trotsky fell in with the Bolshevik Party and joined its central committee. His moment had come.

By the time this photograph of Trotsky was taken in the Georgian city of Sukhumi in early 1924, the Bolsheviks were in control of Russia. However, his ally, Lenin, was dead and Trotsky was falling out of favour. He was about to be rejected (and eventually exiled and murdered) by the regime he had done so much to create.

The Winter Palace

In October 1917, Russia's Provisional Government collapsed under a revolution led by the Bolshevik Party, whose leaders agitated workers, peasants and mutinous troops in Petrograd and beyond with simple, powerful slogans including 'All power to the soviets' and 'Peace! Bread! Land!'

The revolution took place over forty-eight hours, between 25 and 26 October [7–8 November New Style], as insurgents attacked and occupied government buildings across the city. The Petrograd soviet's Red Guards – directed by Trotsky – were prominent in seizing control of bridges, railway stations and telegraph points.

By the end of the first day of the uprising, the leader of the Provisional Government, Kerensky, had abandoned Petrograd. Overnight, the revolutionaries overran the government's headquarters at the former Tsar's Winter Palace and arrested the remaining cabinet members. Contrary to Sergei Eisenstein's later portrayal in his 1928 film *October*, this was not an especially violent siege. The troops defending the palace either slunk away or were ordered to stand down. But there was damage throughout the building, as photographs like this one, of the 'Tsar Alexander II Cabinet', record.

After the revolution, Russia was radically and bloodily reconstituted under Bolshevik rule, with Vladimir Lenin the head of government. On 3 March 1918, in the Treaty of Brest-Litovsk, the Bolshevik government traded peace with the Central Powers for the loss of Ukraine, Belarus, Poland, the Baltic states and more, along with huge coal reserves. Their world war was over. A civil war now loomed.

The War on Hunger

Dwindling food supplies and straitened conditions for ordinary people were not limited to Russia. In Britain, too, wartime conditions were beginning to bite. The British government was bound by the need to feed troops on the front line first, while imports to Britain were heavily disrupted by U-boat attacks on merchant convoys in the Atlantic and North Sea. By late 1917, food shortages combined with rising prices led to queues outside shops, as people competed for goods they could barely afford.

One response aimed at helping those struggling to survive was state-sponsored canteens. Under Lord Rhondda, minister of food control, a system of National Kitchens was introduced. The one shown here is in Bow, in London's East End. Smartly dressed staff and trained cooks served up no-frills, inexpensive but nutritious dishes to diners who bought a ticket and lined up to make their choices. A few of the restaurants were takeaways, but most provided simple seating. They were extremely popular, and some even managed to turn a profit.

In early 1918, the government introduced food rationing across the country. Basic staples including bread, margarine, meat, flour, butter and sugar were limited, and only available with ration cards. This policy, along with the introduction of naval convoys to protect merchant shipping, helped keep Britain fed. In this respect, Britons were significantly better off than their German, Russian, Austro-Hungarian and Turkish counterparts, who suffered malnutrition and in many cases starvation.

The Battle of Cambrai

At the end of 1917, the British public greeted with excitement news of the Battle of Cambrai. This was an extraordinary engagement for several reasons: first because it represented the first mass tank attack in history, and second because the British punctured, albeit only briefly, the long German defensive position known as the Hindenburg Line (*Siegfriedstellung*).

The 400 tanks that swarmed towards this line at Cambrai were the model known as Mark IV. These updated versions of the British tank had been deployed earlier in the year at Passchendaele, but had proved ineffective, as they tended to sink into the sucking mud. However, the ground at Cambrai was harder, and on it the Mark IVs, supported by infantry and aircraft, followed by horseback cavalry, showed their true potential. On 20 November, the British assault slammed through the German defences, along a 10-mile (16km) front, making gains that were (in the context of the Western Front, at least) spectacular.

Momentum soon ran out. Ten days after the battle began, the German Second Army, led by General Georg von der Marwitz, turned the tables, halting the British advance with attacks along their flanks, and using fast-moving stormtroopers to 'infiltrate' and to isolate heavily defended strongpoints. By the beginning of December, the Hindenburg Line had been more or less restored, and the Germans had seized around thirty damaged Mark IVs for their own use. Imitation, in this case, was the sincerest form of flattery.

The Fall of Jerusalem

On 11 December 1917, General Edmund Allenby marched on foot through the Jaffa Gate of Jerusalem's Old City, to take control of it in the name of the Egyptian Expeditionary Force and the British Empire. Allenby walked, rather than rode, as a sign of respect for a city that was holy to Jews, Christians and Muslims alike. On the other side of Europe, David Lloyd George was a little less circumspect: the prime minister called Jerusalem's capture 'a Christmas present for the British people'.

The capture of Jerusalem was a boon for the British and a bane for the Ottoman Empire and their German allies. The Ottomans had already surrendered much ground in Palestine, worn down by the advances of regular Indian, ANZAC and British forces and Arab campaigning, much of the latter masterminded by T. E. Lawrence (see page 115). The Ottoman forces had been bested at Gaza, Jaffa, Beersheba and elsewhere; eventually, the governor of Jerusalem had surrendered the city for fear that 'deadly bombs will hit the holy places' – shrines on the Temple Mount (Haram al-Sharif) and elsewhere.

In this picture, Allenby (*front row, third from right*) is flanked by colonels Philpin de Piépape and Francesco d'Agostino, commanders of small French and Italian detachments respectively. Further right is François Georges-Picot, who would represent French interests in reshaping the Middle East. Not visible, but present, was Lawrence, who called this day the pinnacle of his war.

'Spanish' Flu

By 1918, the First World War had caused as many as 20 million deaths, with a similar number wounded, missing or captured. At least as many people again would die in one of the worst pandemics in world history, which began during the last year of the war and spread rapidly through weak, malnourished and displaced populations.

'Spanish' flu did not begin in Spain (although the Spanish king himself caught it): the name stemmed from the fact that this neutral country's press openly discussed the disease, whereas the belligerents in the war censored newspaper reporting for fear of damaging public morale. The earliest recorded cases appear to have come from an American military base in Kansas; but wherever its origins, the flu was lethal, causing a sharp, wracking cough and a soaring fever, along with bleeding from the ears and lungs. It disproportionately affected those of military age, between twenty and thirty years old. Death could be very rapid, within twenty-four hours of symptoms showing, or could result from a secondary infection of pneumonia, which turned victims' skin an ugly purplish colour.

Despite scrambled attempts by health agencies worldwide to control the spread of Spanish flu, it peaked in the last three months of 1918, when this photograph demonstrating flu protocols was taken at the US Red Cross Ambulance Station in Washington, D.C. By the time the outbreak subsided, tens of millions of people across the globe were dead.

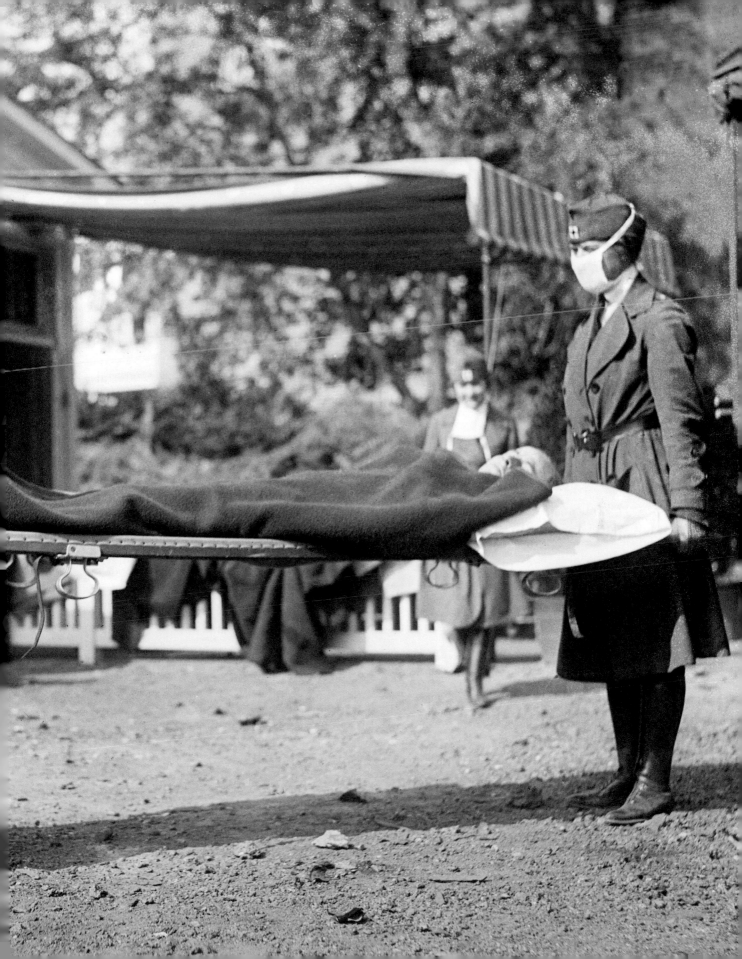

Prisoners of War

Besides monstrous numbers of killed and wounded, the First World War also produced around ten million captives. The sheer size of battles meant men were often taken in far greater quantity than could be handled humanely. POW camps ranging in standard from basic to fatally squalid were therefore a regular sight behind the front lines.

Within these camps were prisoners from a huge range of backgrounds and nationalities. This German photograph shows a group of captured soldiers of eight nationalities. According to the official record filed with the original photograph, these are: 'Anamite [i.e. Vietnamese], Tunese [i.e. Tunisian] Senegalese, Sudanese, Russian, American, Portuguese, and English'.

This diversity among captives was hardly surprising. Britain's war effort alone had drawn in Indians and Canadians, Australians and New Zealanders, and men from the Caribbean and South Africa. By 1918 the Allies also counted among their number thousands of labourers sent from China and fighter pilots offered by the king of Siam; Portuguese divisions and West Africans in France's Force Noire; the 'White' Russian Legion and a Czech regiment, along with Brazilian medics and airmen, North African mounted Spahis and Moroccan riflemen.

German propaganda deplored this broad-based recruitment and railed against the deployment of 'savage' dark-skinned fighters, especially African Americans and men from sub-Saharan Africa. The composition of this photograph, in which subjects are arranged from the short 'Anamite' to the tall Englishman, reflects a mentality of racial and national grading; yet it also reveals how multinational the Western Front had become.

The Finnish Civil War

The collapse of the Russian monarchy and the rise of Bolshevism brought considerable trouble to Finland, which for more than a century had been a Grand Duchy within the Russian Empire. In December 1917, a Finnish declaration of independence heralded a vicious civil war.

The two sides in the war foreshadowed those that would contest the Russian Civil War. On one side were the 'Reds': leftists, urban-dwellers, workers, Russian-speakers, pro-Slavs and some remnants of the Russian Army. On the other were the 'Whites': an alliance of landowners, business owners, Swedish Finns, monarchist-conservatives, pro-Germans and the agricultural poor.

On 27 January, Red Guard paramilitaries staged a revolution in Helsinki, which began the war. They had some success for a month, but soon the amateur nature of Red leadership began to tell. The White forces were better equipped and reinforced by detachments of the German Army. The decisive clash was the Battle of Tampere, which lasted from 15 March to 6 April. White forces besieged the industrial city, reducing some parts of it to little more than a skeleton. This photograph shows Red fighters being marched through Helsinki as prisoners.

By mid-May, the Whites had won the war. Around 37,000 people had been killed, many of them in political murders and executions carried out by both sides to instil terror in the opposition. Nearly 12,000 Red prisoners died in prison camps, and horrifying memories of the war haunted Finnish society for generations.

The Spring Offensive

As Russia abandoned the First World War under the Treaty of Brest-Litovsk, and the United States prepared to join the Allied effort, the spring of 1918 represented the last possible opportunity for German victory. The strategy developed by the German commander Erich Ludendorff was known as the *Kaiserschlacht* ('Kaiser's Battle') or Spring Offensive.

Beginning on 21 March, the Germans' big push was built around five major attacks along the Western Front. The first and largest was known as 'Operation Michael', which surged across old battlefields of the Somme; other attacks hammered British and French positions in Flanders, the Aisne and the Marne. Under the cover of a punishing artillery bombardment – more than a million shells were fired in five hours – and heavy fog, stormtroopers surged across Allied lines. Within a week Operation Michael had gained 40 miles (64km) of territory. Vast, long-range Krupp siege guns bombarded Paris, and panic gripped the French capital at the thought that the city might fall. In Germany, the Kaiser assumed the war was over – and declared an impromptu national holiday.

The war was not over. By the early summer it was clear that the *Kaiserschlacht* had been a pyrrhic victory, which had exhausted German fighting capability and created new 'salients' – bulges in the lines – that were difficult to defend. No final blow was struck, American troops were arriving in ever-larger numbers on the Western Front, and a major Allied counter-attack (the 'Hundred Days Offensive', see page 159) was about to begin. The end was in sight.

Marshal Foch

Ferdinand Foch had established a reputation as a charismatic, hyper-aggressive general early in the war, typified by a situation report he gave at the Marne in 1914: 'My centre's giving way, my right is retreating, situation excellent, I am attacking!' In the face of the Spring Offensive, this bracing attitude seemed to be the Allies' best cause for hope. So on 26 March 1918, with German forces apparently scything towards Paris, Foch was appointed *Généralissime*: Supreme General of the Allied Armies. His mission was simple, if daunting: to halt the German advance, then win the war in the west.

Throughout a perilous and bloody spring and summer, Foch saw through his objective. The turning point came at the Second Battle of the Marne in July 1918, in which a major German advance was halted in its tracks and Allied infantry, tanks and aircraft began a devastating counter-attack. As reward for his command, Foch was awarded the style of Marshal of France, which granted him the right to carry a ceremonial baton decorated with gold stars and the Latin legend *Terror belli, decus pacis*: 'terror in war, ornament in peace'.

Foch was still in position at the end of the war, although he disapproved of the peace terms imposed on Germany. After the war he was fêted and honoured around the world. When he died in 1929, Foch was entombed at Les Invalides, alongside other great French military leaders including Napoléon Bonaparte.

'Pershing's Crusaders'

When President Woodrow Wilson declared war in April 1917, the United States was in no fit state to fight a world war. But by the summer of 1918, Americans were arriving on the Western Front at a rate of 10,000 a day. The overall leader of the American Expeditionary Forces (AEF) was General John J. Pershing, nicknamed 'Black Jack'.

Pershing's first major success came on 12–15 September, when he personally commanded an attack by the US First Army on German positions at a salient around the town of Saint-Mihiel, not far from Verdun. (Orders drawn up before the battle include the first use of the term 'D-day' to denote the start of a military operation.) In pouring rain, aided by artillery, tanks and bomber aircraft, Pershing's troops hunted down retreating German forces and secured the salient. This photograph was taken near Saint-Mihiel the day after the battle was won. It shows American Lieutenant-Colonel R. D. Garrett, signal officer in the 42nd 'Rainbow Division', wearing a British-style Brodie helmet as he tests a captured German field telephone.

After Saint-Mihiel, the AEF moved on to fight a grinding battle through the Argonne hills and forests, which would last until November. Here and elsewhere, US soldiers amply compensated for their inexperience with sheer numbers and a general reckless courage under fire. A patriotic propaganda film issued after the war christened them 'Pershing's Crusaders'. Pershing himself was rewarded in 1919 for his command with the post of General of the Armies – the highest possible officer rank in the US military.

The Hundred Days Offensive

The campaign that won the First World War began on 8 August 1918. It was later known as the Hundred Days Offensive, and it reversed all German gains from the Spring Offensive earlier in the year, punched holes in the Hindenburg Line and prompted rioting and revolution in German cities.

The offensive started with the Battle of Amiens, a devastating Allied assault involving 550 British tanks – mostly improved Mark V models. General Erich Ludendorff called the first day at Amiens the 'black day of the German Army'; by the time the battle was over, 30,000 German troops had surrendered.

The strain of the massive campaigns Ludendorff had ordered earlier in the year now told. His armies were low on supplies and haemorrhaging men. Meanwhile, millions of American troops were bolstering the Allied advance; 1.2 million took part in the battles of the Meuse-Argonne – the biggest and most lethal engagement in American history. This picture of a dead German machine gunner, taken by Lieutenant M. S. Lentz, a photographer in the US Army Signal Corps, was captured towards the end of that series of battles, on 4 November 1918.

The success of the Hundred Days Offensive, the failure of the Hindenburg Line and the general collapse in German morale both on the Western Front and at home was enough to convince the German high command that the war was now unwinnable. All that remained was to negotiate peace. On 9 November, the Kaiser abdicated. Two days later, the war was over.

Armistice

On 11 November 1918, the shooting stopped, as an Armistice agreed in a carriage of Marshal Foch's private train near Compiègne, in Picardy, came into effect. By now, Germany was fighting alone; the other Central Powers had already sued for peace between 29 September and 3 November.

The Armistice – signed at 5 a.m. and executed at 11 a.m. – ordered an immediate halt to fighting, the withdrawal of German troops from occupied territories and the release of prisoners. The exact terms of peace were left to a series of political conferences over the following years.

On the front lines, news of the Armistice was greeted with mixed emotions. In some places there was euphoria; in others, little more than sunken silence, for even the twenty-four hours leading up to the peace had brought 10,000 casualties. Among them was forty-year-old George Edward Ellison of the 5th (Royal Irish) Lancers, who was killed at 9.30 a.m. on 11 November 1918: the last British serviceman to die in action in the First World War.

This photograph, taken on the day after the Armistice, shows two British officers – Captain Paget MC and 2nd Lieutenant Barry MC – reading out its terms to men of the 1st Battalion, Irish Guards Regiment, who were clearly in a celebratory mood. They were at Maubeuge, less than 10 miles (16km) south of Mons, where some among them – the long-serving 'Old Contemptibles' – had fought in the first desperate British encounter of 1914.

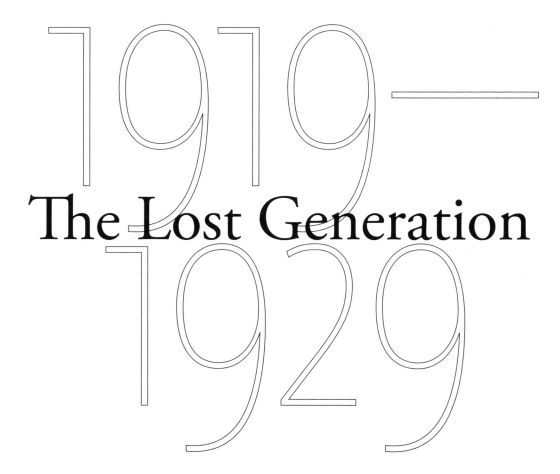

1919– The Lost Generation 1929

Civilization and profits
go hand in hand.

US Vice-President Elect Calvin Coolidge,
speech to Amherst College alumni
(27 November 1920)

The novelist F. Scott Fitzgerald had been commissioned as a 2nd lieutenant in the US Army and sent to Montgomery, Alabama to await deployment to France when, in the summer of 1918, he met his wife-to-be. Zelda Sayre was the youngest daughter of a well-to-do southern family, but she showed precious little regard for typical Alabaman values.

She was a dancer, a smoker, a drinker and a flirt, and her vivacious spirit was exemplary of the age that produced her. She married Fitzgerald in 1920 and gave birth to their first and only child, Frances ('Scottie'), in 1921. This Christmas photograph was taken a few years later; by this time, Fitzgerald had been discharged from the army and begun a career as a novelist and chronicler of the post-war age: a time variously known as the Roaring Twenties and the Jazz Age, whose young people were sometimes dubbed the Lost Generation. His novels during the 1920s included *This Side of Paradise, The Beautiful and Damned* and *The Great Gatsby*. Today, several of his works are considered canonical in American literature, and there has been growing critical admiration for Zelda's only published novel, *Save Me the Waltz*, as well as her paintings.

The world that Scott and Zelda Fitzgerald inhabited, chronicled and – in a sense – created had been profoundly shaped by the experiences of the First World War. For well-heeled Americans and Europeans, the 1920s oozed hedonism:
a devil-may-care cocktail of jazz, parties, flapper dresses and art deco sheen, all helped by a bullish US economy. Behind this glamorous exterior, however, lurked great troubles. The world was at peace, but it was not at ease. The same was true in microcosm for the Fitzgeralds. Both

drank heavily and recklessly; their marriage was plagued by fights, jealousies, serious mental and physical health issues, and acute financial woes. This paradox between the glamour of the post-war age and the miseries that endured was an important theme for many of the greatest artists and writers who emerged during the 1920s.

Many of these creative spirits – including the Fitzgeralds – congregated in Paris. They included the muscular American novelist Ernest Hemingway and the poets T. S. Eliot and Ezra Pound. The key figure in this circle was Gertrude Stein: a writer and art collector who, before the war, had been an important patron of Pablo Picasso. Stein coined the term 'lost generation' to describe this group's collective character, being as they were without a compass, moral or otherwise, caught between cynicism about American self-confidence and displacement in a war-weary Europe.

Besides hosting artists, Paris was also the venue for the momentous political process that settled the war in western Europe. In 1919 the world's most powerful leaders came together at the Paris Peace Conference, which produced the Treaty of Versailles. This – and a series of separate peace treaties agreed with (or imposed upon) the other defeated powers – redrew boundaries, broke up empires, established new nations, and assigned responsibility for the damage done by the First World War. This was far from an easy process. Nor was it perfectly executed, as events would very quickly prove.

In many cases, the end of war was followed immediately by revolution and civil strife. In Germany, the abdication and flight of Kaiser Wilhelm left a power vacuum eventually filled by a tenuous republican government based in Weimar. This government was hamstrung from the outset by the severe terms of

---

28 June 1919

Following the Paris Peace Conference, international delegates sign the Treaty of Versailles (June), which imposes peace terms on Germany after the First World War.

10 January 1920

The League of Nations is founded, to try and preserve world peace, but its principal advocate, President Woodrow Wilson, cannot persuade the USA to join it on his terms.

12–25 August 1920

The Polish Army defeats the invading Russian Red Army at the Battle of Warsaw, and paves the way to confirming Poland's independence and borders.

January 1921

In Russia, the Red Army defeats 'White' counter-revolutionary, separatist and nationalist factions in the country's three-year civil war.

9 September 1922

The sack of Smyrna heralds Greek defeat in the Greco-Turkish War (1919–22), and the creation (1923) of a new Turkish Republic headed by Mustafa Kemal – 'Atatürk'.

Versailles, which included impossibly onerous reparation payments and a 'war guilt' clause. By 1922–3 the harshness of these terms had led to renewed military conflict between France and Germany in the Ruhr, and agitation by violent right-wing firebrands at home – including a war veteran called Adolf Hitler.

Further east, the Bolshevik coup of 1917 that had created Soviet Russia was tested almost to the limit during the Russian Civil War, which pitched Bolshevik 'Reds' against a coalition of domestic and foreign enemies collectively known as the White Army. The civil war and an attendant famine, caused directly by disastrous state requisitioning policies known as 'war communism', killed more Russians than the fighting of 1914–17.

At the same time, the Austro-Hungarian Empire was broken up; Hungary underwent a series of violent socialist revolutions and wars with her neighbours before a peace was imposed by the Treaty of Trianon (1920). Meanwhile, the post-war settlement had recreated the nation of Poland, which had been dismembered during the late eighteenth century. The effective leader of this new state was Józef Piłsudski, a war hero legendary for defending Poland against Russia. Piłsudski exerted his power in Poland as an authoritarian strongman – a type that would become increasingly familiar across Europe during the 1920s, not least in the form of Benito Mussolini, who in 1922 marched a gang of fascist thugs to Rome, and so took the first step on his way to becoming Italy's dictatorial 'Duce'.

While imperial break-up was the order of the day for the defeated empires, it was a different story for the winning side. Admittedly, Britain was forced to grant self-government to Ireland – a process that led to partition on the island of Ireland and a bloody civil war – but in Africa and the Middle East, the British and French were ascendant, asserting their rights to administer former German and Ottoman colonies. The inhabitants were not always happy at swapping one set of foreign rulers for another, as Syria's Great Revolt demonstrated. To Syria's south, European Jews began migrating to British-run Palestine in large numbers, escaping oppression elsewhere but also altering the demographic make-up of the region, and producing conditions for future conflict. Elsewhere, when Greece sent an army into Turkey, the result was brutal ethnic murder by both sides, culminating in the burning of the beautiful city of Smyrna (Izmir).

Of course, not all the post-war revolutions brought hardship: as a direct consequence of the First World War, women won the vote in many European countries and the USA. Overall, though, it is hard not to view the 1920s as an age of extremes. Between the hedonism of the Jazz Age and the cracked fields of famine-struck Russia, everything was in flux. 'I'm not sure about good and evil at all any more', reflected Fitzgerald's Amory Blaine in *This Side of Paradise*. He was not alone.

---

24 May 1923

The 26 counties of southern Ireland that form the Irish Free State win a year-long civil war against opponents who object to continued allegiance to the British Crown.

9 November 1923

In Munich, an attempted putsch led by Adolf Hitler, leader of the small National Socialist German Workers' (Nazi) Party, fails; in prison later, he writes *Mein Kampf*.

21 January 1924

Soviet Russian leader Lenin dies, and afterwards his successor, Stalin, manoeuvres to win succession and to sideline Communist Party rivals, particularly Trotsky.

24 December 1925

Benito Mussolini, Italy's Fascist prime minister since 1922, issues a decree marking the emergence of his personal rule as dictator; he becomes known as Il Duce ('the Leader').

24–29 October 1929

In New York, a stock market crash on Wall Street wreaks havoc on the US economy, and soon sends shockwaves through the global economic system.

German Revolution

Kaiser Wilhelm II abdicated two days before the Armistice that ended the First World War, on the morning of 9 November 1918. He fled to the Netherlands, leaving behind him a defeated army, a mutinous navy, striking workers and a restive German populace.

On the same day, two socialist republics were declared in Germany: one by the moderate Social Democratic Party (SPD) and another by the radical *Spartakusbund*, or Spartacus League, whose leader, the lawyer and anti-war agitator Karl Liebknecht, announced his revolution from the balcony of the City Palace in Berlin, the building photographed here. From this confused state of affairs emerged an interim government, in which the SPD allied with military and right-wing militias known as *Freikorps* to try to keep Germany from dissolving into full, Russian-style communist revolution.

This was not easy. The damage to the palace seen here was done during a skirmish between leftist sailors and army units on Christmas Eve 1918. A few weeks later, in January 1919, a full-blown Spartacist uprising brought running battles to Berlin's streets. During these, Liebknecht and his ally Rosa Luxemburg were captured by *Freikorps* troops and murdered.

By the end of the month, a semblance of order had been restored. Elections returned deputies to a new National Assembly, held in the city of Weimar. The SPD leader, Friedrich Ebert, was confirmed as president. But Germany was far from settled, and the wounds of the war would be a very long time healing.

The Treaty of Versailles

While Germans struggled to form a new internal government, the broader fate of the nation was being decided by the victorious powers. In January 1919 the leaders of Britain, France, the United States and Italy gathered at the Paris Peace Conference to negotiate a treaty that formally ended the war. By 28 June this treaty was ready, and the Palace of Versailles's Hall of Mirrors was packed with dignitaries to witness its signing: the scene captured here.

Germany was denied a negotiating hand at Versailles, and as a result suffered extreme humiliation. Germany lost her empire; Alsace and Lorraine were awarded to France; no German military forces were allowed west of the Rhine. An independent Poland was carved out, with a 'corridor' of land stretching up to the Baltic, slicing East Prussia off from the rest of Germany. A new 'League of Nations' would administer other contested territories. German iron and coal resources were halved, and the German military was reduced to 100,000 volunteers and a token navy, without submarines. No German air force was allowed.

Most contentious was a 'war guilt' clause, which explicitly blamed Germany for causing the war, and in turn justified the imposition of financial reparations set at a staggering 132 billion gold marks (£6.6bn). It was a punishment that invited resentment and revenge, as a few wise heads realized at the time. Treaties with the other old Central Powers followed, but none with such profound ramifications as the Treaty of Versailles.

Women's Suffrage

The peace of 1918–19 redrew the political map of the world and the basic principles on which many nations were founded. Almost inadvertently, conflict and its aftermath had aided the struggle for women's suffrage. Across the west, women had played a critical role in the war, whether on the fighting or home fronts, and their contributions could not now easily be ignored.

So, as post-war reconstruction began, women were granted new freedoms. In Britain, women over thirty were granted the vote in 1918. Female suffrage became an important feature of the revolutions convulsing the defeated nations of Germany and Austria in 1919. Poland, newly reconstituted, allowed women to vote in its very first elections.

In this photograph, women and girls in New York City hold a 'jubilee' to celebrate the ratification of the 19th Amendment to the US Constitution. This amendment, officially adopted after consideration by Congress and state legislatures between 1919 and 1920, brought votes for women across America. 'The right of citizens of the United States to vote shall not be denied or abridged by the United States or by any State on account of sex', it read.

The celebration was mighty because the struggle had been long, dating back in the USA to the 1840s. The war had made change inevitable. President Woodrow Wilson had taken his nation into war in 1917 on the understanding that he was making the world 'safe for democracy'. The time had come to keep the promise at home too.

New Faces

Hundreds of thousands of veterans returned from the front lines of the First World War mentally and physically traumatized. Many were left to deal with their problems alone – but not all. One extraordinary woman who helped return some appearance of normality to veterans was Anna Coleman Ladd.

Ladd was a portrait artist and sculptor who moved to Paris from her home in Massachusetts towards the end of the war when her husband, a doctor, was posted to France with the Red Cross. In 1918 she opened a studio in which she turned her artistic skills to the task of 'repairing' wounded soldiers' disfigured faces by creating lifelike prosthetic masks.

This photograph gives some sense of Ladd's delicate craft, as she carefully paints skin tones on to a mask for one Monsieur Caudron. This was the last stage of a long process, which began when a soldier would visit the studio to have a mould of his face taken. Working from the cast, Ladd and her team next created a thin mask from galvanized copper. This was covered with enamel before, finally, Ladd used her talent as a portraitist to create as true a match to the patient's natural skin colour as possible, and applied, where desired, facial hair and other details.

The limitations of the masks, with their fixed expressions, were obvious. But in helping to gain social acceptability for the patient, this was work that transformed lives.

Irish Civil War

The end of the world war did not bring calm to Ireland. Nationalist sentiment had intensified in the years since the Easter Rising of 1916, and, following the ceasefire in mainland Europe, violence erupted across the island.

Following post-war British elections that gave the republican party, Sinn Féin, a huge majority in Ireland, in January 1919 a revolutionary Irish parliament (the Dáil) declared independence. By September, Sinn Féin and the paramilitary Irish Republican Army (IRA) had been declared illegal by the British government and a vicious guerrilla war had broken out. The IRA assassinated policemen and bombed police stations and barracks. In response, the British reinforced the Royal Irish Constabulary with former soldiers: the Auxiliaries and the 'Black and Tans', the latter so called for their mixed police/army uniforms.

The Anglo-Irish Treaty that brought an end to this war in December 1921 took the momentous step of partitioning Ireland between an Irish Free State with self-governing dominion status (like Canada or Australia) and Northern Ireland, composed of six of Ulster's nine counties, which remained part of the United Kingdom.

This did not by any means end the violence. In the summer of 1922, a civil war broke out in the Irish Free State between pro- and anti-treaty factions. The men pictured here near O'Connell Bridge in Dublin are members of the hastily recruited, pro-treaty Free State Army. Backed by the British, they fought against the IRA in a bloody struggle that lasted until May 1923.

Józef Piłsudski

In 1918, Poland had been a ghost state for 123 years: partitioned by Russia, Prussia and Habsburg Austria in the late eighteenth century and eliminated as a sovereign realm. Under the treaties that concluded hostilities, however, Poland was brought back to life. After the First World War, responsibility for recreating the nation was entrusted to Józef Piłsudski, pictured here.

In his youth, Piłsudski had been a dissident; while a medical student in the 1880s, he was arrested and exiled to Siberia for his supposed connection to a plot to assassinate the Russian Tsar. By the outbreak of war, he was an experienced underground activist, dedicated to building paramilitary organizations that could one day form the basis for a Polish national army. He aligned his forces with the Central Powers but concentrated only on fighting Russia and did not enjoy or desire the full confidence of his German allies. He ended the war as a German prisoner.

In November 1918, Piłsudski was appointed as the effective head of a revived Poland – and given the enormous task of rebuilding a state. He had to do so while simultaneously fighting a war against Bolshevik Russia; perhaps his finest hour came in August 1920 when he beat back an advancing Russian Red Army at the Battle of Warsaw. Soon afterwards he retired from politics, but returned in 1926, heading a military coup that returned him to power as a military strongman, with vast influence over government, until his death in 1935.

The Rif War

In North Africa, a colonial war whose origins predated the First World War exploded during the 1920s, drawing in troops from Spain and France. This war centred on the mountainous Rif region of northern Morocco. At the beginning of the twentieth century, this was land virtually untouched by either Europeans or Arabs, and jealously guarded by the Berber tribespeople who lived there. However, in 1912 the Treaty of Fez had divided up Morocco into colonial 'spheres of interest', awarding Spain theoretical control over the Rif. Subsequent Spanish exploitation of mining rights in the region led to violent clashes and by 1920 these had become all-out war.

The leader of Berber resistance in Rif was Abd al-Karim, a journalist-turned-guerrilla fighter who inflicted several embarrassing defeats on supposedly stronger Spanish forces, including the 'Disaster of Annual' of July 1921, in which thousands of Spanish were killed. This alarming defeat sparked civil unrest and a military coup back in Spain.

The Rif War was ultimately lost when al-Karim overreached and invaded French Morocco. In response, France sent more than 150,000 troops to aid the Spanish. In September 1925 a joint Spanish-French amphibious landing at Alhucemas marked a turning point in the war; by the following year, the Rif rebels had been crushed, this abject prisoner just one among many. Al-Karim was exiled to Réunion in the Indian Ocean for the next two decades. Meanwhile, the Rif War marked an important stage in the military career of Colonel Francisco Franco, future fascist dictator of Spain, who was promoted to brigadier general in 1926 in recognition of his role in bringing the revolt to an end.

Russian Famine

Winston Churchill described conflicts such as Poland's border struggles as 'wars of the pygmies'. Yet the years 1919–22 cost more lives in Russia than the First World War. Millions of Russians died in battle, or through execution, murder, torture, pogroms, sexual violence or starvation.

Following the Bolshevik Revolution of 1917, an alliance of conservative counter-revolutionary forces with international backing, collectively known as the White Army, attacked Bolshevik-controlled western Russia from all directions. At the same time, nationalists in territories previously part of the greater Russian Empire (most notably in the Baltic) tried to seize independence. Fighting was fierce, and in a desperate attempt to survive the war and sustain the Red Army, the Bolsheviks imposed a policy of 'war communism', by which they forcibly requisitioned vast quantities of grain and foodstuffs from peasants in the countryside.

Combined with recent drought, harvest failure and deforestation, the effects of war communism were catastrophic. Between the Volga and Ural rivers, an appalling famine set in, peaking between 1921 and 1922. These starving children were photographed during those crisis years in a refugee camp near Samara. As food vanished, food prices rocketed, black markets sprang up (despite government prohibition) and reports of cannibalism were rife. The famine was an international scandal, and relief efforts were sent from Sweden, the United States, Britain and elsewhere. Despite the efforts of aid agencies, an estimated five million people starved to death or succumbed to famine-related disease.

The Sack of Smyrna

These British citizens posing on the Plymouth dockside in early October 1922 had recently abandoned their homes and possessions as they fled the Turkish city of Smyrna. But they were much more fortunate than the thousands of ethnic Greeks and Armenians who had perished in the city they left behind. The sack of cultured, cosmopolitan Smyrna (Izmir) on the Turkish Aegean coast was the culminating atrocity of the Greco-Turkish War of 1919–22.

This war, like many others, sprang from the ashes of the First World War. In 1920, the Treaty of Sèvres had dismembered the Ottoman Empire. Yet even as this was being negotiated, Greek troops had occupied Smyrna and were trying to conquer further territory in Anatolia for a broader, pan-Hellenistic 'greater Greece'.

At the same time, however, Turkish nationalists who rejected Sèvres were arming and organizing. They halted the Greek army's advance and forced it back to Smyrna. As the Greeks fell back, they exacted brutal vengeance on Turkish Muslim civilians; as Turkish forces advanced, they slaughtered Greeks, Armenians and other minorities.

When Turkish troops arrived at Smyrna in September, the Greeks evacuated. Subsequently, the city burned, with the loss of many lives. Trapped between fires and the open sea, many chose the water over the flames. Tens of thousands of people died and hundreds of thousands became refugees. Surveying the disaster, Smyrna's US consul, George Horton, confessed to a 'feeling of shame that I belonged to the human race'.

Atatürk

Mustafa Kemal 'Atatürk' made his name as a military officer while commanding the Ottoman Fifth Army's 19th Division during the battle for Gallipoli in 1915. He subsequently fought in the Caucasus and Palestine, but by November 1918 he was back in Constantinople, which was now occupied by the Allies.

During the Greco-Turkish War Kemal led the Turkish National Movement, then proclaimed a Turkish government in Ankara and denounced the Treaty of Sèvres. After the Greeks had been defeated, on 29 October 1923 the Republic of Turkey was formed: a single-party state with Kemal as its president. During the next ten years Turkey was reformed and refounded as a modern, secular state from which the last vestiges of the moribund Ottoman Empire were swept away.

This amounted to no less than a cultural revolution. Kemal's reforms jettisoned the roles of sultan and caliph, Ottoman laws, the centrality of Islam, Arabic script, the fez and women's veils. In their place came Western dress, the Latin alphabet, a new calendar and women's suffrage. The Turkish language and Turkish naming conventions were imposed on all citizens. In 1934 Kemal was officially granted the title of 'Atatürk', meaning 'Father of the Turks'.

Atatürk had a complicated marital life and adopted more than a dozen children (including an orphan called Sabiha Gökçen, who grew up to become the world's first female fighter pilot). He was mourned both in Turkey and across the world when he died, aged fifty-seven, on 10 November 1938.

The March on Rome

Italy's would-be reformer during the 1920s was Benito
Mussolini, a blacksmith's son turned agitator-journalist.
In his youth Mussolini was a socialist, but after fighting
with some distinction in the First World War he was
expelled from the Italian Socialist Party, which favoured
neutrality. After the war, Mussolini became a committed
nationalist, and helped establish the *Fasci Italiani di
Combattimento* ('Combat Groups') – nationalist vigilantes
committed to a cocktail of militaristic, imperialist, racist
and reactionary ideas. In 1921 he created the National
Fascist Party as a political vehicle for these beliefs.

Post-war Italy was riven with dissatisfaction. Strikes,
political violence and revolts against landowners were all
underway, while popular sentiment held that Italy had
been let down by the Allies in the peace treaties that
followed the end of the war. There was a latent fear of
communist revolution. Conditions were perfect for
Mussolini's Fascist movement to flourish – yet even so,
his rise to power was astonishingly rapid.

On 27–28 October 1922, Mussolini rallied around
25,000 Fascist supporters – some are seen here in their
signature 'blackshirt' uniforms – for a march on Rome.
(Mussolini himself preferred to take the train.) Fearing
serious civil unrest, King Victor Emanuel III immediately
appointed Mussolini to lead a coalition government. It
was the beginning of a Fascist revolution. By 1925, Italian
party politics was over, and Mussolini was dictator. He
ruled Italy for the next two decades and inspired many
other dangerous European strongmen to follow his
example.

The Ruhr Crisis

In January 1923, the first major crisis in the post-war settlement with Germany unfolded in the Ruhr Valley, a heavily industrialized region of western Germany close to the French and Belgian borders, rich in mines and metalworking plants.

At the root of the crisis lay the vast, punitive and unaffordable war reparations imposed on Germany under the terms of the Versailles treaty, which were owed largely to France, since so much of the damage done in the war had occurred on French soil. By 1922 Germany's new Weimar government had begun to default virtually every month on this huge war debt, failing to deliver both the money and the raw materials (such as coal and timber) that they owed. To the French prime minister, Raymond Poincaré, this breach of Versailles was not just economically damaging, but a threat to the post-war world order. In January 1923 he sent French soldiers to occupy the Ruhr: this photograph shows French troops disarming German police after they marched in. Belgium also sent in soldiers.

Poincaré's assertiveness in the Ruhr set France at odds with her British and US allies, but there was little they could do, since it was perfectly legal under the terms of the Treaty of Versailles. On the ground, meanwhile, more than a hundred German workers were killed during strikes and 'passive resistance' movements, while the crisis also aggravated hyperinflation, which pushed the price of a loaf of bread in Germany to around 200 billion marks.

Adolf Hitler

Resentment at Germany's treatment at Versailles was festering in German society well before the Ruhr crisis. The nation had been humiliated, the economy was broken and many believed a 'stab-in-the-back' myth, which held that Germany was not defeated in the First World War, but had been betrayed by a cabal of subversives, traitors, Marxists, Jews and 'cultural Bolsheviks'. These putrid conditions fostered rancid politics. From them sprang the career of Adolf Hitler.

Hitler had served in the Bavarian Army during the First World War. After the Armistice he entered politics – joining, rebranding and eventually leading the National Socialist German Workers (NSDAP, or Nazi) Party. The Nazis' paramilitary *Sturmabteilung* (SA) were involved in street fighting against other political thugs, as urban violence plagued Weimar Germany.

On 8 November 1923, Hitler – with Germany's former military commander Erich Ludendorff and some two thousand Nazis – attempted a coup in Munich to seize control of Bavaria's state government. The so-called Beer Hall Putsch ended in chaos, with more than a dozen Nazis and four policemen dead. Hitler fled, but was captured, tried and sentenced to five years in Landsberg prison, where this photograph was taken.

Imprisonment was no hardship. Hitler was allowed many visitors, served only a fraction of his sentence, and dictated the text of his autobiographical manifesto, *Mein Kampf* ('My Struggle'), to fellow inmates including Rudolf Hess. When he was released, he was ready to resume what would become the twentieth century's most notorious political career.

The Great Syrian Revolt

In Syria, the imposition of a French mandate crushed Arab hopes for independent rule. It also created new tensions, which in 1925 exploded into popular violence and military confrontation.

Unlike the Ottomans, the French had little sense of the complex local politics of Greater Syria and Lebanon. Rather than governing at arm's length and allowing individual ethnic and religious groups a degree of freedom to decide their own affairs, the French attempted to impose a more hands-on, colonial-style rule. It did not take long for trouble to erupt.

In 1925, the Druze community south of Damascus rose up under the war veteran Sultan al-Atrash and rebelled against French rule, which, said al-Atrash, had 'choked freedom' and 'stolen' Syria. Their uprising soon spread far and wide across the region.

The result was the two-year Great Syrian Revolt. This photograph was taken after the Battle of Rashaya (20–24 November 1925), in which a hilltop fortress held by French Foreign Legion cavalrymen was attacked by a much larger force of Druze fighters, and vicious close-quarter combat took place around the perimeter walls. The French were only saved by support from bomber aircraft and relief on the ground by a force of the French North Africans known as Spahi.

The Great Syrian Revolt was eventually defeated by superior French military technology and numbers. Al-Atrash fled into exile in Transjordan. Thousands of his people were left dead or destitute as a result of the conflict. The French mandate in Syria lasted until the end of the Second World War.

Palestine

As Hitler began his rise, his eventual nemesis, Winston Churchill, was serving as colonial secretary in the British government. In this photograph, taken on 28 March 1921, Churchill is attending a tree-planting ceremony to mark the site for a new Hebrew University at Mount Scopus, Jerusalem.

The onlookers included (*centre*) the Chief Rabbi of Jerusalem, Jacob Meir.

Churchill was in Jerusalem because after 1918 the Ottoman Empire's former possessions in the Near East had been carved up into 'mandates' along lines laid out in the secret Anglo-French Sykes–Picot Agreement of 1916. Britain's mandates included Palestine, Transjordan and Mesopotamia, which was renamed Iraq.

Churchill was personally ambivalent about these mandates, worrying that they were economic and political liabilities. He also had much to wrestle with in the question of Jewish settlement in the region. In 1917, the so-called Balfour Declaration by Britain's foreign secretary had seemed to promise a Jewish National Home in Palestine. Yet at the same time Arab fighters, spurred on by their own desires for liberation, had helped the British push the Ottomans out of Palestine.

The planned Hebrew University at which Churchill planted trees was just one sign of the recent arrival of tens of thousands of Jews into Palestine. Churchill wrote that the immigration 'will be good for the world, good for the Jews, good for the British Empire'. He hoped it would also be 'good for the Arabs… and that they shall not be sufferers or supplanted'. Time would tell.

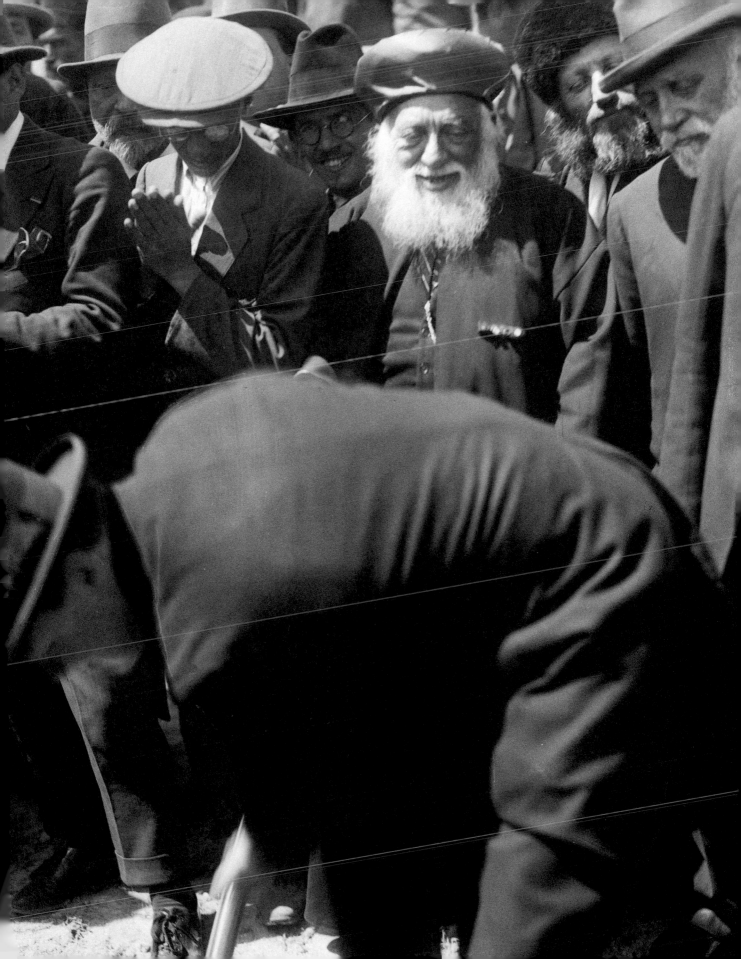

The Rise of Fascism

1930–1936

Come on comrades in strong ranks,
Let's march toward the future
We're audacious and fierce phalanxes
Ready to dare, ready to dare.

First lines of 'La Giovinezza' (Youth),
anthem of Italian Fascist Party

On the morning of 14 June 1934, a Junkers Ju52 aeroplane circled over Venice for several minutes. Adolf Hitler, the chancellor of Germany, did not want to touch down too early, so the pilot, Hans Baur, kept the aircraft airborne, and the brief diversion afforded Hitler an aerial glimpse of Piazza San Marco and the city's other famous buildings, none of which he had ever visited before.

Accompanying Hitler on board the plane was his personal photographer, Heinrich Hoffmann, a committed Nazi party member since 1920. Hoffmann was the man entrusted with capturing and cultivating the image of the Führer. This work kept him busy at public occasions and in the more private spaces of Hitler's retreats, to which he was granted privileged access. There, Hitler was often in the company of his girlfriend, Eva Braun – one of Hoffmann's former studio assistants.

Baur eventually guided the plane down at Venice's airport at noon, exactly on time. The Italian dictator, Benito Mussolini, stood waiting to greet his German counterpart. It was the first time the two men had met, and Mussolini, accompanied by an entourage and an enormous press pack, was dressed in full military uniform. Hitler, perhaps expecting a more discreet visit, was casually dressed; eschewing Nazi paraphernalia, he emerged from the Junkers in rumpled civvies and a brown overcoat.

Hitler saluted. Mussolini did not reciprocate. Instead, he leaned in to shake Hitler's hand – and the subtle power play was snapped by the press. More handshakes would follow, including one during ceremonies at the Piazza San Marco, where this image (*previous page*) was captured by Hoffmann. In all of them, Hitler appeared something of a supplicant.

In June 1934, Hitler had been Germany's chancellor for almost eighteen months. Although the country had already begun to be recast in the Nazi Party's image, Hitler was still some way from achieving the absolute power he craved; the decorated First World War general Paul von Hindenburg, although ageing and ill, still held significant authority as president. By contrast, Mussolini was approaching a decade as Italy's dictator and was the object of a personality cult he enthusiastically encouraged. At Venice, therefore, Mussolini was the senior statesman, whose tactics Hitler had studied, and whose blessing Hitler had sought. The legacy of the Treaty of Versailles meant that Germany was militarily hobbled and forbidden from placing soldiers on parts of her own sovereign soil. Italy, by contrast, was building an empire.

Hitler stayed two days in Italy and it did not take long for relations with his host to sour. With the exception of his service in the First World War, this was Hitler's first ever trip outside Germany or Austria. But he was unimpressed by Italian military displays, and when it came to direct political discussions with Mussolini, the two men had a blazing row about Austria. Hitler made plain that he expected Austria eventually to be absorbed into the German Reich; Mussolini insisted on Austrian independence, which Italy was guaranteeing with troops. 'Little seemed left', said Hitler's pilot, Baur, 'of the warmth with which the two leaders had greeted each other.' Yet despite this awkward encounter, the fortunes of Mussolini's Fascist Italy and Hitler's Nazi Germany would be closely intertwined as the years wore on.

Some of the conditions that allowed these two grandstanding dictators and their totalitarian parties the space to flourish in the 1930s could be traced back to the terrible legacy of the war of 1914–18 and the flawed attempts at peacemaking that had followed. Others were unique to the times. Exhausted and understandably

1930–33	18 September 1931	June 1932	30 January 1933	4 March 1933
In the USA and around the world, economies shrink and unemployment soars during the peak years of the Great Depression; political extremists take advantage.	A Japanese army invades the Chinese province of Manchuria and sets up a puppet state there called 'Manchukuo', against which the League of Nations can do little.	A mutually debilitating three-year war breaks out between Bolivia and Paraguay over their disputed Gran Chaco border region.	President Hindenburg appoints Adolf Hitler as Germany's chancellor; the previous year, the Nazi Party had become the largest party in Reichstag (parliament) elections.	The Democratic Party's Franklin D. Roosevelt is inaugurated as US president and begins his 'New Deal' programme of federal interventions to rebuild the US economy.

gun-shy, Britain and France preferred containment and appeasement to the prospect of a renewed fight with Germany, and many in both those countries reckoned fascism a lesser evil than Russian-style communist revolution. The League of Nations, established as an international arbiter and peacekeeper, lacked the moral authority and muscle to enforce its own mandate.

Meanwhile, after the Wall Street Crash of 1929 the Great Depression tore a hole in the economy of virtually every Western nation, leaving millions of ordinary voters ruined and susceptible to the populist, hateful messages of demagogues like Hitler. The German elites who allowed Hitler to become chancellor in January 1933 underestimated their man until it was much too late. Hitler claimed power through democratic channels; it took him less than a month to start destroying the Weimar polity that had produced him. When Berlin's Reichstag burned down in February 1933, Hitler had a ready-made excuse to rule by *diktat*. Two weeks after his return from meeting Mussolini in Venice, Hitler made another chilling demonstration of his murderous ruthlessness, with the 'Night of Long Knives', in which one of his oldest associates, Ernst Röhm, along with other leaders of the Nazi's paramilitary SA, were killed.

For those who wanted to see the true course of fascism, all was hiding in plain sight in the early 1930s. Hitler was long committed to a racist, expansionist vision of Germany's future, and had already begun to menace Austria's leaders, who in 1934 adopted their own form of fascism, a precursor to full union with Nazi Germany later in the decade. Meanwhile, Mussolini was using the Italian military to realize his own imperial dreams in North and East Africa. His generals imposed Italian rule first on Libya and then on Emperor Haile Selassie's Abyssinia.

Yet at the same time, the balance within the relationship between the two dictators was altering. In August 1934, Hindenburg died and Hitler took full power over Germany. A month later, that year's Nuremberg Rally – the Nazi Party congress – revelled in this triumph. It was commemorated and celebrated in the propaganda film *Triumph of the Will*, whose director, Leni Riefenstahl, found Hitler's charisma irresistible. As 1935 closed, Mussolini recognized the growing power of Hitler and of Germany, and the strategic desirability of a closer relationship. Their partnership would, before the decade was out, lead the world to a second global war.

During all of this, Heinrich Hoffmann continued to chronicle on film Hitler's life and engagements. Hoffmann survived the Second World War, was imprisoned afterwards for several years as punishment for war profiteering and died in Bavaria, a free man, in 1957. Hundreds of his photographs survive today, many of them held in the US National Archives, where they were deposited after being seized by the Allies at the end of the war.

19 October 1933	30 June–2 July 1934	October 1934	3 October 1935	7 March 1936
Germany withdraws from the League of Nations, eight months after Japan has withdrawn in protest at the League's outlawing of the seizure of Manchuria.	In the 'Night of the Long Knives', Hitler's henchmen murder around 200 political and Nazi Party dissidents, including Ernst Röhm, leader of the Nazi SA paramilitary.	In China's civil war, embattled Communists, on the verge of defeat by Nationalist (Guomindang) forces, embark on a gruelling 'long march' to safety in the north-west.	Having already consolidated control of Libya, Mussolini's armies invade Abyssinia (Ethiopia), completing conquest in 1936; again, a weak League of Nations is exposed.	Hitler, having already been increasing German military strength, installs troops in German territory west of the Rhine: both actions breach the Treaty of Versailles.

The Great Depression

At the end of October 1929, the US stock market crashed.
Across several days' trading, between 'Black Thursday' (24
October) and 'Black Tuesday' (29 October), the value of
American stocks dropped by around 25 per cent, wiping
billions of dollars off the market and sparking the worst
global financial crisis in history. In New York, Wall Street
traders were ruined within a matter of hours. In the weeks
that followed, economies across the world collapsed into a
spiralling recession – the Great Depression – which lasted
for more than a decade and produced the conditions for
another general war.

In the United States the recession was particularly
severe, with around one in four workers unemployed – a
situation exacerbated in several Midwestern states where
over-farming and drought combined to create a series of
arid storms known as the Dust Bowl. In the cities, shanty
towns of unemployed migrants sprang up. These were
christened Hoovervilles, in sardonic honour of President
Herbert Hoover, who took office in March 1929 and
oversaw the worst of the Depression.

The misery brought about by this economic crisis
created a surge in popularity for political parties on the
extremes. Membership of the US Communist Party
increased to at least 65,000 during the 1930s. Activists like
these, photographed in San Francisco, found willing
audiences as they protested against evictions of farmers,
and demanded unemployment relief, along with the
guarantee of trade union, labour and civil rights.

FDR

On 5 July 1932 Franklin Delano Roosevelt – or FDR –
was photographed in the office he kept as governor of
New York State. It would not be his office for very much
longer, for his overflowing in-tray contained piles of
messages congratulating him on having been nominated
as the Democratic candidate for the presidency of the
United States. Days earlier in Chicago, on receiving the
nomination, FDR had made a bold promise: 'I pledge
you, I pledge myself, to a new deal for the American
people.' The New Deal would become his signature
policy, associated for ever with the presidency he assumed
in 1933 and relinquished only when he died in office
during his fourth term, in 1945.

Roosevelt was a bona-fide American aristocrat, an
alumnus of Harvard University and Columbia Law
School and an accomplished, experienced politician. He
was physically tough: after contracting polio in the early
1920s he relied on leg braces, a cane and a protective press
to hold him upright. This disability did not stop him
from taking on the most daunting task to face any
American president since Andrew Johnson: Johnson's
challenge had been to take on the presidency in the wake
of the Civil War and the assassination of Abraham
Lincoln; FDR's was to save America from the destruction
wrought by the Great Depression.

Roosevelt's New Deal was a bracingly un-American
scheme of massive federal intervention and economic
stimulus. FDR reformed banks, provided relief
programmes to the unemployed and destitute, and
created jobs with public works schemes. His critics called
it socialism, communism and worse – but FDR dragged
the US through the 1930s and left a lasting legacy to
American politics.

'Manchukuo'

The League of Nations had been established after the First World War with the aim of preventing and settling conflicts like the Chaco War. But by the early 1930s its toothlessness was becoming worryingly apparent. Few incidents better suggested the League's basic weakness than its failure to prevent a Japanese invasion of Manchuria, in north-east China.

Manchuria was a tempting target for Japan, since it was rich in natural resources and offered a possible bulwark against advances in the region by Soviet Russia. On 18 September 1931, Japanese troops invaded, claiming to be taking revenge for the bombing of the Japanese-run South Manchuria Railway at Mukden. By the time this photograph was taken, a day later, Japanese units were already spreading across Mukden – and soon throughout Manchuria. China lacked the military strength to resist, so instead appealed to the League of Nations for help.

This did little immediate good. Japanese forces remained in Manchuria and the province was renamed 'Manchukuo'; the former Chinese emperor Puyi was installed as a puppet ruler. In October 1932 a League of Nations fact-finding commission eventually declared the puppet state illegal and demanded Japanese withdrawal. In response, Japanese delegates walked out of the League. No individual nation had the appetite to intervene, so Japan remained in possession of Manchuria, emboldened even if diplomatically isolated. This territorial grab has even been described as the first conflict of the Second World War.

The Chaco War

As the Depression spiralled out from the United States, in Latin America a savage war broke out between Bolivia and Paraguay. It was known as the Chaco War, after the sparsely populated borderland over which it was fought: the Chaco Boreal.

Following defeats in nineteenth-century wars, both Bolivia and Paraguay were landlocked. This made the Chaco region especially valuable, since it gave access to the River Paraguay, and thereby to the Atlantic Ocean. In addition to this, oil had been discovered in the foothills of the Andes, presenting the tantalizing possibility of vast riches lying beneath the ground for whoever controlled the Chaco.

In 1932, periodic skirmishes between the two countries erupted into all-out warfare. To begin with, patriotic Bolivian reservists, like those photographed here, flocked to be mobilized. But within a year, mass conscription and a series of defeats had begun to sap popular morale. Bolivia began with a larger, German-trained army and a modest air force. However, the draftees, many of them indigenous Amerindians from the highlands, suffered grievously from the diseases in the Chaco's swamps and forests.

Gradually, the Paraguayans gained the upper hand, until, in 1935, an armistice was agreed under pressure from the USA and neighbouring countries. Paraguay was awarded most of the Chaco, while Bolivian access to the river was confirmed in a final treaty, signed in Buenos Aires in 1938. By then, the war had cost 100,000 lives through fighting and disease.

Chancellor Hitler

Adolf Hitler was a convicted criminal who had been born in Austria and was only granted German citizenship in February 1932. Yet less than a year after officially becoming German, he was appointed as chancellor of the Reich. It was a dizzying rise for Hitler and the Nazi Party, and it began the darkest phase in German history.

Against the backdrop of the Great Depression, extremist parties in Germany made huge gains at the ballot box. In 1928 the Nazis held just twelve seats in the Reichstag, yet by 1932 they were the largest party, with 230 seats. The SA, defying banning orders, fought vicious street battles with communist militias, while Hitler and other high-ranking Nazis, including his propaganda chief, Joseph Goebbels, spread the Nazi message far and wide with rabble-rousing speeches. In 1932 Hitler ran for election as German president. He was defeated by Paul von Hindenburg, but garnered 13 million votes along the way. The Nazi creed of national and economic renewal, strong leadership and aggressive scapegoating of blame groups, including Jews, all found a willing audience.

By early 1933 that audience included Hindenburg himself. The moderate centrist parties of the Weimar Republic had failed to form a coalition capable of keeping the Nazis out of power, and Hindenburg was eventually persuaded by politicians, businessmen and generals that the Nazis could be 'managed'. On 30 January – a few weeks before this photograph was taken – he formally appointed Hitler as chancellor. It was a fatal miscalculation.

The Reichstag Fire

On the morning of 28 February 1933, barely a month after Hitler became chancellor, Berlin policemen surveyed the ruins of the Reichstag. The previous evening, the parliament building had been set ablaze. A young Dutch communist called Marinus van der Lubbe was arrested, tried and guillotined for setting the fire; its chief beneficiaries were Hitler and the Nazis, who turned the disaster directly to their own advantage.

Hitler responded to the Reichstag Fire by declaring it a communist plot, and demanded emergency powers from Hindenburg to deal with the crisis. Hindenburg co-operated. Hitler had thousands of political opponents arrested and locked up. A snap election on 5 March, conducted amid a propaganda campaign and intimidation by Nazi paramilitaries, delivered the Nazis 50 per cent of the vote and enough seats in parliament to ally with other nationalists and pass the Enabling Act, which allowed Hitler to rule by decree.

Hitler used his new powers to their fullest extent. The Communist Party was banned, a new Ministry of Propaganda (under Goebbels) controlled the media, and 'undesirables' in the civil administration and judiciary were purged. By May, trade unions had been suborned to a Nazi umbrella organization. In July, a law was passed banning the creation of new political parties. Meanwhile, the Catholic Church was to be allowed to run its schools and institutions in return for retreating from politics. The reality of a one-party state dawned. The Nazification of Germany was to be rapid and smooth.

Italian Libya

The absence of decisive global leadership in the 1930s allowed Benito Mussolini's Italian Army to pursue a long-standing colonial project in North Africa. Twenty years previously, Italy had fought a war with the Ottoman Empire to capture the province of Tripolitania (roughly, modern Libya), which they divided into two territories: Italian Tripolitania and Italian Cyrenaica.

As a young man, Mussolini had opposed war in Libya. But by 1930, he was a dictator with dreams of a 'Second Roman Empire' and had updated his opinions accordingly. He authorized General Rodolfo Graziani to move into North Africa to put down a stubborn anti-Italian rebellion directed by Sheikh Omar al-Mukhtar, a leader of the Senussi movement, nicknamed the 'Lion of the Desert'.

Graziani carried out his orders with extreme prejudice. He incarcerated Cyrenaica's population in concentration camps, mounted air attacks, and constructed a fortified fence to cut off the rebels from Egypt. At least 40 per cent of Cyrenaica's population died, including the seventy-three-year-old Omar, who was captured in September 1931 and hanged.

By 1932 the so-called Pacification of Libya was complete. Cyrenaica and Tripolitania were combined to form Italian Libya, and Italians were encouraged to settle there. Libyans were inducted into the Fascist Party and the Italian Army. Whether the Libyan boy shown here raising his arm in a Fascist salute was mimicking his elders in jest or seriousness is not clear. Whatever the case, it was plain that by the early 1930s, fascism was on the march.

Persecuting the Jews

Hitler's rambling memoir-manifesto, *Mein Kampf*, had made little secret of his dislike for Jewish people, whom he described variously as maggots, vipers and parasites. Yet this was more than dumb, racist anti-Semitism. Hitler conceived of a 'Jewish problem' afflicting the whole Western world; he deemed the very presence of Jewish people to be a societal ill in need of radical remedy. Thus he articulated and exploited a vicious and broad-based European tendency to anti-Semitism that stretched back to the Middle Ages, updating it for the 1930s by suggesting that Jews were to be identified with both greedy capitalists and Marxist revolutionaries.

On taking power, the Nazis turned this cocktail of bigotry and hate into government policy. In 1933 Jews were removed from the German Civil Service, and subsequently banned from other public services and professions, including teaching and medicine. In April, an official boycott of Jewish businesses was enforced at street level by roaming bands of SA men. This graffiti, daubed on a shop window in that year, reads: 'Germans!!! Don't buy from Jews.' And this was only the start. In September 1935 the Nuremberg Laws were enacted. Jews were denied German citizenship, and relationships between Jews and non-Jews were banned, with 'offenders' liable to be paraded in public with placards around their necks. Many Jews began to leave Germany. Those who stayed were pushed to the margins of society. It would not be long before the mass murders began.

!!!
SRAEL.
ht beim
uden

Austrofascism

With Nazi Germany to the north and Mussolini's Italy to the south, it was perhaps unsurprising that in the 1930s Austria moved decisively towards fascism. The country had been severed from Hungary following the First World War and the Austrian economy was crippled by the Great Depression. Conditions were ripe for the rise of hard-line nationalist rule.

In March 1933 the Austrian chancellor, Engelbert Dollfuss, a pugnacious politician who stood less than five feet tall, took advantage of a political crisis to suspend parliament and rule by decree. Political parties including the Communists and Austrian Nazis were outlawed, and a clampdown on civil liberties took place. In early 1934 Dollfuss's dictatorial rule – a form of Catholic corporatism known as Austrofascism – provoked open warfare between government forces and leftist paramilitaries in towns across the country. This photograph was taken in Vienna on 12 or 13 February, at a housing development known as the Goethehof. A few days later the worst violence was over, but more was soon to follow.

Although a fascist, Dollfuss was not a Nazi, and he strongly rejected arguments for a unification of Germany and Austria, appealing to Mussolini to guarantee Austria's borders. He earned his reward on 25 July 1934, when a group of Austrian Nazis burst into his office and murdered him. Dollfuss was succeeded by Kurt Schuschnigg, who tried to resist the Nazification of the state. Ultimately, he also failed. Within four years Germany had annexed Austria into Hitler's Third Reich.

The Night of the Long Knives

Much of the Nazis' success in Germany was rooted in the violence of the SA, led from 1931 by Ernst Röhm – pictured here in his office, in front of an eighteenth-century Flemish tapestry. Röhm had been an early member of the Nazi Party, playing a prominent role in the Munich Beer Hall Putsch of 1923 before leaving Germany to serve as an officer in the Bolivian Army. He returned to take command of the SA at Hitler's special request.

Under Röhm, the SA grew its numbers and ambition: by 1934 there were more than three million members, many of whom agitated for a 'second revolution' of an overtly anti-capitalist nature. Röhm lobbied for the SA to be merged with the much smaller German Army (*Reichswehr*), which seemed to amount to a takeover. Yet at the same time the SA was becoming redundant to the Nazi cause: now that Hitler was chancellor, he controlled the entire machinery of the German state, including the police and armed forces.

Between 30 June and 2 July 1934, Hitler moved against the SA and various other enemies. The smaller elite Nazi paramilitary, the SS (*Schutzstaffel*), arrested and killed around two hundred SA officers, dissident Nazis and former opponents, citing evidence of a plot by Röhm to seize power. Röhm refused to commit suicide, so was shot in a prison cell. The 'Night of the Long Knives' was brutal, efficient and a chilling illustration of Hitler's utter ruthlessness in consolidating his power.

Oswald Mosley

Fascism was not limited to continental Europe. In the 1930s, the blackshirts of the British Union of Fascists (BUF) brought their own brand of thuggish nationalism to the streets of London. Their leader was Sir Oswald Mosley, pictured here (*second from the left*) in 1935.

Mosley was an archetypal establishment figure. In 1918 he was elected as a Member of Parliament aged just twenty-two; two years later he married Lady Cynthia Curzon, daughter of the foreign secretary. In parliament he was a brilliant orator but a permanently restless figure, sitting as a Conservative, Independent and Labour MP before in 1931 founding the New Party, but losing his seat as a result.

In the early 1930s Mosley travelled to Mussolini's Italy, then returned and rebranded his party as the BUF, complete with paramilitary-style uniform, anti-Semitic rhetoric and populist agitation. Fights and ugly protests accompanied BUF rallies and marches, culminating in October 1936 in the Battle of Cable Street, in which police officers fought with anti-fascist protesters and BUF members in a neighbourhood of east London with a large Jewish population.

After Cable Street, some in the BUF split to form the overtly Nazi National Socialist League; these included William Joyce, who would later be better known as 'Lord Haw-Haw' for his radio broadcasts from Nazi Germany during the Second World War. Mosley himself was interned in 1940, along with hundreds of other suspected fifth columnists. After the war, he moved to Paris, where he died in 1980.

The Nuremberg Rallies

Overblown, military-style, quasi-religious rallies were a regular feature of Nazi propaganda, with a history dating back to the 1920s. During the 1930s Nazi rallies became annual fixtures, themed around the Nazis' supposed values, including 'Honour', 'Victory' 'Power' and (rather ironically) 'Freedom'. The rallies were almost invariably held in the Bavarian city of Nuremberg, and involved high melodrama, spectacle, torchlight processions and grandiose speeches. Hitler's address would mark each rally's climax.

The participants photographed here are members of the *Reicharbeitsdienst* (RAD) – a national voluntary labour service. (The spades they brandished were standard issue, as were bicycles.) The military attire and training of the RAD spoke to both the general Nazi obsession with uniforms and discipline and to the means by which Hitler had already begun to circumvent the restrictions of Versailles. The treaty limited the German Army to a strength of 100,000 volunteer troops. Well-drilled, shovel-wielding auxiliaries like the RAD did not count towards that quota.

From 1933 onwards, Nuremberg rallies tended to celebrate major milestones in the Nazi accrual of power over the German state. The rally that year marked Hitler's appointment as chancellor. In 1935 the party cheered the reintroduction of compulsory national service (a direct breach of the terms of Versailles). The following year's rally trumpeted German remilitarization of the Rhineland. It was not difficult to see which way the Nazis, and the country they now controlled, were heading.

Leni Riefenstahl

Nazi Party rallies were major propaganda events, and as such were memorialized for posterity by some of the most talented visual artists in the Third Reich. Heinrich Hoffmann produced photographic souvenir books to capture the pomp of several of the rallies. The most famous documentarian of Nazi festivities was the film director Leni Riefenstahl.

Riefenstahl had been a popular actress in the German genre of alpine-themed films (*Bergfilme*). Hitler enjoyed her directorial debut in 1932, *The Blue Light*, and he asked her to make a short film about the 1933 Nuremberg Rally. Riefenstahl agreed, finding herself captivated by the Führer's stage presence and rhetorical powers. It was however her film about the 1934 Nuremberg Rally, *Triumph of the Will*, that brought her an international reputation. It was seen across Germany and admired across the world for its superlative cinematic technique, despite its lamentable subject matter.

This photograph of Riefenstahl was taken on 12 July 1936 when she was working on a film to document the Berlin Olympic Games. Next to her (*centre*) is Carl Diem, the chief organizer of the Games. The film Riefenstahl eventually produced, *Olympia*, is still considered a ground-breaking sports documentary. It had its premiere on Hitler's birthday, 20 April, in 1938.

Riefenstahl survived the Second World War and worked until her death in 2003, at the age of 101. She consistently denied having ever been a committed Nazi, but questions about her relationship with Hitler, her knowledge of the Holocaust and her true affiliation with the party dogged her all her life.

The Abyssinia Crisis

As the Nazis gathered strength, in Italy Benito Mussolini remained determined to expand his territories in Africa. In 1935 he and his generals set their sights on the empire of Abyssinia (Ethiopia). The history of Italian–Abyssinian conflict stretched back to the 1890s, when Italian troops were beaten at the Battle of Adwa and Abyssinia escaped conquest. By the 1930s, Mussolini was ready to avenge that defeat.

In early December 1934, troops from the colony of Italian Somaliland skirmished with Abyssinian forces at the Walwal oasis. The Abyssinian emperor, Haile Selassie, complained to the League of Nations, and protested against further build-ups of Italian troops on his borders in the following months. It did him no good. On 3 October 1935, Mussolini's invasion began. Italian troops, around 100,000-strong, were heavily outnumbered, but they had air support, machine guns, artillery and mustard gas, while many of Selassie's forces still wielded spears and Adwa-era rifles.

Belatedly, the League of Nations tried to impose economic sanctions on Italy. It was a vain effort. Mussolini ignored the sanctions, secured Hitler's backing for his war, withdrew Italy from the League of Nations, and made private pacts with Britain and France assuring him that there would be no serious punishment. The Abyssinian capital, Addis Ababa, fell in May 1936 and Haile Selassie fled into exile. The international community was shown to be unable or unwilling to intervene against fascist aggression. There was now no going back.

1936—1939

Darkness Falling

Wholesale arson and mass murder,
committed by Rebel airplanes of the German type.

New York Times report (29 April 1937) describing the
bombing of Guernica

n 1938 the American photographer Margaret Bourke-White travelled to Spain, on her way to Czechoslovakia. She was on assignment for *Life* magazine, the photographic weekly launched two years previously with one of Bourke-White's photographs on its first cover. *Life* was destined to become a bestselling, groundbreaking publication, which in its heyday between 1936 and 1972 chronicled the twentieth century's defining moments and employed some of the greatest photographers of the age. During her years working for *Life*, Bourke-White was arguably the greatest of them all.

Bourke-White arrived to find Spain in the middle of a three-year civil war. The simple note scribbled on the back of this photograph only hints at the destruction the war had already caused. It reads: '*Spain – Angeles Gonzalez – 7 years old – refugee from Madrid.*' Like most of Bourke-White's photographs, this one was carefully posed and meticulously constructed – in this case to deliver an emotional message about the nature of the war. (In other pictures in the set Angeles Gonzalez is smiling, and is not holding the bread and potatoes she clasps here.) It is not reportage. But it does speak to a truth perceived by Bourke-White and the many other artists and activists who were drawn to document the Spanish Civil War – among them Martha Gellhorn, Ernest Hemingway, George Orwell, Emma Goldman, John Dos Passos and W. H. Auden. The war fought between Republicans and Nationalists in Spain from 1936 to 1939 was both a proxy conflict for the greater international struggle that lay ahead and a premonition of the immense human suffering that was to come.

Angeles Gonzalez was just one refugee in a war that was generating thousands. Since the late 1920s, Spanish trades unions and republicans, along with separatists in Catalonia and the Basque region, had challenged Spain's

authoritarian, royalist and Catholic traditions. By 1931, following national humiliation in the Rif War (see page 177), popular dissatisfaction reached crisis point. In that year King Alfonso XIII fled the country and a Second Spanish Republic was proclaimed. But this was scarcely any more stable than the collapsing regime that preceded it. By 1936, tensions between the dizzying array of factions on the right and left once again boiled over. On 17 July the leaders of a military coup, including Spain's future dictator, General Francisco Franco, failed fully to overthrow the republic, and a civil war began.

From very early on, the Spanish Civil War was more than a localized struggle. In the context of the unhappy state of European politics, it was seen as a clash of ideologies, which attracted international involvement on both sides. Nazi Germany lent the Nationalist coalition (which included the Falange, or Spanish fascists) an air force and troops, called the Condor Legion. Benito Mussolini also sent planes and Italian soldiers. By 1937, the Nationalists largely ruled the air, and the violence they were able to deal from above shocked the world. The aerial bombing of the Basque town of Guernica on 26 April was memorialized in one of the most famous anti-war paintings ever produced, Pablo Picasso's *Guernica*. But it was far from the only example: six months later, a school in the Catalan town of Lleida was deliberately bombed, leaving dozens of schoolchildren dead.

On the other side, Spain's Republican coalition was supported either overtly or secretly by the USSR, France and Mexico, and by the 'International Brigades': volunteers who travelled to fight from Britain, the United States and elsewhere. Orwell, who was in Spain between December 1936 and the summer of 1937, described his experiences in his memoir *Homage to Catalonia*. 'If you

---

18 July 1936

Dissident militarymen, including Francisco Franco, rebel against Spain's left-wing republican government, beginning a three-year civil war that draws in other nations.

25 November 1936

Germany and Japan sign an Anti-Comintern Pact, opposing the spread of communism; they are joined by Italy (1937), Hungary (1939) and Spain (1939).

26 April 1937

German and Italian aircraft, helping the Spanish rebels, bomb and strafe the Basque town of Guernica; such deliberate targeting of civilians is widely condemned.

7 July 1937

The skirmish called the 'Marco Polo bridge incident' soon escalates into war between China and Japan; by December, Shanghai and the Chinese capital Nanjing are ransacked.

12 March 1938

German troops march into Austria to enact the Anschluss ('union'), which absorbs Austria into the German Reich; many Austrians welcome the development.

had asked me why I had joined the militia I should have answered: "To fight against Fascism",' he wrote, 'and if you had asked me what I was fighting for, I should have answered: "Common decency."' But common decency was a losing cause. When Bourke-White passed through Spain, Orwell had already been forced to leave the country and was back in England. And when she moved on to central Europe, hope for a civilized end to the war was rapidly vanishing. Madrid – the Spanish capital and young Angeles Gonzalez's home town – fell to the Nationalists on 28 March 1939. Franco declared victory four days later. Half a million Spaniards had died and many more would follow in recriminatory executions.

Outside Spain, fascism and militarism were on the march in the late 1930s. From mid-December 1937 to late January 1938, Japanese forces invaded China, ransacking Shanghai and Nanjing, where barely imaginable atrocities occurred. In April 1939, Mussolini's troops conquered Albania. That same month, Spain joined Germany, Italy and Japan in signing the formal alliance of the world's leading hard-right regimes, known as the 'Anti-Comintern Pact'. The belligerent sides in the coming Second World War had now all but taken shape.

Inevitably, perhaps, it was Adolf Hitler who turned alliance-building into all-out war. His ambitions grew throughout the late 1930s. At home, Nazification of Germany proceeded at pace. Increasingly oppressive laws aimed to make life for Jews in Germany so unbearable that they would emigrate; many thousands did so in the months after the night of anti-Semitic vandalism and violence called Kristallnacht. (They included children sent to England as part of the British humanitarian project called the Kindertransport.) Many Jews who did not leave were sent to the Reich's burgeoning concentration camps, where they joined political prisoners, homosexual men and other so-called anti-socials, including alcoholics, prostitutes and homeless people.

Abroad, meanwhile, Hitler was now sufficiently confident to begin the expansion of the Reich of which he had long dreamed. In March 1938 the Nazis marched into Austria, destroying Austrofascism and absorbing the country into the Third Reich. Immediately afterwards, Hitler turned his attention to Czechoslovakia: first bullying the British prime minister, Neville Chamberlain, into allowing him to take the Sudetenland, then in March 1939 sweeping into the rest of the country. In August of the same year, an audacious agreement of neutrality was brokered with the USSR by Hitler's foreign minister, Joachim von Ribbentrop; its aim was to carve up north-eastern Europe between the two powers. On 1 September the Nazis invaded Poland, and three days later, the Second World War began in earnest. Margaret Bourke-White and her fellow *Life* photographers would be on the ground to cover it all.

29 September 1938	9–10 November 1938	2 December 1938	15 March 1939	1 September 1939
British Prime Minster Neville Chamberlain, with Mussolini and French Prime Minister Édouard Daladier, appeases Hitler and allows German annexation of Czech Sudetenland.	An outburst of antisemitic violence sees Jewish temples, businesses and shops destroyed across the German Reich: it is later called *Kristallnacht* for the broken glass.	The first 200 Jewish children evacuated from the German Reich under the humanitarian Kindertransport scheme arrive in Harwich, England.	German troops seize Bohemia and Moravia, as independent Czechoslovakia vanishes; neither Britain nor France intervene, but both offer security guarantees to vulnerable Poland.	Germany launches blitzkrieg on Poland, claiming it is a reaction to Polish aggression; two days later, Britain and France declare war on Germany, beginning the Second World War, while the USA declares neutrality.

Lleida

On 2 November 1937, bombers of the Condor Legion –
the air force supplied by Nazi Germany to support the
Nationalist faction in the Spanish Civil War – bombed
the Catalan town of Lleida, located between Zaragoza
and Barcelona. Several hundred people were killed.
Among them were forty-eight children and their teachers
attending class at the Liceu Escolar.

This scene, captured in the aftermath of the bombing,
was depressingly familiar across Spain during the civil
war that raged from 1936 to 1939. After fighting began,
Hitler authorized the deployment of thousands of
German ground and air troops to the region, along with
transport planes, fighters and bombers. Their presence in
Spain served two purposes: to distract international
attention from German designs on central Europe; and to
provide a test bed for military hardware, which would be
put to use in the general European war that was to follow.
In this context, the civilians of Lleida were nothing more
than collateral damage.

Lleida was a terrible tragedy, but it was not the only
atrocity committed by the Condor Legion during the
Spanish Civil War. On 26 April 1937, German and Italian
bombers laid waste the town of Guernica (Gernika) in the
Basque country, which was targeted in support of General
Franco's campaign against Bilbao. High-explosive and
incendiary bombs destroyed 80 per cent of Guernica's
centre, while fighter planes strafed civilians. The carnage
was immortalized in Pablo Picasso's painting *Guernica*.

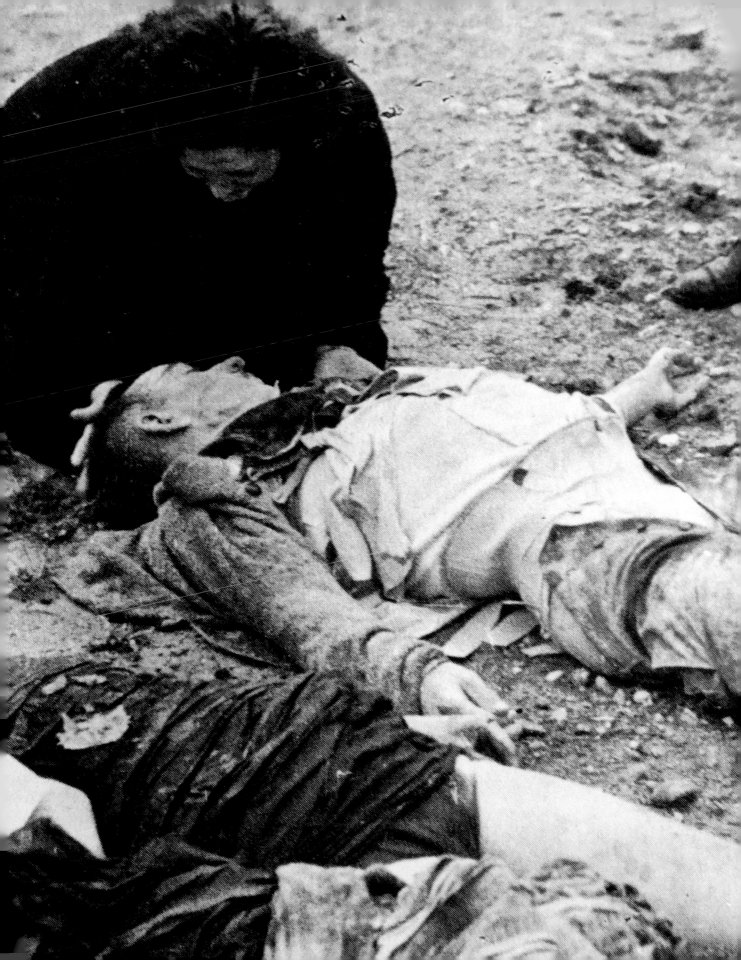

The Battle of Shanghai

On the other side of the world from Spain, a major war erupted in 1937 between Japan and China. The Japanese had occupied Manchuria earlier in the decade (see page 206), establishing the puppet state of Manchukuo; this had been followed by frequent clashes between Chinese and Japanese troops, particularly around Mongolia.

A fragile truce was broken dramatically on 7 July 1937, following an exchange of fire in a village near Beijing – the so-called Marco Polo Bridge incident. Despite attempts to broker a ceasefire, within five weeks troops of the Imperial Japanese Army and Navy had invaded China and descended on the coastal city of Shanghai.

Confident Japanese commanders believed that it would take them three days to conquer Shanghai. In fact, the battle for the city lasted for three months and sucked in approximately one million men. The Japanese attacked with infantry, amphibious landings, artillery barrages, naval bombardment and airborne bombing raids; this photograph was taken on 22 August, and shows Japanese defenders tugging a conquered tank into their lines.

After a ferocious and often desperate Chinese defence, often involving street fighting from house to house, Shanghai finally fell at the end of November. The Japanese immediately marched on Nanjing, the Chinese capital. They arrived so fast, and with such overwhelming force, that in early December the Chinese government abandoned the city. Its fate was atrocious: a six-week orgy of killing, sexual violence and looting known to posterity as 'the Rape of Nanjing'.

The Hitler Youth

While Spain and China erupted into violence, in Germany Hitler was growing more confident with every passing month. He was also enjoying the luxuries and comforts that came with the position of supreme leader. This photograph was taken at Hitler's private holiday retreat in the Obersalzberg: the Berghof, a luxurious chalet in the Bavarian Alps, which Hitler bought in 1933 and substantially rebuilt in 1935.

The Berghof was not merely a place of leisure. Leading Nazis and businessmen, generals, foreign leaders and royalty were welcomed there, along with artists and musicians. The visitors pictured here are members of the Hitler Youth (*Hitlerjugend*), a Nazified perversion of the Boy Scouts, which indoctrinated young men between the ages of ten and eighteen into the tenets of National Socialism and the Führer cult, and trained them in various paramilitary skills, with a focus on physical fitness and basic soldiering.

The Hitler Youth was just one way in which young Germans were trained in Nazi orthodoxy. The movement existed in parallel with a schooling system that emphasized a National Socialist version of history, racial purity and physical education; there was even a tier of 'Adolf Hitler schools' for the most talented pupils. Meanwhile, the League of German Girls prepared girls for the traditionalist roles of housekeeping and child-rearing that were celebrated in Nazi ideology. Brainwashing the young was important because it worked: Hitler Youth fighters numbered among the very last defenders of the Reich in 1945.

The Anti-Comintern Pact

On 25 November 1937 several of Nazi Germany's most important figures visited the Japanese Embassy in Berlin, to celebrate the first anniversary of an alliance signed the previous year, known as the Anti-Comintern Pact. Three weeks earlier, Mussolini's Italy had also joined the pact; Francisco Franco would commit Spain to the alliance in 1939, and other powers joined in the years to 1941.

The Anti-Comintern Pact's members opposed the worldwide spread of communism, which the USSR fostered through the Communist International (Comintern) organization. They also shared ideologically sympathetic, authoritarian governments, aggressive foreign policies and a broad contempt for the League of Nations. The alliance was blatantly anti-democratic and scornful of international law. Joseph Grew, the US ambassador to Japan, described the Anti-Comintern Pact as being 'bent on upsetting the status quo'.

This photograph, taken that evening, includes a number of high-ranking Nazis. Next to the Japanese ambassador, Kintomo Mushakōji (*foreground, left*), is Adolf Hitler himself. To the right, holding court in satin-striped trousers, is the fat, flamboyant, drug-addicted Hermann Göring, head of the Luftwaffe and Hitler's de facto deputy. To the left stands Alfred Rosenberg, an obsessive political and racial theorist, who was influential in concocting key elements of Nazi ideology. Rosenberg advocated the persecution of Jews, loathed 'degenerate' modern art and culture, despised traditional Christianity, and argued for the urgent need for German *Lebensraum* ('living space'), to be conquered from neighbouring countries to the east. Rosenberg edited the *Völkischer Beobachter* ('People's Observer'), the official Nazi newspaper. He was hanged after the Nuremberg trials, in 1946.

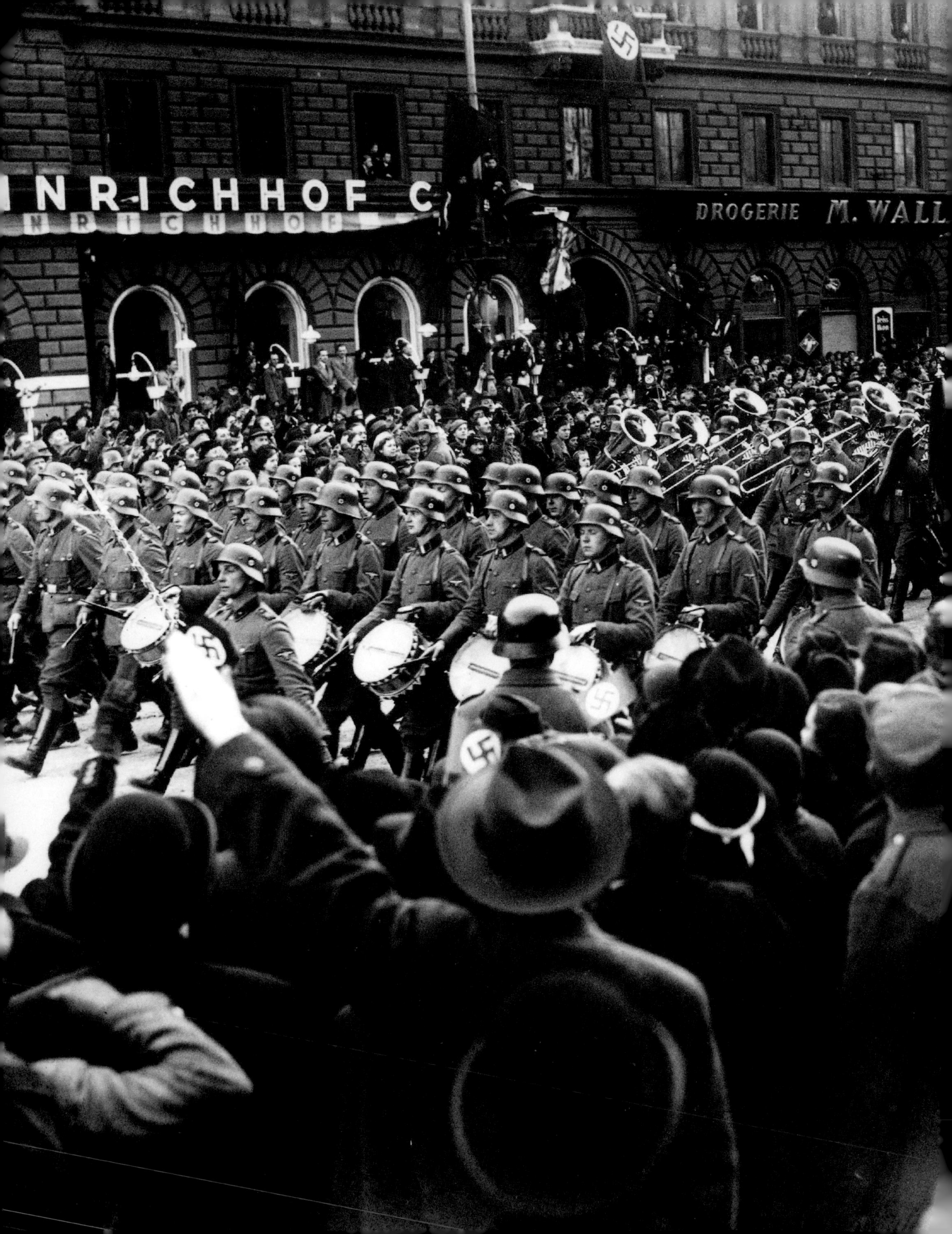
NRICHHOF C
DROGERIE
M. WALL

Anschluss

Expanding the borders of the German Reich was a major theme of Nazi foreign policy in the 1930s, particularly where it could be argued that this would bring 'ethnic Germans' back into their homeland. This policy, which flew in the face of the Treaty of Versailles, was known as *Heim ins Reich* ('Home to the Reich') and it was realized most spectacularly in March 1938, when German soldiers swarmed into Austria to enforce the 'Anschluss': political union between the two nations, with Germany as dominant partner.

'Austrofascism', as established under Engelbert Dollfuss and, later, Kurt Schuschnigg (see page 217), prized Austrian independence. Yet public opinion wavered. As the Nazis (under the Austrian-born Hitler) rearmed Germany, reduced unemployment, enacted public works programmes and began to roll back the humiliations of 1919, a sizeable portion of the Austrian population fell behind the idea of Anschluss.

By 1937 Hitler and Göring had decided that seizing Austria was essential for continued German growth and rearmament. In February 1938 Hitler summoned Schuschnigg to a meeting and delivered an ultimatum: hand powers to the Austrian Nazi Party, or face annexation. Schuschnigg initially agreed, but once back in Austria demanded a public vote. Hitler's patience ran out. On 12 March 1938, a day before Schuschnigg's planned vote, German soldiers marched into Austria. Many of them were greeted with cheers and Nazi salutes. A year later a new plebiscite was held, after which it was announced that more than 99 per cent of Austrian voters had approved the Anschluss.

Appeasement

Prior to the Anschluss, Hitler had defied the terms of Versailles by marching German troops into the supposedly demilitarized Rhineland. No European leader had been willing and able to stop him. Emboldened, Hitler followed up his annexation of Austria by announcing his desire to take over a large, German-majority portion of Czechoslovakia, known as the Sudetenland. If resisted, threatened Hitler, he would go to war. This amounted to a full-blown crisis for Europe's great powers, and the task of dealing with Hitler effectively fell to the British prime minister, Neville Chamberlain, pictured here in Downing Street, in London.

On 29 September 1938 Chamberlain met Hitler at Munich, along with Mussolini and the French prime minister, Édouard Daladier. There, the leaders agreed that Germany could annexe the Sudetenland. In return, Hitler promised that this would be his last territorial demand. Chamberlain returned to Britain claiming to have made 'peace for our time'. During the next two weeks, the Sudetenland was absorbed into the Nazi Reich.

For a brief while, Chamberlain was a hero, invited on to the balcony of Buckingham Palace where he was regaled with rounds of 'For He's a Jolly Good Fellow'. But not everyone was convinced. In private, Hitler found Chamberlain utterly contemptible: a 'silly old man' and a 'little worm'. And in the view of Winston Churchill, the agreement Chamberlain had struck at Munich was 'a total and unmitigated defeat'. He would not have to wait very long to be proven correct.

The Fall of Czechoslovakia

In early October 1938, German troops moved into the Sudetenland to effect its absorption into the Third Reich. They were met by Sudeten Germans like these, photographed on 3 October, who flashed stiff-armed Nazi salutes. Popular enthusiasm for the new regime was apparently confirmed with December election results overwhelmingly in favour of the Nazi Party. Meanwhile, an exodus of refugee Czechs, and some disaffected Germans, headed back into what remained of Czechoslovakia.

At Munich, Hitler had called the Sudetenland 'the final territorial demand I have to make in Europe'. In fact, he had been prepared for the violent conquest of all of Czechoslovakia and had not anticipated such easy British and French willingness to cut a deal. In that sense, the Munich Agreement had been a disappointment.

Nevertheless, Hitler did not have to wait long for what remained of Czechoslovakia to collapse of its own accord. Besides the concessions to Nazi Germany, the Munich Agreement also permitted Poland to annexe the territory known as Zaolzie, while Hungary was awarded part of Slovakia. In March 1939 the rest of Slovakia seceded and became a Nazi puppet state. The Wehrmacht moved swiftly into the Czech heartlands of Bohemia and Moravia to claim what was left. Hitler visited Prague Castle and declared a German Protectorate, and Nazification began in swift and predictable fashion, with the persecution of Jews, a clampdown on press freedom and the introduction of a police state. The Munich agreement had failed, and Czechoslovakia had fallen with barely a whimper.

Kristallnacht

Vienna was where Adolf Hitler had taught himself to hate Jews. The city, home to the majority of Jewish Austrians, had long been a hub of Jewish intellectual and artistic culture – the city of Sigmund Freud, Gustav Mahler and the playwright Arthur Schnitzler. But in the late 1930s the Anschluss gave licence to ancient and ugly strains of anti-Semitism. Austrian Jews were forbidden from voting in the Anschluss plebiscite, and soon the full weight of German anti-Jewish legislation was introduced to the Austrian state. In this photograph from 1938, boys under the direction of a Nazi Party official – or perhaps their schoolteacher – are encouraged in racial prejudice, as one of them daubs *Jud* (Jew) on a property now closed up.

On 9–10 November 1938, popular anti-Semitism was given its head across the Nazi Reich, with a night of violent attacks on Jewish people, properties, shops, schools and synagogues. Nazi propaganda called these assaults a 'spontaneous' outpouring of patriotic anger following the murder in Paris of a German diplomat by a Jewish assassin on 9 November. In fact, what took place was a general pogrom, encouraged by senior Nazis, particularly Joseph Goebbels, and abetted by the SA and police agencies including the Gestapo. Scores of Jews were killed. This orgy of violence later acquired the name Kristallnacht, the 'Night of Broken Glass', in reference to shattered shopfronts and windows that were seen across Nazi-ruled territories. In Vienna, almost all the synagogues and temples were set on fire and left to burn.

Concentration camps

The first Nazi concentration camp was built at Dachau, as soon as Hitler took power in 1933, and used initially to hold political prisoners. During subsequent years many more camps were built across Germany and in other Nazi-occupied lands. They included Sachsenhausen, about 23 miles (37km) from Berlin, which opened in 1936 and is where these prisoners were photographed.

Sachsenhausen was a combined camp, barracks and execution place, designed to house thousands of inmates in harsh conditions. Some were put to work, some were tortured or subjected to cruel medical experiments, and others were killed as the guards and their commanders saw fit. From the 1940s, Sachsenhausen included a purpose-built execution block known as 'Station Z'. The wrought-iron gates at the main entrance were decorated with the notorious phrase *Arbeit Macht Frei* ('Work makes [you] free'): a highly ironic slogan, since the wageless labour of prisoners was exploited by numerous major German industrial companies.

Sachsenhausen's inmates were identified by a system of colour-coded badges. Red badges were used for political prisoners. Pink triangles, as seen on two of the prisoners here, identified homosexual men. Yellow stars were used to mark out Jewish inmates; in the aftermath of Kristallnacht, tens of thousands of Jews across the Reich were rounded up and sent to concentration camps, to be mistreated, overworked, starved to death or murdered outright. During the Second World War, the mass murder of Jewish people in death camps would be systemized as the Final Solution.

Kindertransport

After Kristallnacht there could be no doubt about the Nazis' intentions towards Jews in the Reich. In 1938–9 alone, around 100,000 Jews left Germany and Austria, seeking refuge and survival in other lands. (The total number of Jewish emigrants by the end of 1939 was around 340,000.) But finding a new home was by no means easy – for despite international efforts led by President Roosevelt of the United States, many nations in Europe and beyond were unwilling to accept large numbers of refugees. Germany did not have a monopoly on anti-Semitism.

One exception to this rule was the Kindertransport programme, by which 10,000 unaccompanied Jewish children under the age of seventeen were resettled in Britain between December 1938 and September 1939. One of the first young people who arrived in England under that programme was Max Unger, photographed here wearing his name tag and number. Unger landed on 2 December 1938 at Harwich, along with 200 others, many from a Berlin orphanage attacked on Kristallnacht. The German authorities had allowed them to leave with a suitcase, very little money and no valuables. This photograph was taken at the Dovercourt Bay Camp in Essex, a clearing station converted from Butlin's holiday chalets, from where children were sent to live with relatives, foster families or in hostels and camps. According to an inspection report carried out at Dovercourt in January 1939, the children there 'seemed wonderfully happy, considering all they had been through'.

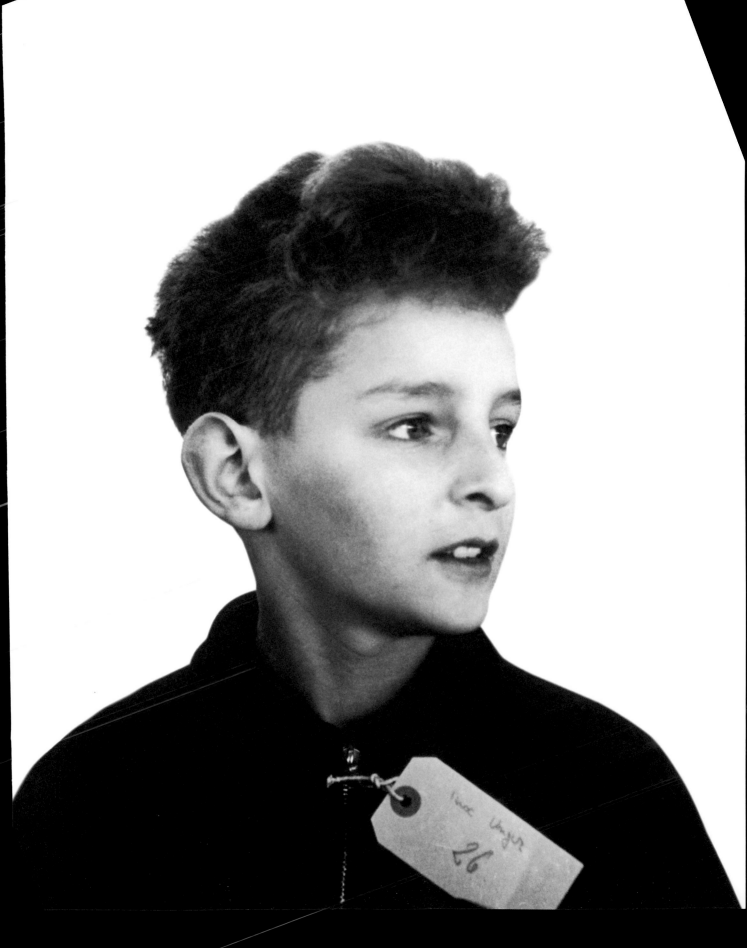

The Great Revolt

During the 1930s around sixty thousand German Jews fleeing the Nazi regime arrived in Palestine. There they joined a growing Jewish population, whose right to settle in the Near East was one of the conditions of British oversight in the region.

With the collapse of the Ottoman Empire after the First World War, Britain had been awarded 'mandatory' control of Palestine. However, the British soon found that they had to juggle two barely compatible sets of demands. On the one hand, Arab nationalists who had helped fight Ottoman rule during the First World War expected the British to favour their rights. Yet at the same time, Jewish immigrants assumed the British would honour the Balfour Declaration of 1917, which promised them a 'national home'. It was not clear how these competing claims could be satisfied. In the late 1930s the result was a major Arab revolt.

The 'Great Revolt' began in April 1936 with an Arab general strike. Eighteen months later, after an official British report proposed the partition of Palestine, protest gave way to armed insurrection. In response, the British imposed quasi-martial law, while the military and security forces brutally suppressed Arab attacks on officials and infrastructure. They were aided in this crackdown by Jewish settlers, including the Zionist paramilitary Haganah. This photograph, taken in 1939, shows Palestinian prisoners inside a British Army prison camp at Jenin, on the West Bank. The revolt cost at least five thousand Arab, four hundred Jewish and a hundred and fifty British lives before its end in 1939.

Nazi America

On 20 February 1939, some twenty thousand American Nazis gathered at Madison Square Garden in New York City to attend the 'Pro-American Rally': a festival of fascism at which the Nazi swastika and the Stars and Stripes were displayed side by side. During the evening, speakers poured scorn on President 'Rosenfeld', shouted 'Heil Hitler!' and denounced Jews and democracy. The date was near the anniversary of George Washington's birthday (22 February 1732), so behind the main stage the rally's organizers raised a huge image of the first US President (whom they called the 'first fascist'), flanked by Nazi insignia. This was, according to one bill-poster, a 'mass demonstration for true Americanism'.

The rally was arranged by the German American Bund, an organization that sought to recruit Americans of German descent to propagandize on behalf of Hitler's regime. Although the Bund never attracted more than about twenty-five thousand members, and was largely disowned by Hitler's regime, it nevertheless provided a focal point for would-be Nazis across the Atlantic. Its leader was a heavily accented first-generation immigrant, Fritz Kuhn, who ran the party as its *Bundesführer* until he was convicted in December 1939 on charges of embezzlement, imprisoned and eventually deported. It had an imitation SA, known as the Order Service, and a Hitler Youth wing. What it never had, though, was anything like mass popular support. The Pro-American Rally mainly served to turn public opinion against the Bund, and its membership rapidly declined with the outbreak of the Second World War.

The Conquest of Albania

As Nazi Germany expanded its borders into central Europe, Mussolini sent Italian troops into Albania, a territory that had long been a target for Italian imperialists who dreamed of rebuilding the ancient Roman Empire. In April 1939 Italian units swiftly overran the country: another blunt sign that the post-war European order was on the brink of collapse.

Since 1922 Albania had been ruled by Ahmed Zogu, who raised himself up from the position of prime minister to the royal status of King Zog I. Albania was a proud nation, but it was also poor, underdeveloped and highly dependent on Italy for trade, financial support, military expertise and defence. Thus it was virtually a client state even before Mussolini decided to invade. That the Italian dictator took the trouble to conquer Albania spoke mostly to his personal pride: as Hitler sent German armies into Austria and Czechoslovakia, Mussolini felt an urgent need to keep pace.

The invasion began on the morning of 7 April. By lunchtime, King Zog had crossed the border to Greece, taking his wife, infant son and a substantial quantity of gold bullion. The following day the Albanian government surrendered. By the middle of the month, King Victor Emmanuel III had formally accepted Zog's vacant crown and Albania had become a fully fledged Italian protectorate.

This photograph, taken in Rome in November 1939, illustrates the new state of affairs. Italian officers are consecrating the flag of an Albanian regiment, on which the distinctive double-headed eagle has been updated with Victor Emmanuel's crown of Savoy.

The Nazi–Soviet Pact

There were smiles all round in Moscow on 23 August 1939 when the representatives of Nazi Germany and the USSR signed a Non-Aggression Pact. Josef Stalin – leader of the USSR since Lenin's death in 1924 – beamed for the camera. Flanking him, the Soviet foreign minister Vyacheslav Molotov (*extreme right*) and his German counterpart, Joachim von Ribbentrop (*arms folded*), exuded satisfaction at one of history's most cynical agreements, made between sworn ideological enemies. Afterwards, they opened champagne.

Hitler loathed communists, as the Anti-Comintern pact had made plain. Stalin saw fascism as an urgent threat to the USSR's security. The Spanish Civil War had been fought as a proxy conflict between Germany and the USSR. Yet now, in this agreement, also called the Molotov–Ribbentrop Pact, mutual contempt was laid aside for expedient self-interest.

The pact promised military neutrality and laid the basis for a trading relationship that allowed both economies to access massive amounts of raw materials and military hardware. Secretly, Molotov and Ribbentrop also mapped out a carve-up of Poland and the Baltic states (Estonia, Latvia and Lithuania), with Finland and part of Romania to be under Soviet sway.

The Nazi–Soviet pact shocked the world. British and French politicians now knew there was no bulwark to Hitler's ambitions in the east. Earlier in the year, they had promised to protect Poland against Nazi aggression. It was hard to see how these promises could now be kept. On 24 August, the Deputy Leader of the Labour Party, Arthur Greenwood, told the British House of Commons: 'The war clouds are gathering.'

Invasion of Poland

A week and a day after the Molotov–Ribbentrop pact was signed, on 1 September 1939, Nazi Germany invaded Poland. Around dawn, a German battleship pounded the Free City of Danzig (Gdansk). By mid-morning, Wehrmacht units were pouring across the Polish border from three directions.

Hitler had challenged his generals to complete the conquest of Poland in just six weeks. The tactics they adopted were known as blitzkrieg ('lightning war'): a ferocious assault of bomber aircraft, tanks, infantry and artillery. The speed of the strike was shocking; it was made much worse on 17 September when, in accordance with the secret protocols of the Molotov–Ribbentrop Pact, Stalin's Red Army invaded from the east. By the end of September, Poland was overrun.

This photograph was taken on the first day of the Nazi invasion. It shows the view from inside a large German bomber plane, a Heinkel He III. The Luftwaffe airman, lying on a cramped platform in the bomber's glazed nose, has a panoramic view of the land below. From here, he could operate a machine gun and aim the bombs.

Hitler knew very well that Britain and France had sworn to intervene to protect Poland. On 3 September both countries declared war on Germany. It was too late for them to save the Polish people from the horrors that had already begun to descend. But the date marked the start of a great-power conflict that had been inevitable, perhaps, since Hitler came to power in 1933. The Second World War had begun.

The Storm of War

1939–1940

We shall fight on the beaches,
we shall fight on the landing grounds,
we shall fight in the fields…
we shall never surrender.

Winston Churchill, speech in the House of Commons
(4 June 1940)

n late May 1940, around four hundred thousand troops – almost all of them British and French – fell back to the exceptionally long sandy beaches around the port of Dunkirk, in north-east France, and contemplated an awful fate. Ahead, above and all around them the might of the Nazi war machine was closing in. Behind them were the chilly waters of the English Channel. There seemed to be no way that more than a bare fraction of the soldiers at Dunkirk could escape death or captivity. The British prime minister Winston Churchill – who had taken office just a fortnight previously – was briefed to expect the rescue of just 10 per cent of the British Expeditionary Force (BEF) trapped there. He – and they – needed a miracle.

Against all the odds, they got one.

Over the course of little more than a week, between 26 May and 4 June 1940, a hastily assembled fleet of Royal Navy ships, aided by a ragtag flotilla of merchant and private vessels – known collectively as the 'little ships' – raced across the Channel to rescue the British and French soldiers pinned down at Dunkirk. Operation Dynamo, as it was known, was planned and co-ordinated at Dover Castle on the south coast of England by Vice-Admiral Bertram Ramsay, a veteran of the First World War whom Churchill had convinced to abandon retirement and serve his country again.

The men on the beaches and those crewing the boats and ships had to endure bombs and strafing by Luftwaffe aircraft – despite valiant sorties flown by Royal Air Force (RAF) pilots to draw them away from the evacuation effort. Fires raged in the town of Dunkirk. The weather was grim. Long, loud, wet, tense, bloody days spent waiting for salvation drove some men to the verge of madness – and others over it. Yet by the time Operation

Dynamo was over, 338,226 Allied soldiers had been saved, two-thirds of them British. It was more than anyone had dared to dream.

On the last day of Operation Dynamo, Churchill gave one of his most famous speeches to the House of Commons. Reporting to his nation and the world beyond what had taken place, he said: 'I feared it would be my hard lot to announce the greatest military disaster in our long history.' And, indeed, Churchill continued, Dunkirk did represent a catastrophe, with huge loss of life and *matériel*. Yet in defeat, the prime minister said he discerned hope. This bleak retreat had convinced him that Britain would be able 'to ride out the storm of war, and to outlive the menace of tyranny, if necessary for years, if necessary alone'.

'We shall fight on the beaches,' he said, 'we shall fight on the landing grounds, we shall fight in the fields and in the streets, we shall fight in the hills; we shall never surrender.'

Dunkirk was not the only rescue mission that took place in early summer 1940. Before Operation Dynamo, Royal Navy ships had partially evacuated the besieged town of Boulogne; in mid-June Operation Cycle saw more than ten thousand men lifted from Le Havre, while Operation Aerial co-ordinated retreats via other French ports, from Cherbourg in the north to Bayonne in the south. The corporal photographed here, being helped up a gangplank, is a member of the Auxiliary Military Pioneer Corps – a reservist corps of British light engineers who were involved in most of the various evacuations that took place during those hair-raising weeks.

This mass, chaotic scattering from the shores of France took place in 1940 because in that spring Hitler's armies had cut a swathe through western Europe. After the fall of Poland in September 1939, there had emerged a 'Phoney War', with relatively little fighting but much military planning and naval blockading. This ended abruptly in April, when the Nazis launched a lightning invasion of Norway, toppling the government, seizing North Sea ports and installing a new regime under a German governor, Josef Terboven, and the Norwegian fascist leader, Vidkun Quisling.

At the same time, Hitler turned his attentions west. On 10 May 1940 the German Army invaded France, Belgium, Luxembourg and the Netherlands. They skirted the Maginot Line – a vast chain of fortresses and weapons posts designed to protect France from German aggression – and with all the usual speed and relentlessness of blitzkrieg, started an advance towards the coast, encircling as they went the hundreds of thousands of troops of the BEF and French armies who would subsequently be evacuated from Dunkirk.

So the war was no longer phoney, and after Dunkirk came further iconic tests for the British. From July until October 1940 an air battle was fought between Hermann Göring's Luftwaffe and the RAF. This was the Battle of Britain: an attempt to establish German air superiority over British skies, so that Operation Sea Lion – a Nazi amphibious invasion across the Channel – could begin. It was by turns audacious, heroic, and deadly, but after the RAF prevailed, the Battle of Britain bled quickly into the Blitz: a heavy night-bombing campaign by the Luftwaffe against civilian and industrial targets in London, Coventry, Bristol, Cardiff, Liverpool and elsewhere. The Blitz lasted until May 1941, and it permanently reshaped Britain's industrial landscape – and collective sense of self.

Elsewhere in 1940, the Allies – as the powers that opposed Hitler were to be known – were suffering.

Belgium and the neutral Netherlands were occupied. Paris fell on 14 June, after which France was also occupied, and given a puppet government, based in Vichy, under the First World War hero Marshal Philippe Pétain. And Italy entered the war, briefly invading France across the Alps, and attacking British interests in Egypt, Mandatory Palestine and British Somaliland.

Elsewhere, the Soviet Union concluded the Winter War against Finland in March 1940, claiming more than 10 per cent of Finnish territory for itself. In the Far East, Japan's war with China ground on into a third year and, after France's surrender to Germany, the Japanese also began to push into French Indochina.

In the last months of 1940, the relationship between Germany, Italy and Japan – the Axis Powers – was cemented in the Tripartite Pact. From this point onwards, the enemy of one was the enemy of all. The world's conflicts had now coalesced into a single world war.

10 May 1940	27 May–4 June 1940	22 June 1940	10 July 1940	7 September 1940
German troops, tanks, aircraft and parachutists invade the Netherlands, Belgium and France, including via the Ardennes forests. The Allies fall back in disarray.	Against all expectation, more than 330,000 Allied troops (two-thirds of them British) escape German encirclement at Dunkirk, rescued by hundreds of naval and civilian vessels.	France submits to German armistice terms, dividing the country into an occupied zone and the client 'Vichy' state. From London, Charles de Gaulle has urged the French to fight on.	The Battle of Britain begins, in which German bombers attempt, unsuccessfully, to destroy British air and sea defences in advance of a planned amphibious invasion.	German bombers, initially in revenge for an RAF raid on Berlin, switch targets to British cities, principally London: the campaign, lasting to May 1941, is called 'the Blitz'.

The Battle of the Atlantic

Although the Phoney War of winter 1939–40 saw little fighting on land, it was a different story at sea. When war was declared, Britain and France imposed a naval blockade on Nazi Germany. Hitler retaliated with a counter-blockade.

For the next five and a half years, the Atlantic Ocean was a battlefield. Merchant convoys travelling from the Americas to Europe and the Soviet Union were menaced by the German navy (Kriegsmarine), while Allied naval vessels and aircraft tried to protect them. In the first four months of the war alone, German vessels sank nearly a third of the British merchant fleet; on 14 October 1939 the battleship HMS *Royal Oak* was torpedoed by a U-boat in the Royal Navy's base at Scapa Flow, with the loss of more than eight hundred sailors. During the course of the Second World War, more than three thousand merchant ships were sunk; anticipating U-boats strikes in the Atlantic was a major goal of British efforts to break the military ciphers used by the Nazis' Enigma machines.

The sailors photographed here were involved in one of the first major naval clashes of the war: the Battle of the River Plate. On 13 December 1939 they were aboard HMS *Exeter* when she, along with HMS *Ajax* and *Achilles*, attacked the German 'pocket battleship' *Admiral Graf Spee* off the coast of Uruguay. *Exeter* was badly damaged, while *Admiral Graf Spee* was later scuttled on her captain's orders. These sailors are celebrating their safe arrival back in Plymouth.

The Winter War

There was no Phoney War in the east, where from November 1939 Soviet troops invaded Finland, aiming to seize territory along the Russian border and create a 'buffer zone' of territory on the approach to Leningrad. This land grab had been agreed under the secret protocols of the Molotov–Ribbentrop Pact, but it resulted in the USSR's expulsion from the League of Nations and proved a chastening experience for the Soviet Red Army.

After the Russian Revolution, the Bolsheviks had become entangled in the Finnish Civil War (see page 150). A generation later, Josef Stalin still yearned to bring Finland into the Soviet fold. So from 30 November 1939, four Russian armies crossed the Finnish border. Stalin's generals poured nearly half a million men into the effort and bombarded Finnish cities with incendiary cluster bombs nicknamed 'Molotov bread baskets', after the hated Soviet foreign minister, Vyacheslav Molotov.

While the Soviets possessed impressive firepower and manpower, the Finns fought fiercely, and were protected by the severity of their climate. Fighters like these Finnish ski troops were more familiar with, and better equipped for, frozen terrain and temperatures that dipped below -40°C. The Red Army suffered terrible losses: tens of thousands of men were incapacitated by frostbite.

Eventually the Soviets' sheer numbers won out, and Finland ceded a large amount of territory in the Treaty of Moscow of March 1940. But Stalin's struggle to conquer an apparently feeble neighbour was noted in Germany. This would have profound consequences later in the war.

The Invasion of Norway

Operation Weserübung was the code name for the Nazi invasion of Denmark and Norway, launched on 9 April 1940. Denmark capitulated easily; more dramatic was the overthrow of Norway's royal government, which was replaced by a pro-Nazi puppet regime under a German governor, Josef Terboven, and the fascist politician Vidkun Quisling.

Norway mattered because its ports gave Germany access to valuable iron ore mined in neighbouring (and neutral) Sweden. Controlling Norway's long coastline would also allow German ships and U-boats to threaten Allied merchant convoys in the northern Atlantic. Realizing this, Britain's naval chief, Winston Churchill, had convinced his colleagues to approve mine-laying in Norwegian waters. But before his operation could make significant progress, Hitler ordered an invasion.

A wide range of Wehrmacht and Kriegsmarine personnel were involved in Operation Weserübung, including paratroopers, who were dropped in to seize airfields in southern Norway. This photograph was taken a week after the campaign began, and it shows two German soldiers – one a platoon commander – in the snowy landscape north of Oslo.

Allied forces rushed to help the Norwegians resist, but the task of containing the Nazi war machine proved beyond them. Although the Royal Navy did permanent damage to the German fleet, on 7 June the Allies withdrew. The Norwegian king, Haakon VII, was evacuated, along with his family, key government ministers and the country's gold reserves. He established a government-in-exile in Britain, and eventually returned to Norway in 1945.

The Battle of France

Allied forces were in no position to defend Norway in June 1940 because by that point Hitler's armies were also racing across western Europe, sweeping past existing defences and pressing Allied troops into a retreat towards the coast.

In France, a huge network of concrete forts, pillboxes and artillery positions known as the Maginot Line had been built during the 1930s to oppose any land invasion by German troops. This line was extended in the north – in theory at least – by the Ardennes, a wooded and hilly region of Belgium and Luxembourg, held to be impassable, even to Nazi blitzkrieg.

On 10 May 1940, however, Germany launched a westward attack against Belgium, the Netherlands, Luxembourg and France. Wehrmacht armoured divisions defied Allied expectations by powering directly through the Ardennes. They were led by General Heinz Guderian, a visionary military planner, pictured here in his command vehicle. Guderian's audacious tactics smashed the French front, and sent the Allies scattering for safety, with the bulk of the British Expeditionary Force heading for Dunkirk in the hope of repatriation across the Channel.

The speed and focus of the German attack resulted in spectacular gains, achieved within a matter of days. The Netherlands surrendered on 14 May, followed two weeks later by Belgium. By 27 May the British were evacuating the continent. Barely more than a month after Hitler's invasion of the west began, the Führer was preparing to enter Paris. There seemed to be no limit to his appetites.

Blitzkrieg

Nazi blitzkrieg against Belgium and the Netherlands showed just what a dangerous military machine Hitler had reassembled during the 1930s. The campaign began with Luftwaffe bombing raids on airfields and an assault by paratroopers in gliders on the imposing Belgian fort of Eben-Emael. On 14 May bombing sorties against the Dutch city of Rotterdam flattened that city's famous historic centre. Incendiary attacks set uncontrollable fires, which burned for days, killing hundreds and leaving nearly 100,000 Dutch civilians homeless.

Overwhelmed civil defence workers and emergency services, like these men, photographed in Brussels at around the same time, struggled against the flames. One of the most potent devices dropped from above was the German standard 'B1' incendiary bomb. It was small – weighing only around 1kg – but could be released in clusters of up to seven hundred at a time. On impact, a small charge heated up a thermite chemical inside, melting the shell casing and setting alight anything in proximity.

Hard-pressed to resist this furious assault, Brussels fell to the Nazis on 18 May, and Belgian political unity disintegrated soon afterwards. On 28 May the Belgian king, Leopold III, surrendered both his armies and himself into German hands. This placed the retreating Allied forces under even greater pressure and earned Leopold lasting opprobrium in Belgium and beyond. The king was placed under house arrest and would remain a prisoner for the duration of the war. In the meantime, the Germans' lightning advance westward continued, sowing chaos as it went.

Prime Minister Churchill

On the same day Germany invaded Belgium and the Netherlands – 10 May 1940 – Winston Churchill became prime minister of the United Kingdom. He replaced Neville Chamberlain, who resigned the post after the Allies had failed to protect Norway from Nazi occupation.

Churchill was now sixty-five years old, but he took to his task with the energy of a man half his age. Under Chamberlain he had served as First Lord of the Admiralty, which gave him a keen sense of what it took to wage a global war. Moreover, he came to high office with an unshakeable sense of historical destiny and his own role in saving Europe from tyranny. His elevated sense of self and 'bulldog' spirit would prove invaluable to British morale, and his timeless rhetoric provided a soaring, heroic commentary on the Allied war effort.

In many ways a throwback to an earlier age, Churchill had been dismissed as a warmonger during the 1930s, when he lambasted those who wished to appease Hitler. Now, as he formed his new War Cabinet, he gave the House of Commons a speech that set the tone. 'I have nothing to offer,' he told MPs, 'but blood, toil, tears and sweat.' Britain's only policy, he said, would be 'to wage war, by sea, land and air, with all our might and with all the strength that God can give us… against a monstrous tyranny, never surpassed in the dark, lamentable catalogue of human crime.'

The Führer in Paris

Two million Parisians had fled their city when Hitler arrived at the end of June 1940. Standing in the shadow of the Eiffel Tower, he could reflect that his armies had achieved in little more than a month what the Kaiser's had failed to do in four years of the First World War. But now, revenge had been served: on 22 June French surrender was confirmed and formalized in the same train carriage that had witnessed the Armistice of November 1918.

Having humiliated the French, Hitler had no wish to raze Paris, although he demolished two statues he deemed anti-German, including one of Edith Cavell (see page 66). In a motorcade of Mercedes cars, he toured the Opéra, before taking in sites from the Arc de Triomphe to Napoleon's tomb at Les Invalides, and Montmartre. His chosen companions on this sightseeing expedition were two architects, Albert Speer (*left*) and Hermann Giesler, along with the sculptor Arno Breker (*right*). Hitler had grand plans for remodelling Berlin and other German cities, so that they might one day outshine Paris.

Although Hitler's visit to the French capital lasted a mere three hours and he never returned, he called it the realization of a dream. But for many in France, Nazi occupation would prove to be not so much a dream as a sustained and terrible nightmare.

Vichy France

Marshal Philippe Pétain was eighty-four years old and serving as ambassador to Spain when he was recalled to France to serve in the Cabinet at the height of the crisis of May 1940. As the commander credited with saving Verdun (see page 98) and restoring French morale in the First World War, Pétain was a national hero. His experience in the Second World War would be very different.

On 16 June, after the government had abandoned Paris to the Nazis, Pétain replaced Paul Reynaud as prime minister. It was his burden to agree the armistice that confirmed German victory in the Battle of France and to broadcast its terms to the nation. The armistice created a German-occupied zone in the north and west of France and allowed a semi-vassal French state to remain in the south, headquartered in Vichy. Pétain became the *Chef* – both head of state and premier – of this new *État Français*.

To conservative traditionalists with authoritarian leanings – like Pétain – Vichy represented an opportunity to wipe the French slate clean of socialist and 'decadent' infection. An extraordinary personality cult developed around the Marshal, and in 1940–41 he made a tour of Vichy France to receive its adulation. Here, he is photographed greeting students in Vichy itself, and receiving bouquets of flowers.

The Vichy regime lasted until the Allied liberation of France in 1944, after which many of its leading members were condemned as collaborators. It existed in opposition to 'Free France' – a state in exile, which organized resistance and fought as one of the Allies.

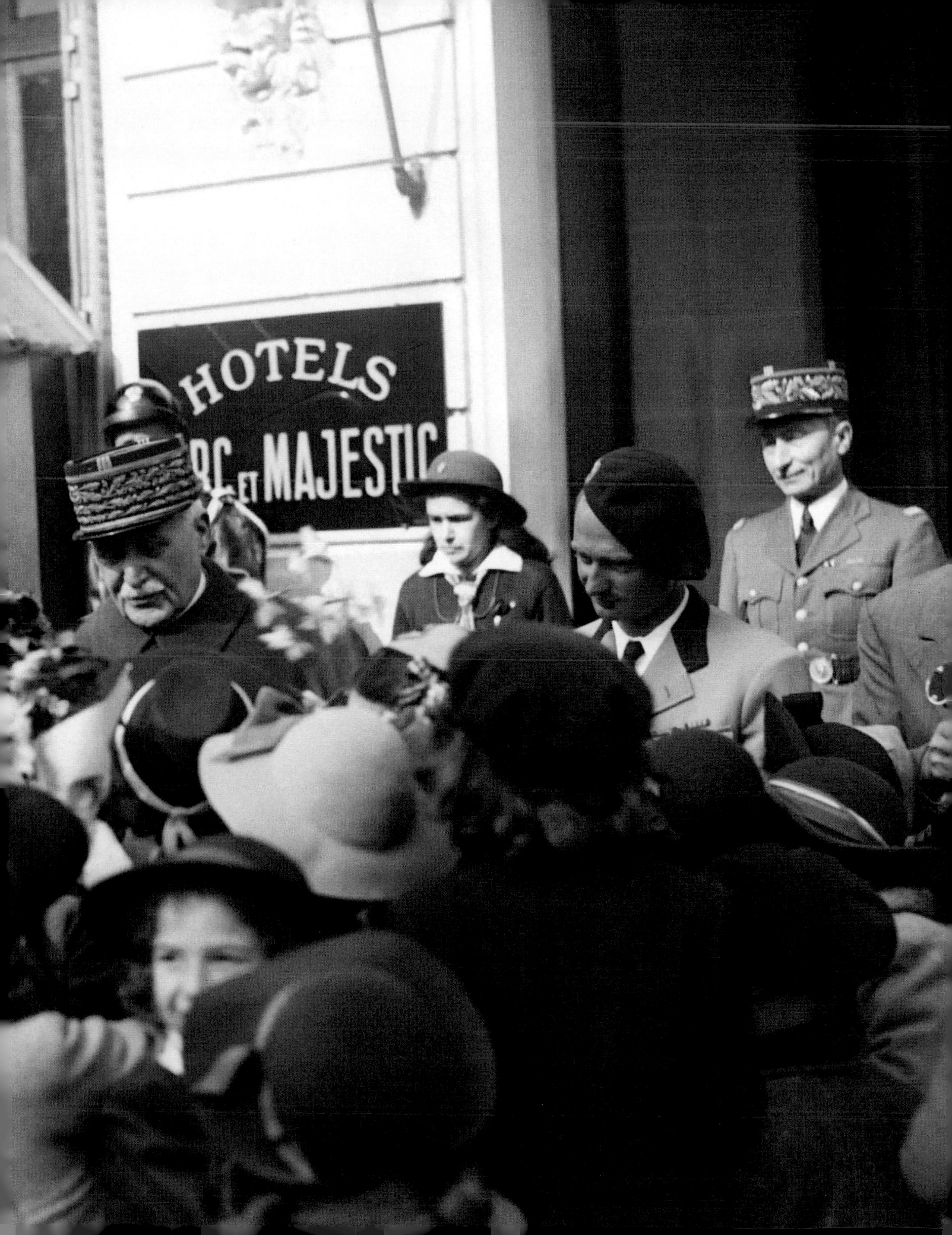
HOTELS
RC ET MAJESTIC

The Battle of Britain

Churchill predicted that the fall of France would be followed by the Battle of Britain. He was right. From July to October 1940, the Luftwaffe attacked. Using newly conquered airbases, German aircraft tried to take control of the English Channel by destroying shipping and ports, and to obliterate the RAF's Fighter Command, leaving Britain helpless against a planned invasion code-named Operation Sea Lion.

To those ends, Hermann Göring, commander of the Luftwaffe, sent waves of German bombers against British targets, while brave but often frighteningly undertrained RAF pilots scrambled to defend the skies. Besides native Britons, the air crews who served in the Battle of Britain included Irish, Poles, Czechs, French, Belgians and even volunteer Americans, as well as pilots from the Dominions. Many flew the Supermarine Spitfire, but even more flew the Hawker Hurricane, which was powered by Rolls-Royce Merlin III engines and sported eight machine guns. The Hurricanes photographed here by B. J. H. Daventry, a press photographer who served in the RAF, were piloted by men of No. 85 Squadron.

By October it was clear that the RAF had successfully defended British skies, and Hitler was forced to cancel Operation Sea Lion. For the first time, the Nazis had been halted in their tracks. In another of his great speeches, given at the height of the Battle of Britain, Churchill said of the RAF: 'Never in the field of human conflict was so much owed by so many to so few.'

Women at War

As soon as the Second World War started, Britain's parliament passed the National Service (Armed Forces) Act. This required all men aged between eighteen and forty-one to register to serve in the military, unless they were ill, involved in essential industries or could prove that they were conscientious objectors. Two years later, after the Battle of Britain and the Blitz, the government extended conscription to British women as well. Unmarried women and widows without children, aged between twenty and thirty, were now also liable to be called up.

Of course, many women had already volunteered, joining organizations including the Women's Royal Naval Service (WRNS) and the Women's Auxiliary Air Force (WAAF). The women photographed here are members of the Auxiliary Territorial Service (ATS). This was the largest women's service of the war, and a quarter of a million British women joined up between 1938 and 1945. This photo was taken in December 1939, at which time Norma Quaye (*centre*) was the only black woman in the service.

Women in the ATS performed a huge range of roles. In addition to cooking, driving and operating telephones or typewriters, ATS women could work at radar stations, on anti-aircraft batteries or as engineers. In the last months of the war, King George VI's elder daughter, the eighteen-year-old Princess Elizabeth (the future Elizabeth II), joined the ATS. She trained as a mechanic and a driver, ending the war with the rank of Junior Commander.

The Blitz

After the Battle of Britain came the Blitz. From
7 September 1940 until May 1941 the Luftwaffe changed
the focus of their campaign, so that instead of targeting
airfields, German bombers began to attack cities and their
civilian populations. The aim was to damage
infrastructure and industrial capacity and terrorize the
British into defeatism.

London was the city hardest hit by the Blitz: at the
start of the campaign it was attacked on fifty-seven
consecutive nights, often with the loss of hundreds of lives
at a time. But the bombs fell far and wide, causing terrible
destruction in Coventry, Bristol, Cardiff, Liverpool,
Birmingham and elsewhere. The dramatic rescue pictured
here took place in Southampton, a city that hosted vital
port facilities, and the main Supermarine factory, where
Spitfire fighter planes were manufactured. On 24
September, Messerschmitt Me 110 fighter-bombers struck
the Supermarine works. Though the damage was light, a
direct hit on an air raid shelter killed around twenty-five
workers and injured many more.

This iconic photograph, once thought to depict
a London scene, was taken in September 1940. It shows a
young man called Albert Robbins struggling to pull a
bomb victim free of rubble. Later the same day Robbins
witnessed a rescue winch slice a girl's legs from her torso.
He was so traumatized that he disappeared from his
family for three days.

Evacuation

The Battle of Britain and the Blitz put civilians squarely
in harm's way. But even before war broke out, a huge
evacuation scheme had been in place, designed to take
vulnerable people – young mothers, the elderly or
disabled and particularly children – out of major cities for
temporary relocation in the countryside. The official
programme was known as Operation Pied Piper and it
moved around 3.5 million people between 1938 and 1944.

The children photographed here were being evacuated
for their second time. At the outbreak of war, they had
been sent to the Sussex coast. When this picture was
taken, on 14 July 1940, they were being moved once more,
to the Home Counties. The tags on their clothes typically
detailed their name, home address, school and a code
number to help the authorities and adult volunteers who
worked at either end of the evacuation process keep track
of the children, who had often been separated from their
parents. The experience of separation could be traumatic
– and memories of being sent abruptly and confusingly
away from home lingered with some child evacuees all
their lives.

Typically, children left their homes with only a few
possessions – clothes, nightclothes and sufficient supplies
to keep themselves clean and tidy. Along with the rest of
the population, they were also encouraged to carry their
gas mask. At the start of the war the government had
distributed millions of black rubber masks to guard
against the possibility of a major chemical weapons
attack. Mercifully, none ever took place.

The Invasion of Egypt

While Hitler's forces were attacking mainland Britain from above, another theatre of war had opened in North Africa. Mussolini's Italian forces, based in Libya, were preparing to attack Egypt.

For the Allies, defending Egypt was vital. Oil reserves in the Middle East were a crucial resource in wartime, while the Suez Canal joined the Mediterranean with the Red Sea, allowing British naval and commercial ships to pass easily between Europe and the imperial territories and dominions in the east. The struggle to keep the Italians out of Egypt was known as the Western Desert Campaign. It began in the autumn of 1940 and continued for more than two and a half years. This Italian flamethrower unit was photographed a few months before the campaign began, near the Libyan–Egyptian border.

Serious fighting started on 9 September, when the Italian Tenth Army, under Marshal Rodolfo Graziani, swarmed across the border and built fortified camps near the coastal town of Sidi Barrani. In early December, however, the British launched Operation Compass, and the Western Desert Force (including Australian, Indian and other imperial troops, as well as some Free French) chased Graziani back into Libya, taking more than 130,000 prisoners and capturing large numbers of tanks and guns as they did so. In January, Mussolini had to ask for German assistance in the desert: Hitler sent him reinforcements, including the Afrika Korps, whose most famous commander was 'the Desert Fox': Field Marshal Erwin Rommel.

Stalemate in China

China had been riven by conflict since 1937. In this photograph, taken in 1940, Chinese civilians line up to form a local self-defence unit; the flag behind them indicates that this is in the part of China still under the sway of Chiang Kai-shek's Nationalist Republic.

Despite the humiliating and bloody defeats of 1937, which had seen the Imperial Japanese Army seize Beijing and Nanjing (see page 235), the Chinese did not capitulate. In a two-week battle fought in the spring of 1938, the National Revolutionary Army managed to inflict a first major defeat on the Japanese at Tai'erzhuang. However, this was followed by another series of setbacks, and by October the Japanese had seized the important city of Wuhan.

The struggle for Wuhan was appallingly deadly. In June 1938 Chiang ordered the destruction of a major dyke on the Yellow River, thereby deliberately flooding vast swathes of the lands along the riverbanks. This failed in its purpose of stopping the Japanese advance, but it destroyed thousands of Chinese villages, flooding farmland and killing anywhere between 500,000 and 1.5 million people.

By 1941 the Japanese occupied large tracts of eastern China, but lacked the capability to push much further onwards. Meanwhile, they and the Nationalists faced a mounting challenge from Chinese communist forces. A stalemate had developed. However, the war in the Far East was about to shift dramatically, as the United States prepared to enter the Second World War.

1941– 1942

Invasion

Once we were there,
it was the most diseased place on earth, I think.
Everything rotted, including your body.

US Marine Theodore R. Cummings,
remembering the battle for Guadalcanal

Ralph Morse was twenty-four years old when he boarded the US aircraft carrier *Enterprise* in Hawaii and headed out into the Pacific Ocean. It was January 1942, and although the Second World War had been raging for more than a year, the United States had been an active belligerent for little more than a month. Morse, who had just been hired as a staff photographer for *Life* magazine, was one of a whole generation of young Americans who were heading far from home to experience battle in lands that many of them had barely even heard of. Few of them would see as much of the war as Morse. During the next four years he travelled from the Pacific Islands to western Europe and captured some of the most arresting images in the history of war photography.

A year after leaving American soil, Morse was on Guadalcanal, one of the Solomon Islands. It was his second visit to the region; on his previous trip he had been caught up in the naval battle of Savo Island: his ship, the USS *Vincennes*, was sunk and Morse spent a night floating in bloody, shark-infested waters waiting to be rescued. On this occasion, however, he was spending the Christmas of 1942 with a group of Marines. Joining them on patrol one day, Morse encountered a tank abandoned in a jungle clearing, with a burned skull balanced on top of it. He knew, he said later, that 'it was just a great picture… to show people who want to go to war what war was like'. He sent the film he exposed back to the USA, sealed in a condom to keep it watertight. Several weeks later, readers of *Life* opened the magazine's 1 February 1943 issue and encountered seven pages of Morse's pictures. The head shot occupied an entire page. 'A Japanese soldier's skull is propped up on a burned-out Jap tank by U. S. troops', read the caption. 'Fire destroyed the rest of the corpse.'

On 7 December 1941, the Imperial Japanese Navy Air Service had conducted one of the most notorious attacks of the twentieth century, launching a massive strike against the US naval base at Pearl Harbor on Hawaii. In the course of around ninety minutes, more than two thousand US service personnel were killed and eighteen ships sunk or seriously damaged. The Japanese attacked as a pre-emptive measure to ensure that the USA could not interfere with planned invasions of American, British and Dutch territories in the Far East. Their actions, said President Roosevelt, marked 7 December as 'a date which will live in infamy'. On 8 December, he declared war on Japan. Four days later, the declaration was extended to Germany and Italy. Just as had happened in 1917, with the entry of the USA into the conflict the whole shape of the war shifted suddenly.

Of course – as in 1917 – the USA had not sat wholly aloof from the war until the point at which it engaged. There had already been violent confrontations between US ships and German vessels in the Atlantic, while US opposition to Japanese imperialism and to the war in China had prompted Roosevelt to prohibit oil sales to Japan. In March 1941, he had agreed a policy of 'Lend-Lease' to supply friendly powers with war materials. And five months later, acting as if Britain and the USA were already wartime allies, he and Winston Churchill issued the 'Atlantic Charter', setting out principles for a post-war order based on global cooperation and liberty. It assumed the defeat of fascism and militarism.

It took time for the USA to shift fully to a war footing, but within two weeks of Pearl Harbor, American 'Flying Tigers' pilots had begun sorties over China, intercepting Japanese bombers in support of Chiang Kai-shek's Chinese Nationalists. On the domestic front there

11 March 1941	27 April 1941	22 June 1941	5 December 1941	7 December 1941
President Roosevelt signs into law the 'Lend-Lease Act', to supply US war-related equipment and supplies to 'favoured nations', particularly cash-strapped Britain.	The Nazi swastika flies over Athens, three weeks after German forces invaded both Yugoslavia and Greece; a vicious collaborationist regime ensues in Yugoslav Croatia.	Operation Barbarossa, the German (and Axis) invasion of the Soviet Union, commences in three main thrusts with the most massive blitzkrieg yet seen.	A Soviet counter-offensive begins pushing German forces back from the outskirts of Moscow; Operation Barbarossa has failed to provide a quick Axis victory, and a brutal winter has set in.	Aircraft of an Imperial Japanese Navy carrier force attack Pearl Harbor, Hawaii, base of the US Pacific Fleet, and within four days the USA is at war with Japan and Germany.

were mass internments of Japanese Americans, many of whom were locked up as potential fifth columnists, amid fears that the US West Coast was vulnerable to foreign invasion. This was a start. But the USA could not summon sufficient might in the first few months of 1942 to fully halt the Japanese advance in the Pacific. In February, a Japanese army crushed British resistance in Singapore, taking around eighty thousand prisoners of war in what Churchill later called 'the worst disaster and largest capitulation' in British history.

By fighting not only Japan but also the Axis powers in Europe, Roosevelt had made a huge commitment to the Allies. Yet he could hardly have ignored affairs in the west. In April 1941, Hitler's armies had swarmed over Yugoslavia and into Greece, supporting Italian efforts in the Balkans and securing the submission of both nations within the month. Then, in June, Hitler launched his most audacious – and fateful – campaign of the whole war. He commenced Operation Barbarossa: a massive invasion of the USSR, which tore up the truce established in the Molotov–Ribbentrop Pact and set an entirely new phase of the Second World War in train. Blitzkrieg eventually stumbled at the siege of Stalingrad. Yet under the cover of the renewed push eastwards, the Nazis began the most terrible phase of the Holocaust (or Shoah): industrial genocide of European Jews. First, Jewish people were crammed into squalid, walled-off ghettos in cities like Warsaw; then the mechanized murder began, and camps such as Auschwitz and Treblinka were used for the programmatic slaughter of innocent people in their millions.

Away from Europe, in North Africa the Axis powers, led by Erwin Rommel, continued to threaten Egypt until two battles at El Alamein began the Allied grind towards regional victory. In November 1942, Anglo-American forces invaded Vichy-controlled Morocco and Algeria; Operation Torch laid the ground for an eventual push across the Mediterranean into southern Europe.

By the end of 1942, then, the tide appeared to be turning. After the Battle of Midway in June, the USA could envisage naval supremacy in the Pacific. After Stalingrad, Hitler was stretched on two fronts, against two rising superpowers. And on Guadalcanal, where Ralph Morse had spent a hair-raising Christmas, US troops were pushing towards victory. Along the way, however, they took appalling casualties, and encountered a Japanese martial ethic of near-suicidal belligerence that would endure until the very last moments of the war.

---

20 January 1942

At the Wannsee 'conference', in a Berlin suburb of that name, Nazi officials make provision for the Final Solution: the industrial methods for killing Europe's Jews.

15 February 1942

Singapore surrenders to Japanese attack, a profound shock for the British Empire; a month earlier, Japan invaded British colonial Burma too, threatening supplies to China.

4 June 1942

The Battle of Midway begins, in which US ships and carrier-borne aircraft inflict serious losses, undercutting Japanese naval supremacy in the Pacific.

23 October 1942

Under Lieutenant-General Bernard Montgomery, an offensive at El Alamein, Egypt, overwhelms the Axis forces of the celebrated 'Desert Fox' Erwin Rommel.

8 November 1942

In Operation Torch, a mainly US amphibious invasion of Vichy French Morocco and Algeria begins: victory is swift, as senior Vichy commanders swap sides.

Lend-Lease

On 11 March 1941, photographers clustered around President Roosevelt's desk in the White House to see him sign the 'Act to Promote the Defense of the United States'. Better known as the Lend-Lease Act, it edged the US away from neutrality by allowing the government to provide friendly nations with 'defense articles' – food, fuel, weapons, vehicles and ships – on the understanding that this was vital to the security of the USA.

The nations favoured by Lend-Lease were all (eventually) on the Allied side: Britain, Free France, China and the USSR. But the act was not the first US contribution to the war effort. Since 1939 the Allies had been able to purchase US arms and armour, so long as they shipped the materials themselves and paid up front (this was dubbed 'cash and carry'). But this scheme had quickly drained Allied funds, and in September 1940 Britain granted the USA a lease on military bases in the Caribbean and Newfoundland to cover the purchase of fifty US naval destroyers.

Lend-Lease answered the desperate need for the Allies to call freely on the US economy's vast resources, and to do so on long-term credit (Britain's final repayment on Lend-Lease supplies from the Second World War was made as recently as 2006). In February 1941, Churchill had made a ringing plea: 'Give us the tools, and we will finish the job!' Roosevelt's signature on the Lend-Lease Act answered that call.

Free France

Among those who benefited from Lend-Lease were the *Forces françaises libres* – or Free French – under their leader, Charles de Gaulle, a First World War veteran who in 1916 had been captured and made a German prisoner of war for nearly three years. When France surrendered to the Nazis in 1940, de Gaulle was in London. He broadcast a speech on BBC radio, declaring that the French had 'lost the battle of France through a faulty military system, mistakes in the conduct of operations, and the defeatist spirit shown by the government during recent battles… Honour, common sense, and the interests of the country require that all free Frenchmen, wherever they be, should continue the fight as best they may.' On propaganda posters, this was later summarized as 'France has lost a battle, but France has not lost the war!'

De Gaulle initially commanded just a few thousand French troops; most of those Frenchmen evacuated at Dunkirk had returned home in June 1940. But the Free French included volunteers from among expatriates in Britain, and (from 7 November 1940) a women's corps too, led by Simonne Mathieu and modelled on Britain's Auxiliary Territorial Service. In this photograph from 1941, some of the *Corps féminin des volontaires françaises* march from the Free French HQ in London's Carlton Gardens. A contemporary report on their appearance noted that they carried themselves with 'the spirit of Joan of Arc'. On their lapels is the Cross of Lorraine – the Free French insignia.

The Warsaw Ghetto

Wherever the Nazis conquered – from the Channel Islands in the west to Odessa in the east – they established an apparatus of oppression, in the form of concentration camps, death camps and urban ghettos. The most notorious ghetto was in Warsaw, where this Jewish couple were photographed in 1942.

After the Nazis overran Poland at the start of the war, they elected to administer much of it as the 'General Government'. This was a lawless zone overseen by a brutal bureaucrat named Hans Frank, who attempted to degrade and desolate the region by systematically deporting, mistreating and killing its occupants, in anticipation of future colonization by Germans. Many of the most heinous crimes of the Holocaust took place within the General Government, which was the site for four extermination camps.

The Warsaw Ghetto was built in the autumn of 1940, as the Nazi occupiers forced the city's Jews to construct 3-metre (10-foot)-high walls around an area of the city measuring less than 2 square miles. Around 450,000 Jews would be imprisoned within these walls, in appalling conditions. Daily rations amounted to fewer than 200 calories per person. Typhus and other diseases connected to unsanitary conditions were rife. Medical supplies were limited. German war profiteers running sweatshop factories used the ghetto inhabitants for cheap or slave labour.

By July 1942, the Nazis had begun removing Jews from the ghetto. This 'resettlement' was in fact mass murder: Jews were packed in their thousands on trains, taking them to be killed in the gas chambers of Treblinka, 50 miles (80km) away.

Alan Turing

By 1942 the Allies knew that behind German lines, millions of Jews were being murdered, both by roving SS death squads and in extermination camps. They discovered this because they could decode intercepted Nazi communications, a task that was spearheaded by Britain's 'Government Code & Cipher School' (GC&CS), based at Bletchley Park. Here, several thousand analysts made sense of encrypted enemy messages, including those sent using the Enigma machine, which the Nazis believed to be impossible to crack. The most sensitive intelligence generated from this high-level espionage was code-named Ultra.

Alan Turing, photographed here, was one of Bletchley Park's most distinguished employees. For a time, he was in charge of 'Hut 8', a department that focused on cracking German naval communications sent using Enigma. His design work on a machine called the Bombe was invaluable in this task; when Turing and others wrote to Churchill in 1941 requesting additional resources for their work and explaining its critical importance in protecting British shipping, the prime minister gave them his firm backing.

Besides working at Bletchley Park, Turing also spent some of the war working on voice encryption systems, both in the United States and in Britain. After the war he was a pioneer of early computer design. He was prosecuted in 1952 for his homosexuality, accepted chemical castration as a punishment, and died two years later of cyanide poisoning, aged just forty-one. His status as an unfairly persecuted war hero has only recently been widely acknowledged.

Operation Barbarossa

Throughout the first half of 1941, intelligence sources across the world briefed that the Nazis were amassing huge military forces in eastern Europe, near the borders of the USSR. It seemed clear to most other leaders that Hitler was planning to tear up the Molotov–Ribbentrop agreement and attack the Soviets. The only person who did not seem to believe that war was imminent was Joseph Stalin.

The Nazi invasion, known as Operation Barbarossa, began on 22 June 1941, when some three and a half million German and Axis troops, supported by thousands of tanks and aircraft, swarmed onto Soviet territory. This photograph shows a German artillery observer watching a shell landing. It was taken at Brest-Litovsk – the site of Imperial Russia's humiliating peace treaty with Germany in 1918.

Barbarossa had been meticulously planned and it was ruthlessly delivered. German troops overwhelmed Soviet defenders in a matter of weeks. In some regions, such as Ukraine, the invaders were welcomed as liberators from Soviet tyranny, and greeted with gifts. But in general, the operation was characterized by the dreadful brutality of the fighting. Wehrmacht troops were ordered to abandon the usual etiquette of war in a campaign of 'annihilation', in which 'subordinate' peoples and Communists were to be eliminated.

When Stalin finally accepted what was happening, he called for a Patriotic War to defend the motherland. He also embraced the need for new allies. An unlikely alliance between the United States, Britain and the USSR was soon taking shape.

Pearl Harbor

On 7 December 1941, more than 350 carrier-launched bombers and fighters of the Imperial Japanese Navy Air Service screamed out of the sky and attacked the US Pacific Fleet where it sat at anchor in Pearl Harbor, Hawaii. No official warning was given of the attack, and although tensions between Japan and the United States were running high, the two nations were not in a state of war. President Roosevelt did not exaggerate when he said the following day that 7 December was 'a date which will live in infamy'.

This photograph shows the USS *West Virginia* being doused by fireboats in the aftermath of the Japanese attack. Despite these efforts the battleship sank, with the loss of 106 lives. In the final reckoning, around 2,400 Americans were killed at Pearl Harbor, nearly half of them when the battleship USS *Arizona* exploded after its magazine was pierced: 1,177 crew and Marines died.

On the same day as Pearl Harbor, Japan also attacked US territories in the Philippines and Guam, and British imperial possessions in Malaya, Hong Kong and Singapore. This amounted to a massive escalation of the war in the Pacific, as well as a major gamble by the Japanese high command, which changed the shape of the whole Second World War. On 8 December Roosevelt declared war on Japan; three days later the USA and Germany were also at war. The Axis powers had at long last awoken the American giant.

Japanese-American internment

Four months after Pearl Harbor, internment orders were issued against 'All Persons of Japanese Ancestry' on the US West Coast. As a result, 50,000 Japanese immigrants (known as *issei*) and their 70,000 US-born descendants (*nisei*) were forced to abandon or sell their homes, leave their jobs and schools, and say goodbye to friends, before being ferried by bus and train to local assembly centres, then onwards to out-of-state 'relocation centres' in Idaho, Arkansas, Colorado or Wyoming. Effectively prison camps, these were secured by guard towers and perimeter fences.

The legal basis for this forced migration was President Roosevelt's Executive Order 9066, issued on 19 February 1942, which allowed the US military to designate zones 'from which any or all persons may be excluded'. Although the order did not specify Japanese Americans as its target, its provisions allowed the military wide discretion and its underlying purpose was clear. In Washington State, Oregon and California, the US Western Defense Command was free to round up residents and American citizens without due process of law and deprive them of their liberty indefinitely.

Internment, particularly for the *nisei*, was a bitter experience. But it reflected a paranoid hysteria stirred up by the attack on Pearl Harbor. In early 1942 seven Japanese submarines had been detected in Californian waters, and one had shelled oilfields at Ellwood, near Santa Barbara. There was a genuine popular fear of a full-blown Japanese invasion of the West Coast.

Flying Tigers

Less than two weeks after Pearl Harbor, US airmen flew their first combat mission against Japanese enemies. But they were not regular US Air Force pilots; they were the Flying Tigers (more properly, the First American Volunteer Group, or AVG): three fighter squadrons sent to help the Chinese Air Force defend strategically vital positions from Japanese conquest.

The Flying Tigers were commanded by Claire L. Chennault, a veteran First World War pilot and advisor to Chiang Kai-shek, nicknamed 'Old Leatherface' for his weather-beaten appearance. They flew Curtiss P-40 Warhawk single-seat fighters – shown here painted with the Flying Tigers' distinctive shark-head design on the nose. Their three squadrons were known as the 'Adam & Eves', the 'Panda Bears' (based in China) and 'Hell's Angels' (based in Burma).

On their first combat mission, on 19 December 1941, fighters from the Adam & Eves and Panda Bears intercepted ten Japanese bombers, downing at least four of them. During the seven months that followed, the Flying Tigers took part in more than fifty fights, over China, Burma, Thailand and French Indochina, and brought down nearly three hundred enemy aircraft. They were retired as a distinct unit on 4 July 1942, but before the year was out, their exploits had become Hollywood material. A film starring John Wayne and Anna Lee was released in October 1942, titled variously as *Flying Tigers* and *Yanks Over the Burma Road*.

The Fall of Singapore

Despite the efforts of groups like the Flying Tigers, the Japanese were ascendant in the east during the first half of 1942. One of their most famous – and notorious – victories occurred on 15 February when the Japanese army captured a crucial British military base at Singapore, taking around eighty thousand British and imperial prisoners of war: the largest single surrender of forces in British history. This photograph was taken on that day.

Singapore was nicknamed the 'Gibraltar of the East', and its strategic location was considered vital for the Royal Navy to project power in the east. But it lacked proper protection, and there were divisions among the various British, Australian and Indian commanders present on the base.

In December 1941, Japanese forces commanded by Lieutenant-General Tomoyuki Yamashita had moved into the Malay peninsula and were soon advancing steadily south towards Singapore. At the same time, air raids on the island itself began. By the start of February, the Japanese were primed and ready to force an amphibious landing against British imperial troops spread too thinly along the coastline. After a battle lasting seven days, the British commander Lieutenant-General Arthur Percival was authorized to surrender, rather than waste lives in an untenable defence.

Surrender brought misery and death all the same. Tens of thousands of prisoners of war were put to work in labour camps and died from their mistreatment, while ethnic Malays and Chinese on the island were murdered in their thousands.

The Battle of Midway

By May 1942, Japanese conquests included Hong Kong, the Philippines, Guam, Thailand, Malaya and Singapore, along with the oil-rich Dutch East Indies (Indonesia) and much of Burma and New Guinea. But between 4 and 8 May the Imperial Japanese Navy suffered a serious setback at the Battle of the Coral Sea, the world's first direct fight between aircraft carriers. This engagement stymied Japanese plans to take Port Moresby in Papua New Guinea and convinced the Japanese naval commander-in-chief, Admiral Isoroku Yamamoto, that the US Navy had to be knocked out in the Pacific.

The result was the Battle of Midway, fought near that tiny island between Hawaii and Japan on 4 June. The American fleet at Midway was heavily outnumbered, and the aircraft available included specimens like the slow and outmoded Douglas TBD Devastator torpedo-bombers photographed here on board the USS *Enterprise*. However, US intelligence had intercepted and decoded Japanese radio transmissions and was able to anticipate enemy plans. When the battle began, waves of more up-to-date Douglas Dauntless dive-bombers attacked and sank all four of the Japanese aircraft carriers present at the battle, with massive loss of life, particularly among experienced Japanese naval pilots.

Midway was a double failure for the Japanese. Not only were the losses at sea terrible and humiliating, the US Navy was now a potent presence in the Pacific, with vastly greater resources of men and shipping soon to arrive in the theatre. It was a critical moment: Japan had lost the upper hand in the Pacific.

The Desert Fox

During the First World War, Erwin Rommel served on the Western Front and the Italian Front, ending the war with the rank of captain and a deep interest in military theory. This brought him to Hitler's attention during the 1930s, when the Führer read Rommel's influential book, *Infantry Attacks*. By the time the Second World War broke out, Rommel was one of the rising stars of the German military, and he commanded the 7th Panzer Division during the invasion of France in 1940.

Rommel's reputation outside Germany was made from February 1941, when Hitler appointed him to lead the Panzer Army Africa (including the Afrika Korps), whose job was to save Italian Libya from the Allies. For nearly eighteen months he did just that, earning the nickname *Wüstenfuchs* or 'Desert Fox' and being promoted to field marshal. In this photograph, he is liaising with the Italian commander Ettore Bastico; Rommel did not hold his Italian counterpart in very high regard.

In 1943 the battle for North Africa would be lost and Rommel recalled to Europe. He was sent to Italy, then redeployed to oversee works on the Atlantic Wall – sea defences to oppose a projected Allied invasion of France. When this invasion occurred – the D-Day landings of June 1944 – Rommel's car was strafed by an Allied fighter plane and he was badly injured. He was then implicated in a failed July 1944 plot to assassinate Hitler, and forced to commit suicide by taking cyanide.

The Dieppe Raid

This photograph, taken in August 1942, shows blindfolded Germans taken prisoner by Canadian forces. It appears to be a victorious moment for the Allies. Nothing could be further from the truth. Operation Jubilee, an amphibious assault on 19 August against the German-occupied Channel port of Dieppe, was in fact a fiasco in which German prisoners were few and far between. Of the 4,963 Canadians who made up the bulk of the expeditionary force sent against Dieppe, more than 900 were killed and nearly 2,000 were captured.

The assault on Dieppe involved more than 230 vessels supported by RAF cover. But the Canadians were spotted by a German convoy before they reached their target, and were let down by inadequate intelligence, which failed to report German gun positions embedded in the steep cliffs around Dieppe and had little clue about German troop strengths. Few of the Allied tanks got very far from their landing craft, the RAF was ravaged overhead, and many of the infantry were cut down on the beaches. Ten hours after it had all begun, the remnants of the battered Allied force were limping back to Britain.

The Dieppe Raid was planned as a demonstration of aggressive Allied spirit, and as a fact-finding experience to help plan a full-scale invasion of France. It was a costly failure. But the lessons that were learned helped influence thinking about subsequent amphibious invasions of North Africa, later in 1942, and Normandy, in 1944.

The Battles of El Alamein

Although the Dieppe Raid was an exercise in failure, within weeks the Allies had a major victory to cheer elsewhere. In Egypt, the British Eighth Army – led by the prickly but brilliant Lieutenant-General Bernard Montgomery ('Monty') – struck decisively against German and Italian forces near El Alamein. The battle inflicted fatal damage on the Axis position in North Africa and removed the threat posed to the Middle East since the first days of the war.

Montgomery arrived to take command in Egypt in August 1942 and oversaw major investment in the Allied forces in the theatre. By late October he had twice as many men and vehicles as Rommel, including hundreds of new tanks. This photograph from 1942 shows Crusader II CS (close support) tanks, armed with howitzers. Swift and agile, these 'cruiser' tanks accompanied infantry into battle.

The Second Battle of El Alamein began on 23 October (the first had taken place in July). Rommel was on sick leave in Germany but he rushed back to Africa to take command. For around a week he tried to coordinate resistance, but eventually yielded to overwhelming force, and on 4 November ordered a rapid retreat westwards, all the way across Libya into Tunisia. Behind him, 30,000 Axis troops were taken prisoner.

In Britain, joy erupted. Monty and his Eighth Army were hailed as heroes. Church bells were rung across the nation, and Churchill called the victory the 'end of the beginning'.

Operation Torch

While the British were driving Rommel out of Egypt, on the other side of the continent a US-led amphibious invasion took aim at Morocco and Algeria. These were Vichy French possessions; securing them would help to squeeze Axis forces out of North Africa and give raw US troops valuable experience of landing and seizing hostile territory.

The invasion, code-named Operation Torch and commanded by Lieutenant-General Dwight D. Eisenhower, began on 8 November 1942. A secret armada of 650 warships, carrying 65,000 troops and protected by substantial air power, landed at three points: two in Algeria and one in French Morocco. This photograph was taken by the Royal Navy photographer Lieutenant F. A. Hudson; it shows American troops of the Centre Task Force in a landing craft heading for the beaches of Oran, in Algeria.

Operation Torch met with limited opposition, thanks in part to careful measures that had been taken to disguise troop movements, and in part to a lack of sustained resistance by Vichy French fighters. The overall commander of Vichy forces, Admiral François Darlan, eventually ordered his men not to resist the landings, and effectively allowed the Allies free rein. (Darlan was assassinated on 24 December.)

After Operation Torch, Hitler ended Vichy's quasi-independence by occupying the whole of France. Meanwhile, Rommel found his northern African troops stuck in Tunisia, sandwiched between major Allied advances on either side. He prepared for a last stand, which would hold out until the spring of 1943.

Stalingrad

The dramatic clashes in North Africa during autumn 1942 were dwarfed by an elemental struggle that took place around the city of Stalingrad (modern Volgograd) at the same time. Hitler invaded the USSR expecting a swift victory. In fact, a long and bitter war developed and Stalingrad epitomized the worst of it. It was the biggest, deadliest and most dreadful engagement in the whole of the Second World War: fought from street to street, building to building, by men and women, with every means available.

Stalingrad was an industrial city that stretched along the western bank of the Volga River. For Hitler, it controlled access to the oilfields of the Caucasus. It was also powerfully symbolic: the city bore Stalin's name, so its capture would be a crowning glory for the Nazis and an intolerable humiliation for the Soviets.

The assault began in August 1942: the Luftwaffe bombed much of Stalingrad into dust, while forces including German, Hungarian, Romanian, Italian and Croatian troops stormed forwards. However, the city did not fall, and in November the Soviet Red Army launched Operation Uranus, which cut off around 250,000 Axis troops in and around Stalingrad. This photograph shows a Soviet artillery crew in action. In early February 1943, after a bleak and bloody winter siege, the German commander in Stalingrad, Field Marshal Friedrich Paulus, surrendered. It was a huge victory for the Soviets, which began to turn the tide in the east. But nearly two million people had been killed, captured or injured in its pursuit.

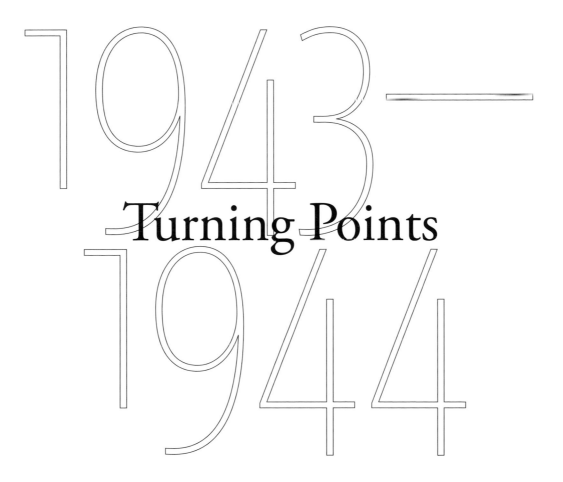

1943–1944

Turning Points

'They had the most immense armaments…
If someone had told me a country could begin
with 35,000 tanks, then I'd have said:
'You're mad!'

Adolf Hitler, lamenting Soviet tank strength to
Finnish ally Marshal Mannerheim
(4 June 1942)

n the first days of July 1943, the land around the Russian city and railway junction at Kursk echoed with explosions and the roar of heavy machinery. Smoke and dust swirled. The ground shook from the blasts exchanged by massive German and Soviet forces: gunshot louder than thunder. Vehicles smashed into one another and burst in giant fireballs. Aircraft in their thousands shrieked overhead. An astonishing two million troops were thrown, with increasing desperation, into a battle that lasted nearly two months. This image, taken during training exercises, shows four Red Army soldiers taking cover in a trench as a Soviet T-34 tank crawls across the shattered landscape above them. It was an experience designed to mimic the horrors of battles like this.

The Battle of Kursk was a pivotal clash in the war on the Eastern Front, in which the limits of Nazi military ambition were finally reached. Hideous casualties were amassed by both sides in one of the biggest land battles ever fought, while Kursk also featured, on 12 July, the largest clash of tanks in the Second World War. At this engagement, known as the Battle of Prokhorovka, around 600 Soviet T-34s took on half as many German tanks; a German eyewitness on that day recalled the enemy swarming 'like rats' over the parched battlefield.

The prelude to Kursk came in the winter of 1942–3, when the German Sixth Army and their allies had been trapped, bombed, starved and frozen into submission at the siege of Stalingrad. By the end of the siege on 2 February, around 91,000 bedraggled German survivors had surrendered, many of whom would die in captivity. In the months that followed, the focal point of the fighting moved north, and by the summer a series of Soviet advances and German counter-attacks

had created a 150-mile (240km) 'salient' – or bulge – at Kursk, in which Soviet lines protruded deep into German-held territory. They were surrounded by Nazi troops on three sides: basic military theory held that this was by definition a vulnerable position.

But Hitler dithered about the best way to proceed. Eventually, in June 1943, Hitler authorized Operation Citadel, ordering attacks at the north and south 'shoulders' of the salient, in the hope of cutting off the Red Army units inside it. The operation was a failure: Soviet intelligence had intercepted many of the planning details, allowing Stalin's men to prepare thoroughly for the Nazi onslaught by planting mines and setting up anti-tank defences. Citadel began on 5 July; but less than a fortnight later, Hitler cancelled it. The Allies had invaded Sicily from North Africa. He was overstretched, and he knew it.

However, if Citadel was over, the Battle of Kursk was not. 'From now on, the enemy was in undisputed possession of the initiative', the German general Heinz Guderian later reflected. On 12 July the Soviets launched a massive counter-attack known as the Kursk Strategic Offensive Operation, and over the course of the next five weeks they drove the Germans back, recovering the cities of Orel (Oryol) and Kharkov (Kharkiv, in Ukraine) which had been lost in 1941 during the Nazi invasion of the USSR. By the time the battle was over on 23 August, the balance of power on the Eastern Front had swung in favour of the Soviets.

The T-34 tank seen here played an important role in Soviet successes during the Battle of Kursk. Its rounded contours and thick armour helped deflect enemy fire. It was agile, could travel at up to 33 miles per hour (53km/h) and was equipped with a powerful 76.2mm gun. Broad

---

2 February 1943

The four-month siege of Stalingrad, witnessing some of the bloodiest scenes of the Second World War, ends with the tables turned and surrender of the German Sixth Army.

19 April–16 May 1943

Armed rebels in Warsaw's Jewish Ghetto stage an unsuccessful uprising against further removals, aware that death camps await those 'evacuated' from the Ghetto.

16–17 May 1943

The RAF's new 617 Squadron attempts to breach three dams and flood valleys in Germany's Ruhr industrial area, using a novel 'bouncing bomb'; it partially succeeds.

5 July 1943

In Operation Citadel, Hitler launches the colossal air and land battle of Kursk on the Eastern Front; it inflicts huge casualties and tank losses, but fails to halt Soviet momentum.

9–10 July 1943

Having quashed the last Axis resistance in North Africa during May, with the surrender of German troops in Tunisia, Allied forces use it as a launchpad to invade Sicily.

caterpillar tracks could cope with the snow and ice of a Russian winter.

German tanks included the heavily armoured and rapid Panther, with a 75mm gun, which debuted at Kursk, and the Tiger tank, which was twice the weight of a T-34 and equipped with armour up to 100mm thick, making it virtually impervious to frontal attack. Yet both these tanks were vulnerable when the lighter, nimbler T-34s got in and around them, as they did very frequently at Kursk, so that horrified eyewitnesses would remember enemy tanks crushed and mangled together, some firing at close and even point-blank range: a sight and sound that lived long with those who survived a battle where the estimated casualties ran to more than a million men.

The decline of Nazi fortunes on the Eastern Front in 1943–4 owed much to the USSR's vast population and their willingness, extending from Stalin downwards, to suffer unimaginably high losses in defending the motherland. Yet Hitler was also stymied in the summer of 1943 by the Allied invasion of Sicily, code-named Operation Husky. These landings required Hitler to divert troops to Italy. Even so, he could not prevent a political crisis in the country, where on 25 July 1943 Benito Mussolini was toppled from power, ending more than two decades of Fascist rule, and setting in train events that would lead to the partition of the country and a nasty guerrilla war.

Although an Allied land invasion of the Nazi Reich lay many months in the future, Germany was suffering nonetheless in 1943, as an Anglo-American bomber offensive sought to destroy German industries, cities and morale. Hamburg was razed, virtually to the ground, and from November a sustained bombing campaign began against Berlin itself. During the course of the war,

Allied bombing altogether killed half a million people in Germany. But this was not enough on its own to cripple the Nazi regime, which continued to commit the most appalling crimes against humanity in its network of ghettoes and death camps across Europe.

The only route to Germany for the Allies in the west was through France. At a conference in Tehran, the leaders decided when the long-anticipated invasion would take place. The day eventually came on 6 June 1944: D-Day, the largest amphibious military landing ever carried out. It was far from the final act in a war that had many dreadful chapters still to be written – not least in the islands of the Pacific Ocean. All the same, it was the beginning of the end for Hitler and his Axis partners.

---

25 July 1943

As Italy is invaded, Mussolini is sacked by King Victor Emmanuel III and arrested; Italy surrenders (3 September) then joins the Allies (13 October), but German divisions have already poured in.

27–28 July 1943

In Operation Gomorrah, RAF night bombing ignites a firestorm that rages through Hamburg; an estimated 40,000 die in this example of the 'strategic air campaign'.

20–23 November 1943

Following Guadalcanal in 1942, the US Navy and Marines experience uncompromising Japanese resistance at Tarawa Atoll, one of the Pacific 'stepping stones' towards Japan.

28 November 1943

Stalin, Roosevelt and Churchill convene in Tehran; they agree a timescale for a second front (invading occupied France) in return for an eventual Soviet declaration of war on Japan.

6 June 1944

With Operation Overlord, the biggest amphibious invasion in history, British, Canadian and US forces gain five beachheads in Normandy, beginning the liberation of France.

Charles de Gaulle

When this photograph was taken on 31 March 1943, General Charles de Gaulle was in London, the city he had made his home since the fall of France nearly three years previously. There was no question of de Gaulle residing across the Channel; in Vichy France he had been sentenced to death in absentia. However, this did not mean de Gaulle was entirely gracious in his exile. He referred to the British, who hosted him, and the Americans, who were engaged in planning to win back France from the Nazis, as the 'Anglo Saxons', and his relationships with Churchill and Roosevelt often verged on being openly hostile.

Nevertheless, de Gaulle occupied a rare status among those working to free France, which made him impossible to ignore. Here, he is meeting young volunteers from the islands of Saint-Pierre and Miquelon – a tiny outpost of French territory off the coast of Newfoundland, which had been liberated from Vichy rule in 1941.

At this point, de Gaulle's residence in Britain was nearly over. Operation Torch had liberated former Vichy French colonial territories in North Africa, and in May 1943 he moved his headquarters to Algiers, elbowed aside his US-backed rival General Henri Giraud and took sole charge of a new provisional government of Free France, known as the French Committee of National Liberation. He would remain a dominant force in French politics until 1969.

The Warsaw Ghetto Uprising

During the summer of 1942 the Nazi rulers of Warsaw deported a quarter of a million Jewish people from the Warsaw Ghetto to be murdered at Treblinka. By the following spring, no more than 60,000 Jews remained inside the ghetto, which had been reduced in size as it was raided, block by block, for victims. Those who remained were desperate. They began to form resistance groups and to improvise bunkers underneath the ghetto's houses.

On 19 April 1943, the eve of Passover, the SS officer and local police commander Jürgen Stroop (*centre, looking up*) led an effort to remove the last inhabitants of the ghetto. He was faced with massive opposition. The flags of Poland and the ŻZW (Jewish Military Union) were raised defiantly over the rooftops, and insurgents pelted the police with Molotov cocktails and fired on them with smuggled guns.

Stroop responded by ordering his men to set fire to the ghetto and dynamite all the bunkers and tunnel networks they could locate. But they were hard-pressed. Stroop had anticipated clearing the ghetto in three days. In the end, it took around a month to suppress the rebellion, a task that was only completed on 16 May, when Stroop shouted 'Heil Hitler' and personally detonated explosives that demolished the Great Synagogue of Warsaw. Afterwards, Stroop composed a pompous, leather-bound report of his actions, illustrated by photographs including this one. He was hanged in 1952 for crimes against humanity.

The Dambusters

Although the Allies were briefed about the atrocities at Auschwitz, the British and American high command decided not to bomb the Nazi death camps to put them out of service. Instead, throughout 1943 they concentrated air power on German industrial targets. On 16–17 May 1943 the RAF undertook a deadly – and now legendary – mission to destroy dams in the Ruhr Valley with 9,000lb (4,082kg) 'bouncing bomb' mines launched from Lancaster bombers (see page 344). The mission was known as Operation Chastise, but the airmen of 617 Squadron who took part in the raid became known as 'the Dambusters'. Their commanding officer was twenty-four-year-old Guy Gibson, photographed here a month after the raid.

In this image Gibson is showing an aerial photograph of the Möhne dam, one of three targeted by the Dambusters. As can be seen, the wall was successfully breached. This caused floodwater to sweep through the valley below, killing around 1400 people (many of them slave labourers in Nazi factories), washing away buildings, roads and bridges, and crippling steel production. The other dams – Sorpe and Eder – suffered less serious damage. The Dambusters themselves incurred heavy casualties, partly a result of flying at just 30-metre altitude to evade radar detection. Although nineteen Lancasters took off, only eleven aircraft returned, and more than fifty-three airmen were killed. After the raid, Gibson was awarded the Victoria Cross and briefly became a celebrity. He was killed in September 1944 when his plane crashed in the Netherlands, while he was returning from a combat mission.

MÖHNE DAM

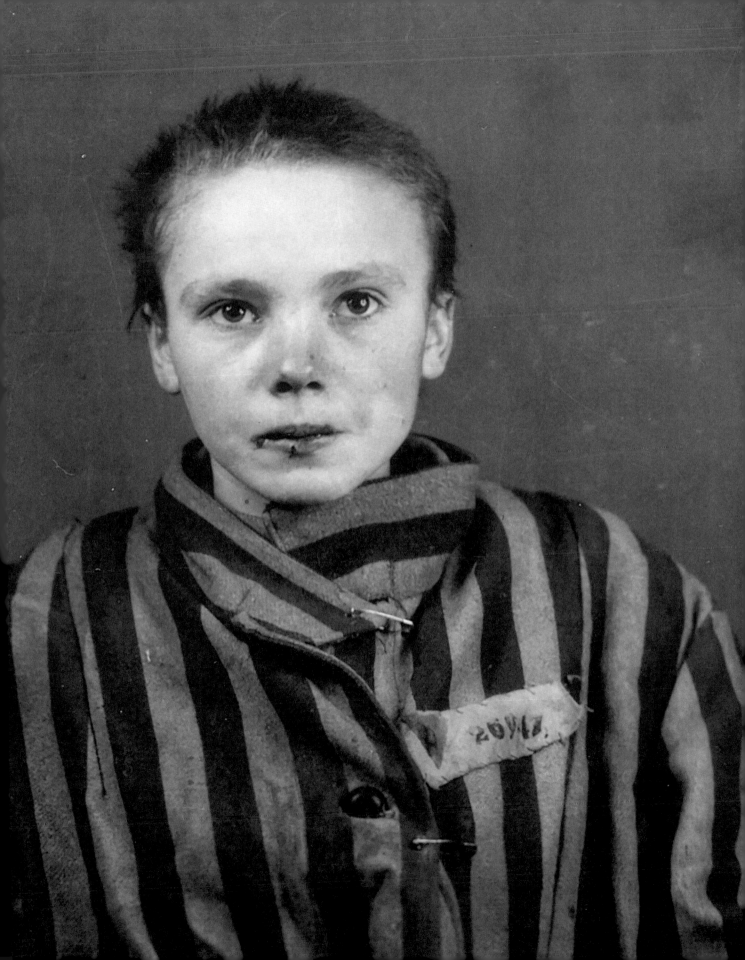

Auschwitz-Birkenau

Czesława Kwoka was born on 15 August 1928 in Wólka Złojecka, a small village in the Zamość region of Poland, which was occupied by the Nazis in 1939. Like her mother Katarzyna, Czesława was a Roman Catholic; their village had been earmarked for ethnic cleansing ahead of future German resettlement. So on 13 December 1942, both were deported to Auschwitz, where they were assigned prisoner numbers 26946 and 26947.

Auschwitz was a concentration camp created by the SS in the spring of 1940. In March of 1942 industrial extermination of Jews in gas chambers began in the camp and most extermination infrastructures were built in the second part of the camp complex, Auschwitz II-Birkenau. During the course of the Second World War, 1.1 million Jews, 140,000 non-Jewish Poles, 23,000 Roma, 15,000 Soviet prisoners of war and 25,000 other people were killed there. They included both Katarzyna, who died on 18 February 1943, and Czesława, who was murdered a month later with a phenol injection to the heart. She was fourteen years old.

These images of Czesława were taken by another Polish prisoner, Wilhelm Brasse, a professional photographer forced to take inmate 'identity photographs'. Brasse later recalled that Czesława was confused and uncomprehending about what was happening to her. A female German overseer beat her angrily with a stick. 'She cried but she could do nothing,' said Brasse. 'Before the photograph was taken, the girl dried her tears and the blood from the cut on her lip. To tell you the truth, I felt as if I was being hit myself but I couldn't interfere. It would have been fatal for me.'

Sicily

The *Life* photographer Bob Landry came ashore at Gela in Sicily a few hours before dawn, on the moonless night of 9–10 July 1943. He was accompanying US troops landing in the first wave of Operation Husky, the Allied invasion of Sicily. In May Tunisia had fallen, completing Allied victory in North Africa; Sicily was part of the region identified by Winston Churchill as the 'soft underbelly' of Axis-controlled Europe.

Machine-gun fire raked the sands as the American landing craft arrived, and Landry and the men he was shadowing had to scramble for cover across uncleared minefields. Over the course of the next forty-eight hours Landry watched and photographed heavy fighting in and around Gela: a tank battle outside the city, Luftwaffe air raids over it, American naval ships shelling Italian and German positions from the sea, and hand-to-hand fighting in the city's streets and squares. By the end of it, Gela was under American control. Landry took this picture on the Via Pisa, near the town hall, where US troops had set up a machine gun on a marble monument commemorating two Italian heroes of the First World War, lauded in the monument's epigram as 'Fascist martyrs' who had died defending Mussolini's 'new Empire of Rome'.

Yet Mussolini's new Rome was about to fall. Within three weeks of the landings at Gela, Allied troops had taken around 80 per cent of the island and were preparing to push north into mainland Italy.

The Fall of Fascism

On the evening of 25 July 1943 – known in Italy as 25 Luglio – Benito Mussolini visited King Victor Emmanuel III at the Villa Savoia in Rome to discuss the crisis in Sicily. The night before, Mussolini had lost the support of his Grand Council of Fascism. Now the king told him he was to be removed from power altogether. Mussolini had been Italy's dictator for more than two decades. But at last, as he had predicted to his mistress Clara Petacci the previous evening, Il Duce had 'arrived at the epilogue'. He was arrested and sent for confinement, first on the island of Ponza and then in the mountain resort at Campo Imperatore. In his place, Marshal Pietro Badoglio – a veteran of both world wars and the Italian campaigns in Libya and Abyssinia – was appointed prime minister. The next day, 26 July, these workmen were smashing away the Fascist insignia from Rome's Ministry of Finance.

Yet this was not quite the end either for Mussolini or for Italy's role in the Second World War. In the south, Allied forces were readying themselves to invade the mainland – a campaign that began on 3 September and resulted in the signing of an armistice which was made public five days later. But Hitler would not allow his Axis partner to melt from the theatre of war. German troops were already deploying through Italy, with the aim of stopping the Allies in the south and creating a Nazi puppet state in the north. Fascism was not quite dead.

The Lancaster Bomber

The Avro Lancaster first flew in 1941. By the summer of
1943, this four-engined strategic bomber, which took off
with a crew of seven men and had a range of more than
2,500 miles (4,000km), was the standard aircraft deployed
by RAF Bomber Command to attack cities, railways,
roads and factories across Nazi Germany. The Lancaster
was frequently used at night, and the dreadful rumble of
its Rolls-Royce engines overhead was the soundtrack to
a merciless campaign, described in Germany as 'terror
raids'. Lancasters were used by the 'Dambusters' in May
1943; and between July 1943 and March 1944 hundreds
bombed Hamburg, Berlin and Bremen, killing tens of
thousands of German civilians, making many more
homeless and reducing Hamburg in particular to ruins.

The Lancaster here is a B Mark 1, flown by RAF 207
Squadron, who were based in Nottinghamshire. On 13
September 1943 it was destined for the city of Bremen,
and its open doors reveal a deadly payload known as a
'usual': one 4,000lb (1,814kg) 'cookie' bomb surrounded
by incendiaries, and four 250lb (113kg) target indicators.
This was not the most powerful ordnance available to
the head of Bomber Command, Air Chief Marshal
Arthur 'Bomber' Harris: by the end of the war, modified
Lancasters could drop 12,000lb (5,442kg) 'Tallboy'
devices, capable of sinking battleships, and 22,000lb
(9,979kg) 'Grand Slam' earthquake bombs, which
could destroy U-boat pens and railway bridges. Like the
Spitfire, the Lancaster was an iconic plane, symbolic of
the British war effort.

Operation Tidal Wave

The German Reich was not the only target for Allied air raids in 1943. This photograph shows a Consolidated B-24 Liberator of the US Army Air Force taking part in one of a series of bombing missions in 1943–4 designed to disrupt oil refineries at Ploeşti, in Romania. The heaviest – and costliest – of these raids was known as Operation Tidal Wave, and took place on Sunday 1 August 1943.

Romania's oil fields were critical to the Axis war effort: nearly a third of the oil needed to fuel vehicles and supply vital industries came from the country. This made them an obvious target for Allied attack as the high command sought ways to prepare for a full-scale invasion of Europe. But attacking Ploeşti was extremely difficult: there were hundreds of anti-aircraft guns around the oil fields, and Romanian fighter planes were stationed nearby, ready to scramble.

On the morning of 1 August, 177 USAAF B-24 bombers took off in five waves from their base near Benghazi, Libya, and flew over the Adriatic towards Romania. They were heading for trouble. On the way to their target, several planes were lost to navigational error and mechanical failure. When they arrived at Ploeşti they faced fierce resistance from both air and ground. And though many of the bombers landed direct hits on the refineries, only eighty-eight aircraft made it back to Benghazi. The USAAF lost 310 airmen killed; another 190 were captured. Romanian oil output soon recovered, and 1 August was later nicknamed 'Black Sunday'.

The Battle for Tarawa

While Allied airmen bombed eastern Europe, US Marines were engaged in a different, very brutal war in the east, fighting troops of the Imperial Japanese Navy for control of islands, atolls and archipelagos in the central Pacific. One of these clashes, pictured here, was the Battle of Tarawa Atoll, part of the Gilbert Islands (modern Kiribati). Most of the fighting, between 20 and 23 November 1943, took place on the island of Betio, just two miles in length and a few hundred metres wide. Yet although Betio was tiny, it was heavily reinforced by 4,500 Japanese with artillery (including old British Vickers guns), deep bunkers and concealed machine-gun positions. The Japanese Rear Admiral Keiji Shibazaki boasted that it would take 'one million men one hundred years' to capture the position from him.

In the end, it took 18,000 Marines about seventy-six hours to take Betio, but at the cost of more than 3,000 casualties. The Japanese fought, quite literally, to the death: just seventeen defenders survived to be captured at the end of the battle.

The human cost of taking Betio shocked the American public, who were exceptionally well informed about this stage of the Pacific war, thanks to magazine reporting, photojournalism and an Oscar-winning documentary shot during the battle, entitled *With the Marines at Tarawa*. The stark reality of modern warfare was made harrowingly plain in this twenty-minute Technicolor film, which included shots of dead Marines littering the beach.

The Tehran Conference

A war with so many belligerents fighting on so many
fronts demanded clear thinking about overall strategy,
so in late November 1943, two major leaders' conferences
were convened. One took place in Cairo, where Chiang
Kai-shek met Churchill and Roosevelt. The second,
pictured here, was held from 28 November to 1 December
in Tehran, Iran. It was the first meeting between
Churchill, Roosevelt and Joseph Stalin.

Stalin disliked travelling outside the USSR, but
on this occasion he did so out of necessity. The Red
Army had been fighting long and hard against the
Nazis on Europe's Eastern Front, and the Soviet leader
wanted the Allies to open a second front by invading
northern France. There were also discussions about the
USSR declaring war on Japan, the post-war borders of
Poland, and relations with Turkey, Iran and partisans in
Yugoslavia.

In keeping with the occasion, gifts and compliments
were exchanged. It was Churchill's sixty-ninth birthday
on 30 November: at one dinner, Stalin toasted his
'fighting friend', while Roosevelt brought a gift of a
Persian bowl. The day before, Churchill had presented
Stalin with a ceremonial sword: a gift from George VI
inscribed to the 'steel-hearted citizens of Stalingrad'.

At the end of the meeting, several major issues had
been settled. Stalin agreed to declare war on Japan
following defeat of Germany, while the Western leaders
agreed a date of May 1944 for Operation Overlord – the
invasion of France.

Chiang Kai-shek

A little over a month after the Chinese nationalist leader Chiang Kai-shek met the Allied leaders in Cairo, he was in India's north-eastern Bihar province, addressing Chinese troops – the scene depicted in this photograph. The terms he had agreed in Cairo were promising: the Allies had agreed to stand together to oppose Japanese expansion in the Pacific and return to China all lands surrendered to Japan since the end of the First World War.

In theory, Chiang was the most important man in the Far East, carrying the titles Generalissimo and Supreme Allied Commander in China. His wife, Soong Mei-ling (or 'Madame Chiang' to Westerners), was American-educated and a popular figure in the United States, where she rallied support for the Chinese cause and was featured on the cover of *Time* magazine. Chiang needed close Allied backing to bolster his position in his sprawling, fragmented nation, assisting him against the Japanese invaders but also against his internal enemy, the Chinese Communists.

Yet the backing Chiang received from the other Allies was seldom unequivocal. Chiang's main point of contact with the Allies in China was American Lieutenant-General Joseph Stilwell, a man appointed Chiang's chief-of-staff and nicknamed 'Vinegar Joe' for his acid tongue. Stilwell freely ignored the Generalissimo, whom he called 'the peanut'. Yet Chiang put up with such insubordination for the sake of the US money, training, warplanes and air cargoes, without which his cause would have been in a parlous state.

'X Force'

Artillery captain Huang Cheun-yu of the Chinese Expeditionary Force's Sixth Army, New 22nd Division, was photographed in Burma in April 1944. Part of the British Empire, Burma had been captured by the Japanese in 1942, cutting off the main supply route between India and China known as the 'Burma Road'. It now fell to men like Captain Huang and their British and American allies to try to fight their way back through Burma, opening a new route: the Ledo Road. Those Chinese troops who undertook this mission from the Indian side of Burma were known as 'X Force'. (Those who approached from the Chinese border were 'Y Force'.) They had been trained by American military advisors, at British expense, and were often accompanied on the ground by US Special Forces.

In contrast with soldiers on the Chinese mainland, who were often abjectly treated and miserably equipped, men of the X Force such as Captain Huang benefitted from modern weaponry, proper shoes and boots, steel helmets, and instruction in skills as diverse as operating radios to firing artillery, as well as superior medical care, welfare and sustenance. And they were of considerable interest in the United States. This image of Huang was captured by William Vandivert, a prolific war photographer who shot stories for *Life* magazine in numerous theatres of the war, from the London Blitz and Bengal famine to the liberation of Nazi concentration camps in 1945.

The Battle of Anzio

By the beginning of 1944, Italy had been partitioned. The official government had agreed an armistice with the Allies. But the north of the country was now a Nazi puppet state, called the Italian Social Republic. Rome was under German occupation. And Mussolini was free, having been broken out of confinement in the mountains by paratroopers led by the SS officer Otto Skorzeny. German defensive lines stretched across the Italian peninsula.

On 22 January 1944 the Allies attempted to storm ashore midway between those lines, landing nearly 400 vessels in and around Anzio, a seaside resort just south of Rome. This photograph, taken by the *Life* photographer George Silk, shows US GIs of the 3rd Infantry a week following the first landings, shepherding captured German infantry to a confinement centre after fighting near Cisterna. But despite this snapshot of American success, Anzio was not a swift, Sicilian-style victory. Rather, it was a long, gruelling battle that produced more than 80,000 casualties across all sides. In Churchill's opinion, the fault for the stalemate lay with the US commander Major General John Lucas, who failed to exploit the surprise of the landing with a swift assault on Rome. 'I had hoped we were hurling a wildcat into the shore, but all we got was a stranded whale,' Churchill commented. Old-fashioned, attritional warfare meant it took four months between the landings and the breakthrough in early June that allowed the Allies finally to advance on Rome.

Operation Overlord

As the Allies in Italy laboured towards Rome, in Britain the long-anticipated invasion of northern France was nearing readiness. Operation Overlord was more than a year in the planning, and involved over two million servicemen from more than a dozen countries, directed by the Allied Supreme Commander, Dwight D. Eisenhower. He is pictured here on the evening of 5 June 1944, meeting US paratroopers of the 502nd Parachute Infantry Regiment at Greenham Common, Berkshire. The invasion, delayed by bad weather in the Channel, would take place the following morning, and Eisenhower's Order of the Day demanded 'nothing less than full victory'. Despite the pressure of the situation, Eisenhower was capable of humanity even in the face of battle: Lieutenant Walter C. Strobel, pictured here wearing the '23' label (indicating the line of parachute-jumpers for whom he was responsible), remembered talking to the general about fly fishing.

Notwithstanding the massive logistical preparations for Overlord, which made it impossible to conceal the Allies' ultimate intentions, elaborate secrecy was imposed to disguise the build-up of troops, while campaigns of deception fooled German reconnaissance and intelligence into thinking the main invasion would occur in Norway or in the Pas-de-Calais area. In fact, the target was the long beaches of Normandy, code-named Gold, Juno, Sword, Omaha and Utah. When the invasion came, the men pictured here were dropped from the air behind 'Utah', detailed to seize gun batteries and two causeways. Strobel survived; many of his comrades did not.

D-Day

From the small hours of 6 June almost 7,000 ships and landing craft crossed the choppy English Channel and around 160,000 soldiers leaped out of them, into the cold sea and on to the Normandy beaches. Ten thousand Allied aircraft swept the skies above, while naval guns blasted German defences dug in to the shoreline. The military called this first day of Operation Overlord 'D-Day'.

This photograph, known as 'Into the Jaws of Death', was taken on the approach to Omaha beach by US Coast Guard photographer Robert F. Sargent. The men shown wading ashore are from the 16th Infantry, US 1st Infantry Division, who had been transported to the beach from the USS *Samuel Chase* on an 'LCVP' (Landing Craft, Vehicle, Personnel). The fighting they were about to encounter was some of the fiercest in all of the landings. While Utah beach, further along the coast, was taken by the US 4th Infantry Division with barely 200 American casualties, Omaha was heavily defended. The infantry took immediate fire from machine gun emplacements, and clearing obstacles on the beach was difficult. High wind and high tides rocked the landing craft; almost all the twenty-nine tanks launched into the water, on their inflatable girdles called 'flotation screens', sank. Several thousand men were killed or wounded and it took until the next day to secure the whole of Omaha beach. But despite these hardships, D-Day succeeded. The Allied invasion of France had begun.

1944–1945

Liberation

You are about to embark on the great Crusade,
towards which we have striven these
many months.

Supreme Commander General Dwight D. Eisenhower,
statement to Allied forces on D-Day
(6 June 1944)

Six months after the D-Day landings, hundreds of thousands of Allied troops were pushing through occupied France and north-west Europe. After facing stiff German resistance during the summer, their advance was now proceeding rapidly, and there were many reasons for optimism among the Allied leadership. Hitler's resources were tautly stretched between defending the Eastern Front, where the USSR was preparing a winter assault, and attempting to stall the Allied invasion in the west. German divisions were undermanned and underpowered; regular Allied strikes on Romanian oil fields were drying up fuel supplies, and the Allies had achieved massive air superiority over the Luftwaffe in France. The Führer's only chance of rescuing his fortunes would be through taking enormous strategic gambles. In December 1944, this is what he chose. The result was a five-week campaign fought in and around the forests of the Ardennes, best known to history as the 'Battle of the Bulge'.

This photograph of a weary and wounded German soldier was taken by the American photographer John Florea during that battle. Florea had made his name taking pictures of Hollywood celebrities, but in 1943 he joined *Life* magazine and shadowed American troops around the world, from training camps in California to aircraft carriers in the Pacific and latterly in France. In December he was stationed with the US First Army, a posting that thrust him into the middle of this last major German offensive, and the biggest and deadliest battle fought by American troops during the whole of the Second World War. The Bulge would cost the United States some 80,000 casualties: a desperately heavy price to pay, even for what Churchill called 'the greatest American victory of the war'.

Hitler's gamble in December 1944 was to throw as many tanks and men as he could muster into the Ardennes, in the hope that he could punch a hole in Allied lines and perhaps recapture their main supply port at Antwerp. He knew that after months of hard-fought combat, the US and British troops in France were tired and running dangerously low on supplies. If they were split and seriously beaten in this northern sector, Hitler reasoned, then there was a chance of negotiating a peace with the powers in the west, which would leave him free to fight on with all his remaining resources against the USSR. That this was largely fantasy was immaterial. On 16 December, amid heavy snowstorms in the Ardennes, his generals commenced their attack.

The initial shock and speed of the German assault caught thinly spread US troops in the region by surprise. More than 400,000 soldiers and 1,400 tanks were hurled into the first phase of the assault, backed up by heavy artillery bombardments. The ferocity of this offensive allowed the Germans to create a large, triangle-shaped 'bulge' into Allied lines around the Belgian towns of St Vith and Bastogne; it was from this that the Battle of the Bulge gained its name.

After initial successes, however, the German advance soon began to fail. Chronic fuel shortages, along with the Allies' ability both to commit large numbers of reinforcements and to take advantage of the tough terrain, meant that in the days after Christmas 1944 the drive towards Antwerp was halted. By late January, US forces had regained all the territory lost in December. The 'bulge' was no more, and the Germans were retreating again, falling ever faster back towards the Reich.

Florea documented the hard fighting at the Battle of the Bulge with terrifying clarity. Besides this photograph

---

10 June 1944

A Waffen SS unit murders 642 villagers in Oradour-sur-Glane, northwest of Limoges, in the most notorious of revenge murders for French resistance in the aftermath of D-Day.

15 June–9 July 1944

US forces capture the island of Saipan, from which B-29 bombers will be able to target Tokyo; and the US Navy ravages enemy ships and aircraft in the neighbouring Philippine Sea.

20 July 1944

Hitler narrowly escapes assassination when a bomb planted by a dissident army officer explodes in a conference room of the Führer's Wolf's Lair HQ, in East Prussia.

1 August–2 October 1944

Insurgents in Warsaw, including the Polish Home Army, rise up against German occupation; they are brutally suppressed, and advancing Soviet forces provide little aid.

4 August 1944

The German Jewish teenager Anne Frank is arrested with her family, while hiding in Amsterdam; she will die in Bergen-Belsen camp, but her diary brings posthumous fame.

(the young man here was wounded while trying to attack an American fuel depot), he also captured the horrifying sight of the 'Malmédy massacre' of 17 December. In this, around 150 unarmed US prisoners were gunned down in cold blood by a body of SS troopers. At least 84 died. Florea was by this stage an experienced war photographer. But he later recalled of Malmédy: 'I felt someone had hit me so hard – I actually cried. It was the most shocking thing I had ever seen.'

Of course, there was no shortage of shocking things during the second half of 1944. Ordinary Germans had to accept the reality of their Führer's war collapsing everywhere. Italy was slowly being prized out of Fascist hands. The Nazis abandoned Vichy France following Allied landings on the Mediterranean coast. Soviet troops, tanks and aircraft sent German armies reeling back across Belorussia and Poland to Warsaw; they also penetrated the Baltic States, and forced Romania, Bulgaria and Finland to swap sides, while besieging the Hungarian capital, Budapest. German control of Yugoslavia, Greece and Albania collapsed. Hitler, ever more isolated from his people, his generals and reality, demanded fights to the death and scorched earth strategies. In July, a plot to assassinate him narrowly failed, but implicated such senior figures as Field Marshal Rommel.

On 25 August 1944 Paris was liberated by the Allies – a moment of triumph and relief for many citizens, and one that attracted great (and would-be great) war correspondents, including the American novelist Ernest Hemingway. Yet with liberation came vengeance: men and particularly women who were accused of collaboration with the Nazi occupiers were humiliated, beaten and abused. Fears and resentments that had built up during the long years of war would not simply evaporate with the prospect of peace.

Meanwhile, far away from Europe, in the Pacific, the war was also running away from Hitler's Japanese allies. US Marines won critical battles on the island of Saipan and in the Philippine Sea, although they faced enemies who embraced death and strove to take the maximum number of enemy lives as they did so. Just as 'doodlebug' pilotless rockets created havoc in the west, so suicidal *kamikaze* pilots were a bane in the east. The weapons of war were becoming more ingenious, destructive and terrifying – and worse was still to come. The last chapter of the war may have been looming, but that did not mean there would be a happy ending.

25 August 1944

Paris's German commander disobeys Hitler's orders to destroy the city, and instead the French capital is liberated by the French 2nd Armoured Division and US infantry.

17–26 September 1944

Montgomery's Operation Market-Garden misfires: its unfulfilled aim was to capture bridges over the Meuse and Lower Rhine rivers and speed up the invasion of Germany.

16 December 1944

Hitler launches the 'Battle of the Bulge' through the Ardennes, to divide Allied forces and then to retake Antwerp; facing US reinforcements and resistance, it will fail.

27 December 1944

The Red Army begins besieging Budapest, Hungary's capital, having already rolled across Romania, Bulgaria and Yugoslavia since August 1944.

January 1945

As the Red Army enters German soil and commences its full-scale invasion of East Prussia, German fears of the systematic rape, torture and murder of civilians are realized.

Cherbourg

As Allied forces worked to secure the Normandy beaches during the hours and days after D-Day, the US VII Corps were sent to take control of Normandy's Cotentin Peninsula and its port of Cherbourg. The deep-water harbour there offered the possibility of unloading vehicles, troops, supplies and other necessary materials directly on to the French mainland, rather than transporting them via landing craft and improvised floating harbours. By 21 June, the US forces were on the town's perimeters, and for the next week they fought in the streets and suburbs, while US and British naval guns fired at the coastal defences.

On 26 June the German commander of Cherbourg's garrison, Lieutenant-General Karl Wilhelm von Schlieben (*centre*), surrendered, to the joy of Cherbourg's inhabitants and to the disgust of Hitler, who pronounced him a 'disgrace'. By contrast, Hitler awarded Rear-Admiral Walter Hennecke (*far right*) the Knight's Cross for having ordered the deliberate destruction of port facilities in Cherbourg before the city fell. In Hitler's words, this was 'a feat unprecedented in the annals of coastal defence'; in practice, it prevented the harbour from coming into use for the Allies until August.

This photograph shows von Schlieben being escorted off a landing craft on to British soil. According to one newspaper report from the time, he had been afforded 'every courtesy' on his Channel crossing, including a haircut. Both von Schlieben and Hennecke were imprisoned in Britain until the end of the war before being sent home to Germany.

The Battle of the Hedgerows

Fighting their way through Normandy, Allied soldiers discovered that the characteristic local landscape of narrow sunken lanes, surrounded by banks and thick hedgerows – known as *bocage* – could be a deathtrap. The nature of this Norman *bocage* made it perfect territory for concealment and ambush; hidden machine guns could spray a column of marching men; tanks could lurk around any corner, camouflaged by trees or tangles of vegetation. During the summer months of 1944, therefore, a sort of guerrilla-style war developed, as US and British troops adapted their own tactics – and equipment – to the local surroundings. Some Allied tanks were fitted with prongs at the front, recycled from German anti-tank obstacles; this effectively turned them into armoured ploughs, which could drive through undergrowth.

These US soldiers are firing a 105mm HM2 howitzer, which they have disguised under camouflage netting. The men pictured were fighting around Saint-Lô, where one of the most ferocious encounters of the Normandy campaign took place. The town was considered strategically vital to securing lower Normandy, and heavy bombardment added to damage that had been done earlier in the war. Saint-Lô was taken for the Allies between 7 and 19 July, but virtually the entire city was left desolate. The Irish writer Samuel Beckett visited later and described it as the Capital of the Ruins. 'When we got there, there was nothing at all,' he wrote. 'The whole of Saint-Lô was blotted out.'

'Doodlebugs'

Unmanned flying 'V-1' rockets of the type pictured here
were known in German as *Vergeltungswaffe 1* or 'Revenge
Weapon 1'. To ordinary Britons they were 'buzz bombs'
or 'doodlebugs'. The first were launched on 13 June 1944,
and their purpose was straightforward: to fly across the
Channel from launch sites in occupied France and the
Low Countries, and fall wherever their engines ran out of
fuel, blowing up whatever (or whoever) they landed upon.
To begin with, V-1s were aimed at London and south-east
England, though as the Allied invasion of western Europe
gathered pace, many were also launched towards Antwerp
and other mainland targets.

The noise made by a doodlebug overhead – a pulsing
drone – was unnerving. More troubling still was the
engine falling silent, since this meant that the bomb was
soon to crash-land and detonate. On 18 June a V-1 fell on
the Guards' Chapel of Wellington Barracks in London,
killing 121 members of the congregation at morning
service.

Although doodlebugs killed more than 6,000 people
in Britain, many veered off course, while fighter planes
and anti-aircraft guns became increasingly adept at
shooting them down. Eventually, the continental launch
sites were overrun. By the time this damaged V-1 was
displayed in London, on 31 October 1944, smiles were
justified, for the danger was largely over. Unfortunately,
in the meantime, the Nazis had developed a new weapon
– the V-2. This was a supersonic rocket that plunged
to earth without warning and without possibility of
interception.

Operation Valkyrie

Despite the development of weapons like the V-1, by mid-July 1944 it was evident to many in the German high command that the war situation was dire. The Allies had invaded Normandy, while in the east German military positions in Belorussia were collapsing. Among some high-ranking German officers, Hitler's leadership was now seen as a grave impediment to any hope of avoiding national catastrophe. As early as the winter of 1942–3, Army dissidents had been considering a plot to assassinate the Führer. By the summer of 1944 this plan, code-named Operation Valkyrie, was ready for execution. The aim was to kill Hitler, along with Hermann Göring and Heinrich Himmler, by detonating a time bomb during a meeting. This would be the prelude for a military coup, which would displace the Nazi regime.

On 20 July one of the plotters, Colonel Claus von Stauffenberg, joined Hitler's conference in his East Prussian bunker complex, the *Wolfsschanze* (Wolf's Lair). Von Stauffenberg was a disillusioned officer who had served the Reich well, and bore the scars to prove it: an amputated hand and an eye patch.

Having brought the bomb into the room in a briefcase, von Stauffenberg left the room and the device exploded. But the briefcase had been moved, and a solid oak table support protected Hitler, who suffered only shredded trousers and frayed nerves. Within 24 hours, von Stauffenberg was shot by a firing squad. Other plotters committed suicide or were captured.

The Liberation of Paris

The plotters who failed to kill Hitler were not the only Nazis convinced that the Führer no longer deserved their obedience. In Paris, the commander of the German garrison, Dietrich von Choltitz, had concluded, as he later put it, that 'Hitler was insane'. As Allied troops approached the French capital in the middle of August 1944, von Choltitz had a choice to make. He could follow Hitler's orders, which were to burn and bomb the city to the ground, so that it could not fall into enemy hands 'except in complete debris'. Or he could surrender the streets to the French Resistance.

The day for deciding was not long coming. With the Allies advancing out of Normandy, on 15 August Parisians rose in readiness for liberation. First came a series of strikes; next, French Resistance fighters known as the Forces Françaises de l'Intérieur (FFI) erected barricades in the streets and began to fire on German occupiers. Then, on the night of 24/25 August, General Philippe Leclerc led the French 2nd Armoured Division into Paris; here they are seen being greeted by crowds on a corner of the rue Guynemer. Behind them came the US 4th Infantry Division. Von Choltitz formally – and sensibly – surrendered on 25 August at the Hôtel Meurice. The same day, Charles de Gaulle gave a speech announcing that 'the French vanguard has entered Paris with guns blazing' and calling for national unity under his leadership. After four years, Paris was free.

Americans in Paris

Along with the fighters came the reporters. The liberation of Paris was a historic moment, irresistible to men like two of those pictured here. On the left is the photo-journalist Robert Capa, often ranked as the greatest war photographer of all time. Capa had been in the Spanish Civil War in 1937 and the Japanese invasion of China in 1938, in Naples during the Allied invasion of Italy in 1943 and on Omaha Beach during the Normandy landings, when he took a series of blurred but dramatic photos later nicknamed 'The Magnificent Eleven', filed to *Life* magazine. He was in Paris on 25 August, photographing stand-offs as soldiers and Parisians sheltered in doorways and behind barricades

On the other side of a driver (*centre*) is Ernest Hemingway (*right*), who was reporting from France for *Collier's* magazine. On the eve of Paris's fall, he was 40 miles (65km) away at Rambouillet, supposedly embedded with US troops but in fact comporting himself as self-appointed leader of a local resistance militia. On 25 August, he rushed to Paris, celebrating French freedom with champagne at the Travellers' Club, before heading to 'liberate' the Ritz Hotel, where his group was said to have run up a bill for fifty-one martinis. Despite Hemingway's fondness for the idea of himself as a great war reporter, he was in fact far better at drinking and showing off, unlike his wife of the time, Martha Gellhorn, a far more talented and serious correspondent.

Operation Dragoon

As Paris fell, Allied troops landed at beaches in southern France, opening a second French front and heralding the end of the Vichy regime. Although planned to coincide with D-Day, Operation Dragoon was ultimately delayed until the beachheads in Normandy had been secured.

The landings began on 15 August, when US, French and Canadian forces converged on France's Mediterranean coast from bases in Italy, Corsica and Algeria. They met with only moderate resistance: by the end of the month the Allies had secured Toulon and Marseilles. This photograph shows civilians literally kicking the occupiers out of Toulon. By 14 September, German forces had abandoned the French south altogether and retreated to the Vosges Mountains. Marshal Pétain and the Vichy government were evacuated to Germany, to be set up as a government-in-exile in the southern German town of Sigmaringen.

However, if the collapse of Vichy France was swift, it left behind a legacy of cruelty and violence. In the weeks and months before D-Day, Nazi officials had carried out revenge attacks against the resistance fighters known collectively as the *Maquis*. In one notorious incident, at the village of Oradour-sur-Glane near Limoges, on 10 June 1944 a Waffen-SS unit murdered 642 men, women and children, and destroyed the village. There had also been bitter fighting between French factions, as the *Maquis* battled with the collaborationist *Milice* paramilitary. After Allied liberation, many ex-*miliciens* were subjected to harsh reprisals, in the form of official treason proceedings and unofficial beatings and executions.

Collaboration and Shame

Reprisals across France were notably severe against women accused of *collaboration horizontale* – sleeping with the enemy. Some Parisian prostitutes were kicked to death after liberation. And throughout France, from Brittany to Provence, an estimated 20,000 women were subjected to a ritualized form of ostracization for consorting with Germans: their hair was shaved off in public. Some were then daubed with swastikas and stripped to their underwear, before being paraded through the streets, barefoot or in open-topped vehicles, to be jeered and spat at by their compatriots.

This process – seen taking place here – was known as a *carnival moche*, 'ugly carnival', and it was a method of publicly shaming women that had a grievously long European history. It had its roots in the Middle Ages, when it was sometimes used as punishment for adultery. But the ritual had been revived throughout Europe during the world wars: in the Rhineland after the First World War, during the Spanish Civil War, and in Nazi Germany, where women accused of having sexual relations with 'impure' foreigners or men not deemed to be of 'Aryan' blood were subjected to this depersonalizing ordeal.

Needless to say, this rough and misogynistic form of mob justice often targeted women who were unable to defend themselves, or who had been the victims of unhappy or impossible circumstances. It was bound up with rumours of collaborationist women working as assassins for the retreating Germans. And it was barely policed by the liberating army. In this photograph, several soldiers wearing US-style helmets can be seen posing among the mob.

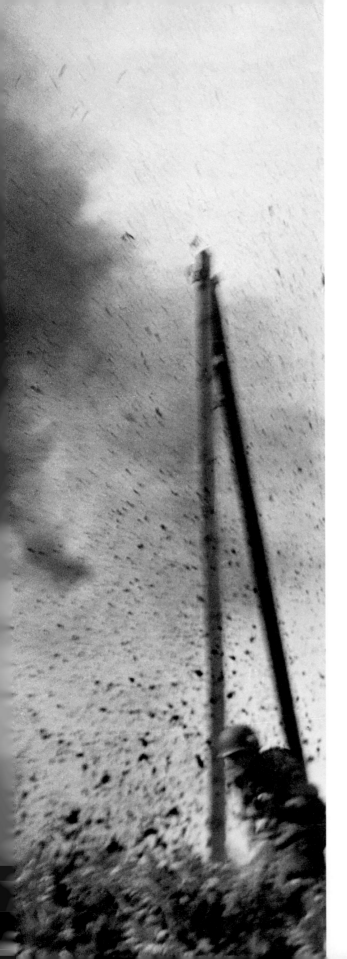

Operation Market-Garden

In the minds of British and American generals, liberating Paris in the summer of 1944 was less important than the rapid drive towards Germany. In that regard, the Allies had to find a way to deal with Germany's version of the Maginot Line, the Siegfried Line or *Westwall*: defensive fortifications stretching along the German border between Switzerland and the Netherlands. Field Marshal Bernard Montgomery developed an ambitious plan to circumvent the *Westwall*. It resulted in scenes like this, in which US paratroopers narrowly evade a shell burst in a soggy Dutch field.

On 17 September 1944, two US airborne divisions, one British and the Polish Parachute Brigade dropped and glided into occupied Holland, north-east of Eindhoven. The goal of Operation Market was to secure vital bridges over the Meuse and Lower Rhine tributaries and hold them long enough for the British XXX Corps to arrive overland (Operation Garden), consolidate the gains, and open a path into Germany's industrial heartland, the Ruhr.

Initial success soon faded. Lightly armed British paratroopers landed short of the furthest bridge, at Arnhem, to find two Panzer divisions in the area; Allied equipment went astray; and the XXX Corps were slowed down by fighting, the difficult landscape, and bad weather. By 25 September, Arnhem was lost, as were three-quarters of the British troops, mostly captured. The Lower Rhine still lay in German hands. Despite territory gained and many heroic individual actions, Montgomery's gamble was a failure.

The Ruins of Aachen

With the failure of Operation Market-Garden, there was little choice for the Western Allies but to press on with a slow and steady direct advance on Germany. On 21 October 1944, US forces captured Aachen, the country's westernmost city. When they entered the city, much of it lay in ruins. This photograph was taken in Aachen's ancient cathedral.

Although Aachen was situated on the Siegfried Line, it had little other significance to the German war effort. It did, though, have deep historical resonance. In the ninth century, Aachen was the seat of power for Charlemagne's Frankish empire, and his Palatine Chapel, now part of the cathedral, became the emperor's resting place. For hundreds of years afterwards, German kings were crowned in the chapel, to which the choir, seen here, was added in the thirteenth century.

These US serviceman, gazing up from the rubble-strewn floor, would have been unable to appreciate the vibrant colours once thrown by the stained-glass windows, which gave the choir the name *Glashaus*. A US military field report baldly stated: 'All valuable windows destroyed. The south and west portions of the cloisters are badly damaged.' It took two years from 1949 to restore the glories of the Glashaus.

Outside the cathedral, Aachen was semi-deserted, most of its people having been evacuated east. Hitler's orders for defence of the Reich betrayed ruthless intent: where Germany could not be defended, everything of value should be destroyed before the invaders could claim it.

Greek Liberation

In 1941 Greece had been swiftly conquered by German and Italian armies. On 27 April of that year, the swastika had flown above the Acropolis – the birthplace of democracy – and the country had been partitioned between the Axis powers, with Bulgaria seizing a large portion of land in the east. When Italy fell to the Allies in 1943, Nazi control had been extended over most of Greece.

The occupation had caused widespread misery and hardship, ruining Greek industry and leaving tens of thousands of people dead. Understandably, therefore, there was jubilation when, in October 1944, German troops abandoned Athens and a British task force arrived to oversee the return of the Greek government. This photograph shows a parade in the Greek capital, with citizens celebrating in traditional dress.

However, these celebrations masked new troubles. Greece was deeply divided between political factions on the right and left, which had been manifested under Axis rule by armed resistance groups who fought one another as often as the occupying powers. In December 1944 rioting (the so-called *Dekemvriana*) broke out in Athens, and a civil war was soon underway. This pitted the Greek government, backed by British troops, against Greek communists, who were encouraged from afar by leaders including Josip Broz 'Tito', the partisan leader and communist revolutionary recently elected as prime minister of Yugoslavia. Although it was eventually won by the Western-backed government, civil war would plague Greece until the end of the 1940s.

Saipan

The Allies were keen to bring the war against Germany to a close as quickly as possible so that they could concentrate their efforts on defeating Japan in the east. That became a real possibility from the summer of 1944 after a ferocious battle between US Marines and the Imperial Japanese Army on the island of Saipan – one of the Northern Mariana Islands, not far from Guam.

Saipan was a vital target for US forces, because it could serve as a launch pad for air raids, putting Toyko within reach of new American long-range B-29 Superfortress bomber planes. The Japanese, under Lieutenant-General Yoshitsugu Saitō, were determined to defend it to the death. On 15 June 1944, 600 US landing craft arrived and three weeks' hard struggle began. The battle wiped out the 30,000-strong Japanese garrison on Saipan, and cost 5,000 US lives. On 7 July, the last 3,000-odd Japanese soldiers, armed with guns, sticks and knives, threw themselves into a mass *banzai* suicide charge. Saitō ritually disembowelled himself.

This photograph shows US Marines treating a wounded child during the battle for Saipan. It was taken by W. Eugene Smith, who covered many of the campaigns in the Pacific for *Life* magazine (and later lived for a time with his wife in Japan). Thousands of civilians died on Saipan in 1944, including around 1,000 who killed themselves by jumping from cliffs after a broadcast ordered by Emperor Hirohito promised them reward in the afterlife for doing so.

Kamikaze

All the men pictured here intended to commit suicide. They are *kamikaze* pilots. The word, meaning 'divine wind', evoked a typhoon that saved Japan from a Mongol invasion fleet in 1281. Six and a half centuries later, in autumn 1944, Japanese Rear Admiral Masafumi Arima created *kamikaze* culture when he crashed his Yokosuka D4Y dive-bomber into a US aircraft carrier, killing himself but damaging the vessel in the process. Arima's example was used to promote the concept of honourable suicide in the service of emperor and the homeland. The official name for the *kamikaze* divisions that were thereafter deployed in the Pacific theatre was Tokubetsu Kōgekitai, or 'Special Attack Unit'.

Kamikaze pilots were typically trained to do one thing, once: crash their planes into enemy ships. Their aircraft, loaded with high explosive and extra fuel, became flying bombs. At the moment of impact, pilots were told to yell *hissatsu!* ('certain kill!'); they were assured that at this moment they would see their mothers' faces.

Kamikaze attacks began at the Battle of Leyte Gulf (23–26 October 1944), during the recapture of the Philippines. On 25 October, the USS *St. Lo,* a small aircraft carrier, was the first US vessel sunk by *kamikaze* action. On this occasion, *kamikaze* tactics were not enough to force victory. The battle was another disaster for the Japanese, who lost twenty-seven ships, including their last four aircraft carriers in active service. But the *kamikaze* programme was just beginning. By 1945, suicide pilots would be flying 'cherry blossoms': rocket-powered piloted torpedoes.

The Lapland War

Far away from the Pacific, in the scrub and tundra of the Arctic Circle, came a new twist in the war. In October 1944, Soviet winter troops like these were fighting in Finnish Lapland – on the side of the Finns. Even their sub-machine guns, the PPSh-41s seen here, were based on a Finnish design.

This represented a major shift in alliances. Three years earlier, in 1941, matters had been very different. As Hitler prepared for Operation Barbarossa, a deal was struck between Nazi Germany and a group of senior Finnish politicians, by which Finland would invade Russian territory at the same time as the Wehrmacht. From that summer, therefore, Finland was at war with the USSR, in a conflict known as the Continuation War.

The Continuation War ended in September 1944, having cost by that point around one million casualties. However, the deal that ended hostilities, known as the Moscow Armistice, demanded that Finnish troops remove every trace of the German military presence from their borders. For the next seven months, therefore, Finnish troops with Soviet backup were engaged in chasing German units through Lapland towards Nazi-occupied Norway.

By April 1945, the retreat – and the war – was over. Lapland, however, had been ruined. Roads, buildings, bridges and railway lines were wrecked and the Wehrmacht left tens of thousands of mines hidden in their wake. Ten years after the end of the Lapland War, the clean-up operation was still going on.

The Race to Berlin

By the time these Soviet artillerymen were photographed dragging a field gun across the River Oder, around 31 January 1945, the end of the war against Nazi Germany was in sight. Allied troops had won the Battle of the Bulge and were planning their advance into Germany across the Rhine. On the Eastern Front, the Red Army was surging forward: swallowing the Baltic States, surging across Poland and heading unstoppably towards the German capital. They traversed – and created – a hellish landscape. In July 1944, Soviet troops discovered Majdanek death camp, the first of the Nazi camps to be liberated. Its horrors were widely publicized – although the Soviet NKVD secret police repurposed Majdanek to imprison Polish nationalists.

Red Army troops committed many atrocities during their advance. In late October 1944, during the first Soviet incursion into East Prussia, villagers were murdered, and women raped and killed. The full-scale invasion of the same region in January 1945 continued in the same fashion, amounting to a systematic campaign of rape, murder and pillage. The twenty-six-year-old Alexander Solzhenitsyn, an artillery captain on the East Prussian front, was appalled at his compatriots' cruelty. Years later, as a dissident in the Soviet Gulag system, he turned the horrors into the narrative verse of *Prussian Nights*. 'The little daughter's on the mattress', he wrote. 'Dead. How many have been on it / A platoon, a company perhaps?'

For ordinary Germans, a long-threatened nightmare was coming true. The artillerymen photographed here were one tiny part of it. Across the Oder, Berlin lay barely 50 miles away.

Downfall

1945–1946

The enemy has begun to employ a new
and most cruel bomb, the power of which to
do damage is, indeed, incalculable,
taking the toll of many innocent lives.

Emperor Hirohito of Japan, the 'Jewel Voice' surrender broadcast
(14 August 1945)

At 11.02 a.m. on 9 August 1945, a nuclear bomb nicknamed 'Fat Man' fell several thousand feet through a gap in thick clouds above the Japanese city of Nagasaki. When it was a little more than 1,500 feet over the city, it detonated. The plutonium core of the device exploded in a nuclear fission chain reaction, which released energy equivalent to 21,000 tons of TNT. The explosion, including the massive 'mushroom' cloud pictured here, was spectacular. The destruction wrought on the city was even more so: around 40 per cent of the buildings and houses in Nagasaki were destroyed, including the Mitsubishi Steel and Arms Works and nearby torpedo factory.

Perhaps 40,000 people – almost all of them civilians – were killed instantly when Fat Man blew up, and within the next six months roughly the same number again would succumb to the effects of exposure to massive doses of radiation. When people first started dying of acute radiation syndrome, their symptoms were described as 'atomic bomb disease'. But by that time the Second World War was over. The United States had demonstrated battlefield capability with the deadliest weapon in the history of humanity, and in the days after the bombing, American aircraft littered Japan with leaflets warning of their intention to repeat the atomic blasts over and over again until Emperor Hirohito surrendered to the Allies. The emperor duly did so on 14 August, bringing peace to the Pacific theatre. But peace was not the same as harmony. The world itself was now infected with atomic bomb disease. A new, potentially apocalyptic era of warfare had begun.

The bomb that devastated Nagasaki was the third nuclear weapon ever to be detonated, and the second to be used in warfare. The first atomic explosion occurred in New Mexico on 16 July 1945: this was the so-called Trinity Test of a 'Fat Man'-style plutonium bomb, and it demonstrated the success of the Manhattan Project, the American nuclear arms program overseen on the scientific side by the physicist J. Robert Oppenheimer.

The Trinity Test established that the USA had won the nuclear arms race with Germany and the USSR, and it made the deployment of an atomic bomb in warfare overwhelmingly likely. Japan was proving an obstinate enemy in the Pacific theatre: 14,000 American troops had been killed invading the tiny island of Okinawa in the spring, and the projected casualties for an invasion of mainland Japan (known as Operation Downfall) were intolerably high. US President Harry S. Truman – who had succeeded to office on Franklin D. Roosevelt's death in April 1945 – was all too glad to sanction the use of a weapon that could obliterate Japanese cities with minimal danger to American lives, while sending a message to the USSR about America's potential post-war military supremacy. On 6 August a uranium 'gun-type' bomb nicknamed 'Little Boy' was used to vaporize much of the Japanese city of Hiroshima. The device dropped on Nagasaki three days later finished the job.

When Hirohito broadcast a message to the Japanese population announcing his surrender, it was the first time an emperor had ever addressed his people, albeit in a speech delivered in classical, courtly Japanese that was unintelligible to most of them. He gave the reasons for his decision. 'Should we continue to fight,' he said, 'not only would it result in an ultimate collapse and obliteration of the Japanese nation, but also it would lead to the total extinction of human civilization.' He was not very far from the truth.

The final throes of the Second World War were as

---

27 January 1945

Soviet troops arrive at the Auschwitz death-camp west of Cracow, which has consumed a million lives; most of the remaining 66,000 prisoners have been force-marched west.

13 February 1945

Dresden is turned into an inferno by RAF Lancaster bombers; later, on 9–10 March, US B-29 bombers devastate a large section of Tokyo, killing an estimated 100,000 people.

4 April 1945

Shocked US troops liberate their first German concentration camp, Ohrdruf, a sub-camp of Buchenwald; on 15 April, the British uncover the horrors of Bergen-Belsen camp.

25 April 1945

In a symbolic moment prefiguring victory over Germany, Soviet troops from the east and US troops from the west greet one another at the River Elbe, south of Berlin.

28 April 1945

Mussolini, his mistress and politicians of his puppet state are arrested by Italian partisans and shot; their abused bodies are later hung upside-down in Milan.

terrible as anything that had preceded them. When 1945 dawned, Allied troops advancing on Germany from the west and their Soviet counterparts arriving from the east saw at first hand the sickening reality of the Nazi death camps. Auschwitz-Birkenau was liberated by the Soviets in January and Bergen-Belsen by the British in April. Yet as the camps fell, many prisoners were being removed towards the interior of the Reich by sadistic SS officers, who organized 'death marches' on which thousands of weak and starving victims perished. The survivors were herded into other, overcrowded and disease-riddled camps hidden away from the collapsing front lines.

The only small mercy was that eventually there were no front lines left to hide behind. And before long there was no Nazi Party ruling the Reich, either. Between 16 April and 2 May Soviet forces overran Berlin, devastating the city with massive loss of life on both sides and committing numerous crimes against civilians. Finally accepting that the end had arrived, Adolf Hitler committed suicide in his bunker on 30 April. Josef Goebbels and his wife killed themselves and their children the following day. Heinrich Himmler took cyanide after he was captured by the British, and Martin Bormann was killed while trying to escape Berlin. Other high-ranking Nazis, including Hermann Göring, were captured and tried for war crimes at Nuremberg in 1946. Göring killed himself before he could be executed, but other Nazis and generals tried at Nuremberg, including Joachim von Ribbentrop, Alfred Jodl, Karl Dönitz and Wilhelm Keitel, were hanged for their crimes.

One of the war's other instigators, Benito Mussolini, died when he was beaten and shot by partisans in late April – his body was hung upside down in Milan alongside that of his mistress Clara Petacci. The Japanese prime minister and general Hideki Tojo was hanged for war crimes in 1948. Emperor Hirohito was not forced to abdicate, but his status was downgraded from that of imperial sovereign (implying divinity and descent from the gods) to constitutional monarch, a role he continued to play until his death in 1989.

And so the war was over. But the announcement of VJ (Victory over Japan) Day, on 15 August 1945, was as much a cause for awful contemplation as it was for celebration. The Second World War had killed between 70 and 85 million people – roughly 3 per cent of the world's entire population. Like the First World War, it had harnessed all the greatest technological advances of its time and turned them to vicious and diabolical ends. The world would take decades to recover, and the only consolation was that for a time – to the present day, at least – people would recall its horrors and say to one another: never again.

---

30 April 1945

In his bunker under the Reich Chancellery, Hitler commits suicide with his wife Eva Braun, having married her the previous day, shortly before dictating his will.

8–9 May 1945

Following several regional and partial German surrenders agreed since 29 April, a full German unconditional surrender to the Allies, signed in Berlin, comes into force.

21 June 1945

In the Far East, the US capture of the island of Okinawa, after three months' fighting, has been an even more gruelling and costly operation than conquering Iwo Jima (March).

6 and 9 August 1945

US atomic bombs dropped on Hiroshima and Nagasaki finally shock Japan, at the behest of its emperor, into surrender on 14 August. The Second World War is officially over.

30 September 1946

Following landmark trials for war crimes held at Nuremberg, leading Nazis, including von Ribbentrop and Göring, are sentenced to death. Göring commits suicide.

Liberating the Camps

As the Allies captured Nazi-occupied territory, they saw at close hand the concentration and death camps whose existence had generally been known outside the Third Reich only from reports. In late January 1945 the Red Army arrived at Auschwitz, to find around 6,000 prisoners in dreadful condition. The rest had already been evacuated by the SS and were on a lethal march towards the German interior.

In the west, troops of the 6th Armored Division of the US Third Army arrived at Buchenwald concentration camp on 11 April. Here over 20,000 prisoners remained, although an epidemic of typhus had killed many more. Four days after his troops arrived, General George Patton, commander of the Third Army, demanded that civilians from the nearby town of Weimar be brought to the camp to witness the abysmal sight of bodies stacked naked in heaps and human beings reduced to living skeletons.

The photographer Margaret Bourke-White arrived at Buchenwald concentration camp at the time of these citizen tours, on 15 April. She took this famous photograph that day and noted that although she used a flash, not one of the traumatized prisoners before her flinched or reacted to the light. She later recalled being grateful to have had a camera in her hands: the lens provided a form of psychological barrier from the horrors of the camp. The whole experience was profoundly unnerving. 'I hardly knew what I had taken until I saw prints of my own photographs,' she said.

Iwo Jima

The volcanic island of Iwo Jima ('Sulphur Island') lies roughly 650 miles (1,000km) from Tokyo, halfway between Japan and the Mariana Islands. An airbase on Iwo Jima had allowed the Japanese air force to disrupt long-range US bombing raids from Saipan, so in February 1945 US Marines arrived to conquer it. They faced one of their most challenging and costly battles, against a garrison of 22,000 Japanese defenders hidden in deep bunkers and tunnels, particularly around the extinct volcano Mount Suribachi, at the extreme southern end of the island.

The Marines' assault began on 23 February, and although they took heavy casualties fighting their way ashore on steep beaches of rock and black sand, they secured Mount Suribachi the same day. This is one of several images captured by Staff Sergeant Louis R. Lowery, who took photographs for the Marine Corps' *Leatherneck* magazine. The Marines shown are switching the first US flag that had been planted on the mountain for another, larger one, which could be seen from further away. A similar image of the same event (taken by Associated Press photographer Joe Rosenthal) became famous across the world, being used to sell US war bonds and even featuring on a postage stamp in 1945.

Despite this triumphant scene, it took another month to win Iwo Jima. During a battle fought with flamethrowers and phosphorus grenades, the Marines suffered 23,000 casualties. Twenty-seven Medals of Honor were awarded after the fighting was over.

Dresden

On the night of 13 February, more than 700 RAF Lancaster bombers arrived over the city of Dresden, in Saxony, on a mission to support the Soviet ground assaults on Germany with a campaign of firebombing from above. The aircraft carried payloads of high explosives and incendiary devices. RAF Bomber Command's justification for attacking Dresden was the city's use as a wartime transportation hub. But the massive firestorms that ensued from the attacks, in which temperatures reached 1,000°C, destroyed far more than just military targets. This photograph was taken from the viewing platform of the Rathausturm – the tower of the City Hall: it shows the wreckage caused by the firebombing, which burned out some 1,600 acres of the city and killed between 20,000 and 25,000 people. The statue in the foreground of this photograph, offering up this vista of abject ruination, is known as *Güte*, or Goodness.

Queasiness over Dresden's incineration began with Churchill, who in March 1945 said that 'the destruction of Dresden remains a serious query against the conduct of the Allied bombing'. Some German propagandists have gone much further, deliberately inflating the death toll and arguing that the bombing of Dresden should be considered a war crime. That this is highly dubious should not detract from the miseries experienced by the people of Dresden. The American writer Kurt Vonnegut, who was trapped there as a prisoner of war during the attacks, called the experience 'carnage unfathomable'.

Crossing the Rhine

As US Marines fought on Iwo Jima, the American armies in Europe were arriving at the banks of the Rhine. Crossing this great western German river would be a symbolic act; even at the end of the First World War in 1918 the Allies had not made significant incursions on its eastern banks. Now, however, German defeat was to be unambiguous, so the river would be crossed.

The Rhine was heavily defended. Although a US tank patrol seized Ludendorff Bridge at Remagen, most other permanent crossings were blown up on Hitler's orders. The Allies were therefore forced to use improvised pontoon bridges or landing craft. This photograph was taken aboard one of the latter: it shows troops of the US 89th Infantry Division crossing the Rhine near St Goar. The US Signal Corps photographer who took the picture recalled his bad luck at being assigned to a landing craft. 'We all tried to crawl under each other because the lead was flying around like hail,' he noted.

Despite stiff resistance, by 24 March the river was so secure that General Patton could stop while driving over one pontoon bridge to 'take a piss in the Rhine'. The next day, Churchill visited and conducted himself with a little more decorum. 'We landed in brilliant sunshine and perfect peace on the German shore, and walked about for half an hour or so unmolested,' he wrote. Ahead of him, Nazi resistance was petering out.

The Battle of Berlin

Berlin lay in eastern Germany, closer to the Red Army than the Allied armies approaching from the Rhine. Stalin's forces were already rampant: they took Budapest on 13 February and Vienna on 13 April. Knowing that Berlin had been weakened by USAAF and RAF bombing raids, and that the Allied Supreme Commander, Eisenhower, was ambivalent about forcing a march to reach the German capital first, Stalin whipped his own generals to make all haste to take it. The 'race to Berlin', between Marshals Georgy Zhukov and Ivan Konev, brought more than 1.5 million Soviet troops to the outskirts of the city on 16 April. Their arrival began one of the most ferocious battles of the Second World War, in which the Red Army suffered some 350,000 casualties as they battered at the Nazis' last ring of defences.

Stalin's willingness to absorb such awful losses of his own troops remained undimmed by the war's impending end. So, after a confused and desperate fight, in which many regular German units flocked west to surrender to the Americans or British rather than the Soviets, leaving the defence of some streets to the Hitler Youth, it took just two weeks for Berlin to fall. On 2 May Red Army soldiers were in control of the Reichstag, mounting the roof and flying the Soviet flag with glee. By then, the Nazi garrison had given up. General Helmuth Weidling signed the instrument of surrender. Adolf Hitler had shot himself dead on 30 April.

The Führerbunker

'It is all lost, hopelessly lost,' Hitler said to his secretary, Traudl Junge, on 22 April, as news reached him that the Soviets had broken Berlin's defences. Two days previously the Führer had celebrated his fifty-sixth birthday in this bunker within the besieged capital – a lair within the Old Reich Chancellery that had lately become his permanent home. For months he had been in denial about the hopelessness of the German war effort and the implosion of the Nazi regime, insulated as he was from reality by layers of security and a long-standing addiction to powerful drugs. He had ranted about betrayal and issued orders to his generals that veered between absurd and fantastical.

Now, though, truth dawned. The war was lost. Even loyal lieutenants like Himmler and Göring were abandoning him. The Red Army was in Berlin, and the Western Allies were closing. On 29 April Hitler married his girlfriend, Eva Braun; the next day he poisoned his dog, Blondi, then Braun took cyanide and Hitler shot himself. Josef and Magda Goebbels, also in the bunker, murdered their six children and killed themselves. Hitler left a will and testament true to his lifelong bigotry and delusion: he blamed Jews for the war and demanded a struggle to continue Nazism. Fortunately, Nazism as a political force died with him. He left behind a legacy of pointless hatred and destruction and this pitiful room, photographed after it was pillaged on 1 May 1945.

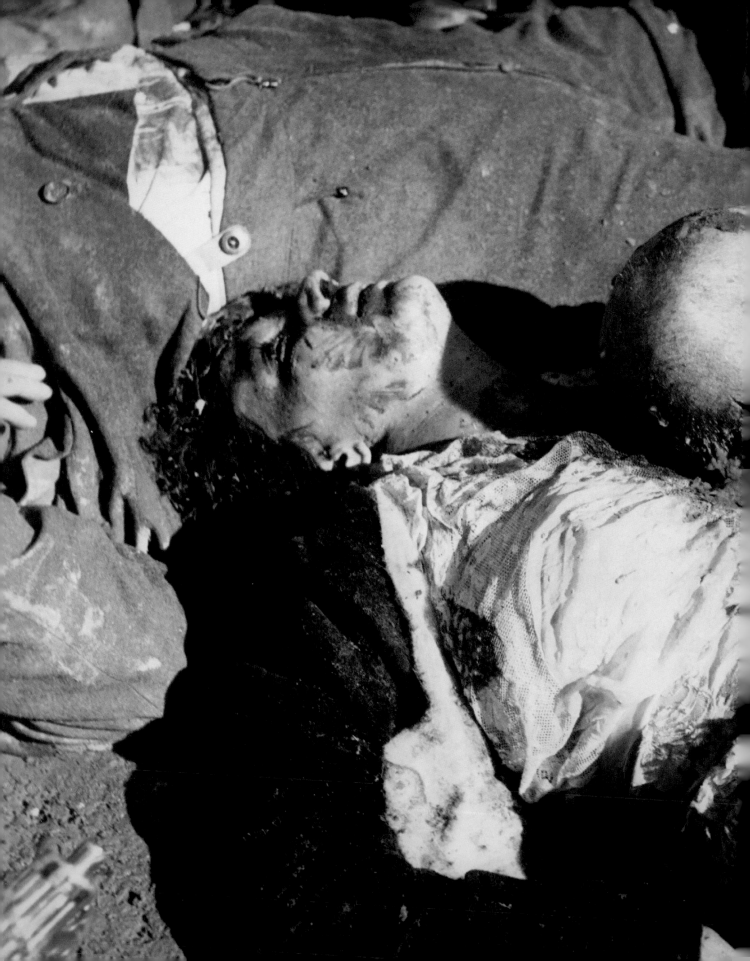

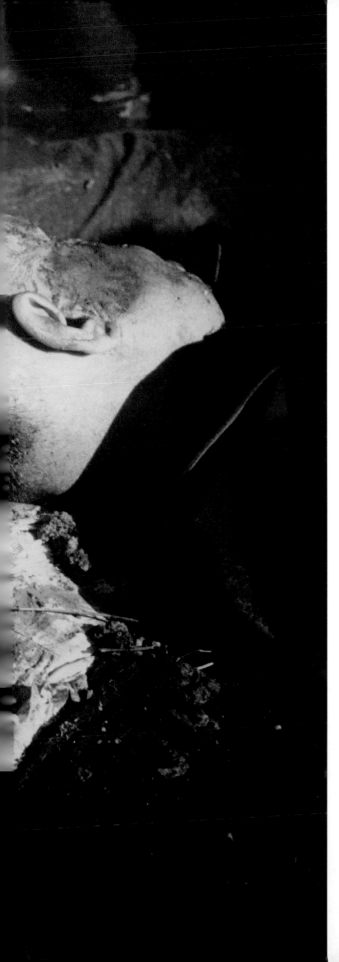

Mussolini's Death

Two days before Hitler committed suicide, on 28 April, his erstwhile fellow dictator Benito Mussolini was captured by Italian partisans and shot dead, along with his girlfriend Clara Petacci. They died near the village of Dongo, not far from Lake Como, but their corpses – photographed here – were brought to Milan on 29 April, where they were abused by crowds before being hung upside down outside a petrol station. Fear of similar ritual humiliation had lain behind Hitler's orders that his and Eva Braun's bodies should be burned after their suicides.

Mussolini's capture and death were preceded by the collapse of the Italian Social Republic – the Nazi puppet state over which he had nominally ruled since late 1943. This rump Fascist regime had been under pressure from its first moments, riven by factionalism and under attack from both the Allies and armed insurgents. By the end, Mussolini had been able to offer its citizens nothing but empty promises and bravado. As Allied troops swept through northern Italy in the spring of 1945, Mussolini had raved about a grand last stand for Fascism, either in Milan or the alpine passes known as the Valtellina. In the end, nothing of the sort happened. Milan fell to partisans on 25 April; within the week Il Duce's broken body was dangling there on public display and the SS commander in Italy, Karl Wolff, had negotiated surrender with the Allies.

Surrender

Hitler's will cancelled an earlier order that Göring should take over the Nazi state in the event of his demise, and instead named Admiral Karl Dönitz, Supreme Commander of the Kriegsmarine, as the new Reich president. But Dönitz's time in office, during which the government relocated to Flensburg in northern Germany, lasted less than a month. In May 1945 various groups of the German military began to offer their surrender to the Allies, and the process of halting the war in Europe and dismantling the Nazi state began.

This photograph shows Dönitz's successor as head of the navy, Admiral Hans-Georg von Friedeburg (*centre*), on the evening of 4 May, signing an agreement to surrender all forces in north-west Germany, the Netherlands and Denmark to the British commander in that sector, Field Marshal Montgomery (*seated, right*). The scene was witnessed by reporters and photographers, including a newsreel film crew from Pathé. Despite this public ceremony, it was not the last such document to be signed.

After several days of tense negotiation, a fuller instrument of unconditional military surrender – satisfactory to the Allied Supreme Commander, Eisenhower, as well as the Soviet high command, represented by Marshal Zhukov – was formalized on the night of 8/9 May in Berlin.

During the following weeks, the Flensburg government was rounded up and arrested. Admiral Friedeburg took a cyanide capsule and died on 23 May, avoiding the certain fate of being tried for war crimes.

The United Nations

US President Franklin D. Roosevelt died on 12 April, before he could witness the final collapse of the Axis forces he had devoted his last years to defeating. But among his many great legacies was the name he coined for the organization founded in 1945 to police the world and prevent future global wars. The United Nations (UN) was voted into existence at an international conference in San Francisco held between April and June; it was officially constituted on 24 October.

This photograph was taken at a sub-committee meeting of the San Francisco conference by Gjon Mili, the Albanian-born photographer who also pioneered freeze-frame 'stop-motion' photography to capture movement and light too fast to be seen by the naked eye.

The face illuminated on the far left, smoking a pipe, belongs to Edward, Lord Halifax, the British Ambassador to Washington, who, in 1940, had declined the position of prime minister in favour of Churchill. The figure smoking a cigar is John Foster Dulles (*second right*), a career diplomat from a family of high-flying US public servants. Dulles had promoted American membership of the UN's ill-fated predecessor, the League of Nations, and was keenly involved in drafting the terms on which the new organization was built.

In later years, as secretary of state to President Eisenhower, Dulles was a staunch opponent of the USSR, and he continued his commitment to international alliances by advocating for the North Atlantic Treaty Organization (NATO).

Okinawa

With Germany and Italy now out of the war, Japan remained the only Axis power left to be defeated. Yet the scale of that task was dauntingly bloody, as proven by the dreadful battle for Okinawa, a Pacific island just 106 miles (170km) long, but with an airstrip considered critical to the planning of Operation Downfall – the envisaged capture of Japan proper, pencilled for late 1945.

The joint US Army–Marines task force (with British naval support) sent to take Okinawa staged the largest amphibious assault of the whole Pacific war, involving around 200,000 combat troops. More than 14,000 of them died in a battle that lasted from 1 April to 21 June and was nicknamed the 'typhoon of steel'. This photograph was taken during that battle, and the nonchalance evinced by the Marine in the foreground is understandable, even if shocking. As Japanese defenders dug into hillsides all around the island, and *kamikaze* pilots hurtled out of the skies at US and British naval vessels, the death toll spiralled. Around 100,000 Okinawan civilians were killed or committed suicide, and around the same number of Japanese military personnel also died. Nearly every building on Okinawa was destroyed and the tropical landscape was churned by heavy bombardment. The result was an Allied victory but at appalling cost to both sides. Conservative estimates suggested that the final stage of the Pacific war – if this meant invading Japan – might cost 200,000 American lives. It was a sobering thought.

Potsdam

The solution to the Japanese question was already forming in the mind of new US president Harry S. Truman (*seated, centre*) when he attended a conference in the Berlin suburb of Potsdam, which convened between 17 July and 2 August. Previously, US hopes had been pinned on persuading the USSR to join the war against Japan. Now, Truman hinted to Stalin (*seated, right*) – cryptically, he thought – that the US had 'a weapon of unusual destructive force' that might do the job on its own. In fact, spies had already briefed Stalin about the Manhattan Project, and the Soviet dictator was unruffled. On 26 July the Allied leaders issued an ultimatum warning Japan to surrender immediately or face 'prompt and utter destruction'. One way or another, the end was in sight.

So was the future. There were new faces at Potsdam, as this photograph shows. Besides Truman, a British general election had ousted Winston Churchill from office; he had been replaced mid-conference as prime minister by his former deputy, Clement Attlee (*seated, left*). Behind them stand, *left to right*, US Admiral William Daniel Leahy, new British Foreign Secretary Ernest Bevin and US Secretary of State James Byrnes.

These new men had pressing matters to discuss. Carving up and occupying defeated Germany, agreeing war reparations, drawing new borders for Poland, restraining Stalin's ambitions for communism in eastern Europe and managing mass post-war migrations were all on the table. The rest of the century was coming rapidly into focus.

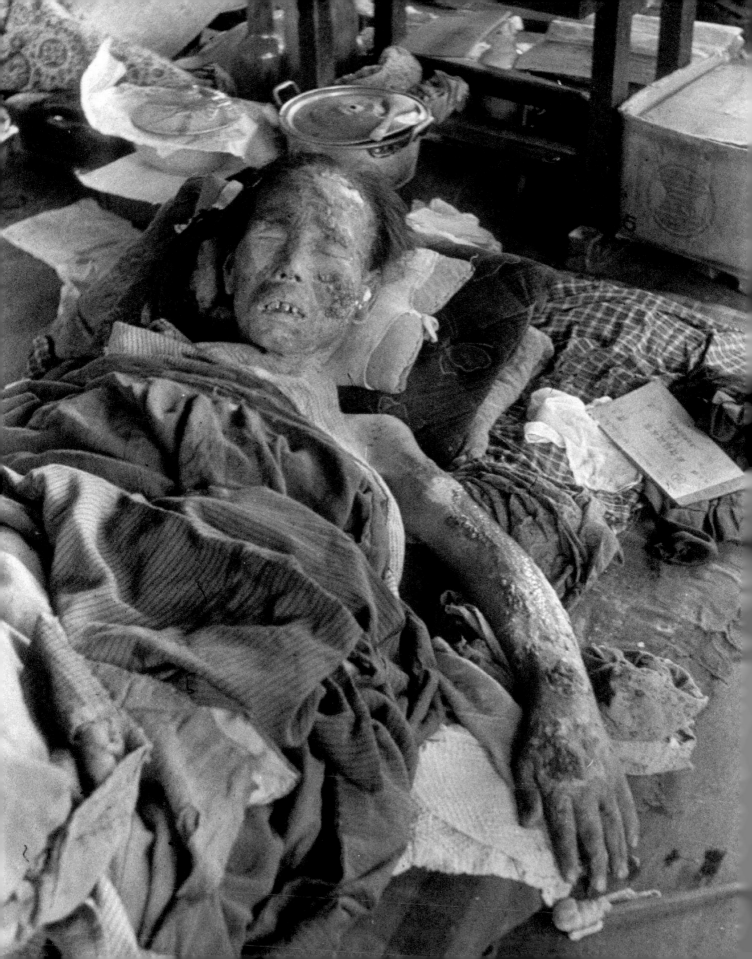

Hiroshima and Nagasaki

A USAAF B-29 Superfortress bomber named *Enola Gay*, after the pilot's mother, dropped the 'Little Boy' nuclear bomb over Hiroshima at 8.15 a.m. on 6 August. When it exploded, in the words of one eyewitness, 'Hiroshima just didn't exist'. Temperatures reached around 3,000°C in the blast zone and between 70,000 and 80,000 people died.

Yet this was not enough to coerce the Japanese high command into surrender. On 8 August the USSR finally declared war on Japan and sent 1.6 million troops into occupied Manchuria. Then, on 9 August, 'Fat Man' was detonated over Nagasaki. (Its original target had been Kokura, but adverse weather required a late change of plan.) Once more, tens of thousands of people were killed instantly, and the same number again suffered fatal radiation poisoning. British airman Leonard Cheshire, who was aboard the B-29 *Bockscar*, which dropped the Nagasaki bomb, called the blast 'obscene in its greedy clawing at the earth'. This photograph shows just one of the victims of the blast: a child suffering from terrible burns, clinging to life at an improvised hospital in a Nagasaki elementary school.

Despite the horrors of the blasts, and the threat of further attacks – the United States was capable of at least seven more strikes, which President Truman called 'a rain of ruin from the air, the like of which has never been seen on this earth' – it took until 14 August for Emperor Hirohito to announce the Japanese surrender.

VJ Day

Owing to the difference in time zones, it was evening on 14 August when news broke in the United States that Japan had quit the war. President Truman stated, cautiously, that formal surrender terms would not be signed until 2 September. But joy immediately swept the country. People ran into the streets to celebrate with spontaneous parties. This photograph shows the Brazilian performer Carmen Miranda dancing on a convertible car in the streets of Los Angeles. Miranda was famous for her roles in variety shows and Hollywood films, in which she was usually cast as a generic Latina type, often with a large basket of fruit on her head. On VJ day, she gave an impromptu performance across the street from Grauman's Chinese Theater, at the intersection of Hollywood Boulevard and Orange Drive. (Today, a square there is named in her honour.)

Of course, VJ day was not only celebrated in the USA. In Britain, Prime Minister Attlee announced a three-day public holiday, telling his people: 'You have earned rest from the unceasing efforts you have all borne without complaint through so many dark years.' There was dancing in the streets of London, and military parades were held in British outposts from Nairobi to Colombo.

In Tokyo, however, humiliation and misery reigned. Japan's capital had been wrecked by Allied firebombing raids in March. Now there was nothing for the dejected citizens to do but stand in the streets outside the Imperial Palace and weep.

The Nuremberg Trials

In 1943, Churchill, Roosevelt and Stalin signed a joint declaration condemning the 'atrocities, massacres and cold-blooded mass executions which are being perpetrated by Hitlerite forces in many of the countries they have overrun'. The Allies vowed to pursue the perpetrators 'to the uttermost ends of the earth' after the war. This promise was realized at the International Military Tribunal, which opened in Nuremberg on 19 November 1945.

Charges of war crimes and crimes against humanity were drawn up against twenty-four leading Nazis; this photograph shows most of the defendants in the dock. (Hitler's confidant Martin Bormann was already dead but was tried in absentia and another high Nazi official, Robert Ley, committed suicide early in proceedings.)

The men in the front row here include (*from left*) Hermann Göring, Joachim von Ribbentrop and Wilhelm Keitel, the chief of the Wehrmacht high command. In the back row can be seen (*far left*) Admiral Karl Dönitz, Hitler's successor as head of the Nazi state, (*fifth and sixth from left*) General Alfred Jodl and Franz von Papen, a Weimar chancellor who served as German ambassador to Austria and Turkey, and (*eighth from left*) Albert Speer, Hitler's friend, architect and minister for armaments.

Twelve of the accused were sentenced to death by hanging, including Göring, Jodl, Keitel and von Ribbentrop. Others, such as Dönitz and Speer, were given long prison sentences. But many prominent Nazis escaped the noose. Justice was served – but not completely.

Escaping Justice

Göring was found guilty of all charges at Nuremberg. The judges called him 'the moving force, second only to [Hitler]... the leading war aggressor... director of the slave labour programme and the creator of the oppressive programme against the Jews and other races... His guilt is unique in its enormity. The record discloses no excuses for this man.' His request to be executed by military firing squad was turned down.

But Göring did not hang. On 15 October 1946, the night before his execution day, he obtained a cyanide capsule and killed himself in his cell. This photograph shows his corpse before it was burned and his ashes thrown in the Isar river.

Many other Nazis also cheated justice. Hitler shot himself. Josef Goebbels committed suicide. Heinrich Himmler took cyanide while in British custody. Heinrich Müller, chief of the Gestapo, disappeared and was never found. Dr Josef Mengele, who performed cruel human 'experiments' at Auschwitz, fled to Brazil and died in 1979. Perhaps the most famous case of a Nazi evading justice – for a time – was that of Adolf Eichmann, a senior SS officer who played a leading role in organizing the Final Solution. Eichmann escaped a US detention camp in 1945, fled to Argentina and was only captured by Israeli intelligence agents in 1960. He was hanged after a trial in Jerusalem in 1962. 'To sum it all up', he reflected in an interview with the journalist and former SS man Willem Sassen, 'I must say that I regret nothing.'

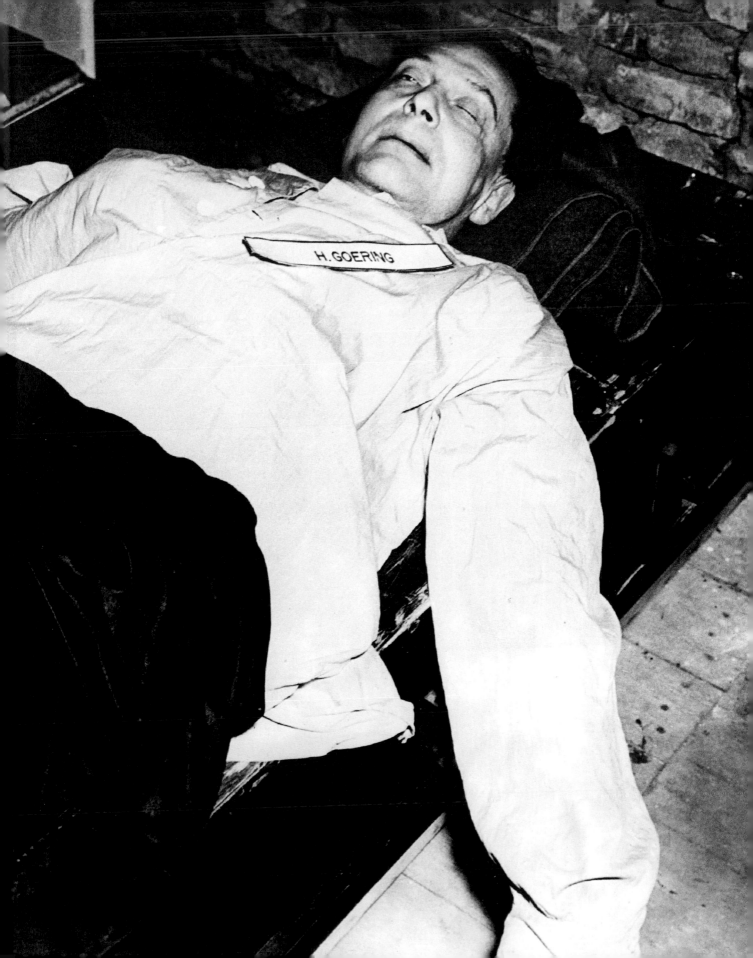

Index